Scrip.

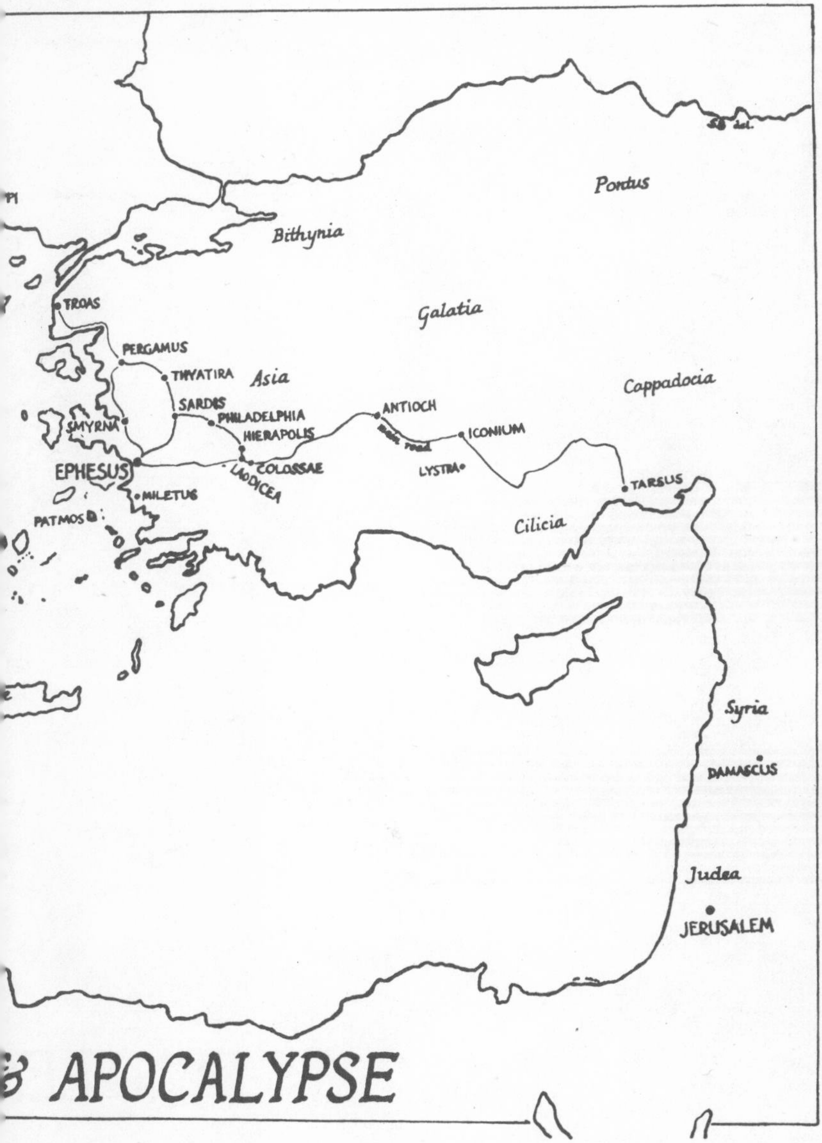
Pontus
Bithynia
Galatia
Asia
Cappadocia
TROAS
PERGAMUS
THYATIRA
SARDIS
PHILADELPHIA
HIERAPOLIS
SMYRNA
EPHESUS
COLOSSAE
LAODICEA
MILETUS
PATMOS
ANTIOCH
ICONIUM
LYSTRA
TARSUS
Cilicia
Syria
DAMASCUS
Judea
JERUSALEM
& APOCALYPSE

St. Paul

the Missionary

Saint Paul

The Missionary

❖❖❖❖❖

by Justo Pérez de Urbel, O. S. B.

Translated from the Spanish by
PAUL BARRETT, O.F.M.CAP.

THE NEWMAN PRESS · WESTMINSTER, MARYLAND
1957

This is a translation of SAN PABLO, APOSTOL DE LAS GENTES
published by Ediciones Fax, Madrid, Spain

Nihil obstat: FR. HILARIUS A CARLOW GRAIG, O.F.M.Cap.
Censor theol. deput.

Imprimatur: FR. JACOBUS A MITCHELSTOWN, O.F.M.Cap.
Min. Prov. Hib.

die 4 Junii, 1956

Nihil obstat: EDWARD A. CERNY, S.S.
Censor Librorum

Imprimatur: FRANCIS P. KEOUGH, D.D.
Archbishop of Baltimore

September 27, 1956

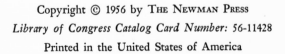

NOTE

I should like to express my deep indebtedness to the Very Reverend Father Hilary, O.F.M.Cap. for comparing this translation with the original Spanish text and for making many valuable suggestions. I am also very grateful to Mrs. Marian F. Gough of La Canada for typing the manuscript, doing a great amount of research work and offering much constructive criticism.

The New Testament quotations herein are taken from the Confraternity Edition with the permission of the Confraternity of Christian Doctrine, holder of the copyright.

To these and to all who assisted me in any way I am indeed thankful, and I pray that St. Paul may be their strong defender on earth and their loving companion in heaven.

PAUL BARRETT, O.F.M.CAP.

La Canada, California
Ascension Thursday, 1956

v

CONTENTS

One day, two friends and I were discussing St. Paul when one of them turned to me and asked: "Why don't you write a life of St. Paul?" My reply was not encouraging. Veritable mountains of books have been written about the great Apostle: heavy folios, now mostly smothered in cobwebs; learned and painstaking commentaries on which men renowned for their holiness and genius spent their lives; historical studies full of erudition; literary flights rich in poetry and color; exegetical treatises compiled with the sincerity of those who wish to understand; voluminous biographies, written with knowledge and love; psychological analyses, some of them inspired by pedantry and impiety; hypercritical works, cold, cautious, destructive books, the idealistic investigations of historical innovators pledged to undermining the sacred texts, to multiplying interpolations, to bringing forward fantastic hypotheses, and to destroying incontrovertible facts. From St. John Chrysostom to Loisy, through Theodoretus of Cyrus, Maldonatus, Foire, Prat, Lagrange, Baumann, Strauss, Renan, Norden and Ramsay, innumerable authors have written about the Apostle of the Gentiles, commenting on his Epistles, weighing each one of his sentences, describing his appearance, relating his deeds, and studying the problems which his unique character presents. What could I add to that rich literature, in which some authors have won fame by virtue of their genius and endeavor, while others have failed despite long years of preparation? How can one say anything new where so much has already been said?

"But it's not a question of saying something new," my friends told me. "All we ask you to do is to show the giant stature of St. Paul, make your readers love him, recall his great thoughts, wake their drowsing spirits with the example of this man of sublime passion who became what he was through struggle and triumph." There is nothing comparable to this inspiring story for awakening noble enthusiasm, keen desires and high ambition. It is spirit and life, not a vain shadow; it is a heart beating with love, not the empty echo of a dead system of thought. The world is becoming filled with Epicureans, content to wallow in the mire and root in their dunghills. There are Pharisees who do all they can to impose on others the cult of mechanical formulae and the dead religion of convention. Exultant and filled with self-esteem are the modern Sadducees, those sceptical opportunists and deniers of a future life, those self-opinionated pursuers of dignities and high position. Increasing in number daily are the advocates of Communism and anarchy, those poor dreamers who are looking for a paradise without Christ or the things of the spirit, devotees of spiritualism and magic, modern gnostics and Illuminati, believers in a universal religion without creed or commandment, stoics, full of pride, who try to forge their own destiny and that of the world without any guide save their own small minds, without any strength save that of their own puny arms. The world is returning to paganism and the soul-confining narrowness of unbelief. If St. Paul came back to earth today, he would find in our cities as many shameful things as he did in Paphos or Corinth, as many vendors of amulets as in Ephesus or Antioch, as many idols as in Rome, as many pedants and sophists as in Athens, and as many hatreds as in Jerusalem. Some would laugh at him like the elders of the Areopagus; others would throw him into jail like the magistrates of Thessalonica; some would listen to him merely to pass the time like King Agrippa; and others, like the Roman proconsul, would say to him ironically: "Paul, thou art mad. Thy great learning is driving thee to madness." But St. Paul would go forward, preaching his Lord in every place, seeking out the elect in the streets and the inns, following the busiest highways and appearing in the great commercial centers of the world from Marseilles to New York, from New York to Buenos Aires, from Buenos Aires to Shanghai. His fearless voice would be heard striking terror into the souls of tyrants, awakening men's consciences, transforming their hearts, and showing them the star-strewn path to heaven. And many, from among the stevedores at the docks to the ministers at the altars of pleasure, would listen to that jubilant invitation which filled the Ephesians with joy: "Awake, sleeper, and arise from among the dead, and Christ will enlighten thee."

All this means that St. Paul is for us the Doctor of the Gentiles and the teacher of salvation, as he was for the contemporaries of Nero and Caligula. It means that if the modern world is to be spiritually renewed, it must return to the school of that extraordinary man who shed his light upon and enkindled the ancient world. The great Pauline dogmas are precisely the remedy which is needed to cure us of our spiritual ills and restore our sanity. We need to learn the doctrine of original sin to rid us of the foolish optimism of Rousseau's "infinite perfectibility of man" which has been responsible for so many of our ill-fated Utopian experiments. We must substitute for it the only optimism possible, the one which begins by recognizing humbly our fallen nature, and which then affirms the existence of a Redeemer who restores us and makes us sons of God. We need to saturate ourselves with the strong and virile dogma of predestination, in order to free ourselves from that fatalism which leaves the soul indifferent to its destiny, weakening it and weighing it down in its struggle with the material world. We are constantly hearing of that sad travesty on the Communion of Saints—Communism— which seems to be the only remedy materialistic metaphysics can supply to relieve our distress, but which contains nothing humanly intimate, nothing vital, since it can offer only the mechanical union of atoms in a mass. St. Paul would teach us the true way to peace. He would show us that the wages of sin is death; he would unfold to us the knowledge of love, and would give us in his moral teaching the secret of strength, the joy of interior peace and the blessing of harmony between peoples. . . .

I do not offer here any historical novelty, nor do I offer anything that will enlighten the learned or surprise the specialists. Even if I could do so, that is not what was asked of me. I have simply tried to outline the story of the great missionary's life, endeavoring to penetrate into his soul, to grasp the essence of his thoughts, to see his actions against the background of his age, and to present his gigantic character in all its rugged sublimity and sanctity.

May the example of the Apostle, "against hope believing in hope," always awaiting in patience and love the hour of justice and the glorious coming of Christ—may his example sustain and enlighten us in the days that lie before us.

St. Paul

the Missionary

CHAPTER I

A Young Man Named Saul

"**B**ehold I send you forth as lambs in the midst of wolves," our Lord had said to His disciples. "You will be hated, mocked, scourged, cast out of the synagogues; they will kill you, thinking that they are doing a work pleasing to God." These prophetic words began to be fulfilled very soon after the birth of the Church on Pentecost, for the minions of Caiphas still kept a close watch on these teachers of new doctrine, and the same tribunal that had judged the Master now condemned His disciples. Peter and John were brought before the Sanhedrin; the Twelve were persecuted and thrown into prison, but a voice was raised in their defense, that of the Rabbi Gamaliel, the great authority on rabbinical learning. Moreover, these Galileans, sons of working men, former fishermen and despised publicans, had not in their eyes the flashing fire of their Master, nor did they speak as He spoke. The rabbis concluded that these fools, with their insane pretensions, would soon come to grief, and that the people would see that their work was not of God.

Contempt begets toleration. Consequently, the chiefs of the synagogue, who, like Annas, paid more attention to politics than to religion, considered that there were other

1

things much more important than suppressing a handful of stubborn, ignorant, fanatical and, on the whole, inoffensive country louts. Thus the small group of disciples was left to grow and organize, and the Spirit of Christ continued to live among them, while His words filled them with confident, joyous enthusiasm. He had said to them: "Therefore do not be anxious, saying 'What shall we eat?' or, 'What shall we drink?' or, 'What are we to put on?'" Wherefore, in blind faith, they despoiled themselves of all their possessions, placing them at Peter's feet and living in an ingenuous and joyful communism, convinced that there were no riches comparable to love. They had but one purse, one soul, and one heart.

Their deep happiness in poverty awakened admiration and sympathy for their ideals, with the result that more and more people every day came to hear them speak of Jesus and to ask for baptism. The majority of these converts were Jews of the Diaspora, Hellenized Jews, who used to come from their ghettos, scattered all over the Empire from the Atlantic to the Euphrates, to present their offerings at the Holy City on the great solemnities of the Mosaic Law. These strangers' foreign ways, their lax interpretation of the ancient rites, and even the fact that they were businessmen, merchants, industrialists and bankers, begot suspicion and disdain among the puritanical Hebrews who had never set foot in a Gentile land nor sullied themselves by dealing with the uncircumcised. Furthermore, the foreigners did not know the language of the sacred writings, but used instead *Koiné*, the international Greek dialect of that time, both in their religious functions and their everyday life. Accustomed as they were to their own synagogues without altars, Ark of the Covenant, cherubim or sacrifice, the Jews of the Diaspora were more easily able to understand the spiritual nature of the new religion, the worship "in spirit and in truth," the prophecy of the destruction of the Temple, and the parable of the piece of new cloth sewed to an old garment or of the new wine poured into old bottles. In fact, the first seven deacons chosen by the Twelve to help in serving at the tables, in preaching and baptizing, were taken from among these Jews of the Diaspora.

Little by little, the conversions began to make notable inroads on the synagogues of the Hellenized Jews. The members of these synagogues were zealous for the Law, as were the Jews of Jerusalem; they were influential, aggressive, and passionately devoted to their traditions. Even though they had ceased to practice some secondary points of ritual, their dealings with the Gentiles had made them prouder than ever of their blood and had deepened their belief in their religion, but while the Pharisees of Jerusalem shut themselves up in an inviolable isolation of caste, these Hellenized Jews, calculating nationalists that they were, dreamed of the universal rule of the Mosaic Law. They were intelligent, astute, wealthy; they had a veneer of Greek culture, but they also had ambitious schemes for converting the Gentiles, and, while their business connections offered opportunities for missionary work, the missionary work itself was a new means of gaining influence and making profits.

But here was this new sect spoiling their plans, robbing them of success, sowing confusion among their converts, and stealing their best preachers. The newcomers seemed harmless enough, and people even remarked upon their charity and lack of self-interest. The atmosphere of brotherly love that surrounded them was commented upon enthusiastically, and their champions pointed out that, far from fighting against the established religion, many of them observed its practices strictly, going to the Temple to pray, attending the ceremonies and even offering sacrifices. And although they insisted on believing that the Messias had already come, their stubbornness in holding to their belief injured no one. Nevertheless, their enemies realized that if this movement were to continue unchecked, a revolution in the history of Israel was inevitable. Even during Jesus' life, His adversaries had seen this danger, pointing out that the teachings of the Carpenter of Nazareth had stirred the multitudes, lessened the prestige of the Temple, reduced the authority of the priests, and threatened the very foundations of Jewish society. If the Messias had come, Israel's mission was finished and the Chosen People would cease to exist, like the desert bush that has grown to its full height and produced its purple blossom. Had the nation borne for centuries the humiliations inflicted on it by the *goyim*, that is, the Gentiles, the instruments of Jahweh, merely to fade away like that? For thousands of years the story of the world's origin had been told and retold in Israel's tents. She retained the savor of divine food snatched from heaven by her prophets, and she alone, in the midst of a world sunk in error and given over to idolatry, had preserved the treasure of the true religion, the idea of a monotheism that was totally opposed to all idols and to all deformation of the Divinity. But the Countryman from Galilee had come, proclaiming Himself the herald of a new religion, the greatest of the prophets, the Only-Begotten Son of God. He had announced that one day He would reappear in glory in the clouds of heaven; He had arrogated to Himself the title of Supreme Judge and demanded that men worship Him as God. What could all this mean except the dethronement of Jahweh or the setting up of a rival deity?

In addition, the disciples of the Carpenter were spreading all kinds of subversive ideas clothed in popular language. In the spiritual brotherhood which these disciples were trying to propagate, all dreams of grandeur had to be renounced. No longer was there to be a ruling nation; no longer were there to be subject peoples. The first were to be the last, the workers who came at the eleventh hour would receive the same wages as the rest, pagans were to be treated as equals with the Jews. No longer were there to be privileges, an Ark of the Covenant, or a priestly caste, and victims could be immolated anywhere in the world as effectively as in Jerusalem. All the greatness of Israel, all her dreams, all her special prerogatives were to be destroyed and brought to nothing.

One of the most ardent preachers of these new doctrines was a convert from among the Hellenized Jews, and the very prestige which this new follower of Christ had enjoyed among his former co-religionists spurred him on to unheard-of daring. He went back to their synagogues, won over their most devout members, and argued with their learned men, refuting their objections, humiliating and confounding them. When he spoke of the pre-eminence of Christ over Moses and proclaimed the abrogation of the levitical prescriptions, his ringing words re-echoed in the minds of his hearers, convincing them that the greatest miracles were possible. No one could resist the wisdom of the Spirit who spoke through the mouth of Stephen the deacon. His eloquence and intrepidity stirred up all the synagogues which the Jews of the Diaspora had in Jerusalem—the synagogues of the Libertines of Rome, the Alexandrians, the Cyrenians, the Asiatics, and also the synagogue of Cilicia, which counted among its members a young man named Saul, a fanatical Jew whose burning hatred and indignation were fanned to a white heat by the blasphemies of the fearless new preacher.

By this time, three or four years had passed since Christ's death, years of an iron Roman dictatorship devoted to maintaining peace and limiting the independence of the provinces. From his island of Capri, a tall, bent old man with feeble limbs, bald forehead, and a face half-eaten away by ulcers and covered with plasters, sent edicts of proscription and death to Rome. However, the people had some reason to be thankful for the lonely old emperor's strong measures, for his reign of terror assured political order, he suppressed rebellions ruthlessly, and caused the governors of the provinces to tremble as much as their subjects. In Palestine, Pontius Pilate continued to exercise his office of procurator in the same way as he had in the days of Christ, alternating between weakness and brutality; and Caiphas still wore the ephod of the high priests.

Personalities and hatreds were the same as they had been during our Lord's life, but now the doctors of the Law, humiliated by Stephen's eloquence and itching to punish his audacious blasphemy, thought themselves strong enough to act on their own initiative and put into force their national laws.

Following the same pattern they had used in their plotting against our Lord, they began by stirring up the crowds, repeating their old accusation: "This man ceases not to speak against the holy place and to contemn the Law." In their eyes, no crime could be worse: the Law was the glory and pride of Israel; the Temple stood for the stability of the nation, enshrined its traditions, and was the source of great material gain to the city. Without the Temple there

would be no pilgrimages, no sacrifices, no Talmudic teaching, no history, no religion, no fatherland. To speak of its
downfall was to speak of the destruction of the Chosen
People.

Stephen's enemies well knew how to play upon the
emotions of the crowd by skillfully combining violence
with hypocrisy. Their efforts were rewarded with the out-
break of a riot in which it was easy to see the hand of the
rabble-rouser. But the instigators of the disturbance wanted
to give the proceedings the appearance of legality to satisfy
their scrupulous consciences, so they seized the blasphemer,
"rescued" him from the mob, and threw him into prison.
Meanwhile, the great tribunal of the nation, the Sanhedrin,
had begun to meet in the Temple. In the center sat Caiphas,
he who had condemned Christ and who still, as high priest,
wore on his forehead the plate of gold and on his breast the
rational, or breastplate, studded with rubies and diamonds.
Around him were gathered the seventy judges, and at his
feet, in three rows, sat the most famous disciples of the
Judaic schools, the future Sanhedrists and pastors of Israel.
Undoubtedly, there too sat Saul, the hope of the Cilician
synagogue, transfixing the prisoner with looks of hatred.

Impassively Stephen listened to the accusations brought
against him, impressing even his enemies with his candid
expression and magnificent serenity, for his face was like
an angel's, reminding his audience of the ancient prophets.
"Is it true what the witnesses say?" the high priest asked
him, as if inviting him to defend himself. Stephen, the true
disciple of Christ, did not keep silence as five years before
his Master had done, nor did he burst forth into agitated
speech. Instead, he delivered a sublime discourse, his last
call to men of good will and his challenge to the hard of
heart. His inspired words caught the minds of his listeners

and led them through the history of Israel, stripping the veil of mystery from the ancient allegories and revealing the symbolic character of the most important personages in that magnificent story. He spoke of Moses; he painted the picture of Abraham leaving the land of the Chaldees; he traced the history of Joseph, ill-treated and sold into bondage by his brothers; he recalled the bush that burned without being consumed; he reminded them of the Temple of Solomon and the glory of Jahweh's throne, skillfully making allusions to the Just One whom they had condemned and crucified.

A shock of surprise ran through the crowd: the prisoner was liable to be sentenced to death, and yet he did not defend himself or even deign to look at his accusers. The aged Pharisees began to stir in their robes and broad phylacteries. Raising their eyes in order to fix them on the accused, they "saw his face as though it were the face of an angel." He was young, handsome, eloquent; the Holy Spirit was working in him, inflaming his heart and his words, and he spoke as one having power.

Perhaps his hearers did not immediately grasp the drift of the first part of Stephen's discourse: before the pact of circumcision, God looked upon Abraham and regarded only his faith. Faith, obedience, and love were all that mattered. Race and lineage meant nothing, and a purely material confidence in the Temple was simply idolatry. This was the argument that was to be later developed so compellingly by the young man named Saul who was now listening, with hate-filled heart, to the deacon Stephen.

The speaker's interpretation of Israel's history grew more and more vehement, arousing the audience to fury. Far from fearing their rage, Stephen added fuel to it by gazing about on them with scornful indignation as he

uttered his scarifying indictment: "Stiffnecked and uncircumcised in heart and ear, you always oppose the Holy
Spirit; as your fathers did, so you do also. Which of the
prophets have not your fathers persecuted? And they killed
those who foretold the coming of the Just One, of whom
you have now been the betrayers and murderers, you who
received the Law as an ordinance of angels and did not
keep it" (Acts 7:51-53).

A wild clamor shook the august tribunal, and the speaker
was not allowed to say more. ". . . they gnashed their
teeth at him"; for the words they had just heard cut them
to the heart. In their fury, the like of which is found only
in Oriental mobs, they became like a pack of wolves. But
the accused seemed to be unaware of their strident voices,
their slavering mouths, their shrieks of anger, their fierce
eyes, their claw-like, threatening hands. It was as if he were
already surrounded by the joys of paradise. And when the
tumult began to die down, he fixed his gaze like a dreamer
awakening on a vision which only he could see, and exclaimed: "Behold, I see the heavens opened, and the Son of
man standing at the right hand of God." In the ears of his
hearers this was another blasphemy, the proclamation of
Christ's glory and of the triumph of the Nazarene.

Goaded beyond endurance by these words, and in the
grip of an insane rage, the tribunal rose as one man. Stopping their ears and shouting furiously, they threw themselves on Stephen, crowding him toward the door. No need
to pass sentence—the well-known text of Leviticus was
doom enough: "Bring forth the blasphemer without the
camp. . . ." The prisoner had to die the death prescribed
—execution by stoning outside the city. Surrounded by the
howling mob, he was hurried through the Golden Gate
and along the Valley of Cedron to a point opposite Geth-

semane which was chosen as the place of execution. Following the prescriptions of the Law, the witnesses cast the first stones, whereupon, as at a signal, a hundred arms flashed upwards, paused a moment and came crashing viciously down, their missiles crushing the holy deacon to the ground.

Saul was there among the others, but perhaps because he was more fastidious or because he had more authority than the rest, he did not wish to cast a single stone. Enough for him to be present at the execution, which possibly he, with his impetuous zeal, had brought about. The witnesses were acquaintances of his, perhaps his tools, which was the reason why, before approaching the prisoner to fulfill the legal preliminaries, they had given him their cloaks to watch lest they lose them in the tumult and confusion. He viewed the horrible performance with complacency: "And Saul approved of his death."

Neither Stephen's ecstasy nor the dignity of his bearing in the face of death could abate Saul's hatred. Yet some spark from the furnace of Stephen's love must have lodged in the recesses of the young Pharisee's heart, later to be fanned to an all-consuming fire, although at the moment Saul was conscious of nothing but his passionate zeal for the Law. With the din of the mob ringing in his ears, he felt the secret satisfaction of justice done filling his soul, and the victim's bravery, his meekness under the executioners' blows, his forgiving eyes and his undaunted words in the midst of suffering served only to increase Saul's hatred. Overwhelmed with blows, the martyr drew his last breath and, following Christ's example, exclaimed in a voice of power: "Lord, do not lay this sin against them." Having said this, he fell asleep in the Lord. It was a perfect sacrifice, the sacrifice of one who pardons his enemies and offers himself as a holocaust for them. Perhaps while saying those last words, Stephen was thinking of the young man from Cilicia who was present at the martyrdom with murder in his heart—the man for whom that martyrdom was paving the way to the most fruitful of apostolates.

At the time, however, Stephen's death marked the beginning of a cruel persecution. Even as his friends were sadly carrying away the body and burying it, new measures were being taken in the Council of the Ancients against the worshippers of Christ. The procurator was absent from Jerusalem, and if he did get news of the crime just committed, he probably thought it more prudent to turn a blind eye on it. This first attempt of the proud Pharisees to recover their lost rights was so successful that they became even more insolent. No longer was Gamaliel's counsel of moderation able to restrain the fanatics, among whom Saul soon emerged as a leader, for his zeal in the recent events had drawn attention to him; he had shown everyone that he was vehement, fearless, and a great lover of Israel's traditions. His qualities as a commander of men were so evident that, in spite of his youth, the members of the Sanhedrin did not hesitate to give him the office of inquisitor, an office which he proceeded to exercise with all the fury of a zealot. The victims of his wrath were above all the Nazarene innovators, with their disrespect for the Temple, their indifference to the Law, and their desire to cut all the ties that bound them to Judaism. The schismatic tendencies of these Hellenizers, at a moment when every true patriot should have united against Rome, almost drove Saul insane and made him a rabid persecutor of the despicable traitors, his youthful impetuosity urging him on to crush them. Filled with hatred for these enemies of Israel and believing that he had been delegated by God to annihilate them, he went from synagogue to synagogue, he spoke in the streets, he pushed his way into dwellings, forcing the weak to renounce their new faith, imprisoning the stubborn and threatening them with the lash, with torture, and with death. As he himself said later: "And I persecuted this way even to the death, binding and committing to prisons both men and women. . . ." And St. Luke uses these significant words: "Saul was harassing the church." In his hatred for the innovators, he did not hesitate to throw them into prisons, drag them before the tribunals, and send them to their death. He was, as he later put it, "a blasphemer, a persecutor and a bitter adversary. . . ."

Pascal once observed that evil is never done so completely and joyfully as when it is done as a matter of conscience, an observation that helps us to understand Saul's psychology during this period of his life. His cruelty was born of burning zeal and a profound conviction of the truths he was defending. Speaking later to his disciple Timothy, perhaps in a moment of inner disquiet, he was able to say: ". . . but I obtained the mercy of God because I acted ignorantly, in unbelief." And when writing to the Galatians he expressed himself in this manner: "For you have heard of my former manner of life in Judaism; how beyond all measure I persecuted the Church of God, and ravaged it. And I advanced in Judaism above many of my contemporaries in my nation, showing much more zeal for the traditions of my fathers" (1:13-14). He was urged on by a mystical passion akin to that which had inflamed his forefathers when they commanded fire to come down from heaven, when they inveighed against the sacrifices of Moloch, or when they beheaded the priests of Baal before the altar of their false god.

In Saul the exaltation of the patriot combined with the

sectarian fanaticism of the ardent Pharisee, and his youthful intolerance lent added vigor to his naturally passionate and fiery temperament. His was undoubtedly a misguided zeal, but all his violence was motivated solely by sincerity and pride in the name of Jahweh. He was not then aware that the devil was lending strength to his arm, but no doubt he realized it later when his experiences of diabolical influences led him to exclaim: "For our wrestling is not against flesh and blood: but against the Principalities and the Powers, against the world-rulers of this darkness, against the spiritual forces of wickedness on high" (Eph. 6:12). At the time we refer to, however, he was not conscious of this, for he was blinded by hatred of the Galilean Rabbi whom he had never even seen, but whose doctrine, as he understood it, seemed to be the ruin of all the hopes of Israel. The Galilean's interpretation of the great Messianic prophecies enraged and scandalized him. As a Pharisee, he was bound to oppose the Man who had launched such terrible anathemas against his whole caste; and as a descendant of Abraham, he had to protest against the new universalist movement which proclaimed the superseding of the Old Law by the New, which threatened the future of Israel and abrogated the privileges of the Jews as the Chosen People.

CHAPTER II

At the Feet of Gamaliel

When Saul suddenly appeared on the stage of history in the Synagogue's first pitched battle with the Church, he was hardly twenty-five years old. This is not to be wondered at, since in crises of terrorism youth always takes the lead. Hitherto the fiery young man had lived in obscurity; we can only guess at the events of his childhood and youth. However, he himself has told us something of his first years: "If anyone else thinks he may have confidence in the flesh, yet more may I; circumcised the eighth day, of the race of Israel, of the tribe of Benjamin, a Hebrew of Hebrews; as regards the Law, a Pharisee . . ." (Phil. 3:4–5); "I am a Jew from Tarsus in Cilicia, a citizen of no insignificant city" (Acts 21:39). In later years, when he spoke to Jews, he used to stress his Jewish origin, but when he had to defend himself before the officials of Rome, he emphasized the fact that he was by birth a citizen of one of the most important cities in the Empire. In the eyes of the law and of society, this title of citizenship placed him among the aristocracy of the province, for it was an honor not easily granted, even at that period of the Empire's history. It was a mark of distinction, a sign of material prosperity and a key which could unlock many doors for its possessor.

Saul derived his civic rights from no less a city than Tarsus, that rich storehouse of knowledge and wealth, one of the great cities of the East, justly proud of its wide tracts of fertile land yielding abundant crops, and of the favors which Rome had showered upon it. Tarsus was a cross-roads at which civilizations met, for the ships of the Mediterranean could sail up the Cydnus to the very walls of the city, and the trade-route along which the caravans from Asia Minor entered Cilicia ended here. In the city's markets the rarest products of India were on sale side by side with merchandise from the West. It was by working in this cosmopolitan atmosphere, along the colorful wharves and amid the din of the markets, that Saul's father earned the proud title which he was to leave as a heritage to his son.

However, in the stormy beginning of his active life, Saul considered that no title of nobility or citizenship could compare with his claim to being a son of Abraham. Later he came to count all such pretensions "as dung," but at the time we are speaking of, his pride of nation and race knew no limits. He called himself "a Hebrew of Hebrews" with the same arrogance as the members of the priestly families in the cities of Asia called themselves "priests, and sons of priests." It is true that he had been born outside of Palestine, and that he was a member of one of those numerous Jewish colonies which sprang up all over the ancient world as a result of the Jews' instinct for trade, their love of money and their flight from persecution. But he had lost none of his devotion to the traditions of his race or the memory of his ancestors. In his veins pulsed the blood of the patriarchs undiluted by intermarriage with the Gentiles, the blood of Benjamin, the beloved of Jacob, the founder of one of the Twelve Tribes—the only tribe, apart from that of Juda, which had helped to raise the walls of Sion after the Babylonian Captivity. The family atmosphere in which he was reared was as purely Jewish as the blood in his veins, for no breath of paganism was admitted to that puritanically orthodox household. No tendril of Hellenistic culture took root there; the surrounding Graeco-Roman world was a place in which to trade and thereafter to avoid. Rigid Pharisaism was the rule in that Jewish home in Tarsus. In later years, when Saul wished to lay stress on the fidelity to the Law in which he was educated from birth, he could with truth say that he was "a Pharisee, the son of Pharisees," a member of that privileged class who kept apart from the common herd of the faithful, who wore broad phylacteries and fulfilled the smallest precepts, who loved to be honored in the market places and at banquets and to be called "Rabbi" by the people.

Tarsus was a university city, rivalling Athens in its rhetoricians, its philosophers and men of learning. The Romans, lords of the world, looked to this city in Cilicia for teachers, so that it is possible that Saul knew the aged Athenodorus, the Stoic philosopher who had taught the young Augustus and who, laden with riches, had come home to his native city to die. But Saul's preceptors were not men of Athenodorus' stamp, for he attended the Jewish school at Tarsus, one of those schools of orthodoxy which the Jews set up in every important city. Here, and perhaps also at home, he learned Aramaic, which he came to speak as fluently as his native tongue. In the streets and at the synagogue, he learned Greek, the common language of the country, but instead of Thucydides, Plato and the fables of Homer, his reading-book was the Sacred Scriptures in the Septuagint translation. Later on, he would not disdain to include in his epistles and discourses quotations from the classical writers such as Aratus, a Tarsian like himself, the comedian Menander, and the satirist Epimenides. But these quotations are nearly all proverbial sayings current at the time, and, even if they are taken to indicate that he had some interest in profane literature, they certainly do not argue a profound knowledge of the subject.

Saul learned Greek and learned it thoroughly. His Greek is not, as some have said, transposed Aramaic, but neither is it the artificial Greek of the grammarians. His is the language of business, of the market place, of the busy seaport; it is *Koiné,* the dialect in which the rabbi read and explained the Scriptures to him, the dialect which his father used in selling cloth woven from goat-hair, the language he and his playmates used in their games. It is the language of conversation and not of the schoolroom; it is vivid, picturesque, full of images, flexible, expressive and original, far richer in shades of meaning and more vigorous than the language of a Jew completely ignorant of all Greek culture, or of a rhetorician confined by the rules of grammar. This dialect was to serve him later as a weapon; in his youth, however, it was the channel through which Greek thought began to exercise its influence on his mind.

According to the rabbinical traditions, a Hebrew had to begin learning the Scriptures at the age of five; at ten, he began to learn the Mishnah; at thirteen, to observe the precepts; and at fifteen, to study the Talmud or commentaries on the Law. The most famed teachers of the complicated Talmudic lore had their schools in Jerusalem, and it was there that Saul went at some time between his twelfth and fifteenth year with the ambition of one day becoming as renowned as his masters. It is not surprising that he was sent to Jerusalem for further study, since exiled

Israelites like his father rarely forgot the land of their ancestors. Although they were tireless travellers, drawn by the lure of gain to all parts of the ancient world from Gades to the cities of Persia and Mesopotamia, and though they adopted any country where they could set up their stalls, these wandering Jews still regarded the Promised Land as their spiritual home and the focus of all their religious ambitions. At least once in their lifetime they visited Jerusalem to adore in the only temple in which Jahweh accepted the Mosaic sacrifices, and, if their social position and family circumstances permitted it, they remained there to steep themselves in the knowledge of their national traditions, seeking out the leaders of Israel from whom they learned the skills of the scribe.

This profession of scribe was the recognized preparation for all careers. It was a twofold profession which opened the door to every honor in the political and religious life of the Chosen People, for a scribe was at once a counselor-at-law and an attorney, a magistrate and an expert jurist, a preacher and a teacher, a grammarian and a rhetorician—in a word, both churchman and man of law. At the rabbinical school in Jerusalem, classes were held within the Temple or in its outer porches, and were taught by the great rabbis, the intellectual descendants of Hillel and Shammai, those two illustrious doctors who flourished a century before Saul's time, and who founded the two most famed schools of Talmudic knowledge, which rivalled each other more in prestige and in their efforts to attract the youth of the nation than in differences of doctrine. It is true that one of these schools, that of Hillel, had the name of being broadminded and liberal in contrast to the rigor and conservatism of the other; however, they disagreed only on minute details of ritual and insignificant points of observance which did not affect the essence of the Torah. For example, in reply to the question: "May one eat on the Sabbath an egg laid the same day?" the disciple of Hillel would say "Yes," while the follower of Shammai would answer "No." It was due to problems like this, impossible to solve either by metaphysical arguments or appeals to authority, that disagreements, rivalry and even hatred arose between the two schools.

As a student in Jerusalem, Saul was a follower of Hillel, despite his puritanical character which soon made him a fanatical Pharisee. At that time, the school of Hillel was mainly represented by the Rabbi Gamaliel, the grandson of the founder and a renowned teacher who, in spite of his defense of Christ's followers, was considered by his compatriots the exemplar of the true Israelite. "Since his death," says the Mishnah, "there is no more respect for the Law. The purity of Pharisaism died with him." He combined knowledge and virtue, prudence and goodness. Moreover, while the other rabbis condemned Greek as a channel of corruption and idolatry, he spoke it and recommended its study to his pupils. His rivals, the followers of Shammai, used to tell their pupils, "You may learn Greek when it is neither day nor night,"—that is, never. And they would add, "He who delights in the honey of Greek fables will find the milk of the Scriptures bitter."

We must not forget that St. Paul was a Hellenist, a fact which helps us to understand his enthusiasm for the doctrine of his renowned teacher, who looked with a compassionate smile on his first bursts of fervor. "I am a Jew . . . brought up at the feet of Gamaliel," he tells us himself. Seated on the ground, with arms clasped around his knees, silent, with eyes fixed on his teacher's face, he heard day after day that voice warmed by an almost prophetic fire revealing to him the literal and allegorical meaning of the Holy Books in all their aspects, historical, grammatical, ethical and theological. In that school there were no classes in mathematics, physics, the exact sciences, or philosophy. Everything was reduced to morality, the positive law, and sacred history—in a word, the Sacred Scriptures. The student learned from the Holy Books how to read, how to write, how to argue, and how to live. In them was sought the concept which an Israelite ought to have of the world and of life. The idea of God, His infinite transcendence, His creative power, His fatherly goodness, the doctrine of man's last end, as well as the teaching of revelation on the origin of the world, the resurrection of the dead, the last judgment, punishments and rewards—such were the main points in that theological system which Christianity had but to amplify and complete.

However, this doctrinal foundation was accompanied by hair-splitting casuistry and subtle dialectics reminiscent of the pagan rhetoricians. The pupils were taught a method for interpreting the Scriptures which, in its essentials, had been evolved by the great Hillel, the Aristotle of rabbinical logic. Every student had to learn the seven arguments developed by this great teacher, and to practice, under the direction of the rabbi, the use of syllogisms, analogy, parallelism, contrast, context, reasoning from the universal to the particular and from the particular to the universal. The teacher would propose a question such as, "Must the zizith, the multi-colored shirt, be worn at night?" The disciples would discuss the point, marshalling their arguments pro or con, and the teacher would pronounce judgment on the matter. There was no problem too difficult for these debates, which were actually only literary exercises full of ingenuity and refined subtlety, more concerned with adroit casuistry than rigid logic. For example, it might be asked if it were lawful to sacrifice the Paschal lamb on a Sabbath that coincided with the full moon of the month Nisan. The rabbi would unhesitatingly reply with an *a fortiori* argument: "Although the daily sacrifice can be omitted without the punishment of excommunication, it takes precedence over the Sabbath. How much more, then, should the sacrifice of the Paschal lamb take precedence over the Sabbath, since its omission *is* punishable by excommunication."

Along with these rabbinical methods, which were frequently paradoxical and puerile, the young student from Tarsus learned the most important texts of the Law and the Prophets, the ritual formulae and the better-known solutions evolved by Pharisaical casuistry. These studies demanded a gigantic effort of memory, since neither the *haggadah*, that is, historical tradition, nor the *halakah*, juridical tradition, was written down, and since the students were forbidden to take notes on the rabbis' decisions or discourses. Infinite were the ceremonies, the prayers, the customs, the traditions and the rites which the teachers of Israel guarded jealously, and which won for them the admiration of the multitude. The rabbis knew the words which had to be pronounced in blessing before sitting down to eat radishes which had been cut into small pieces, as well as the words required to invoke the blessing of heaven on radishes which had been cut lengthwise into strips. They knew that on a Sabbath one could go as far as the olive-garden of Gethsemane but no farther. They knew that one had to wash one's fingers before drinking but were not agreed on the precise ritual, since the disciples of Shammai said that the hands ought to be washed before pouring the drink, while the followers of Hillel maintained that the ablution should take place after the liquid had been poured. The most minute details were provided for in their scrupulous quibbling which left its mark on the Asiatic student who had come to their schools at what was perhaps the zenith of their ingenuity and casuistry. At this period more than any other there was justification for the proverb: "If you lose your purse, pray God that a moralist doesn't find it." The Talmud relates a story about the wise, virtuous and venerable Gamaliel which, if true, is reminiscent of the delicate irony of a sophist from the school of Gorgias: "On a certain occasion, the rabbi went to take medicinal baths at Accho where there was a temple to Aphrodite which was supported by the money left by the bathers. A pagan named Proclus ben Philosophos asked him why he went to bathe in a place devoted to the service of an idol when the Mosaic Law definitely forbade him to do so. To which the Rabbi Gamaliel replied: 'It is not I who go into the domain of the idol, it is the idol that comes to me. The establishment was not built in honor of Aphrodite; on the contrary, it is Aphrodite who serves as an ornament to the establishment.' "

Gamaliel's solution to the problem is similar to that which his disciple later gave in the case of meats sacrificed to idols, although while Saul was still a stiff-necked Pharisee, he would not have thought as Gamaliel did. From his teacher Saul learned the biblical commentaries, the use of rabbinical arguments, which he was afterwards to employ to the full, as well as the precepts of the Law with their innumerable distinctions and interpretations which he later rejected as useless burdens. However, he did not learn to imitate his master's sweetness of character, forbearance and broad-mindedness. Perhaps he was even scandalized by Gamaliel's wise and generous liberalism, for it often happens that a pupil adopts an attitude contrary to that of his teacher. That was the case with Saul, and it is an indication of his forceful, independent character. Although he undoubtedly admired Gamaliel's knowledge, he raised his voice in protest against his moderation and in vehement defense of integral Judaism, rejecting all dangerous mitigations and refusing any toleration of innovators, cowards and blasphemers. Instead of following a policy of disdainful non-intervention based on a fatalistic view of Providence, Saul wished to leap into rapid, energetic and ruthless action. "Leave them alone," Gamaliel said in later years, referring to the disciples of Christ, "because if their work is simply human they will fail utterly; if it is of God, your efforts will be in vain." Actually, this was an unanswerable argument, because if the claims and mission of Peter and his companions were not divinely inspired, then there was neither rhyme nor reason to them and they were certain to fail. However, as a young student and even later, Saul was guided only by the vehemence of his faith, the violence of his character, and the interests of the cause to which he had dedicated his life.

At this period in Saul's career, the good tidings of the Gospel had not yet been preached in the fields of Galilee. Christ was still working silently in His carpenter-shop, waiting for His hour which was soon to come. And Saul, his course of studies finished, had returned to his parents' house without an inkling of the nearness of the great religious revolution. He returned rich in knowledge and full of Pharisaical pride. He knew the Scriptures almost by heart; he knew how to interpret them literally and allegorically; he had assimilated the historical and canonical traditions of his people; he was now a scribe, a theologian and a man of letters. He felt that he was more of a Hebrew than ever; he recited the words of David and Isaias with greater fervor and recalled with deeper gratitude the wanderings of the prophets, mysteriously guided by the voice of Jahweh. With iron will power and heroic tenacity he set out to make himself worthy of the saints and prophets, and to help bring to pass the predictions of heaven by his irreproachable conduct. He was of the race of Abraham, that race which had been chosen for a providential mission, which had been thought worthy to receive the tables of the Law and which was to dominate all nations with that Law, as the Lord had promised. Such were the feelings which possessed his soul and inspired his conduct. He wanted to observe the Law, to observe it as completely as the most devout Nazarite, as the most ardent and inflexible Pharisee. He was a zealot, haughtily and fearlessly virtuous; he was a Pharisee of such scrupulous correctness that later he could say: "I was zealous for the Law . . . According to the strictest sect of our religion I lived a Pharisee. . . . As regards the justice of the Law, leading a blameless life" (Acts 22:3; 26:5. Phil. 3:6).

Sustained by mystical exaltation, he was happy beneath the yoke of that slavery and, caught in the net of the six hundred and thirteen prescriptions of the Mosaic Code and the innumerable precepts which the casuists had been adding thereto for centuries, he had the deep satisfaction of being able to pray, like the Pharisee in the Gospel: "O God, I thank thee that I am not like the rest of men. . . ." This state of mind was the natural result of the miserable formalism to which religion had been reduced—a collection of mechanical rites that paralyzed inner spontaneity, enchained the spirit, deadened the highest aspirations of natural morality, and convinced man that he alone was the architect of his own justice, the "justice" of one who fasted twice in the week and paid tithes on mint and anise, disdainful of the repentant sighs and humble words of the publican who in one instant attained true justice. Such was the psychology of the Pharisee which, with its presumption, its hatred and its hypocrisy, took possession of the mind of the young man from Tarsus. But even the most alert brain and strongest will were incapable of always fulfilling all the demands of the Pharisaical code, with the result that omissions and infractions multiplied, casuistry flourished, and ideals were lowered. This duality of belief and practice is described by our Lord in the Gospel: "And they bind together heavy and oppressive burdens and lay them on men's shoulders; but not with a finger of their own do they choose to move them" (Matt. 23:4). The Pharisees felt that they had to uphold their reputation for virtue before the common people whom they despised, yet feared; they had to compensate for their inner poverty by exterior intolerance. Thus Saul, enslaved by the ritual of his caste and goaded on by zeal, pride, hypocrisy and remorse, gradually became a fanatic, a persecutor and a murderer.

Now that he was in Tarsus again, his formal studies completed, he breathed in the austere atmosphere of his home and considered his future. He went to the synagogue with exemplary regularity; he took part, perhaps, in the religious services; enthusiastically he sang the psalmody of the *Hallel;* with profound respect he gazed upon the scroll of the Law when the rabbi unrolled it before the eyes of the congregation, and when, on Friday evenings, the lamps of the day of rest were lighted, he recalled with grateful heart the favors God had showered on his people. His teachers in Jerusalem had told him that every good Israelite ought to know how to work with his hands, and he could not forget the holy eccentricity of the Rabbi Shammai who used to wear an earring in the shape of a miniature hammer to symbolize his trade of carpenter. Therefore Saul set out to acquire a trade too, and in time became a tent-maker. Even to this day the inhabitants of Cilicia have retained their skill in this art. In the country villages one can still find large lean-to shelters filled with the happy voices of the tent-makers. In each workshop one of the craftsmen is busy turning a wheel from which hang the ends of a stout cord. At his waist he has a pouch from which he draws out, one by one, the goat-hairs or camel-hairs which he is plaiting into the cord hanging from the wheel. As he spins the strong hard thread, he moves slowly backwards from the interior of the shelter to the doorway where his fellow-workers, sitting on sheep-skins, ply their wooden knives as they weave the coarse cloth that will soon be made into tents for shepherds and farm workers, or hair shirts for ascetics. Following the advice of the rabbis, Saul worked at this trade in his youth and he kept it up throughout his life, earning his own living, for the business was, and continued to be, profitable. Moreover, because the process was purely mechanical and unvarying, it left his mind completely free, so that he was able to meditate on the last chapter of Scripture that he had read or on the last meeting in the synagogue or, in later years, on the affairs of the churches.

It was during this visit to his native city that Saul came into closer contact with Graeco-Roman culture. Apparently neither art nor nature ever made any profound impression on him. Tarsus had its porches and temples in the Corinthian style, its palaces, its public baths, its open squares and its gardens adorned with statues. There Grecian culture combined with relics of Phoenician and Babylonian civilization; Zeus and Baal were merged into one on the city's coins, and Greek elegance added a new seduction to oriental sensuality. In the city's port, Cleopatra had stood on the golden prow of her galley, listening as the sails of perfumed silk stirred and whispered overhead, watching for the coming of Antony's victorious ships. At a little distance from the port loomed the gigantic dancing statue of Sardanapalus, inviting the traveller to read and follow the advice given in the cuneiform inscription on the plinth: "Eat, drink and be merry; everything else is worthless." From the city one could see the fertile plain and the smiling riverbanks, the dark-colored countryside criss-crossed by canals, and the quiet pine-shaded nooks in the mountainside where herds of goats and bulls grazed. Farther off, on one side gleamed the white sails of the Mediterranean, and on the other towered the snowy peaks of the Taurus range, from which gentle breezes blew over the city.

However, none of this natural beauty seems to have had any great influence on the young Israelite's imagination. In future years, he will see breath-taking panoramas, he will pass through the most picturesque regions of the ancient world; he will visit cities redolent of the magic of poetry and history: but his face will not light up with admiration, his heart will not be touched by emotion, nor will his language be enriched by the memory and impact of these scenes. It was not that he was unobservant, but simply that the external world mattered very little to him. Occupied as he was with the interior battle that raged within him, he had no time to listen to the language of inanimate things. Of all the great mystics, he alone does not refer to the whole of nature in his ecstatical descriptions. The prophets relate their visions with a wealth of imagery; our Lord's parables are filled with the perfume of flowers and fields. But psychology is Saul's domain; the inanimate world interests him only in its relationship to man. His commentators have observed that his metaphors are taken from the whole of human activity—the exercises of the Roman legionary, full of agility and strength; the graceful skill of the games in the circus; the clamor of the seething market places; the deadly combats in the arena that thrilled and made partisans of the populations of great cities; the glittering spectacles in the theatre; and the imposing architectural achievements which revealed the genius of men.

In the streets of Tarsus and in the porches of the public places, Saul often saw groups of men with unkempt beards and shabby, trailing robes, who focused the crowd's attention on themselves with their maxims and paradoxes. These were the Stoic philosophers, an unwashed but proud coterie who had made the capital of Cilicia one of the leading centers of thought. Saul looked upon them with a mixture of disdain and curiosity, for, although they were full of vanity, evil-smelling in body and rotten in soul, he found them not wholly despicable, since some of their maxims coincided with his deepest convictions, and also because their methods of arguing were not without merit. Afterwards, when he came to preach and write, he combined analogy, as taught him by the rabbis in the Temple, with the diatribe, a kind of mixture of dialogue and sustained discourse which the Stoics used in teaching morality. Nor did he, at times, disdain to make use of their terminology. But that is all he owed to these men with whom perhaps he argued more than once beneath the porches of Tarsus. Theirs was the philosophy of the street, not of the academy or of books. Seneca had begun to publish his writings about this time, but Saul, although his later style occasionally resembles this philosopher's, had no inclination to read him, or may never even have heard of him. He had no interest, either, in the Jew Philo who lent lustre to the School of Alexandria, and whose exegetical method he later used in his Epistles. Nor can we imagine him reading the Dialogues of Plato, much less the works of the poets. However, endowed as he was with a keener eye for ideas than for scenery, he listened to and observed what went on around him, absorbing the atmosphere in which he lived, analyzing, comparing, and arriving at an exact concept of the pagan world, its aspirations, its rites, its ideas, its religious and social practices. These influences will appear in future years in his discourses and writings, expressed not in a classical vocabulary but in the common language of the people, in what St. Jerome will dub "Cilicianisms," and in which the latest discoveries of inscriptions and papyri reveal to us idioms and expressions which, when they are not from the Septuagint version of the Old Testament, are of popular origin. The Scriptures in this version remained the principal object of his reading, study and meditation, the main source from which he drew his ideas and his language, the subsidiary one being his observation of the world in which he lived. Just as he had learned his theology by listening to the doctors of the Law in Jerusalem, so now, also by listening, he increased his skill in Greek, that cosmopolitan Greek which was spoken in Athens and Antioch, in Alexandria and in Rome. It was thus that he acquired his style, certainly a defective one if we view it in the light of rhetoricians' rules, but one which is nevertheless highly personal, full, rich and vigorous, suited to convey the highest ideas and produce the most miraculous effects.

CHAPTER III

On the Road to Damascus

Six, seven, perhaps eight years passed and Saul was again in Jerusalem, where his education and natural inclination led him to move in clerical rather than in commercial circles. He sought the company of famous teachers and venerable members of the Sanhedrin, for he already had his eyes on their pulpits and professorial chairs. Gradually he began to put on the airs of a doctor of the Law, and well he might, since his religious enthusiasm, his knowledge of the Scriptures and his energetic character undoubtedly augured a brilliant future for him.

It is possible that he had a hand in provoking the persecution which broke out against Christ's disciples, fomented by the Hellenists among whom he held a prominent position. Stephen died under the stones of the mob, and Saul became a leader among the oppressors of the new sect. His violent onslaught had the effect of scattering the disciples far and wide, so that soon there were many Jews in Damascus, Samaria and Antioch who invoked the name of Jesus. But the thought of these fugitives gave him no rest. Accustomed as he was to analyzing his religious ideas, he understood better than had his teacher how important for Judaism was the annihilation of the remaining handful of lunatics. Four years had passed since Gamaliel had given his views on Christ's disciples, and yet, far from dying out, the madness had spread, become organized and found followers among the novelty seekers, both Jews and proselytes.

Fortunately, the most important congregation of Christ's followers, that in Jerusalem, could be regarded as wiped out, since many of its members were in prison and others had disappeared into the shadows, no longer daring to speak boldly in public as Stephen had done. Even the leaders of the movement seemed to have conformed meekly with the rest of the Jewish nation in their devotions and exercises of piety. No longer did they fail in respect to the Temple, for they were frequently seen entering the Beautiful Gate, descending the marble staircase and praying with arms extended in the direction of the Holy of Holies, the repository of all that was most precious to God's people. But Saul still could not forget the fugitives who had escaped him. He knew that a good number of them had taken refuge in the capital of Syria, and "breathing out threats of slaughter against the disciples of the Lord, [he] went to the high priest and asked him for letters to the synagogues at Damascus, that if he found any men or women belonging to this Way, he might bring them in bonds to Jerusalem" (Acts 9:1-2). It was a propitious moment for the Sanhedrin to attempt to regain its cherished rights, for although Syria was then ruled by King Aretas, the father-in-law of Herod the Tetrarch, the Jews maintained a close relationship with him, and therefore he would not prevent an emissary of the high priest from carrying out orders among the Jewish community. When this new nest of rebels had been destroyed, the world

would see how vain had been their Master's prediction:
"The gates of hell shall not prevail against you."

Saul was confident that he was strong enough to show
everyone how ridiculous Christ's claim was, and, humanly
speaking, his confidence seemed well-founded. How could
that handful of nonentities resist him, armed as he was with
the authority of the Jewish leaders, supported by his
brawny escort and grimly determined to put an end to the
heresy once and for all? Christ's followers, however, had
no doubt as to the outcome of the struggle; they remembered their Lord's words, and they could not imagine for
one moment that the Church would perish in these first
days of its expansion. In fact, things were happening just
as He had foretold, and those who had had the great blessing of seeing and hearing Him kept in their hearts the
memory of His serene countenance as He confronted His
enemies. Only He knew how this new surge of persecution
would end, but they were confident that His word could
not fail.

The nightmare of terror did indeed come to an end, but
in a most unexpected way, with a miracle as inexplicable
in its cause as it was fruitful in its results. The dying patri-
arch, Jacob, had foretold that "Benjamin a ravenous wolf,
in the morning shall eat the prey, and in the evening shall
divide the spoil" (Gen. 49:27). His prophecy was about
to be fulfilled in the young Israelite of the Dispersion, the
most illustrious member of the tribe of Benjamin. As St.
Augustine interprets Jacob's words, Saul, in the fiery morning of his youth, darted out like a ravening wolf to devour
Christ's little flock and, in the evening of his life, ranged
through the world feeding the hungry with the bread of
salvation. It is St. Luke, himself a disciple of St. Paul, who

tells us the awe-inspiring story of the apparition from heaven which worked the transformation.

Saul and his armed escort were on their way to Damascus, the hooves of their mounts steadily eating up the miles and kicking up a plume of dust behind them to mark their swift passage. The travellers' faces were drawn with fatigue and their eyes bloodshot from the sun and wind-blown dust of four days' hard riding. But off to the north they could already see mountains patchily clad with vegetation; they could discern the first palm trees and feel a touch of freshness in the wind that hitherto had scorched them with its breath. They knew that they would soon see the great oasis itself, watered by the Abana and Pharphar Rivers which Naaman the Leper esteemed more than the Jordan. There, nestled among scented orchards of pomegranate, lemon and orange trees, amid groves filled with the murmur of flowing fountains and the music of singing birds, lay Damascus the fair, so aptly described by the Arabian poet as a network of pearls on an emerald carpet.

When the travellers at last sighted the turrets and ramparts of the city's walls, their tired eyes brightened with joy and their animals, sensing that they were near the journey's end, quickened their pace. Saul, small in stature but proud and authoritative in bearing, looked around triumphantly at his companions. His face was untroubled, even joyful, showing no signs of preoccupation or uncertainty. He was not thinking of the serene gaze of Stephen the deacon, nor was he aware of the sun's rays which were now beating fiercely down upon him; nor was he recalling to mind the glory of the nearby city whose kings had so often humiliated the conquered sons of David. One idea alone obsessed him—he was going to wipe out the last nest

of the hated innovators. Soon he would know the names
of the apostates, he would fall on them before they could
flee, he would drag them behind his camels to Jerusalem
and bury them in the dungeons of the Fortress Antonia.
Nobody would be able to resist him, for he would present
his letters from the Sanhedrin, signed and sealed by Caiphas,
and the ancients of Israel in Damascus would place themselves at his orders. The officials of King Aretas would look
with favor on his efforts, for it would not be good politics
for them to arouse the opposition of the fifty thousand Jews
who lived in the city just when the king had established his
rule there. Thus buoyed up by the thought of assured success, Saul was happy. The cavalcade was already wending
its way through the outer fringe of cultivated land which
surrounded the city drowsing under the heat of the sun.
Riding at the head of his retinue, proudly erect on his
Arabian steed, he hugged his dream of glory—victory
almost within his grasp, the city resounding with his name,
the praise of his fellow-Jews, the congratulations of the
Sanhedrin and the annihilation of the Galileans.

Suddenly a great brightness shone round about the
travellers and, like a bolt of lightning, it concentrated upon
the leader, throwing him to the ground, paralyzing him
and freezing the very blood in his veins. Then a voice, afar
off and terrifying, thundered in the vault of the sky, saying,
with love and reproach, compassion and irony: "Saul,
Saul!" Saul opened his eyes and there in the heavens, surrounded by light and glory, he saw the Son of Man whom
Ezechiel had seen clad in linen, His face flashing like
lightning and His arms white as bronze in the fire, He
whom John was to see later in Patmos among the seven
gold candlesticks, clad in a long tunic and golden girdle,
His eyes like burning coals, His head white as snow, His

face like the sun in all its brightness, with seven stars in His hand, a two-edged sword in His mouth, and His voice like the sound of many waters. (Cf. Apoc. 1:12–16.) As Saul looked with awe upon the vision, he saw that bright flames were springing from the pierced feet, and that in His side was a red wound opened by the blade of a lance.

Crushed and blinded, Saul sought to escape the searing radiance by burying his face in the dust of the road, but the Unknown One continued to speak, bending over him to ask gently: ". . . why dost thou persecute me?" Saul did not answer; the light which had dazzled his eyes was now stealing into his heart; he had a sudden intuition as to who the speaker might be, but he was not certain. Therefore, with incredible audacity, he asked: "Who art thou, Lord?" He had to know who had so rudely cut short his journey; as a worthy son of Jacob who had wrestled with the angel, he was not going to submit without at least knowing the name of his conqueror. This was the natural reaction of a man whose will was so strong that he retained control over himself even in such a crisis. Saul's whole soul was in that question; he would not bow down before mere brute strength, but only before truth. The Unknown deigned to reveal His name in these words: "I am Jesus whom thou art persecuting"—a name which awoke a last spasm of hatred in the young scribe's breast. Torn with doubt, he shied away from the truth as an unruly horse shies from his master's touch. But the Voice that breaks the cedars of Libanus and makes the mountains tremble continued to speak, decisively and threateningly: "It is hard for thee to kick against the goad." And immediately Saul surrendered.

His whole being had been illuminated by an ineffable and transforming revelation, a flash of divine fecundity. He saw that Stephen and all his other victims had been, not mad fanatics, but true servants of God, as were the prisoners suffering in Jerusalem and the Israelites fearfully awaiting his arrival in Damascus. He realized that his hands were stained with innocent blood, that his heart was far from God and that his devotion to the Law had served only to make him sin against his fellow-men. The Voice still ringing in his ears accused and pardoned him at the same time; it traced out for him a norm of conduct and strengthened him to undertake every sacrifice and penance. Saul was indeed transformed, his hatred becoming pure and passionate love, his bloodthirsty ambition being changed into a deep desire for expiation and obedience. "Lord," he implored, "what wilt thou have me to do?" And his Lord replied, "Arise and go into the city; and it will be told thee what thou must do."

Obediently Saul staggered to his feet, his body trembling, his mind in a turmoil. His companions had heard the Voice, but not understanding what had happened, they looked at him in fear and expectation, awaiting his orders, anxious to leave this bewitched place for the safety of the crowded city. However, something was wrong with their leader— he had his arms stretched out in front of him, feeling his way toward them, stumbling on the road like a blind man. Although the merciless rays of the sun were beating down on his upturned face, he was surrounded by night. He opened his eyes as wide as they would go, and still he could not see. His servants regarded him with frightened and questioning expressions as if to say, "What angel has visited him? What spirit has spoken to him?" Without a word he resignedly stretched out his hands to them, allowing them to lead him into the city like a child, a prisoner, or a soldier in defeat. The subdued company made its way along the street called Straight, the main thoroughfare of

Damascus which ran through the city in a straight line from east to west, dividing it into two parts. Slowly they moved along the hundred-foot-wide street, past the Corinthian porches which lined it on either side and under the triumphal arch at the center of the city.

The man who had pictured himself entering Damascus in triumph now shamefacedly groped his way along, unable to see the passersby looking at him with a mixture of curiosity and pity. He asked to be led to the house of Judas the Jew, situated in one of the aristocratic parts of the city, and though Judas received him with open arms, placing his whole house at his disposal, Saul was so shaken in body and soul by his recent experience that he could neither eat nor drink, but fasted and prayed without ceasing, refusing to receive or speak to anyone. The thought of the faithful whom he had persecuted, the cries of his victims under torture, the blood of Stephen, his last words and piercing glance—all these memories now returned to crush his heart beneath their insupportable weight. And the voice of Jesus re-echoed in the depths of his being with a bitter sweetness that caused him new torments: "Why persecutest thou me?"

Yet at the same time, he felt himself bathed in a consoling light, the lingering rays of that brightness that had shone about him on the road to Damascus. He could still visualize the face of Christ, and the same thought kept running through his mind—that obscure carpenter who had been crucified some years ago was not a blasphemer or an impostor. He was the hoped-for Redeemer; He still lived on, and He had spoken the truth. With a shock, Saul realized that hitherto he had understood nothing in the Scriptures.

Saul's conversion, accomplished in a few seconds on the road outside Damascus, is unique in the annals of religious history. Another great convert, St. Augustine, an authority on such occurrences, says that "turning a sinner into a just man is a greater achievement than creating heaven and earth." [1] But of all conversions, none is so well-known and so miraculous as Saul's. So instantaneous and reverberating was it that, as a miracle, it is comparable only to the Resurrection of Christ, and is as well proved by the testimony of historical documentation. The event is described no less than three times in the Acts of the Apostles, and the three descriptions agree so closely with each other that they have confounded all the malevolent ingenuity of the enemies of the supernatural. Not only that, but St. Paul has left us a record of Christ's own words, explaining to him the reason for the vision: ". . . for I have appeared to thee for this purpose, to appoint thee to be a minister and a witness to what thou hast seen, and to the visions thou shalt have of me; delivering thee from the people and from the nations, to whom I am now sending thee, to open their eyes that they may turn from darkness to light and from the dominion of Satan to God; that they may receive forgiveness of sins and an inheritance among those sanctified by faith in me" (Acts 26:16–18).

The experience engraved itself so deeply on his mind that the whole of his life from that point on seemed to be moved by the force of his first contact with the Crucified. It was the point of departure of his whole apostolate, the explanation of his heroic endeavor, the beginning of thirty years of devoted, unceasing and untiring activity, unequalled in history. In the midst of anxieties, persecution and sufferings, he was to remember that moment which had marked him with the seal of the elect, and he was to refer to it often in his Epistles and sermons: "It pleased [God] . . .

[1] *Tract. 72 in Joan.*

to reveal his Son in me," he wrote to the Galatians (1:15). To the Ephesians he wrote: ". . . you have heard of the dispensation of the grace of God that was given to me in your regard; how that by revelation was made known to me the mystery . . ." (3:2-3). "Am not I an apostle?" he asked the Corinthians; "Have not I seen Jesus our Lord?" (1 Cor. 9:1). Yes, he had seen Him in human form transfigured and glorified by the Resurrection, His face resplendent and His body bearing the wounds of His Passion. Christ had deigned to show Himself to him, the Apostle who had been born out of due season, suddenly brought forth from the darkness of error into the broad daylight of truth.

But there are philosophical systems which are, to put it mildly, incompatible with miracles, since they teach that the supernatural is impossible and that the intervention of Providence in human affairs is an old wives' tale. It is on the basis of this assumption that many critics have tried to explain away the conversion of St. Paul as described in one of the most authentic and best-documented books of antiquity. The simplest thing for them to do would be to deny entirely the apparition on the road to Damascus. But then how could they explain the other greater miracle in the moral order? For if the apparition of Christ is denied, Saul's conversion becomes inexplicable. Faced with this dilemma, the enemies of God cudgelled their brains and produced a series of over-subtle, extravagant, puerile, ridiculous or insufficient hypotheses, some of which were as lengthy and as fictional as any novel and acceptable only to shallow minds wholly undemanding in the matter of historical criticism. However, these writers would go to any extremes to provide a purely naturalistic explanation for the miracle of Saul's conversion.

One critic, the leader of the Tübingen school, who devoted himself to explaining away the Gospel miracles, found that his imagination failed him when he came to this incident in the Acts of the Apostles. In fact, one of his disciples, speaking at his graveside, was able to say: "Baur spent his life eliminating the miracles of Jesus, yet he confessed that Paul's conversion resists all historical, logical and psychological analysis. By admitting this miracle he allows all the others to stand. Therefore his life was a failure." In the face of this confession, the leading rationalists became alarmed. They examined, discussed and analyzed the evidence once more, and finally proposed so many solutions, presented them so ingeniously and wrapped them up in so much scientific verbiage that it would be easy to fill a large volume with them. One writer described the violence of the storms in the deserts of Syria as dramatically as if he had been a member of Saul's escort. His theory was that the vision was the result of an electrical discharge in the occipital cortex of Saul's brain, or even a trick of his subconscious which, after a long, silent process, had been precipitated by the external conflict of a storm. Another critic went to great pains to describe the effects of a severe sunstroke on a sick man with a propensity to hallucination, such as he imagined Saul to be.

A fixed idea, says one writer, must infallibly lead to autosuggestion. No, replies another, Saul's mind was a battlefield on which two ideas had been struggling for supremacy until one of them suddenly gained the victory, of which the vision was only a symbol. Renan could not allow himself to be left out of this display of misguided genius, so he, too, advanced a theory. According to him, the whole thing was simply a physical accident caused by Saul's passing abruptly from the burning plain into the cool shadows of the oasis.

And, he went on to say, it is not unlikely that a sudden storm added to the upheaval. Still another of these self-satisfied commentators asserted that Renan's theory was a gratuitous assumption. What really happened, he said, was that despite himself Saul's mind was filled with the thought of the Man he was fighting, and the ensuing psychical crisis suddenly produced an hallucination that was strong enough to overthrow his reason and his will power and to subjugate him completely. All of this happened, continued this theorist, after an inner process of feverish activity, a long series of combats and dissensions in the depths of his psyche. The thought of Christ was brought to the surface by a sudden phenomenon, a cerebral upheaval that is more a subject for psychiatry than for rational psychology.[2]

These explanations of Saul's conversion are pure fantasies, unfounded theories that are in contradiction to the facts of history and frequently to common sense, since they make a mockery not only of the texts but also of all the possibilities of man's mental processes. The Apostle's whole life, his convinced Pharisaism, and the unshakeable firmness of his faith, prevent us from viewing him as weak or unbalanced. His writings reflect his clear mind, his strength of will, his ability to deal competently with all the demands of practical life. For thirty long years after his conversion he remained consistently lucid, forceful, and wise in his words and actions. Not for one moment did doubt trouble his mind, and in his last hour, under the shadow of the sword, he proclaimed his faith as serenely as he had done during his life. No hallucinations, however strong, could serve as the inspiration and foundation of St. Paul's missionary career, the greatest epic ever lived out by a mere

[2] Loisy, *Commentaire des Actes*, p. 399.

man. Even Sabatier, who was no champion of the supernatural, wrote that it would be illogical to accept Christ's
Resurrection and deny that He appeared to His Apostle.[3]

Furthermore, he who insists on denying both events as
impossible leaves the historical order and takes refuge in
the metaphysical, since the historical order demands that
we accept Luke's testimony, which coincides with St.
Paul's own account, as readily as we do the events related
by Tacitus or Thucydides. History demands that we
accept the facts as they occurred, without deforming them
by our personal prejudices.

The facts are undeniable—the persecutor of Christ's
disciples was conquered, the synagogue lost one of its most
zealous defenders, and the Church won over the most
terrible of its adversaries. Transformed by an almost irresistible grace, Saul placed all his powers of mind and body
at the service of the new religion, all his passionate sincerity, all his sweeping eloquence. His conversion was the
greatest victory of the new-born Church, a victory that
was won with the speed of lightning. The convert's life itself was to be thereafter a continuous flash of lightning that
would crackle year after year across the face of an empire.
Those dazzling rays which blinded Saul gave us also an
insight into his character. St. Augustine was convinced and
conquered by a book; the Magi were guided by a star; but
Saul was cast to the ground and blinded by a sword of light
in broad day, on a busy road within sound of a large city.
The man of action was dominated and dedicated instantly
and completely by the direct action of God. He heard the
voice of Christ reproaching him, and that was enough.
Though taken by surprise, cast to the ground and conquered, he lost no time in observing and analyzing what

[3] Cf. *L'apôtre Paul*, p. 51.

was happening around and within him. He could think of one thing only—that his old way of life had gone forever and that he had to find a new one, the true one. But what was he to do? Whatever it was, he was ready to do it with all his strength. In the history of mankind, there has never been a more complete transformation. Although he was still the man of deep emotions and iron will, nothing remained of his former thoughts and feelings; his pride, his hatred, and his thirst for blood had vanished beneath the gentle gaze of the One whom he had persecuted.

CHAPTER IV

The Vessel of Election

The news of Saul's accident quickly made the rounds of the Jewish colony in Damascus, and sensation-seekers hovered about Judas' house, eager to hear more about the Sanhedrin's trusted agent. Saul himself would receive no one, but left his host to deal with the callers as best he could. "He is totally blind," Judas told the visitors. "He doesn't eat or drink or sleep. He doesn't even want to talk to anyone. His accident has completely prostrated and exhausted him." Saul's condition, of course, was not caused by the fall from his horse, but by the vision which he had seen and which still held him spellbound. As St. John of the Cross has said, the voice of God is as strong as the rolling of thunder, yet is ineffably sweet; it is music so delightful and enchanting that it raises the soul above the earth in a transport of ecstasy. This was the music which now resounded in Saul's heart and which was to continue echoing there for the rest of his life. He had heard the voice of Christ; he had spoken with Him and had been drawn close to Him in those few moments of intimate conversation. The very sound of that divine voice had given him an insight into a new world so full of wonders that, in spite of the crowding memories of his former life, his soul was filled with joy. Remorse is always for things past; forgetting all that had gone before, he now pressed on toward the future with all his strength, reaching out toward that resplendent panorama which had unfolded itself so suddenly before his eyes and which had taught him in one moment more than all the rabbis in Jerusalem. He now saw that the Son of God was the foundation-stone of salvation and of the spiritual life, for he had grasped the fundamental idea of the Divine Sonship of Jesus. He knew that Christ had saved man by His death on the Cross, that He had risen again from the dead, and that He remained present on earth even after the Ascension as the Leader and Head of the Church which He had founded.

Saul was blind, but he willingly suffered the loss of his sight in exchange for that inner vision which he now possessed. In this new interior light, he saw that the madness of his former victims was in reality the highest wisdom. Joyfully he recalled some of the phrases he had heard on his prisoners' lips as he haled them before the tribunals or put them to the torture. The innovators were right after all —Christ *was* the Ruler of wills, the Lord of the living, the Conqueror of death. He was the Son of God, yet He ". . . emptied himself, taking the nature of a slave and being made like unto men," and in order to free the wicked from death, "he humbled himself, becoming obedient to death, even to the death of the cross" (Phil. 2:7, 8).

This, indeed, was a mystery of infinite love and compassion. The whole of love was contained in the sublime wisdom of the Cross, which was a scandal to the Jews and madness to the Gentiles, "For scarcely in behalf of a just man does one die; . . . but . . . when as yet we were sinners, Christ died for us" (Rom. 5: 7, 9). Saul knew now that Christ had loved him from the beginning, had chosen him, revealing to him His eternal counsels, converting him from persecutor into apostle. Wherefore this excess of God's predilection for one who had so raged against Him? He found the answer later, when he realized that just as the potter is master of the clay, so God is master of souls, and showed His glory and omnipotence by choosing him from his mother's womb, making a vessel of mercy out of a vessel of dishonor. (Cf. Gal. 1:15; Rom. 9:21.) But now, in the first sweet savoring of Christ's identity, he could only adore, give thanks and humble himself before the unfathomable mysteries of divine goodness. He offered God his whole being in a jubilant and ardent act of oblation. In his breast an immense fire of love already burned, a fire of love so intense that he could later say: ". . . neither death, nor life, nor angels, nor principalities, nor things present, nor things to come, nor powers, nor height, nor depth, nor any other creature will be able to separate us from the love of God, which is in Christ Jesus our Lord" (Rom. 8:38–39).

Love now began to claim its sacrifices, beginning with his intellect, for he had to bow down before the wisdom of God, since there are many things which reason cannot understand. But no matter, because, as Pascal says: "Reason's last resource is the recognition that there is a multitude of things above reason." Or in St. Paul's more energetic phrase: "If anyone of you thinks himself wise in this world, let him become a fool, that he may become wise" (1 Cor. 3:18). In a word, the renunciation of human prudence is the first step toward the highest wisdom. That was the resolve which Saul now made, and, inspired by the light which he discovered in the depths of his inner darkness and drawn on by its far-off beckoning glow, he plunged himself into the abyss of divine faith.

He still had a far more painful sacrifice to make, the sacrifice of all he had loved so ardently: the religion of his fathers, the Temple that was the pride of his race, the religious hierarchy, the holocausts, the customs and the ceremonies of Israel. The glorious past had to be blotted out forever. From the very start, he recognized that this was the natural consequence of his new-found faith, although the rest of the disciples of Christ could not yet clearly see that it had to be so. Peter and the others still did not realize that to be Christians they had to stop being Jews. But Saul's keen mind saw that there was a radical opposition between the Gospel and the Law. He had seen this opposition even before his conversion; in fact, that was why he had persecuted the disciples with such energy. Now, after his conversion, he made no attempt to bring the two opposing forces into harmony with each other. Instead, he was from now on to reject the Law, and to love the Cross with the same ardor which he had shown before in persecuting it.

That was the hardest sacrifice of all for him to make. An idealist such as he could joyfully renounce honors, or riches, or the glorious future which his talents promised him. It was much more difficult for him to abandon forever the atmosphere and surroundings in which he had lived his whole life, to cut himself off from his friends, his teachers, the religion of his infancy and youth, in which he was just beginning to win distinction for his ardent proselytism. He could hear the cries of rage that would echo in the porches of the Temple when the Pharisees heard that he had gone over to the enemy. He could imagine the wrath of the venerable members of the Sanhedrin, the disgrace which would fall on his family, the scandal his conversion would be to the young men who had been students with him. He would be hated, anathematized, branded as a renegade, and upon his own head would fall the punishment with which he had persecuted the disciples of Jesus. And how would his new brothers in Christ receive him? True, their religion bound them to forgive injuries; but even if they brought themselves to believe in his sincerity, would they be able to overcome their suspicions and forget their natural hatred of their former persecutor? Thus, in exchange for all he was giving up, he could see before him only an immense void. Doubt, uncertainty, and darkness pressed upon him from all sides; yet not for one moment did he think of turning his back on the sublime vision which had conquered him. He had believed, and though faith is an act of free obedience, once it is made it places the believer in a new world of rights and duties, of obligations and privileges. He had seen the ineffable ideal, and from that moment his gaze remained fixed on his Divine Model and nothing in the world could separate him from his new-found Lord. As he himself said later: ". . . I count everything loss because of the excelling knowledge of Jesus Christ, my Lord. For his sake I have suffered the loss of all things, and I count them as dung that I may gain Christ . . ." (Phil. 3:8).

This was the conviction which brought him swiftly to the heights of sanctity; yet he fully realized that his conversion and sanctification were miraculous, and that his only merit was that of hearkening to the divine call. From this truth he was later to deduce one of the main doctrines in his theology: "By the grace of God, I am what I am," he repeated again and again, thus affirming his powerlessness, in contrast to the boasting of the Stoics of Tarsus who never ceased to praise and exaggerate their own self-denial and deeds of virtue.

The first days which he passed in Judas' house were ones
of fruitful solitude, of enlightenment and resolution, of
peaceful rapture and sublime ecstasy, of divine outpour-
ings, intimate communion with God, secret tears and acts
of love to his Lord. At the end of this time, he had a new
vision in which a man seemed to approach him and put his
hands upon his head. Therefore when, soon afterwards, a
stranger came to Judas' house asking for Saul of Tarsus,
Saul received him gladly.

The heavenly forewarning was necessary because, if the
visitor had arrived unannounced, it is very likely that Saul
would not have received or listened to him. The stranger,
Ananias, has left us an account of how he, in his turn,
received a mysterious message from a voice which suddenly sounded in his ears calling: "Ananias!" Surprised and
alarmed, he answered: "Here I am, Lord." The voice went
on: "Arise and go to the street called Straight and ask at the
house of Judas for a man of Tarsus named Saul. For behold,
he is praying." But Ananias was a disciple of Christ, one of
those men whom Saul had come to drag away as prisoners
to the Holy City, and he had heard of this persecutor, of
his hatred, power and cruelty. Therefore, fearing to fall
into a trap, he answered apprehensively: "Lord, I have
heard from many about this man, how much evil he has
done to thy saints in Jerusalem. And here too he has
authority from the high priests to arrest all who invoke thy
name." But the voice insisted: "Go, for this man is a chosen
vessel to me, to carry my name among nations and kings
and the children of Israel. For I will show him how great
things he must suffer for my name's sake."

When at last Ananias stood before Saul, he placed his
hands on the young man's head and said to him: " 'Brother
Saul, the Lord has sent me—Jesus, who appeared to thee on

thy journey—that thou mayest recover thy sight and be filled with the Holy Spirit.' And immediately there fell from his eyes as it were scales: and he received his sight" (Acts 9:9–18). Saul's first act after his cure was to look up gratefully into the face of the friendly visitor whom the Lord had used to restore light to his eyes, and whom he later feelingly described as "an observer of the Law, respected by all the Jews who lived there" (Acts 22:12). Ananias was indeed a true Israelite, one who observed all the Mosaic practices, but who also bore in his face that look of gentleness which Saul had so often noticed among the disciples of Jesus, and which spoke of peace and pardon. Ananias' words, like his face, were peaceful, for had he not called his former enemy "Brother"? Saul gazed at his visitor in astonishment, at a loss how to thank him for his fraternal welcome to the ranks of the Lord's disciples.

Weakened as he was by his long fast and overcome with emotion, he was unable to express his gratitude in words, but lay in silence as Ananias continued: "The God of our fathers has appointed thee beforehand to learn his will and to see the Just One and to hear a voice from his mouth; for thou shalt be his witness before all men of what thou hast seen and heard. And now why dost thou delay? Get up and be baptized and wash away thy sins, calling on his name" (Acts 22:14–16). With Ananias' assistance, Saul arose and made his way to the courtyard where there was a fountain surrounded by rose bushes and orange trees. Here the man who had restored his bodily sight now gave new life to his soul, baptizing him in the name of the Lord Jesus. Afterwards he ate and rested, gradually recovering his strength.

The disciples at Damascus who before had feared his coming, now received him with joy, giving thanks to God for the miraculous change, which was not only a victory for their cause but a confirmation of their faith. Here was a new witness to the Resurrection of Christ, a new testimony to His conquest of death, coming, not from a disciple on fire with love and overcome by the magic of Christ's presence, but from an enemy and persecutor of the cause. This was involuntary evidence, confirmed by a series of miracles to which the whole city could testify. In consequence, the disciples never tired of asking the new convert about the minutest details of his strange adventure, and his eloquent descriptions summoned up before their eyes the image of their invisible Lord and increased their love for Him. As he spoke, many of Saul's listeners could already see in him the future champion of the Gospel. While they listened to his words, they tried to penetrate the meaning of the mysterious message which Ananias had heard concerning him—that he would argue with the Jews, preach to the Gentiles, and appear before kings as the instrument of God's glory. Certainly his physical presence was not impressive, but his speech was ardent, his eyes shone, his actions showed his indomitable energy and, above all, the grace of God had descended upon him.

Saul, in his turn, listened eagerly to what the Lord's disciples had to say about the "good tidings." He was inspired by Christ's parables, meditated on His miracles and stored in his memory the teaching and events of the Gospel. For him, newly born of water and the Holy Spirit, this was the milk of spiritual infancy. Strengthened by this divine food, his faith gained vigor and ardor, and he began his long career of preaching by proclaiming in the houses and synagogues that Jesus was the Son of God, that He was Christ, the Messias promised to Israel. In his preaching he was fearless, "acting boldly in the name of the Lord" (Acts 9:27). The central theme of his discourses was Christ considered not so much in His earthly life as in His glorious Resurrection, His continued nearness to His disciples and His unceasing guidance of His Church. Certainly there is no divergence between the historical Christ and the glorified Savior. Truly, "Christ died for all: that they who are alive may live no longer for themselves, but for him who died for them and rose again. . . . And even though we have known Christ according to the flesh, yet now we know him so no longer" (2 Cor. 5:15–16). Christ's death was wholly effective in itself, but His Resurrection and glorification teach us to see Him in a new spiritual and transcendent light, the light of the Holy Spirit.

These first sermons of Paul's were composed on a pattern which he was to follow all his life. He preached Christ crucified and risen from the dead. He spoke in the synagogues, for as a born Jew he still loved his fellow-Jews, the members of his race. Therefore it was natural that, following the example of Christ Himself, he should bring the good tidings to them first of all. But in the synagogues he found not only Jews but another group of listeners who from the beginning drew his attention to them as they sat near the doors. These were the friends of Israel, proselytes from paganism, hungering for spirituality and weary of the aberrations of idolatry. The historian Josephus has recorded that at this time, in spite of its austerity, the Law had spread all over the world. Thousands of souls, tortured by doubt, came to seek enlightenment in the teachings of the synagogue and to take part in its psalmody and ritual. These people were of all classes—country folk and army officers, slaves and patricians. However, the majority of them were women, since it was they who felt most profoundly the universal attraction of the Jewish religion, for they were unable to satisfy their religious yearnings in the cold, silent temples of Isis, Jupiter, Cybele, and Bacchus, or overcome their repugnance to the degradation of their womanhood in the ritual orgies of pagan worship. So many of the finest women in the pagan world attended Jewish services that Ovid was able to tell the dissolute young men of Rome that if they wanted to see the most famed beauties of the city, they had only to wait outside the synagogue on the Sabbath.[1] Similarly in Damascus the majority of the women, from the aristocracy down, had joined the ranks of the proselytes.[2]

From the very beginning, Paul placed his greatest hopes in these non-Jewish members of his audience. Through observing the effects of Stephen's preaching he had learned that these proselytes were not drawn to Judaism by the practices of the Law, by circumcision, the ablutions, or by the sacrifice of bulls and goats. Rather they were drawn by the sureness with which the Law solved the knottiest problems, by the sweetness of its poetry and hymns, by the nobility of its moral code, the purity of its worship, the loftiness of its dogmas and the fraternal spirit that reigned among the Chosen People. But the new religion also possessed these good things, purified, idealized, and freed from the innumerable fetters of the Mosaic Code which hampered many men of good will. Moreover, Paul knew now that justification did not come from the Law, but from faith in Jesus Christ, and it was this message which he bore to the synagogues of Damascus when he appeared in them to tell the story of his conversion. No one had kept the Law more rigorously than he, who had been among the purest of the pure observers, a fanatic among fanatics; yet he had re-

---

[1] *Ars amat.* i. 76.
[2] Josephus *Bellum judaicum* ii. 20. 2.

mained in the blindness of his impiety until God deigned to reveal His Son to him.

At first, the Jews of Damascus listened to him with a mixture of curiosity and amazement, remarking to each other: "Isn't this the man who persecuted the followers of Jesus? Didn't he come here to take them away as prisoners to the chief priests? And now he's preaching their doctrine!" Their very astonishment at the change led them to give Paul a hearing, and he was enormously successful as an advocate of Christianity, armed as he was with such extraordinary proofs to lay before his listeners. In fact he was so successful that the leaders of the synagogues became alarmed at the number of Jews who began to follow him. It was not long before their alarm turned to hatred and Paul began to hear himself called a renegade, a traitor, and an apostate. Soon the news of his success as a preacher of Christ reached Jerusalem, where the Sanhedrin were probably already discussing the means to be taken in dealing with the effects of his scandalous desertion. Finally, the atmosphere in Damascus became so threatening and charged with danger that he resolved to leave the city. "But when it pleased him . . . to reveal his Son in me . . . without taking counsel with flesh and blood, and without going up to Jerusalem . . . I retired into Arabia" (Gal. 1:15–17).

Once more he withdrew into silence—not so much to escape the revenge of his former co-religionists as to devote himself to recollection and solitude. After all that had happened, he wished to enter into himself and be alone with God. To this end he went to Arabia, that is, to the Sinaitic peninsula where Moses and Elias had conversed familiarly with God on the mountain-tops, for he wished to listen to the eloquence of the desert before returning to the great cities of the world. He already knew his destiny, but he did not hurry to accomplish it, knowing that God would call him at the opportune moment. Meanwhile he would sound the depths of his being, meditate on the Sacred Scriptures, mortify his body and strengthen his will. Far from the noise of the world, amid the silence that reigned around and within him, he would be able more surely to hear the murmur of the inner voice of God.

Like all great mystics, Paul loved solitude, and although by temperament he was a man of action, yet he became a hermit and hid himself from men's gaze. For three years he disappeared from sight—three years that seem to us like a blank space in his life, years about which we can know nothing, but which must have been supremely fruitful. They were years of intensive preparation, of prayer and re-flection under the guidance of the Holy Spirit, of unceasing effort to understand the true sense of the Old Testament. In those years of silence, Paul discarded the Pharisaical interpretation of the Scriptures which he had learned as a student, and strove to understand ever more fully the divine plan of salvation by faith and to see the history of humanity in the light of the Gospel.

The religious re-education of such a man could not be accomplished in a day or a week. True, his reforming had begun with a sudden crisis, but from that point on it developed gradually. The complete system of Pauline theology was the fruit both of lengthy reflection and slow, prolonged revelation in which divine intervention was constantly evident. First came the vision on the road, then the message of Ananias, next, Paul's acceptance by the church at Damascus, and finally, the heavenly communications which he received in the desert. After he had been three years in Arabia, he again heard the mysterious voice—

this time in the Temple at Jerusalem, and he was to continue to hear it at all the important junctures of his life. From his conversion to his death, heaven continually enlightened and guided him, pointed out to him his field of action, warned him of danger, strengthened him, counselled him, inspired him, protected and instructed him. Christ Himself was his teacher: "For I give you to understand, brethren," he wrote to the Galatians, "that the gospel which was preached by me is not of man. For I did not receive it from man; nor was I taught it; but I received it by a revelation of Jesus Christ" (Gal. 1:11–12). "I know and am confident in the Lord Jesus that nothing is of itself unclean . . ." (Rom. 14:14). "For I myself have received from the Lord what I also delivered to you," regarding the manner of celebrating the Eucharistic sacrifice. (Cf. 1 Cor. 11:23.) "For this we say to you in the word of the Lord, that we who live, who survive until the coming of the Lord, shall not precede those who have fallen asleep" (1 Thess. 4:14). Therefore, taught as he was by God Himself, Paul was a witness at first hand to the doctrine which he preached.

Thus he could, with verity, speak to us of his "Gospel," the mystery of salvation, the body of truths which were the "good tidings" and which he expounded with an originality and vigor of style possessed by no other disciple of Christ. His was the same message as that of Peter and John, the great truths which Jesus had taught His followers: the equality of all men in the plan of redemption, the admission of the Gentiles to the Church, the abolition of the Mosaic Law, the meaning of Christian liberty, the justification of men by faith, the incorporation of the faithful into Christ by baptism, the doctrine of the Mystical Body of Christ. But Paul shed new light on all these concepts, impressing on them the seal of his personality, particularly when preaching to pagans. His gospel was truly the "good tidings," the secret hidden from the beginning of the ages, which he brought from the heart of Judaism to the Gentiles, the apostolic teaching which, with his sense of reality—that characteristic of great minds and men of action—he was able to adapt to the mentality of his hearers. Sometimes he presented it in a simple and elementary form, while on other occasions he spoke in detail of the sublimest Christian concepts, or clothed his thoughts in the luminous and profound language of poetry. Whenever he spoke or wrote, he chose his words according to the existing circumstances, so that if we wish to see the reason for his variations in style, we must study the historical background of his discourses. Here too, Fénelon's maxim holds true: "Nearly everything in Christianity is historical."

If an idea belongs to him who best knows how to expound it, defend it and make it triumph, then no one has as much right to speak of "his Gospel" as Paul. No one has explained more beautifully the grandeur and poetry of the mystery of redemption. No one has described more vividly paradise regained, that immense drama in which the actors are the Creator and His creatures, the visible world and the world invisible—a drama in which the ebb and flow of action begin and end in the unfathomable depths of eternity.

CHAPTER V

The Voice in the Temple

Paul's long sojourn in the desert had given him a deep serenity of soul and had prepared him for the great work of his life. His high destiny had been revealed to him and he was now able to gaze in rapture on the heavenly light which before had blinded him. He was master of himself; peace reigned in his soul and his heart was filled with confidence. During the long years of silent meditation his analytical mind had crystallized the teaching of Christ into the precise, dogmatic formulae which were to be the foundations of the towering theological structure he was to build in the future. His deep thought and communion with God had given him a clear concept of the relationship between the physical world and the world of the supernatural, and he had brought his speculative ideas, his interpretation of man's history and destiny into full harmony with the interior reality of his faith. His love and faith had identified him with Christ, had made him a member of Christ's Mystical Body, living in and for his Crucified Lord. He lived now in close union with Him who was not only the cause but the ever-present Guide of his spiritual life and of his very thoughts. This nearness to his Lord strengthened him to bear every toil and suffering, leading him to undertake gigantic tasks and preparing him to embark on super-human ventures. He knew that he would have much to suffer for the name of Jesus, and though he had already felt the weight of the Cross, he was not deterred but was only the more determined to "fight the good fight." "For to me . . . to die is gain," he would say later, as he could now say: "For to me, to live is Christ," and he was confident because "if God be for us, who is against us?"

The time had come for him to go out and conquer the world, to appear once more among men and share with them the interior riches he had garnered during his long retreat in the desert. However, his first appearance was only an experiment, a preparation for future campaigns, and it seemed to end in failure. To make amends and restore the balance of justice, the former disciple of the Pharisees wished to glorify the name of Christ in the very place where before he had been bent on persecuting those who invoked it. Accordingly he presented himself in Damascus once more, ready to struggle and to suffer. During his short stay there three years before, his main theme had simply been an explanation of what he had heard and seen during and after his vision of Christ. But now, on his return, his speech was forceful and full of light as he "confounded the Jews who were living in Damascus, proving that this [Jesus] is the Christ" (Acts 9:22). His addresses took the form of regular Pharisaical expositions in which he combined arguments from Scripture with the dialectical methods he had learned from the rabbis in Jerusalem. On the Sabbath days he went to the synagogues, opened the scrolls of the Holy Books and, pointing out the passages referring to the Messias, he would prove that all the prophecies were fulfilled in the Prophet of Nazareth. This was the method he adopted when speaking to an audience of Jews, and he continued to use it for many years. He developed his thesis along the following lines: "God spoke to our fathers through the prophets, but finally, in these our days, He has spoken through His Son, the splendor of His glory, the figure of His substance, the Expiator and Pardoner of sin, nobler than the prophets and higher than the angels. To Him alone were addressed the mighty words: 'Thou art my son; this day have I begotten thee.' And it was He whom the psalmist had in mind when he sang: 'In the beginning, O Lord, thou foundest the earth: and the heavens are the works of thy hands. They shall perish but thou remainest: and all of them shall grow old like a garment. . . . But thou art always the selfsame: and thy years shall not fail' (Ps. 101:26–28). To which of the angels or prophets were such things said?" (Cf. Hebr. 1:1–12.)

These arguments of Paul's greatly angered the Jews, for they were unable to understand how their prophecies could have been fulfilled by the despised Carpenter from Nazareth who had died on a cross. Moreover, although the aggressive young preacher did not declare that the Law was abolished, he considered it valueless for producing interior holiness. But the worst feature of all was that the renegade found many eager listeners in the synagogues, particularly among those Gentile proselytes, the society women of Damascus, whose love for the Scriptures was a guarantee of Jewish influence and prosperity in business. No wonder then that the Jewish doctors did their best to discredit and refute his arguments; but he always emerged the victor from these verbal battles, leaving his opponents humbled and in shame-faced confusion. Finally, when none of the scribes or rabbis dared to debate further with him, they resorted to violence. Paul faced their persecution cheerfully, but in the end life in Damascus became impossible for him and he was forced to think of fleeing the city. The Jews had succeeded in getting the authorities to support them, and at their instigation the ethnarch of King Aretas, who was in charge of the city guard, had ordered a watch kept at all the gates of the city, so that soon Paul could scarcely venture out into the streets for fear of assassination. However, when all chance of escape seemed lost, someone suggested an ingenious means of getting him out of the city. One of the disciples, whose house adjoined the wall, smuggled the missionary into his home and in the darkness of the night lowered him in a wicker basket through a window in the wall. It was a humiliating procedure, but there was no other way to escape the enemy's grasp. As much as twenty years later, Paul was to recall this moment as one of the darkest of his life: "If I must boast, I will boast of the things that concern my weakness. The God and Father of the Lord Jesus, who is blessed forevermore, knows that I do not lie. In Damascus the governor under King Aretas was guarding the city of the Damascenes in order to arrest me, but I was lowered in a basket through a window in the wall, and escaped his hands" (2 Cor. 11:30–33).

Paul had no wish to court death, but neither did he fear it. Persecutions never deterred him from doing his duty, and on escaping from one danger he often boldly put himself into greater peril for the sake of souls. This was the case now, for, having eluded the vengeance of the Damascene Jews, he did not go into hiding, but headed for Jerusalem where he knew he would be confronted with the wrath of the outraged Sanhedrin and the anger of the Pharisees. The scenes of his former blasphemy and of the last days of Jesus were calling to him, but above all he wished to see Peter, the head of the Apostles, "to look upon him as one looks upon something miraculous and worthy of being sought diligently: he wanted to contemplate, study, and admire him who was his senior and greater than he." [1] He wished to ask him about his preaching and at the same time to meet St. James, the Lord's "brother," and St. John, who were considered the pillars of the Church (Gal. 1:18; 2:9).

Once more he was travelling on the road outside Damascus, but now he went wearily on foot where before he had ridden swiftly, spurred on by hatred. Everything had changed: before, he had led an armed escort in triumph towards the city; now he was crossing the desert alone, a fugitive, looking back at intervals to see if he were being followed. When at last he arrived at the Holy City, he found himself surrounded by coldness and suspicion. Although it was some time before the members of the Sanhedrin knew he was in Jerusalem, the disciples of Christ were not slow in recognizing their former persecutor. Some of them did not know of the wondrous change that had been worked in him; others had forgotten him, but soon his uncompromising attitude aroused distrust, particularly among the conservatives who clung to their old traditions. "He was dangerous as an enemy," they said, shaking their heads, "but it seems that he may be even more dangerous as a friend." They remembered the time when he had dragged them from their houses and thrown them into prison, "and they were all afraid of him, not believing that he was a disciple" (Acts 9:26). He did his best to reassure them but they did not trust him, fearing that his friendliness was a trap. We can visualize him trying to make friends with the disciples, asking their pardon for his cruelty to them,

[1] St. John Chrysostom, *Comment. in Ep. ad Galatas*, I, II.

attempting to join in their meetings and to take part in their religious functions. No doubt many a door was slammed in his face, and if he did succeed in gaining entry he probably had to be content with a seat in a corner of the room, cut off from the company and furtively watched by eyes full of distrust.

This severe trial was brought to an end by an educated and warm-hearted man named Joseph, a native of Cyprus and a member of the Diaspora, who perhaps had sat with the student from Tarsus listening to the teaching of Gamaliel. With his gentle and noble character, this man understood the stranger who trusted him and to whom he offered his support in gaining the confidence of the disciples. His vouching for Paul carried great weight, for he had won the affection and gratitude of all by his kindness and generosity. He came of a distinguished family and had been a rich man, but when the community had fallen on evil days, he had sold all his lands and had placed the money at the feet of the Apostles. Moreover, since he was a member of the tribe of Levi and was well-instructed in the Sacred Scriptures, he had been charged with preaching to the faithful after the reading of the Law and the Prophets. So fervently, so beautifully and with such persuasive eloquence did he speak that the brethren began to call him "Barnabas, the son of prophecy," and it was under this title that he was to distinguish himself in the history of the Church.

It is likely that Paul became acquainted with Barnabas on the occasion of one of these discourses on the Sacred Books. Soon they were fast friends, for they had much in common since both were Hellenists and could understand each other perfectly. It was not long before Barnabas saw his new friend's plight, and "took him and brought him to the apostles, and he told them how on his journey he had seen the Lord, that the Lord had spoken to him, and how in Damascus he had acted boldly in the name of Jesus" (Acts 9:27).

Thus it was that Paul and Peter, two men destined to change the world, came to meet each other. Peter was a real Galilean, open, generous and spontaneous, and his naturally kind heart joyously welcomed this stranger in whom he could see the same love of Christ which he felt himself, the same enthusiasm for the Lord's work, the same vigorous faith, more reasoned if perhaps less strong than his own. On his part, Paul was captivated by the somewhat rough nobility of the chief Apostle, that brusque and fervent man in whom he, the keen judge of men, discovered from the very start a moving candor coupled with passionate loyalty and headlong impetuosity. At Peter's side stood John, the beloved disciple, with a gentle smile of welcome for the new brother, and there was another Apostle present, one who was perhaps slow to be convinced of Paul's good intentions, St. James, the Lord's "brother," the last defender of the Law within the Christian community, always intent on harmonizing in his life the Law and the Gospel.

St. James was already coming to be recognized as the principal personage in the local community, and his conservative attitude must have caused the new disciple great mental conflicts. When Paul had become a follower of Christ, he had renounced all that he had formerly loved, but St. James, on the contrary, had remained the perfect Israelite. Which trend was the correct one and which ought to prevail? The question must have arisen as a result of this first visit which Paul made to the Apostles. The former persecutor of the Church needed the approval of those who were considered the pillars of the Church. He had come to them to tell them about the method he used in his apostolate, to learn more about the Gospel traditions, to find out more about Christ from those who had eaten and drunk in His company after the Resurrection. He was the only one who saw—or at least the one who saw most clearly—the problem of the Gentiles' vocation to the Church. Obviously, justification was not a monopoly of the Jews, for all men were called to do penance, all had a place at the banquet in the kingdom of heaven. That was the clear interpretation of Christ's parables, as all agreed. But what would be the difference between the circumcised and the uncircumcised in the new society? Peter was in doubt as to the answer, for he had not yet had the vision at Joppa. (Cf. Acts 2:5–18.) Still held captive by his national prejudices, he observed the distinction between clean and unclean animals, and debated in his mind whether or not he had to ask the pagans to bear the whole weight of the levitical prescriptions. Paul defended the broader view, but did so timidly at first, partly because he felt that as a newcomer he had no right to speak out boldly, and also because his position conflicted with the rigorist opinions of St. James.

But whatever disagreement there might be among them was always without bitterness or stubborn pride. The new Apostle now lived in an atmosphere of friendliness, for the disciples' suspicions had changed to lively admiration. Those who had first followed the Lord realized what a precious gift heaven had sent them in the person of this man whose fiery eloquence held them spellbound. Moreover, he too had seen Christ in a miraculous manner and had heard from His lips the Gospel which they preached. As a result, Paul "moved freely among them in Jerusalem, acting boldly in the name of the Lord" (Acts 9:29). He accompanied them as they went about the city, sat among them at their public meetings, and was shown every mark of friendship and esteem.

But Paul's happy sojourn among kindred spirits was not destined to last long, for before two weeks had passed, his former co-religionists realized that in him they had not only lost a supporter but were confronted with a new adversary, perhaps the most formidable of all. Paul was now addressing the congregations in the synagogues where he had shone so brilliantly only a few years ago. He preached to the Jews of the Diaspora, the Hellenists from Syria, Cilicia and Cyrene, and with burning eloquence reminiscent of but even more vehement and illuminating than that of the deacon Stephen, he spoke to them of Jesus and His teaching, of the fulfillment of the Messianic prophecies, and of the new way of salvation that was open to all men.

His sermons were always well received by the proselytes from paganism, by the Gentiles of the Roman cohorts and the officials of the Roman administration. But his victorious eloquence filled the Israelites with hatred, for it wounded their national pride and laid bare their vices. Paul knew his enemies well, and could foresee the result of his audacious attack on them, so that he was not surprised when, a few weeks after his arrival in Jerusalem, his friends reported that the Pharisees and the Sanhedrin were plotting his death. Yet he continued to preach fearlessly in the synagogues because he regarded himself, with all humility, as a living witness to the truth of the Gospel, so much so that a warning from heaven was necessary to make him think of fleeing from the daggers of his enemies. The admonition came to him as he was praying in the Temple where, in an ecstasy, he had a vision of the Lord and heard Him say: "Make haste and go quickly out of Jerusalem, for they will not receive thy testimony concerning me." The words of Christ disconcerted the young preacher, for whom would they believe if they did not believe him? Was not his very presence among them the proof that his teaching was true? So great was his desire to repair the damage he had done to the Church that he ventured an objection: "Lord, they themselves know that I used to imprison and beat in one synagogue after another those who believed in thee; and when the blood of Stephen, thy witness, was shed, I was standing by and approved it, and took charge of the garments of those who killed him." The conclusion that Paul wished to draw from this line of reasoning was that no testimony could be more authoritative than his, but the Voice interrupted him: "Go, for to the Gentiles far away I will send thee" (Acts 22:17-21).

When God speaks, says St. Teresa, His words so impress themselves on the hearer's mind that he cannot forget them, no matter how hard he may try.[2] God had spoken again to His Apostle when he least expected it, setting aside all his plans. This was to happen many times in Paul's life in unsought-for and unforeseen visions, for his soul, at once impetuous and sensitive, needed sometimes to be held in check and at other times to be spurred on, and the Voice was always there to console, strengthen, or restrain him. His visions were not wrapped in apocalyptic imagery as John's were, but were markedly intellectual and almost always devoid of exterior signs. He was less a visionary than a man who possessed the mystical presence of God, one who lived in the intimacy of the Spirit, and who was once lifted up by Love even to the third heaven where he heard words which no mortal man could repeat.

In obedience to Christ's command, he left Jerusalem,

---

[2] *Life*, chap. 25; *Interior Castle*, chap. 3.

which he now definitely knew was not to be the scene of his life's work, and accompanied by a group of the disciples as a safeguard against attack by the Jews, he hurried on without stopping and without preaching in any of the synagogues along the road. Later, when writing to the Galatians, he said: "And I was unknown by sight to the churches of Judea which were in Christ. But they had heard only that he who formerly persecuted us, now preaches the faith which once he ravaged. And they glorified God in me" (Gal. 1:22-24). When he reached Caesarea he boarded a ship which, after calling at the coastal ports of Ptolemais, Tyre, Beirut and Seleucia, brought him finally to the mouth of the Cydnus.

CHAPTER VI

The Years of Silence

Paul was once more in his native city of Tarsus, but we do not know why he returned or what he did there, for long periods of his life are hidden from our eyes, like the waters of a river which disappear into the crevasses of a mountain only to reappear elsewhere more powerful than before. So it is that we now encounter another span of silence in the Apostle's career, during which perhaps he prepared himself for the great mission foretold by the Voice in the Temple, or deepened his interior life, or awaited the Lord's definitive summons to preach to the Gentiles.

No doubt he wished to know still more about that world which he was called upon to conquer, and his natural prudence led him to study its rites and customs, to delve deeper into its psychology, and to improve his knowledge of its language. If that was his purpose in returning to Tarsus he had chosen well, because the city was one of the best vantage-points from which to view the field of his future battles since it was, as Xenophon called it,[1] "a great and happy city," a storehouse of ideas as well as a trading center, a focus of spiritual culture and a breeding-ground for superstitions and schools of thought. Undoubtedly it

[1] *Anab.* i. 23.

was during this visit to his native city that Paul, inspired
partly by missionary zeal and partly by his thirst for
knowledge, decided to accost the philosophers and grammarians who, as Philostratus expressed it, chattered like
flocks of birds on the quays along the Cydnus.[2] He lingered
thoughtfully at the doors of the temples, looking with compassion on the well-meaning devotees who flocked about
their false prophets to hear them speak of happiness and
salvation. Often he would see in the streets groups of
initiates celebrating the feasts of their gods with all the
trappings of lights and flowers. At one season of the year
the devotees of Dionysus would meet in the moonlight on
a hill near the city, where after lighting the sacred lamps,
they would clash cymbals, ring bells, and rend the air with
the sound of Phrygian flutes. To the accompaniment of this
savage music they performed the sacred dance, shouting
incoherently as they whirled in a mad frenzy until exhaustion forced them to stop. Then they rushed down to the
city in ragged groups, their long hair flying in the wind
behind them as they ran, shouting hoarsely, chewing ivy-
leaves whose bitter juices cause intoxication, brandishing
daggers and the sacred serpents of Sabazius, and waving the
leafy wands of Dionysus.

At another season of the year, the spring equinox, the
feast of Attis, the beloved of Cybele, took place in imitation of the rites held on the banks of the rivers of Pessinus.
The worshippers sang songs about the god's beauty and
misfortune and about his faithfulness to his goddess. They
observed fasts in memory of his sufferings and sorrows, and
mutilated those who wished to be his priests—the *Galli*—
who, they held, ought to emulate him in his horrible sacrifice. Finally, casting off their sandals, they carried the god-

[2] *Vita Apollonii* i. 7.

dess Cybele's image down to the river where they bathed it in the flowing waters.

Yet another feast was celebrated after the June solstice, the feast of Adonis, the youthful god over whom Aphrodite and Persephone quarreled. This anniversary was commemorated by funereal processions and rites amid the lamentations of the women, as well as by banquets, oblations, and public homage in which the worshippers carried clay and waxen images of the god while they sang, prayed and mourned. It was the feast of vegetation, a farewell to the splendors of spring, the season of Aphrodite, and the announcement of autumnal sadness and winter cold, during which the goddess of the lower regions ruled. At other times the city streets rang with the chants of the devotees of Mithra, the Persian god whom the successors of Alexander had Hellenized. Some of the citizens of Tarsus celebrated the liturgy of Isis and of Osiris, who taught agriculture to the peoples of the Nile valley, the latter afterwards falling victim to the envy of his brother Typhon.

Thus there was in the city an almost unbroken round of ablutions and bloody rites, of processions which ended in orgies and of fasts succeeded by banquets. These were the religions of mysteries, in which the people took refuge from the sterility of their cold traditional cults. Such religions promised them freedom from punishment, the good will of the gods, and a more or less secure guarantee of safety in the terrible journey to the world beyond the tomb. But what connection had Paul with all these religious manifestations? It is hard to know, but undoubtedly he often came across the noisy gatherings of the worshippers and saw in some sacred cave the statue of Mithra, youthful and athletic, his Phrygian cap on his head, grasping with one hand the nostrils of a bull while his other plunged a dagger into its shoulder. Paul must have often discussed religion with the believers in these Oriental gods, and also encountered many times the travelling soothsayers who, with the book of Museus or Orpheus under their arm, called at the houses of the rich or appeared among the crowds in the market places, looking for clients to absolve and purify with their rites of initiation and their magic formulae.

However, it never occurred to Paul to study these formulae, to analyze the genealogies of the gods and their role in the origin of the universe, much less to take active part in the liturgies which were a complete negation of all he believed, although an analogy could be drawn between some of the beliefs they expressed and the doctrine which he preached.

He never refers to these pagan rites in his Epistles, unless we wish to see an allusion in such passages as the following from his Epistle to the Romans: "For while professing to be wise, they have become fools, and they have changed the glory of the incorruptible God for an image made like to corruptible man and to birds and four-footed beasts and creeping things" (1:23). He regarded all such idolatry as an abominable and infernal practice, a diabolical deceit and a lie, to be avoided like a quagmire waiting to engulf the unwary. In later years he warned his disciples: "Do not bear the yoke with unbelievers. For what has justice in common with iniquity? Or what fellowship has light with darkness? What harmony is there between Christ and Belial? Or what part has the believer with the unbeliever? And what agreement has the temple of God with idols?" (2 Cor. 6:14–16). These are the five points wherein he demonstrates that Christianity is incompatible with paganism. In the first place, there is a moral incompatibility between the two, for Christianity is justice, while paganism is injustice and impiety. Secondly, there is an intellectual gulf between them, since the light of wisdom shines in the Gospel so that all who believe in it live in the light of the Lord, whereas idolatry is darkness because God "has blinded their unbelieving minds" (2 Cor. 4:4). Furthermore, the Author of Christianity is totally different from the author of paganism; each is the captain of an army which he leads against the other in a battle to the death. Hence there is a fundamental opposition between the followers of Christ and the worshippers of false gods, between the faithful and the infidels.

Yet some theorists have tried to picture St. Paul as a sympathizer with idolatry, as one who wished to harmonize Jewish monotheism with Greek paganism. With unbelievable temerity these writers depict the Apostle as studying the pagan mysteries, adopting the theories of the philosophers in order to combine them with the doctrines which he learned in his home at Tarsus and in the schools of Jerusalem, thus forming a splendid synthesis of all the trends of religious thought in the ancient world. He is supposed to have found most of his main teachings in paganism—the doctrine of baptism and the Eucharist, the belief in the union of the soul with the deity, the idea of a divine death which extended its power to men of all ages. The initiates of Eleusis also purified their bodies by bathing in the waters of the Cephisus; the devotees of Isis were carried to the public baths before the priest introduced them into the goddess' sanctuary, and those who were being consecrated to Dionysus Zagreus wore white tunics as a symbol of the purity which they sought. In the cult of Attis, the worshiper was showered with the blood of the bull which had been sacrified. There was even mention of the new light, the splendor which guided the initiates, the character, seal, or sacred mark which was the sign of union with the divinity, and there was promise of regeneration, eternal rebirth, as a result of divine influence.

Paul is supposed to have adopted all these beliefs, combining them with Mosaic theodicy, simplifying, spiritualizing and universalizing them. In reality there are only external similarities between these pagan rites and tenets and the Christian sacramental system; it is a question of outward signs which on the surface sometimes resemble each other, but which have completely distinct meanings. It is false to say that in the pagan mysteries salvation was assured by the initiates' ritual participation in the trials, sufferings, death and resurrection of the gods who bestow immortality, as is the case in the Christian faith. In the mysteries of Eleusis, for example, there is no mention of death; Demeter and Persephone were too authentically Greek to die. Dionysus, Osiris and Adonis do die, it is true, but none of them accepts death willingly or looks upon it as a sacrifice to the divinity, and none of them rise again; therefore it would be fruitless to ask their devotees to undergo a mystical death and resurrection, as St. Paul interprets the sacrament of baptism. Osiris, torn limb from limb by Typhon, finds life and kingship in the regions beyond the tomb, and Adonis escapes each year from the wintry prison of Hades to live and love again for a time. But these are only vague analogies connected with the rhythm of the seasons, and even when they are given an eschatological significance by regarding them as figures of human destiny, they indicate only a hazy awareness of the invisible world, a confused desire for happiness, man's deepest yearning expressed in terms of his lowest instincts, in bloody rites and scenes of debauchery and vice.

Even the Dionysian religion, which in its Orphic form possesses a background of doctrine concerning man's destiny, and which is the only pagan cult which counts for anything in the history of religious thought, is not a religion of active virtues, of love of God and social beneficence. It deals only with the freeing of the heavenly element in man, with breaking the bonds of sin and the body and with cleansing his stains. These are the liberations and purifications to which Plato referred, and which are completely negative in character. What mattered primarily was to redeem oneself from the fatal chain of rebirths so that one could arrive at rest in Hades; that is to say, purity was desirable merely as the necessary condition for escaping the treadmill of matter. That was the meaning of the triumphant cry of the Orphic initiate: "I am pure and I come among the pure to thee, O queen of Hades, O Eukles, O Eubulus, and all ye other immortal gods. Now I have the good fortune to belong to your happy race. Destiny held me captive, but now I have broken the dire and mournful circle and with swift feet I have fled to the cherished crown."

But even the fable of Dionysus Zagreus, in which some wish to find an image of the Redeeming Sacrifice and even a source of the doctrine of original sin, is really only a legendary account of a violent death by murder. The story is this: one day when young Dionysus was happily engaged in playing the games of childhood and was looking at himself in a mirror, he was attacked by the Titans who had been incited by the envy of Hera, for the goddess was enraged because her brother had been given dominion over the world. Dionysus fled, assuming the shapes of various animals, but when he resumed his own appearance his enemies recognized him, cut him to pieces and devoured him. But Athena, his sister, was able to rescue his heart and took it to Zeus, who ate it, thus begetting a new Dionysus, the Theban Zagreus. Then the god launched his thunderbolt, burning the Titans to ashes from which men were born to continue expiating the crime of the deicides. One could rid oneself of this hereditary stain only by being initiated into the mysteries by means of air, water and fire, and by entering the sacred chamber with covered face, or by allowing one's body to be covered with a layer of mud and then submerging oneself in water.

The Christian doctrine of redemption which St. Paul teaches is completely different from such mythological meanderings. Christ died because He wished to do so in order to expiate the sins of the world, but Dionysus was killed without his foreknowledge or consent, and so his death was without merit in intention or in reality. Furthermore, the fable contains a complete absurdity in that the crime is its own expiation, since Dionysus' death is both the original sin and the remedy thereof—a contradictory idea that is repugnant to the Greek concept of justice, and which substitutes a physical contingency for that which in Christianity is the expression of a moral law of human solidarity, the Christian doctrine of divine sonship.

It was not from such fables that St. Paul evolved his doctrine of redemption, nor did he construct a system out of thin air. Instead, he used materials that existed before his time and before all the pagan religious mysteries were conceived. From the sacred books which he had heard read from his childhood he knew that the fall of Adam had brought death into the world, and all other Israelites were aware of it, too, for they sang David's great psalm in their synagogues: "For behold I was conceived in iniquities: and in sins did my mother conceive me" (50:7). He also knew that in due time a redeemer would come on earth to blot out sin and reconcile man with God. All the literature of his race spoke of this redeemer, extolling his greatness, his mighty kingdom, his goodness and his marvelous appearance. He had waited thirty years, from infancy to manhood, for the savior to arrive, until finally he was convinced that the Messias, so often proclaimed down through the ages, was none other than Jesus of Nazareth, Son of God and Son of Man, who had humbled Himself even to taking the form of a servant in order to make us sons of God, and that He had become sin to expiate our offenses. It was then that he understood the logical and psychological relationship between sin and forgiveness and was able, as far as was possible to human intelligence, to understand the magnificence of the divine plan and to explain it better than anyone else.

He could have learned nothing of these sublime concepts from studying the pagan mysteries, since they were but empty shadows of a sublime reality or, in the words of St. Justin and Tertullian, poor imitations employed by the devil to keep good men from the glorious truth. Even the doctrine of purity which some of the pagans seemed to recommend was totally unlike the morality taught by St. Paul. For example, for all its vaunted striving toward freedom from matter, the Orphic religion was a phallic cult, and while the Apostle regarded the human body as the temple of the Holy Spirit, the Dionysian initiate regarded it as an unclean prison from which one had to escape as quickly as possible. Thus for the pagan there was a basic opposition between flesh and spirit, and the two were united only transitorily in order to expiate the sins of former existences. Sanctity therefore consisted in liberating the divine element and destroying the human; it was a Buddhist sanctity, the aim of which was to free oneself from visible things, from the oppression of the physical world and the influence of the heavenly bodies. Exterior purity was sought by means of washings, sprinklings and corporal penances; all contact with carnal things was forbidden; the initiates were not allowed to attend weddings; it was a sin for them to touch dead bodies; abstinence from flesh meat was recommended, and the begetting of children was regarded as an accursed practice—all with the purpose of breaking the cruel circle of birth, death and rebirth.

Such pagan beliefs could not have served as a starting-point for St. Paul's theology, even when we consider them in their highest form, the form they took after Christianity had already begun to spread through the Roman Empire and to influence the various cults with which it came in contact. The pagan rites never dealt with freeing man from sin by pardon, but only at best the attaining of a happy immortality. The main thing was to avoid the dangers of the world beyond the grave, to escape the snares of evil spirits, to evade the miseries of life such as sickness, wars, adversity, shipwreck, or loss of fortune. Thus the pagan teaching on life after death was purely material, utterly different from the eternal life which, as St. Paul teaches, the Christian already possesses in germ in this world. The rites practiced by the initiates were regarded as infallible means of obtaining occult powers and of working salvation by magic, the favor of the gods being automatically gained by the prescribed physical actions. In the Eleusinian mysteries the devotees' sacred marriage with Demeter was so efficacious that no one could doubt that man had been united with the divinity, and in the mystery of Attis when the ritual lamentation had been pronounced and the leader of the ceremony had cried: "Rejoice, you are free of your punishments!" all those consecrated to the god were sure that they could look forward to a happy eternity. The same was true of the ceremony of the Tauro-bolium, which has been so admirably described by the poet Prudentius. In this ritual, the high priest descended into a grave dressed in his pontifical garb, and upon him spurted the blood of the decapitated bull, saturating his garments, staining his hands, flowing into his eyes and mouth, pouring down his cheeks, and inundating his whole body. In that way he was consecrated because the god, hidden in the victim's blood, penetrated into his veins, sanctified his lips, made his words fruitful and gained immortality for him. He was convinced then, or at least those who had offered the sacrifice were convinced, that his prayers could ensure fertility for the fields and could conquer the terrors of destiny, for he was no longer really a priest but a magician whose words could effect what they signified.

Similarly, when the initiate of Eleusis had been allowed to contemplate the sacred green ear of corn and had pronounced the formula, "Prosperity! Light!" he believed that he had helped to assure the success of the next harvest, or even that he himself had been translated to the bright regions of the immortals. The latter was Apuleius' conviction when, on the tenth day of his initiation into the mysteries of Isis, he went into the most sacred place in the sanctuary to attend the dramatic representation which, in the midst of the shadows, laid bare before his eyes the picture of heaven and the lower regions: "Listen and believe that which is the truth; I have approached the kingdom of death, I have set foot on Persephone's threshold and have come back across the elements. I have seen the sun shine at

night in all its splendor; I have arrived at the presence of
the gods of the lower regions and the gods of heaven; I have
seen them face to face and have prostrated myself before
them." [3]

We find nothing of this kind in St. Paul's teaching on
Christianity. For him, salvation is never gained automatically, but only psychologically, by the submission of man's
will to faith, by turning one's back on dead works, and by
the use of the means which God has given to man. Works
of virtue and belief in the revealed truths must accompany
the use of the sacraments, and we follow a divine plan of
salvation drawn up by God Himself, instead of using magic
to force the gods to be propitious. There is no significance
in the fact that both Orpheans and Christians used the
metaphor of divine light, since in paganism it was only a
meaningless term, while in Christianity it refers to a strict
reality. "You are light in the Lord," St. Paul used to say to
those who had been baptized, to remind them that formerly
they were in darkness and death, although they might have
prostrated themselves before the statue of Sabazius, or
covered their bodies with mud, or been sprinkled with the
sacred flour or come forth from the ritual cleansings shouting joyously: "I have fled from evil; I have found security!"

Why would the Apostle go looking in such superstitious
cults for doctrine and rites that were so contrary to his
concept of the world and of man's life here and hereafter?
No doubt he smiled pityingly at the blind confidence of
those who thronged about the gates of the temples of Isis,
"the one who is all things," the most eminent of the divinities, she who, according to her litanies, combined in herself
the attributes of all the other deities. She certainly was not

[3] *Metamorphosis* xi.

the infinite and personal God whom he had seen on the road to Damascus, but rather only a symbol of omnipotent nature who, instead of loving her worshippers and suffering to redeem them, was merely a cruel stepmother to them. And if in his travels about the world, he happened to discuss religion with a priest of Osiris, we can be sure that his faith was not shaken by the very vague resemblance between the Egyptian gods and Christ, "the image of the invisible God, the firstborn of every creature. For in him were created all things in the heavens and on the earth, things visible and things invisible. . . . that through him [God] should reconcile to himself all things . . . through the blood of his cross" (Col. 1: 15–16, 20).

Did Osiris or Attis or Adonis suffer death for love of their followers or pass on to them the splendors of their second lives as did Christ for those who believe in His Gospel? If these fables of pagan mythology had not been a hindrance to his preaching, Paul would merely have shrugged them off. He must have seen on many occasions how these legends, instead of preparing souls for "the mystery which has been hidden from eternity in God," rather stood in the way of the victory of the Cross by temporarily satisfying religious yearnings with what seemed like a noble mysticism. Then, too, it was very convenient for men to be able to gain salvation and eternal happiness by external ceremonies, without the necessity of interior struggles, ethical considerations, personal sacrifices and self-denial. It was so pleasant to adore a happy goddess or a handsome young god who gave everything and asked for practically nothing except an offering of fruit, a dove, a goat, a bull, or a few days of abstinence that gave one the right to indulge afterwards in orgies of all kinds.

However, not everything in these cults was bad and

diabolical, nor can one, as Tertullian hints, explain them simply as a devil's parody on true religion. Origen gave a more profound explanation of the undoubted analogies that exist between St. Paul's theology and the religions of the mysteries when he observed that yearnings for purification, expiation and union with the godhead have their roots in the very nature of the religious man. These desires are aspirations of the soul that arise, as St. Augustine remarks, "from that inner consciousness which spurs on the best of men to look for God and serve Him." [4] But outside Christianity these concepts were so clouded over, so adulterated with shameful ideas and so demeaned by ridiculous, childish practices, that what ought to have been a joyous and luminous progress toward the Heavenly Father became merely an aimless wandering in the dark.

Paul's anger was aroused by the statues, the temples and the rituals of the false gods who had usurped his own God's place in so many men's hearts. So great was his wrath that he would never allude to these trappings of paganism, nor sully the pages of his Epistles with their names; neither did he make use of the resemblance of some of their myths to the truths of the Gospel. For he held that he who has received the liberty of the sons of God should not submit himself to what he calls "the elements of his world" (Col. 2:20). The teachings of the philosophers also had superficial resemblances to his doctrine, since the Stoics, like him, despised riches, fled from shameful pleasures, and showed courage in suffering. Yet their attitude filled him with anger and disdain, for their outer poverty was only a cloak for their refined pride, and they were immoral, egotistical scoffers, foul-mouthed in their abuse and implacable

[4] *De utilitate credendi* 16.

in their hatred. They prided themselves on their knowledge, their sole occupation was the discussion of ideas, their only god was reason. It is true that they extolled liberty of spirit, boldly opposed despotism, and cheerfully bore the blows of fate, but their virtues were centered on themselves, for they believed that the source of all peace and justice lay within them, and that their own minds were the measure of the absolute good.

Like the mysticism of the pagan cults, the religious yearnings of Stoicism failed to rise above the earth, and although both pagan and Stoic felt a vague nostalgia for union with divinity, they confused divinity with the forces of nature and called it by various names—Isis, Mithra, Demeter, Adonis, or the Great All. Though the philosophers sneered at the devotees' rituals, they, too, believed that the soul was a spark from the creative fire in which it was destined to lose itself once again. This was simply pantheism, or belief in a god who creates destiny, yet is subject to it, who is the underlying reality in all things and who encompasses the world. Consequently, since man was a participation in the divinity, he must be naturally good, and his vices were either not born with him or were simply a matter of opinion.[5]

In the streets and in the schools of Tarsus, Rome, Athens and Corinth, Paul must have frequently met the teachers of these doctrines, men who wore ragged beards and torn mantles and who, like himself, had travelled throughout the civilized world. No doubt he argued with them and tried to convert them to the ascetical practices of the Gospel, for if they already were so mortified as to sleep on the ground, to eat frugally, to suffer poverty and fatigue, what would they do when they knew that a free and personal

[5] Cf. Seneca *Epistolae ad Lucilium* xliv. 53.

God had come on earth to teach these practices as a means of gaining immortality? It is possible that more than one philosopher came to the Jewish preacher, curious to know the teachings of the man who went from city to city making converts and arousing such animosity. But the result would always be the same: they came expecting to find a philosopher like themselves and found instead, as they thought, a melancholy story-teller, a deluded reciter of myths such as they had already rejected as fit solely for slaves and foolish women. They saw only the man, small and insignificant; they heard only his unpolished speech; and they found his teaching ridiculous, for he held that their philosophy was useless, that the one aim of life was to seek the glory of God, that virtue consisted in imitating simply and humbly a man who had died on a cross, that it was necessary to submit one's reason to a revealed tradition, and that perfection did not consist in the exaltation of one's personality but rather in self-abnegation, self-surrender, and sacrifice inspired by spiritual love. On hearing this doctrine these men, proud of their knowledge, went away smiling disdainfully, and considered the speaker insane.

To Paul, who was announcing to the world the unity of God's kingdom and revealing the secret of real love, the cold, confident doctrines of the intellectuals of his day, the haughty and purely rational solidarity of the Stoics, must have seemed completely sterile, yet possessed of a certain austere beauty, like moonlight on snow. With their systems founded on pride in their own impeccability and justice, they appeared to present greater obstacles to the spread of the Gospel than did the priests of the mystical religions with their seductive promises and idolatrous fanaticisms. Yet the philosophers were only blind leaders of the blind, outwardly free but inwardly the slaves of their perverse instincts. They were not among those who were pre-destined to realize the glorious conquests of the Gospel: "Where is the wise man? Where is the scribe? Where is the disputant of this world? Has not God turned to foolish-ness the 'wisdom' of this world. . . . [He] has given them up to shameful lusts. . . . And as they have resolved against possessing the knowledge of God, God has given them up to a reprobate sense . . . and they receive in themselves the fitting recompense of their perversity" (1 Cor. 1:20; Rom. 1:26, 28, 27).

Thus does St. Paul anathematize the leaders of those schools of thought, the degenerate successors of Plato, Zeno and Aristotle, of Pythagoras and Epicurus, and his words seem to bring to our ears the echoes of bitter dis-putes and stern accusations. Heir to immense treasures that he was, he had no need to go begging for spiritual riches among such peddlers of vicious truths and brilliant lies, and if he did happen to see a jewel sparkling on their moth-eaten robes, he claimed it unhesitatingly as something that belonged by right to his Lord. Far from preparing the way for the Faith, these philosophers hindered its growth, since they gave false consolation to the noblest men of the time, men who were disgusted with the despotism of the em-perors and the servility of the subjects. Such a philosopher was Apollonius of Tyana, a contemporary of Paul's, who studied the teachings of the Brahmins in India and then travelled through the Western world lecturing in the theaters, preaching against vice from the steps of the temples, and restoring peace in the cities. He did not lack hearers who, torn by a confused but keen desire for good-ness, resolved to live without sinning and to die bravely with no other consolation than the knowledge of their own virtue or the hope of an impersonal immortality. Even the most sincere souls did not think of striving to find a better-defined deity and a more hopeful future. Such was the case with Seneca, whom Tacitus calls "a spirit marvellously adapted to the tastes of his time," a divided man in whom the thinker and the mystic seemed to be continually at war. As a philosopher, Seneca taught that God is the soul of the world, the infinite force, immanent in the universe, the Great All in which the very personality of the human soul is submerged and diluted. But at the same time he introduced into his philosophy a kind of mystical enthusiasm unknown to the Romans, which he inherited from his Iberian ancestors. He held that God is a Father, the friend of our souls, ever-present and ever-vigilant, and that adoration and love are the best homage we can offer Him. We should beg Him to aid us in rooting out vice, since this life is a battle in which we strive to win virtue in union with our brothers, the rest of mankind. Therefore we should not fear death, since it is a liberation—a true birth into life eternal. But unfortunately these beautiful thoughts were clouded by such a tumult of doubts, uncertainties and contradictions that they compare very sadly with the security, the strength and the Catholic dogmatic firmness of St. Paul's theology.

These hidden years which the Apostle spent in his native city must have been years of observation and discussion, of trial and labor. Once again he sat upon the sheepskin, weaving goat's hair into rough cloth for the tents; once again he wielded the wooden knife to separate the tangled threads, but now, as he stretched the woof of the cloth with sharp blows of the carder, he could speak to his companions of the Faith he had found in Damascus. Gradually he built up a Christian community in Cilicia, a church which he always thought of as peculiarly his own, which he later visited many times, and which testified to the intense and fruitful apostolate of his silent years in Tarsus.

After a series of adventures which had spread his name through the ghettos of the Jews of Asia, he had heard the call of his native land and had returned to the scenes of his childhood. During the first years of his conversion, God's summons had been so urgent that, as he himself tells us, "without taking counsel with flesh and blood . . . I retired into Arabia. . . ." But soon he had felt himself drawn by the call of his blood and race, for who had more right to the first fruits of his preaching than his own family and boyhood friends? Accordingly, he had gone back to Tarsus and his father's house, and when the family gathered together in the evenings, he had told them about his miraculous vision and had spoken to them about Jesus. On the eve of the Sabbath when his mother lighted the ritual lamp, he had explained the Messianic passages in the prophets and proclaimed the salvation of the world through the blood of Christ Crucified.

We do not know how his family reacted to his preaching, since he does not once refer to the matter in his Epistles. It is more than likely that he was unable to break down the wall of their Pharisaical resistance and that they regarded him as a prodigal, a rebel, an unworthy descendant of the ancient patriarchs. We can well imagine the hostile atmosphere in that home—discussions, threats, recriminations, and heart-breaking sorrow for all. The son of the house, who had been regarded as a future ornament to the Mosaic cause, had turned out to be a shame to his family; he had become an enemy of the nation's traditions, a member and defender of a sect of ignorant fanatics. In his Epistle to the Philippians, the Apostle tells us that: "For his sake I have suffered the loss of all things, and I count them as dung that I may gain Christ . . ." (Phil. 3:8), a declaration which seems to cast some light on the events of these years in Tarsus and to show us the conditions under which he had to pursue his apostolate. Although he was a member of a rich and influential family, he found himself reduced to dire poverty and compelled to work hard to earn a living. We can picture how he had been rejected by his father, disinherited, cast out of his home and cut off from all the joys and love he had once known there. He never forgot the sorrow this repudiation by his family caused him, and in later years he did all he could to foster a happy relationship between fathers and sons. Writing to the Ephesians, he advised: "Fathers, do not provoke your children to anger, but rear them in the discipline and admonition of the Lord" (Eph. 6:4), a counsel which he repeated on several other occasions, with an added warning to parents not to be over-strict lest they break their children's spirit. (Cf. Col. 3:21.) At the same time, however, he insisted that children were bound to obey their parents and to show them every mark of honor and respect.

In a certain house in Tarsus there is a well which is still called "St. Paul's Well," and on a mountain near the city there is a cave which is traditionally believed to be the place to which the Apostle retired to live in contemplation and penance. If we are correct in assuming that he had to leave his father's house, perhaps he found shelter in that cave while he awaited God's definitive summons to his new mission-field. There is no strictly historical proof that the well and the cave were actually used by St. Paul, but the persistent tradition may serve to throw a little light on these hidden years during which the Apostle may have lived partly in retirement as a hermit in the mountains, and partly in teaching and preaching. At any rate, these years were an intensive preparation for the fufillment of the task assigned him by Providence, years during which the call of the Jewish world sounded ever more faintly in his ears, while his thoughts gradually turned toward the lands ruled by the Caesars. And, significantly enough, it was about this time that his Jewish name of Saul began to be eclipsed by the name Paul which he used as a Roman citizen.

CHAPTER VII

The Third Heaven

During the years which Paul spent in Tarsus, the disciples of Christ had continued to increase in number and to found new communities in many places. "Throughout all Judea and Galilee and Samaria," St. Luke tells us, "the Church was in peace and was being built up, walking in fear of the Lord, and it was filled with the consolation of the Holy Spirit" (Acts 9:31). By driving the Nazarene's disciples out of Jerusalem, the persecutors had hastened the spread of the new religion. One of Stephen's companions, the deacon Philip, had fled from the Holy City and had organized an important gathering of converts in Samaria, while similar groups had sprung up in the most important centers in Palestine. The religion of the Crucified God, which seemed for a time to have only a social significance, now triumphantly began its spiritual conquest of the world.

Since it was necessary to maintain a close connection between the central community at Jerusalem and the new foundations, Peter had to travel throughout Judea and Samaria, for it was he who, as chief of the Apostles, inspected, directed and arranged the Church's first plans of organization. He visited the disciples at Lydda, then went on to Joppa where he raised the charitable widow, Dorcas, from the dead, and finally he arrived at Caesarea, where he was confronted for the first time with the problem that was to trouble the Church in these, the first days of its existence: must one be an actual descendant of Abraham to gain entry to the kingdom of the Messias? At first glance the answer did not seem difficult, since the doors of the Church were not going to be narrower than those of the Synagogue, which were wide enough to afford entrance to a large number of Gentile proselytes. Yet there were some who protested, thus starting a controversy which divided the early Christians into two factions. When Peter, while in Caesarea, entered the house of the Gentile centurion, Cornelius, ate with him and baptized him, the conservatives were troubled and asked him for an explanation. To quiet their fears, he described the vision which he had seen before Cornelius had invited him to his house, the vision in which God answered his objection to eating anything common or unclean with the words: "What God has cleansed, do not thou call common." (Cf. Acts 10:10–16; 11:4–10.) Nevertheless, the argument continued, for Cornelius was a proselyte "of the sanctuary," one of those God-fearing men who had fully accepted the Mosaic Law and had submitted to the rite of circumcision, and thus the problem now became: Was it necessary to pass through the synagogue to enter the Church? Yes, replied the party "of the circumcision"; no, answered the more liberal element—it was enough for a prospective convert to be a proselyte "of the gate," that is, a person who observed some of the ritual ceremonies like abstinence from blood, from meat that had been sacrificed to idols or killed by strangling, and from marriage within the degrees forbidden by the Law.

While the controversy continued, alarming news was brought from Antioch, whither a large group of disciples had fled after Stephen's martyrdom for, not feeling safe even in Damascus, they had continued their flight along the Mediterranean coast to the capital of Syria. There, protected by the cosmopolitan outlook of the citizens, they had been free from the intrigues and violence of the Sanhedrin. Today, Antioch is a dead city, in which a half-dozen minarets rise above a shapeless collection of gray houses huddled below the arid crests of Mt. Silpius. In the background the Amanus mountains raise their peaks like the towers of a giant citadel, and among the steep foothills the muddy yellow waters of the Orontes flow sluggishly along to end their journey from Lebanon in the Mediterranean Sea. The river is spanned by an old bridge with narrow low-slung arches, and near the riverbank one can still see the ruins of the large amphitheater in which the greatest charioteers of the past competed. But no longer does one find the temple of Zeus Keraunios which protected the Acropolis from lightning, nor the Pantheon which sheltered the statues of all the gods, nor the gigantic images of the Dioscuri on their rearing chargers, which the Emperor Tiberius commanded to be erected.

At the beginning of the Christian era, however, Antioch was the third city of the Empire. Plains and mountains, the myrtle-trees of the gardens and the pines of the woods, the palaces of the patricians and the caves of the anchorites, the marvels of Greek art in the baths, circuses, law-courts, temples and theaters—all combined to complete the beauty of that landscape of enchanted islands, fragrant hillsides, pleasant nooks, and mountain gorges and precipices which echoed with the thunder of cascading waterfalls. Along the streets of the city and beneath its miles of Corinthian colonnades the noisy, motley crowds surged in multi-colored waves: caravans from the Euphrates laden with the riches of Asia, native Syrians, white and negro slaves, Jewish merchants, and lively Greeks. Finally there were the wealthy, indolent Romans drawn thither by the beautiful climate and the charms of nature, but above all by the prevailing licentiousness that had made Antioch a city of dissipation, proud of its sacred gardens with their gaudily-clad courtesans who were insatiable for pleasures, for plays and concerts, for feasting and every kind of diversion.

In that whirlpool of humanity, the fugitives from Jerusalem were thrown together with Jews from Cyprus and Cyrene, who were more used to the cosmopolitanism of the Roman world than their brothers from Palestine. Slowly the small group increased in numbers, flourishing in the liberal atmosphere that tolerated all kinds of ideas, and even all kinds of aberrations. In a provincial setting or in a tribal or village society, the spreading of new ideas is always difficult and dangerous, because such communities are almost completely closed to outside influence and are thus more resistant to innovations. In a large city, however, changes take place imperceptibly and the mass of the populace scarcely adverts to them, or, if they do, they are so used to novelties that they take little interest in them. At most, they just smile mockingly at the new ideas and turn away to wait for the next day's surprises. That is what happened at Antioch; yet the time and place were favorable to the spread of the Gospel. A rhetorician of the city, the pagan Libanius, described the existing conditions of his time in one sentence: "Religion consists solely in defiling oneself with a thousand infamies and in stripping oneself of the last traces of virtue." [1] No wonder, then, that men of noble character were filled with disgust and were ready to

[1] *Opera* iii. 333.

accept a pure religion, although it might demand of them all the heroism of the ascetics.

So great was the success of the preachers from Cyrene and Cyprus that soon the pagans of the city realized that the followers of Christ were distinct from the Jews, with whom they had hitherto confused them. Thus it was that in the capital of Syria, the disciples began to be known by a Greek name with a Roman ending, a name that was not without a touch of irony—"*Christiani*," the disciples of the Anointed One. But the brethren in Jerusalem held divided opinions about this new community which, if they only knew it, was soon to outshine all others. While some praised such rapid expansion of the Gospel teaching, others who clung stubbornly to the Mosaic tradition criticized the liberality with which the disciples there conferred baptism on the pagans, for it was alleged that they indiscriminately received circumcised and uncircumcised converts, prose-lytes of the sanctuary and of the gate, and even Greeks who had had no connection at all with the synagogue. The very name by which the followers of Christ were being distinguished from other Jews was interpreted by the critics as a definite indication of separation from the Law. In actual fact, the coining of the name "Christian" marked the solemn moment in which the Church cut free from Judaism.

In order to judge the case and ascertain what was to be done, the leaders of the church in Jerusalem decided to send Barnabas to inquire into the spirit of the new com-munity. Barnabas' selection as emissary seems to have been a conciliatory measure, for it was he who had introduced Paul to the company of the Apostles, and he was a Hellen-ist, "a good man and full of the Holy Spirit and of faith" (Acts 11:24), who had gained the affection of all the brethren by his generosity, his devotion and skill in explaining the Scriptures, and by his noble presence.

In Antioch Barnabas "saw the grace of God" (Acts 11:23), for the new disciples, mostly converts from the darkness of paganism, were producing many fruits of sanctity, and both Greeks and Jews were striving with equal enthusiasm to practice the evangelical virtues. Filled with admiring wonder, Barnabas sanctioned and approved the converts' baptisms, "and exhorted them all to continue in the Lord with steadfast heart" (Acts 11:23). His words not only encouraged the members of the church but reached the ears of outsiders, so that many Gentiles came each day to ask for baptism. Nevertheless, contradictions were not lacking—opposition from the rabbis, public debates, and arguments in the streets and in the synagogues. In the midst of the turmoil Barnabas remembered Paul, whom he had found such a formidable controversialist some years before, and who was quite close at hand in his birthplace, Tarsus, on the other side of the Gulf of Commagene, later known as the Gulf of Alexandretta. Now was the time for his friend to come out of that mysterious retirement in which his fiery soul was being tempered. So, in the first months of the year 42, Barnabas decided to seek out Paul, and started on his voyage—a day's sailing from the mouth of the Orontes to that of the Cydnus, and then two or three days by land over the mountains and passes. He did not tell anyone the object of his journey, perhaps because he was not sure he could persuade his friend to accompany him back to Antioch. Yet he had what he considered an unanswerable argument; the voice of God had chosen Paul to bring the Gospel to the Gentiles, and here were the Gentiles in Antioch beginning to swarm about the doors of the Church. Therefore there could no longer be any doubt as to where he should begin his divinely appointed task. Paul gave in to his friend's persuasion, influenced more by the conviction that it was his duty to accept the invitation than by his naturally active temperament. The burden of the apostolate dismayed him; yet in the depths of his heart he heard the admonishing words: "Woe to you if you do not preach the Gospel!" (Cf. 1 Cor. 9:16.)

He began his ministry by joining his ardent discourses to the gentle words of Barnabas, "the son of consolation." Although he had been more favored by heaven than any of the evangelizers, he humbly submitted his actions to the direction of others, repressing the impulses toward independence which arose out of his fiery personality. Thus in brotherly harmony with the disciple from Cyprus, he spent several years teaching and winning souls to the Gospel and, what was more difficult, molding the weak, inconstant and pleasure-loving Syrians to the precepts of Christ. However, he was no longer content to preach in the synagogues, but went out into the streets and squares where the charlatans sold their magic formulae and peddled the lastest novelty or the newest fashions in clothes. Even as late as the sixth century the Antiocheans used to point out the spot where St. Paul preached to the crowds, an elevation in Singon Street, one of the busiest thoroughfares of the city which climbed toward the hill of the Acropolis. There, near the Forum and the Pantheon, amid theaters and statues of the gods, on the avenue along which flowed the foolish multitudes flocking to the gate of Daphne's temple and to the bacchanalia in the sacred olive-groves, the Apostle began his gigantic struggle against paganism, "opening to the Gentiles a door of faith" (Acts 14:26). For the first time he had a varied audience, one very different from that which he had faced in the synagogues of Damascus and

Jerusalem: some were dressed in the short Roman cape, others in the Greek mantle, still others in the brief tunic of the countryman; there were idolaters, tired of their soulless gods, and God-fearing men who were shackled by the rigidity and self-righteousness of Judaism. When speaking to such a gathering, Paul laid aside the stone tablets of Sinai, replacing them with "the Law written in their hearts" (Rom. 2:15). He changed his method of approach by casting aside the remnants of his Pharisaical education, throwing off the yoke of the synagogue and joyfully proclaiming the liberty of the sons of God. The growing Church, stimulated by the vast horizons which he and the other preachers opened before it, gained new strength, and though people might derisively call the disciples by the hybrid nickname "Christians," which the malice of the crowd had pinned on them,[2] they were determined to make it a glorious title for the sake of which they were willing to bear insult, tortures and even death itself. Paul was to carry this name like a torch across the face of the world, and when he came to write his Epistles he made each page glow with its heavenly light.

Very soon the brethren in Antioch gave the disciples in the Holy City palpable proof of the sincerity of their faith. Although they had not pooled their possessions in a dangerous communism, they still regarded earthly goods with the detachment which their Savior so often stressed. Now it happened that a prophet named Agabus, when invited to speak one day before the assembled disciples, foretold that a great famine would lay waste the world, and described so vividly the misery that would afflict the church in Jerusalem that the congregation hastened to gather funds among the Christians of Antioch to aid their brothers in the Holy

---

[2] "*Quos vulgus christianos appellat.*" Tacitus *Annales* xv. 44.

City. Paul and Barnabas were assigned to bring the money to the mother-church, but before the famine came, another calamity struck the church in Jerusalem: the persecution started by Herod Agrippa who had recently ascended the throne of Palestine.

This man, the grandson of Herod the Great, combined the adaptability of his race with a genius for intrigue and for insinuating himself into the good graces of the Roman rulers of the world. Under the patronage of Rome, he had succeeded in adding new strength to his grandfather's realm. By a whim of Tiberius he had been removed from the court and cast into prison, while a whim of Caligula had brought him from the dungeon to the throne. He was zealous for the Mosaic Law, but more for political reasons than out of conviction, and he had beautified Jerusalem and hung in the Temple the gold chains which Caligula had given him as a remembrance of his imprisonment. He assumed the airs of a mystic, paid tithes of cumin and mustard-seed like the most scrupulous Pharisees, went to the sanctuary with the customary small basket of first fruits, wept with emotion when the Levite read the words of the Law, and sacrificed thousands of victims in one day. The Jews rejoiced at his apparent zeal for the Temple and regarded his reign as a renewal of the splendor of David's rule. Yet the strictest of the Pharisees were uneasy about one thing—the stubbornness of the disciples of Jesus; and Agrippa, urged on by the zealots, resolved to wipe out the Christians. He began by persecuting the leaders, beheading St. James, the son of Zebedee, and throwing Peter into a jail from which he was later freed by a widely-acclaimed miracle.

Thus, when the envoys from Antioch arrived in Jerusalem, the faithful of the mother-church were still in a state of alarm. The persecution had lasted several months and already the famine, foretold by Agabus, was harassing the city and was to continue afflicting it for a long time to come. Josephus speaks of the rigors of the famine and of the generosity shown by Queen Helena, who came from her kingdom on the Euphrates River to help the poor in Jerusalem. In addition to the queen's alms, the disciples in the city had the money brought from their brethren in Antioch by Paul and Barnabas, who remained among them, encouraging and consoling them, acting as administrators of the relief funds they had brought and preaching the word of God.

During all this time, Paul continued to visit the Temple, for although he was convinced that the Gospel had superseded the Mosaic Law, he could not entirely forget the holy places in which he had prayed and studied in his youth. Here, more than anywhere else, he felt himself surrounded by the presence of God; here he had his visions and revelations and listened to the mysterious voice which guided him. Perhaps it was in the Temple, too, during this visit to Jerusalem, that something happened to him which engraved itself on his memory. One day while praying, he felt an irresistible force raising him with incredible swiftness to dizzy heights, where he heard an ineffable language and where a marvellous panorama was spread before his eyes, a new and undreamed-of world, a vision of divine beauties. His whole body trembled with the excess of joy that surged within him, and he fell into an ecstasy (that sublime phenomenon of the mystical life so minutely described by St. Teresa and St. John of the Cross—the rigid and immobile body, the shallow respiration, the closed eyes, the loss of bodily sensation, the weak pulse and the memory swept clear of all earthly things). He later wrote of this experience in words that are pregnant with divine things: "I know a man in Christ who fourteen years ago—whether in the body I do not know, or out of the body I do not know, God knows—such a one was caught up to the third heaven. And I know such a man—whether in the body or out of the body I do not know, God knows—that he was caught up into paradise and heard secret words that man may not repeat" (2 Cor. 12:2-5).

This was not only a vision of Christ, whom he had seen in his former ecstasies; it was a flight of his spirit up to the very throne of God, a few moments in which he felt himself plunged and lost in the depths of the Godhead, and in which he caught a faint glimpse of that sublime happiness, that heavenly reward which eye has not seen, nor ear heard, nor heart of man conceived. Now all the sufferings of the apostolate—the insults, scourgings, imprisonment, labors, shipwrecks, chains and the sword—would seem insignificant and fleeting. He had scaled the heights, and the wondrous intuition of the truth that had been granted him left in his soul an inexhaustible store of joy and light. This marvellous ecstasy marks one of the culminating points in St. Paul's life, for it gave his preaching a conquering certitude that was to sustain him in the face of all obstacles, and an accent of conviction that would open hearts to receive his teaching.

The turn of events at that time confirmed St. Paul's own interior experiences, for Peter had been miraculously freed from prison a few days before he was to have been brought out to his fate, and the other Apostles, who had been driven from Jerusalem by the persecution, were preaching the name of Jesus outside the city. Finally Herod Agrippa, the persecutor, was snatched away by a death that must have seemed to the disciples a new proof of God's assistance. He had retired to Beirut, the Phoenician city built on the slopes of the Libanus mountains within sound of the sea, and had tried to forget the failure of his maneuverings against the Christians. He occupied himself in building circuses, baths and colonnades, for he loved the arena and the amphitheater as passionately as any patrician of Rome or Athens, and it was in the arena that his hour of agony came upon him.

It happened in Tiberias, near the Sea of Galilee, where Peter had heard Christ's call. The crowd roared its acclamation of the king, and when he addressed them they shouted: "It is the voice of a god, not of a man!" Immediately, St. Luke tells us, the "angel of the Lord struck him down . . . [and] he was eaten by worms. . . ." The historian Josephus writes of an owl, the harbinger of misfortune, which the king had seen over his head in the course of an idolatrous feast, and the chronicler acknowledges that the petty tyrant was finally punished for his impiety by the raging fire which burned within him for five long days before it consumed him totally. Herod Agrippa died in the autumn of the year 44, while Peter, with whose death he had wished to put the seal on his popularity, was making his way to Rome to lay the foundations of a new world-wide empire.

CHAPTER VIII

"Set Apart for Me Saul and Barnabas"

Herod Agrippa died, says St. Luke, and "the word of the Lord continued to grow and spread" (Acts 12:23–24). The community at Antioch had become a church, "the church at Antioch," a flourishing congregation with an abundance of teachers, one which was visited by the Spirit and which was increased daily by numerous conversions. The initiative now came from the capital of Syria and not from the Holy City where, in the absence of Peter, the opinion of the zealots for the Law prevailed among the Christians. The leader and principal teacher in the church in Jerusalem at this time was St. James the Apostle, the kinsman of the Lord, a man of austere character who, though admirable for his unyielding strictness of life, was devoted to the narrowest puritanism. "There is no salvation without circumcision" was the watchword and motto of the conservatives, who were still held prisoner by the confining circle of their national traditions.

In the church at Antioch, however, the spirit of universalism prevailed, and Gentiles of all nations rubbed shoulders in its assemblies, so that in a meeting of the

Christians there was a cross-section of cosmopolitanism. Even the teachers of the church belonged to the most diverse nations, for besides Barnabas, a native of Cyprus, and Paul, who represented Cilicia, there was an African from Numidia named Lucius of Cyrene, as well as a proselyte from Ethiopia, Simon, "called Niger," and a foster-brother of Herod Antipas, Manahen, who was a Hellenist, although he came from Palestine. These were the principal prophets and teachers of the church and it was they who, when moved by the breath of the Spirit, revealed the will of God, judged the truth of doctrines and traced out the path along which souls should be guided.

In St. Luke's account Saul is mentioned last, since he did not as yet have the decisive influence which he was to wield a little later on. His widely-acclaimed conversion, his educational background and his burning eloquence gained him a place among the doctors, but, unlike the others, he had not received the fullness of the priesthood at the hands of Peter. And although God had enlightened him with extraordinary revelations, he did not claim a higher place, but remained subject to the elders of the church and, above all, to Barnabas, to whom he was united by bonds of gratitude.

Nevertheless he prepared himself, waiting for the decisive moment and thinking much about the missions, his eyes straying impatiently toward those lands which spread beyond the Amanus Mountains and those which were hidden beyond the sea. He spoke many times to his companions about the impulses of grace which were urging him toward the Gentiles, but none of the elders made the decision to send him thither, for it was necessary that everything be done in fraternal harmony and that the current of divine strength which he felt pulsing in his heart be approved and directed by the will of the brethren under the guidance of their pastors.

This was the way the matter stood when the time of a solemn festival came around, probably the feast of Tabernacles, a period of "ministering to the Lord and fasting" (Acts 13:2). The faithful of Antioch came together, fasted, invoked the Lord, broke bread and were about to bring the sacred mysteries to a close when a voice was heard throughout the assembly saying: "Set apart for me Saul and Barnabas unto the work to which I have called them." This was the undoubted expression of the will of God and was accepted as such by the congregation, which forthwith redoubled its prayers and continued its fast, imploring the grace of God for the two chosen ones. Finally, the elders who already possessed the priestly order imposed their hands on Saul and Barnabas before the gathered assembly, giving them the solemn consecration of the apostolic powers.

It was clear that the two friends were to leave Antioch, but in what direction were they to turn their steps? Paul thought of Asia Minor, and it was there he went later when he assumed direction of the expedition. But Barnabas preferred Cyprus, his native land, the nearest of the Islands of Cethim, the center of the Gentile world for the sons of Israel, the land which on clear days could be seen from the coasts of Syria across the dark waves. There stood the great temple of Paphos in which multitudes of pilgrims presented their offerings to Aphrodite, and there also the two missionaries would find thousands of Jews who had been attracted by the riches of the island, the vineyards and olive groves on its hills, the fertility of its plains watered by the ancient canals. And if their fellow-countrymen refused to listen to the Gospel, the two preachers could turn to the many slaves who worked in the copper-mines or in the pine-woods from which they hewed keels and masts for ships, or on the castles, citadels, aqueducts and amphitheaters that were being built at the instigation of the Roman administration. Since Barnabas was senior to him in the Church as well as being the most venerated leader of the faithful in Antioch, Paul concurred with his wishes. Only one thing mattered to the disciple from Tarsus: that the name of Christ be brought to the ends of the earth, as the Church desired. Wherever he had to go he would spend his strength and even his life in spreading the teaching of Christ. The divine adventure which now lay before him filled him with joy, and never did a conqueror press forward to the unknown with more generous enthusiasm.

After having received the kiss of peace from the brethren, the two missionaries left Antioch, travelling on foot in accordance with the Gospel teaching, and accompanied by a young man named John Mark who had come with them from Jerusalem a short time before. Mark was a relative of Barnabas and had family connections in Cyprus, although his mother, Mary, lived in Jerusalem where her household was noted for its faith, its hospitality and generosity, as well as its large, well-furnished guest room which, after the Cenacle, was one of the principal sanctuaries of the disciples of Christ. It was in this house that the Prince of the Apostles took refuge on the night when the doors of the prison were miraculously opened for him and Herod's chains fell from him to the ground. At that time Mark had been only a growing boy who had been frightened by Peter's loud knocking at the door, and since he still was not old enough to undertake the ministry of preaching, he was appointed financial agent and put in charge of the material affairs of the missionary expedition, administering the funds, receiving alms, arranging for lodgings, paying the expenses and otherwise helping the missionaries as much as possible.

In one morning's journey the travellers crossed the strip of country that lay between Antioch and the port in Seleucia. The road they took was a winding and picturesque one that followed the course of the Orontes River and ran between hills on which sycamores and evergreen oaks mingled with myrtle and laurel. As they neared the coast, the mountain opened out like a fan, and in the distance behind a broken line of towers and walls, they could see the heaving green plain of the sea. Paul had never before travelled the trackless expanse of the ocean, and it certainly held no charms for him. Yet, though he feared it as a thing unknown, he was not daunted by its dangers. Beyond the threatening waves, men still walked in the shadow of death and souls suffered shipwreck, and to reach them he had to cross these alien depths. But to him the sea was, and remained always, an obstacle, an enemy, a monster which in a moment could put an end to his life and, what really mattered, to his apostolate. It is not surprising therefore that he did not embellish his writings with metaphors or similes drawn from its surging waves, its mirrored surface, or the majestic beauty of the ships that sailed upon it. Actually, he was a typical Hebrew, unmoved by the awesome splendor of the sea, a man solely taken up with the magnificence of the world invisible. But the heavenly Jerusalem awaited its sons who were scattered in the immensity of the waters, as the prophet had said, and the hour had struck in which the kings of Tharsis and the islands were to come before the Messias with their gifts. (Cf. Ps. 71.) The islands leaped with joy on that day when the three travellers, covered with dust, poorly clad, without staff or scrip or store of wealth, crossed the wharves of Seleucia to board the ship that awaited them. Nothing like this had been seen before on these seas, so rich in mythological memories.

After a few hours' sailing, when behind them the far-off Pierian mountains were blending with the evening mists, the ship approached a neck of land which resembled a finger pointing toward the coasts of Asia Minor, and entered a spacious harbor where war-like triremes and peaceful merchant vessels lay at anchor. This was the port of Salamis, the most important city on the island, where the industrious Greek colonists had supplanted the original Phoenician immigrants. It was a good haven for ships, a flourishing commercial center, an important Jewish colony containing several synagogues, and therefore a strategic starting-point for missionary work. At first Barnabas and Paul preached to their compatriots, who listened without hostility and even with interest, for these exiled Israelites were so much taken up with business affairs that they were both less fanatical and more tolerant than the Jews of Palestine. The speakers were neither insulted nor threatened, but although the seed fell on good ground, no attempt at organization was made at that time.

The missionaries went from synagogue to synagogue, "passing through the whole island," no doubt following the coastline and visiting the most important centers of population, cities with poetic and sweet-sounding names—Idalium, Citium, Amathus and Paphos. This was a land furrowed by pleasant valleys and shaded by cool groves, the land of the goddess Venus who had risen from its waters in a chariot fashioned of mother-of-pearl and drawn by dolphins and white doves. The very gardens still flourish in which, under the title of Cypris, she was adored with ritual orgies, and one can still hear the cooing of the sacred doves. There Paul understood, even better than in Antioch, the burden that had been placed on his shoulders when he was given the difficult task of converting the Gentiles. In the future, he was always to associate idolatry with lewdness and impurity, remembering no doubt the licentious processions of Paphos, the grove at Idalium, and the shapeless stone, crude symbol of the power of generation, before which devotees always placed flowers and burned incense. But he did not shrink before the superhuman difficulties that confronted him, and it was actually in the city of Paphos, the center of corruption, at the foot of the hill on which rose the temple of Aphrodite, that he won the first of his victories. This city of Paphos was the political capital of the island, where the proconsul resided and quartered his cohorts. At that time the destinies of the island were directed by a Roman of noble family named Sergius Paulus, whose name appears in St. Luke's narrative and also in a local inscription of the period.[1] Sergius was a cultured person, interested in philosophy and theosophy, and a delver into the mysteries of the occult sciences. As governor of the peaceful and pleasure-loving island he had few cares of state and was able to engage freely in the pursuit of his favorite studies. Moreover, this was the home of far-famed soothsayers, renowned magicians, astrologers and mathematicians, who claimed to know the formulae by which men could be changed into beasts, and who prided themselves on possessing the magic words which could open both palaces and hearts to them. Nor was that all, for they also mixed love-potions, compounded irresistible unguents, and sold poisons and their antidotes.

[1] D. G. Hogarth, *Devia Cypria*, p. 114.

In Cyprus there were two schools of magic: the first was the native school of the island, the more recently-founded according to Pliny,[2] which was connected with the dark genius and the impure, bloody and evil practices of the Phoenicians; the other school was of Jewish origin and claimed to know the secrets with which Moses had confounded Pharaoh's magicians. Like Josue ben Hananiah, the rabbi mentioned in the Talmud, the disciples of this school promised to change staffs into serpents, cucumbers into deer, gourds into young goats and stones into calves.[3]

Sergius Paulus had had himself initiated into the secrets of astrology, just as had the Emperor Tiberius some years before when he was in retirement on the island of Rhodes. Sergius' teacher was a Jew named Bar-Jesus whose knowledge had earned him the title of Elymas, "the Sage," and who was not a common fortune-teller or a cheap quack but an illustrious representative of his profession, which was partly scientific and partly religious.

This man was a member of the proconsul's retinue, his fortune-teller, interpreter of dreams, and miracle worker, as well as a consultant in all branches of learning, skilled in the use of plant-juices, able to utilize the secret powers of nature. He was both chemist and alchemist, astronomer and astrologist, a daring investigator of the philosopher's stone and the elixir of life, and a researcher into the properties of the lodestone and the laws of biology.

Like the priests of the Asiatic empires, Elymas combined genuine science with fraudulent deceit and religion with superstition, but his personality was so powerful that the crowds regarded him with respect and the proconsul himself consulted him and favored him with his friendship. All

[2] *Historia naturalis* xxx. ii. 6.
[3] Mishnah, *Sanhedrin*, 7, 11.

in all, he represented the strongest force that the Roman Empire had to employ against Christianity—the worldly influence of the Oriental religions, that was more to be feared than the shameful practices of the groves of Daphne and the hills of Paphos. Hence the great interest of the strange scene that was soon to be enacted under the colonnades of the proconsular palace when the missionaries confronted the magician. In Paul's life we find many occasions when powerful forces clashed in a battle for the right to free or enslave men's souls, but none as impressive as this encounter in Cyprus.

The proconsul had heard of the two preachers who were spreading a new doctrine, and, lover of theories that he was, he wished to test the strangers' powers and hear the philosophy they were teaching concerning the nature of God and His relationship with man—the two points which were the core of their belief. Perhaps Elymas, too, was interested in hearing original systems of thought and in seeing prodigies such as those which he himself produced by his magical practices. At any rate, he was sure that this was an occasion on which to display his art and demonstrate the power of his incantations before an admiring audience.

When all was in readiness, Barnabas and Paul began to expound their doctrine, the story of the God-Man whose death had given men a guarantee of immortality. As one of the variant texts of the Acts puts it, the proconsul "listened with great pleasure" to them as they advanced what were to him wholly new ideas, with profound conviction and telling force. It was not merely the enjoyment of a novelty that held his attention, but the growing belief that he had at last found the truth he had so avidly sought. Elymas saw the effect the strangers were having on the proconsul, and, fearing the loss of his prestige and influence, made ready for the struggle he knew was to come. The proconsul listened to Paul and Barnabas telling in simple words of the world's redemption by the blood of Christ, and his mind was swept clean of the fables of mythology. Elymas could sense that his hold over Sergius was at an end, for his system of religion, based perhaps, like that of Simon Magus, another Cypriot, on vague gnostic concepts culled from Pythagoras and Plato, could not stand against the clear and forceful arguments of the strangers. Hitherto, with the empty ostentation of a pseudo-prophet, he had proclaimed a false spiritual ardor and had pretended to enlighten his followers with high-flown mystical mouthings. Now all that was finished; no one would listen to him once the truths of Christianity had been heard.

But human nature does not resign itself easily to defeat and humiliation, and so Elymas made frantic efforts to nullify the effect which the strangers' words were having on the proconsul. Throwing caution to the winds, and forgetting the laws of courtesy and the respect due to the Roman magistrate, he interrupted the speakers with objections and scornful laughter, "trying to turn away the proconsul from the faith" (Acts 13:8). Finally Paul, struck with a sudden inspiration, turned on him with blazing eyes and silenced him with the terrible utterance: "O full of all guile and of all deceit, son of the devil, enemy of all justice, wilt thou not cease to make crooked the straight ways of the Lord? And now, behold, the hand of the Lord is upon thee, and thou shalt be blind, not seeing the sun for a time." Instantly, darkness fell upon the sorcerer; he could no longer see the light of the sun, and the onlookers watched in frightened wonder as he groped about him for a friendly hand to guide him. "Then the proconsul, seeing what had happened, believed and was astonished at the Lord's teaching."

With these words St. Luke ends his wonderfully concise account of St. Paul's first missionary labors among the Gentiles. He draws no conclusions, makes no comments and adds no corollaries, but simply sets down the bare outlines of an astonishing event that was to have a unique importance in the first years of the Christian Church. He also shows us the Apostle's conquering faith and the impetuosity of his character, for not for one instant did Paul doubt that at his word God would strike the blasphemer. But, always compassionate, Paul inflicted only a temporary punishment until the soothsayer should have a change of heart, renounce his magical practices and cease to exploit his knowledge. Yet here, in his condemnation of Elymas, we catch a glimpse of the Saul of former years, with the same fire in his eyes, the same ring in his voice, and the same energy in action as when he, the fanatical scribe, launched anathemas at the enemies of the Law and cut down or imprisoned anyone who stood in his way.

At last Paul was in his element, for he had come into contact with the Gentiles and his first efforts had been crowned with a resounding success. An illustrious Roman had yielded to the power of the Gospel and to the evidence he had put before him. The head of a senatorial province, who had the privilege of being preceded by lictors carrying axes and fasces, had become one of the brethren of the Lord. Truly a magnificent future had been opened up by this first conquest, and soon the prefects and even the emperors themselves with their retinues of philosophers and their swarming legions, would knock at the doors of the Church. Rome would be the center of that immense renewal, just as it was the meeting-place and goal of all the roads that crossed the Empire. Undoubtedly, the purifying blood of the martyrs would first have to flow, the serene voices of the apologists be raised, and the greatest psychological drama of all time be slowly enacted, but the Apostle foresaw even now the victorious end of the struggle in the final submission of the city which had conquered the world with the sword. Knowing that God, who is eternal, "makes times and ways His own," Paul did not plan to start a revolution in high places. It is true that he had just won to his cause an influential official through whom he could reach high political circles, but he was not tempted by the magnificent impatience which St. Francis Xavier felt centuries later, and he did not aspire to change an empire by converting one man. But he did turn his gaze on the golden city that dominated the world and, later, when he passed as a prisoner through its streets, he was to write to the Philippians with holy pride: "The chains I wear for the sake of Christ have become manifest as such throughout the praetorium and all other places" (Phil. 1:13). Even then, however, when he had made disciples in the Emperor's household, he did not dream of suddenly transforming the court or of changing Nero's heart, but was content to sow broadcast the seed of faith and to combat the pride, idolatry, false philosophies and brutality which had made the Caesars what they were, for he considered this the best way to bring them to their knees at the foot of the Cross. He knew, too, that the soul of a slave such as Onesimus was worth as much as, if not more than, the soul of a Caligula.

He did realize, nevertheless, that the political structure of Rome with its organization, its inherent discipline and its well-guarded roads, offered him a providential field in which to develop his course of action, and from that moment on, the son of Abraham gave place to the Roman citizen. When recalling the words with which the Apostle confounded the magician, St. Luke points out the transformation in a terse but eloquent phrase: "Saul (also called Paul)." Up to this point, we have seen Paul as a Jew among Jews, using the Hebrew name by which he was known in his home and during his years of studying in the Temple. But now he found himself in the presence of the proconsul and had to answer the Roman official's questions in an interview which began with the customary formulae: "What is your name? Where do you come from? What is your business?" It was with similar questions that Ulysses and his companions were received by the Cyclops in the *Odyssey:* "Strangers, who are ye? From what land do ye come sailing to these shores? What enterprise or adventure have ye undertaken?"

Paul remembered his privileges as a citizen of Rome, his Roman name and his origin in Tarsus. In later years he described in stirring words the method he used on such occasions: "I have become to the Jews a Jew that I might gain the Jews; to those under the Law, as one under the law . . . to those without the Law, as one without the Law; . . . I became all things to all men that I might save all. I do all things for the sake of the gospel . . ." (1 Cor. 9:21-22). With one stroke of wonderful historical precision, the author of the Acts uses a very simple phrase to show us the stand that Paul took from then on when dealing with the Romans: "Saul (also called Paul)"; and from this point in the Acts, Paul is constantly before our eyes. That confession of a double identity on the part of an Oriental teacher who suddenly emerged as a free citizen of Rome, would have awakened the curiosity of any Roman magistrate. But for a man with the tastes of Sergius Paulus it had a twofold appeal, because it both aroused his interest as a judge of men and assured him of his guest's sympathy with the name of Rome which he represented in that senatorial province.

With the assumption of his new name the Apostle's soul appears in all its grandeur. Until now he had journeyed with Barnabas as a subordinate, and Barnabas' name had appeared first when the two were mentioned together in the Acts—Barnabas and Saul brought the alms to Jerusalem; Barnabas and Saul took John Mark with them on their journey from Jerusalem; Barnabas was the first of the prophets of Antioch, Saul the last; Barnabas and Saul were chosen by God; Barnabas and Saul were invited to the proconsul's audience. But suddenly Paul assumed the responsibility of the mission, while Barnabas was content to second and approve his plans. No longer do we hear of Barnabas and Saul, but of Paul and Barnabas; Paul and his companions sail from Paphos to Pamphylia; Paul and Barnabas address the pagans at Antioch in Pisidia; Paul and Barnabas contend with the Judaizers. . . . This new order of names is reversed on two occasions only: once when the two friends were in Jerusalem to consult the Apostles, for here they were among Jews who were respectful of the hierarchical order of antiquity; and again when they were in Lystra and the Lycaonians singled out Barnabas because of his striking appearance (Acts 15:12-25; 14:12-14).

Thus we see the exquisite delicacy of St. Luke in his narrative and the supreme art with which he depicts the new facet of Paul's personality; we realize that the hour had struck for the expansion of the Church among the Gentiles —that hour foretold so long ago. The historian marks as a psychological peak that moment in which the Apostle confronted the magician before the governor of Cyprus, for in this conflict of two religions in the presence of Roman law, Paul not only asserted his claims as a citizen of the Empire, but assumed a commanding position in the new Church, a position which was recognized both by heaven and by those in civil authority.

CHAPTER IX

"Behold, We Now Turn to the Gentiles"

On the mainland, across from Cyprus to the north, lay Tarsus, with its childhood memories for Paul, the din of its markets and its pride in its schools; to the south lay Alexandria, boasting of its harbor, its wise men, writers and artists. Here were two wide fields for the sowing of the Gospel seed, capable of attracting the most enthusiastic missionary, but Paul did not allow himself to be drawn either by the splendor of centuries-old civilizations or by the nostalgic appeal of his homeland. Later he was to visit Cilicia, but only briefly and in passing, and he was never to see the shores of Africa. Now, however, turning his back on the privileged position and the reputation as a prophet which his victory over the Israelite sorcerer had won him, he sailed to the north, led on by the breath of the Spirit and followed by his companions, who had come to regard him as the leader of the expedition. The provinces of Asia Minor still possessed their old appeal and challenge for him. He was not daunted by the narrow mountain paths which more than once caused Alexander's army to tremble with fear, or by the arid plains of the interior or the rough-

117

ness of the roads, nor did he fear the monstrous gods of the region—Jupiter Labrandeus of the heavy beard and woman's breasts, Sabazius with the terrible aspect of an Asiatic Zeus, or the many-breasted Diana who lacked every vestige of the grace that characterized the divine huntress among the Greeks.

The mountains of Cyprus had not yet sunk into the sea behind them when they saw from the ship the purple heights of the outer ramparts of the Taurus range. Onward they sailed for some hours more, with land in sight to the right and left, for here the coast of Asia Minor seems to have reached out to embrace the soft waves of the sea. To the left stretched the plains of Lycia, watered by the Xanthus of the blood-red waves of mythology; to the right lay the threatening cliffs of the Cilician coastline. They put into harbor in a dark and inhospitable land which boasted no great cities, famous markets or illustrious schools, but only small ports where the main traffic was in the spoils of piracy and smuggling, and the traders were the mountain dwellers of the interior, men of many different tribes and dialects. The Greeks appropriately called this region Pamphylia, the land of many diverse races, and the missionaries saw the truth of the name in Attalia, the first center of population they encountered, a town which even today recalls by its appearance and its name (Adalia) its great antiquity, for it consists of groups of poor houses huddled in the shadow of steep rocks, fragments of battlemented walls, and here and there a lone minaret.

Paul and his companions did not tarry here, perhaps because Attalia already possessed a Christian community founded by those pilgrims from Pamphylia who had heard St. Peter's discourse on the day of Pentecost in Jerusalem.

The ship continued on its way, breasting the current of

the Kestros River, and in about two hours more it came to rest near another city, somewhat more populous and aristocratic in appearance than Attalia. They had arrived at Perge, the center of local government, where there was an arena with Corinthian colonnades, a spacious theater, and a temple of Artemis which was the most frequented sanctuary of the region and whose ruins can still be seen today. No doubt there was also a synagogue in such a prosperous community, and Paul believed that here he had found a strategic place from which to develop his work in the territory. But he had to alter his plans, perhaps because of the summer heat which in that low marshy country made the atmosphere so heavy and unhealthy that a stranger unused to it was almost certainly bound to be overcome by the unbreathable air laden with the miasmas of the stagnant swamps. Even the natives of the region had to leave when the heat began to mount, and in summer the villages emptied and the cities were virtually deserted. The yearly flight from the region was a picturesque sight, as the many-colored caravans left the palm-and-cactus-dotted plain to take refuge in the mountains and pitch their tents amid the towering green walls of aromatic pine and majestic cedar. The men led the procession, walking beside their high-piled wagons; the young shepherds drove the flocks before them; while the women, with their babies in wicker baskets on their shoulders, trudged along behind.

It was probably the time for this annual migration when the three missionaries penetrated that unhealthy region. They had come to preach, but something must have happened to alter their plans, something incidental and passing, since we shall see them stop there again on their return to sow the seed of the Faith. Undoubtedly they had to defer their preaching because of the confusion caused by the seasonal exodus from the villages and cities, but Paul was able to adapt himself to any circumstance. Now they were confronted with a dilemma; should they give up their plans or follow the emigrants on their journey? John Mark favored the first solution, but Paul considered such a course cowardly, and Barnabas was inclined to agree with him.

The problem was suddenly further complicated by Paul's becoming seriously ill. The enervating effect of the unhealthy climate added to the fatigue of his toilsome journeys of the past months, the continual strain of missionary work, and his supreme exertion at Paphos, permanently affected his health with a lasting malady, so that from then on his life was to be a constant martyrdom, a daily death. (Cf. 1 Cor. 15:31.) In all his Epistles he mentions this chronic disease which hindered his apostolate, humbled him in the eyes of the Gentiles, and tortured him incessantly: ". . . always bearing about in our body the dying of Jesus" (2 Cor. 4:10). The illness first appeared while he was in the low-lying lands of Pamphylia and, to judge by the evidence, must have been a continuous affliction which in its most violent manifestations caused splitting headaches and spasmodic attacks of ague which left him prostrate. There are many ancient inscriptions in which this type of sickness is regarded as a punishment of the gods, and anyone suffering from it was deemed impure and was not allowed to enter the sanctuary. It was for this reason that the Apostle looked upon it as a humiliating stigma and was later to be always grateful to the Galatians: ". . . on account of a physical infirmity . . . though I was a trial to you in my flesh, you did not reject or despise me, but you received me as an angel of God, even as Jesus Christ" (Gal. 4:13-14).

The new turn of events gave John Mark an added argument for his point of view, since it seemed that the most reasonable thing for them to do now was to abandon temporarily an expedition that appeared doomed to failure, and return to the pleasant banks of the Orontes, where Paul could be placed under the care of famed physicians and recuperate in that healthy climate, amid the cool groves of Antioch. However, in spite of his illness, Paul would not hear of retreating, but proposed instead a new course of action in which the demands of his ill-health could be met without abandoning the duties of the apostolate. He pointed out that they could follow the caravans of the emigrants across the mountains and penetrate into the higher regions of Pisidia, where there was a far-famed city, also called Antioch like the capital of Syria, with prosperous markets and an important Jewish colony that had all the requirements for the formation of a nucleus of converts. In regard to his health, Paul argued, the city would be an ideal place for him to recover from his fever, since it was more than three thousand feet above sea level, there was a beautiful plain to the south of the city with orchards and gardens that rivalled those along the Orontes, while to the north a wall of mountains protected the city and the plain from the cold winds.

But Paul argued in vain, for his young companion would not allow himself to be convinced, asserting that if the others would not listen to him, he was prepared to return home alone rather than plunge into a mad venture. Further discussion left the position unchanged, so that the only solution was to allow John Mark to retrace his steps. His departure was a sore blow to Paul, who felt he had been mistaken in the young man and discovered that he was indocile and lacking in spirit, ". . . inasmuch as he . . . deserted them . . . instead of going on with them to their work . . ." (Acts 15:38). The disappointment which the Apostle then felt still remained several years later when John Mark, repenting of his momentary weakness, wished to take part in a new expedition. If Paul had been hurt by the defection on his companion's part, he had long ago forgiven the injury, but even so he did not want any timorous souls in his company. There was no question of personal pique, but only of principles. Later, the Apostle came to understand fully the nobility of Mark's self-effacing and sincere soul, and to appreciate the value of his services in the cause of the infant Church. In the Second Epistle to Timothy, written in Rome, we find the instruction: "Take Mark and bring him with thee, for he is useful to me in the ministry" (2 Tim. 4:11). Actually, the whole cause of the misunderstanding was that Mark was not able to approve fully of Paul's apostolic daring, for he had been a member of the church at Jerusalem, had been brought up in strict Judaism, and was therefore alarmed by the increasingly powerful tendency to abandon the Mosaic traditions. He preferred the moderation of the other Apostles and that concept of Christianity which allowed him to harmonize this new Faith with all the things he had learned to love from infancy. He later found his place by the side of Peter, whom he was to follow on his journeys as his assistant, his interpreter when preaching, and as the secretary to whom he dictated his Epistles. Finally, with his Gospel, Mark continues to be the echo of the Prince of the Apostles down through the ages of the Church.

While John Mark was boarding the ship to return to Attalia, Paul and Barnabas were hastening to leave the humid, torrid regions where they had reaped only sorrow. Before them reared the silvered ramparts of the steep mountains which they had to cross to reach the interior.

The journey cost them several days of hard travelling over unknown territory where they were increasingly beset by hazards and sudden dangers—the hostility of fierce tribes, the rapacity of bandits, impassable roads, the sudden gush of torrents that tore away the paths before them, bridges washed out by the rivers and battered by storms; ". . . in perils from floods, in perils from robbers . . . in perils in the wilderness . . . in labor and hardships" (2 Cor. 11:26–27). When they reached the Pisidian uplands the country opened out gradually, and here they found only miserable villages and scattered herds of goats that wandered over the steppes. At nightfall, they were forced to seek shelter in the black tents of the shepherds, where they huddled around the fire and talked while the milk for the evening meal was being heated.

Beyond these uplands the monotonous countryside became gentler in character and the rocky mountain-slopes gave way to green inclines upon which oak and pine trees grew and which were dappled by flocks of white storks from the banks of the Nile. Then the Lake of Egherdir appeared, its blue waters reflecting in sharp relief the white plumage of the wild swans that glided over its calm surface. The missionaries skirted the lake and soon came in sight of the walls of Antioch and, on a nearby hill, the arches of an immense aqueduct which even today still stand amid ruins that recall the grandeurs of the past.

Paul had come here both to recover his health and to preach, as he later wrote to the churches of Galatia: "You know that on account of a corporal infirmity I preached the gospel to you" (Gal. 4:13). But the interests of the Church came before every other consideration. The inhabitants of Antioch in Pisidia were numerous and varied, for the city contained an important Jewish community, and many Western Europeans had been attracted there by the privileges of an Italic colony which the city enjoyed. As was their usual practice, the two missionaries waited until the Sabbath before appearing in the synagogue to invite the Jews into the Church and to gauge the possibilities of conversion.

At the very first meeting in the synagogue great hopes were awakened in their hearts, for they saw that many proselytes had come to hear the Law being read, and that they seemed to be motivated by sincere devotion. Particularly notable was a large group of women who, to judge by the richness of their attire, were ladies of high social standing who had been admitted to the group of "those who feared God." These were souls who thirsted for the truth, who were no longer satisfied with the worship of the moon under its masculine form, the thick-bearded Lunus, titular god of Antioch, and who preferred the rabbis of Israel to the god's cohorts of priests.

Prior to their appearance in the synagogue, Paul and Barnabas had begun to speak of Jesus in the houses and in the streets, so that soon the news of their arrival spread through the city with the result that the members of the synagogue, hearing that one of the strangers was a Levite and the other a doctor of the Law and a disciple of Gamaliel, conceived the idea of asking them to address the gathering. Thus it came about that on the Sabbath, when the services were finished and the leader of the synagogue saw they were present, he addressed them in the customary manner: "Brethren, if you have any word of exhortation for the people, speak." They, being strangers, had taken their seats on a bench in the background and did not realize that the leader was speaking to them, but the messenger from the president, the *hazzan*, crossed the hall to them with the rabbi's formal invitation to address the assembly.

The incident caused some murmured comments among the gathering, but Paul rose, motioned with his hand for silence, and began to speak. St. Luke, in summarizing this discourse, has preserved for us an example of the Apostle's preaching to the Jews. The tone of his voice was grave and even somewhat severe, and it seemed as if the orator felt confined by Pharisaical etiquette and by respect for the leaders of the synagogue who were regarding him with cold impassivity. The opening of the discourse followed the usual pattern of Jewish oratory and resembled the sermon preached by Stephen before the Sanhedrin. Then, building upon the Scripture texts that had just been read, the Apostle firmly and forcefully developed his thesis that Christ was the Messias foretold by the prophets, and that in Him alone could men be saved and justified. His audience listened gladly to the first part of his discourse, for it dealt with the divine vocation of Israel, the mighty figures of the prophets and many of the glorious events of their national history. But when he came to speak of David, the orator changed from a panegyrist of the Chosen People to a herald of Christ.

The Apostle saw that his words were arousing opposition among the majority of his listeners, and he repeated his opening statement in equivalent terms: "Brethren, children of the race of Abraham, and all among you who fear God. . . ." But he did not hesitate to go on to tell them the full truth, that Jesus, the Son of David, who had been crucified not long ago in Jerusalem, was the promised Redeemer; that in Him the prophecies were fulfilled and the regeneration of the world accomplished; that His divine mission had an irreproachable witness in John the Baptist, the prophet and wonder-worker, who did not consider himself worthy to loose the Messias' sandals; that there was the impressive multiple testimony of the many men and women still living throughout the world who had broken bread with Him, had heard Him preach and had seen Him after His death. "Be it known therefore to you brethren," the Apostle concluded, "that through him forgiveness of sins is proclaimed to you, and in him everyone who believes is acquitted of all the things of which you could not be acquitted by the Law of Moses." Then he pronounced a stern warning, a veritable threat, in words taken from Habacuc: "Beware, therefore, that what is said in the Prophets may not prove true of you, 'Behold, you despisers, then wonder and perish, because I work a work in your days, a work which you will not believe, if anyone relates it to you'" (Acts 13).

The effects of this speech were varied; some of the listeners were disconcerted by it, others were openly opposed to the doctrine it contained, while a fairly large number seemed disposed to accept its message of salvation. While speaking, Paul had been aware of little else besides the murmuring and half-voiced protests of those who considered him a heretic, but when the meeting broke up, he was encouraged to see a group of Jews and proselytes drawing near and following him to his lodgings, eager to hear more about Christ. The stream of the curious and the devout continued during the ensuing days, keeping the two missionaries constantly busy with teaching and explaining the Gospel.

Throughout the city the two strangers and their message of salvation were the whole talk of the day, and pagans as well as Jews impatiently awaited another discourse on their strange doctrine. The enthusiasm of the crowd and the willingness with which many Gentiles listened to the preachers aroused the suspicions and jealousy of the doctors of the Law. The more learned rabbis prepared their defense, consulting Scripture for texts and formulating arguments in support of their ancient traditions, for they foresaw a stormy and heated discussion. On the next Sabbath, when people began to flock to the synagogue, the regular attendants were surprised to see there many people who had hitherto shown no interest in the teachings of Moses. "Almost the whole city" was there, so that the synagogue and the street in front of it were crammed with eager listeners.

When the reading of the passages from the Scriptures had ended, the *hazzan* approached the preachers of the Gospel and invited them to speak. And speak they did, fearlessly expounding the mystery of the grace given through the blood of Christ to all believers, Jew and Gentile. However, a great part of the audience had come for the express purpose of undermining the influence of the two missionaries, and these troublemakers broke in on their speeches, protesting loudly and shouting insults to the name of Christ in threatening voices that drowned out the preachers' calm exposition of the Gospel truths. Then Paul and Barnabas, angered by the Jews' resistance, launched this awful indictment against their compatriots, an indictment that they were to repeat often in similar circumstances in the future: "It was necessary that the word of God should be spoken to you first, but since you reject it and judge yourselves unworthy of eternal life, behold we now turn to the Gentiles. For so the Lord has commanded us. 'I have set thee for a light to the Gentiles, to be a means of salvation to the very ends of the earth'" (Acts 13:46-47).

These fearless words were a further blow to the Israelites, but awoke among the pagans new interest in these men who were opening to them the gates of heaven without subjecting them to the trammels of the Law or imposing on them the humiliating rite of circumcision. As a result, the fame of Paul and Barnabas spread far beyond the city and was carried through all the district, so that the name of Jesus was discussed even in the fishing boats on the near-by lake, in the shepherds' huts on Mount Paroreia, and among the tribes of the highlands who were continually rebelling against Roman rule. Many who heard the Gospel teaching realized that it was the word of the Lord, "and glorified [it], and all who were destined for eternal life believed."

The Jews were enraged by the success of the two men whom they thought to crush by casting them out of the synagogue, and they brought into play all the resources of their influence to put a stop to the increasing triumph of these strangers. By dint of intrigue, they convinced the authorities that the preachers were rabble-rousers and a danger to the peace of the city. The rich merchants, the magistrates, and even the officers of the Roman garrison were deceived by the specious claim, but the high-born Jewish women of the city were the principal instruments of the rabbis' hate. This was not Athens or Corinth, but the provinces of Asia Minor, where the women were the religious organizers, bringing their menfolk to the festivals, ablutions and ceremonies.[1] Hence it came about that a group of fanatical women joined forces with the rabbis, went to the palace of the city governor and had the strangers imprisoned and tortured. Perhaps it was here in Antioch in Pisidia that Paul first felt the blows of the rods with which he was scourged three times by the lictors of the Roman colonies. After the scourging, a municipal order

[1] Cf. Strabo viii. 3.

was issued expelling them from the city and its environs, and, mindful of Christ's command, they shook the dust of the city from their feet as a sign of divine reprobation. (Cf. Matt. 10:16.)

CHAPTER X

The Testimony of Blood

Present-day Konia, formerly known as Iconium, is still a flourishing city in which domes, palaces, bastions and stout gates recall the time when it was the capital of the Turkish Sultans, the destroyers of the Empire of Baghdad. However, at the time of the Roman Caesars it did not yet possess such courtly splendors, although it did have an important Jewish colony, an indication of commercial activity, and it undoubtedly boasted an amphitheater, a market place surrounded by porches, some monument in honor of its protectors, the Claudii, and a number of palaces, richly adorned with mosaics and columns, the dwellings of rich colonists from the west.

After being expelled from Antioch in Pisidia, Paul and Barnabas came to Iconium, having followed the broad highway which connected the principal cities of the Roman province of Galatia, and which was known in those days as "the royal road." They had been travelling for three or four days heading east, and gradually approached the borders of Cilicia across a wide arid plateau on which wild asses shied at their passing and coarse-wooled sheep grazed peacefully.[1] When the missionaries entered the city, it must

[1] Cf. Strabo xii. 6.

130

have reminded them forcefully of Damascus, for it, too, possessed many fountains and groves, it was criss-crossed by canals and small streams, and it abounded in bright and luxuriant tropical vegetation. To the north rose the snow-capped peak of a mountain, while outside the green circle of the city stretched the dry sands of the plain.

According to an old legend which is actually a packet of lies containing a few grains of truth, the Apostle and his companion met a man named Onesiphorus, who fell on his knees before them and invited them to share the hospitality of his house. Paul accepted his invitation, and when he arrived at the door, all within greeted him with the words: "Welcome, servant of the true God." Smiling at his host, the Apostle replied: "May the grace of the Lord be with thee and thy house." Then he knelt, broke bread and spoke the word of God concerning continence and the resurrection.

There is nothing improbable about this part of the legend, for the borders of Lycaonia and Cilicia run together, and it could well have happened that Paul had known Onesiphorus during his years in Tarsus. The story goes on to say that Paul preached daily in the house of his generous friend, that listeners came and went—some believing, others incredulous—and that when the sun went down each evening, Paul would still be preaching. Opposite Onesiphorus' home there was a large, well-appointed house in which lived a young maiden who never tired of listening to Paul, and who, in order to do so, remained motionless at her window all day and all night without eating, drinking, or sleeping. As she watched, she saw that many women and girls visited the stranger, and she longed to enter his presence.

This maiden's name was Thecla. She lived with her

mother Theoclya and was visited from time to time by a young man called Thamyris, to whom she had been promised in marriage. Alarmed by the way Thecla remained at the window as if in a trance, the mother hastily sent for Thamyris. Not knowing the reason for the summons, the young man answered it joyfully, and when he arrived at the house, he said eagerly to Theoclya: "Where is my promised bride? I want to see her!" But the mother answered worriedly: "Thamyris, I have something strange to tell you. She has not left that window for three days to eat or drink. She seems overcome with an insane joy, as if she were spellbound by that stranger who is teaching his insidious doctrine. Thamyris, I tell you this man is causing an upheaval in the city of the Iconians and my daughter is fascinated by him. All the women are coming to hear him and he tells them things like this: 'You must fear God, the one true God, and you must live chastely.' My daughter, too, is caught in his net. There she is, glued to the window like a cobweb. Go and talk to her."

Trembling with love and frightened by the strange behavior of his betrothed, the young man approached her. "Thecla, my beloved, what has happened to you? Why don't you look at me as you always did before? What strange passion has taken hold of you? Turn around to me: this is Thamyris! Oh, have a little shame!" The mother joined her pleas to his, but in vain, for Thecla did not move or reply, or even look at them—she had ears only for the voice that came to her from the house opposite. Everyone around her was reduced to tears: Thamyris because he was losing his bride, Theoclya because she was losing her daughter, and the slave girls because they were losing their lady.

As a result of the way he had entranced Thecla, con-

tinues the legend, Paul was denounced, condemned as a
wizard and deceiver, and thrown into jail. Only then did
Thecla leave her post at the window, and one night, taking
off the bands of gold which encircled her arms, she used
them to bribe the gatekeeper to let her out of the house.
When she came to the jail she was at a loss as to how she
would gain entrance to see the prisoner, until she remembered she had a silver mirror with her. This she gave to the
jailer and, full of joy, entered the Apostle's cell where,
after kissing his chains, she seated herself at his feet and
listened for hours as he spoke of the greatness of God.

Soon Thamyris' love changed to hate, and Theoclya, the
girl's own mother, aroused the governor against her. Paul
was scourged and exiled, and a great fire was built in the
market place to burn his convert, but Thecla was miraculously saved from the flames. She fled from the city in
search of the man who had taught her the science of life,
and, upheld by the promise of the happiness of heaven,
she travelled through the world as a prisoner of divine love.

The figure of the virgin of Iconium shed light and joy
on the primitive Christian communities. People spoke about
her visions, her ecstasies and her journeys; they talked of
her beauty and her wisdom, and she came to be regarded as
the living embodiment of Paul's teachings. Soon the facts
of her life became lost in a labyrinth of fables, and the
legend "The Acts of Paul and Thecla" was composed, consisting of pious discourses, embellished with extravagant
prodigies and full of unlikely events. St. John, who at that
time was still directing the churches in Asia Minor, condemned the fable, and it was consigned to the limbo of
apocryphal literature. But the figure of Thecla continued
to shine in the dawn of Christianity, and her holy extravagance was regarded as one of the most glorious manifesta-

tions of the folly of the Cross which her teacher had preached so well. Adorned as she was with the double crown of virginity and martyrdom, she was the precursor of the Cecilias and Eulalias of later years, while her ecstasies, born of the ardor of her love, the joys of self-renunciation and the hope of a blessed eternity, are like an anticipation of the mystical experiences of St. Teresa of Avila. The martyrs invoked her name in the midst of the flames, her wisdom was famed throughout Asia Minor, and all the Fathers of the Eastern Church sang the praises of her virtues and victories. The virgins in St. Methodius' *Convivium decem virginum* exclaim: "To her belongs the most beautiful and fragrant crown because she shone above all others in the heroism of virtue." [2]

St. Paul would have undertaken this mission to Asia Minor solely for the sake of winning such a soul for Christ, but his labors in Iconium were being rewarded in many other ways as well. He heard from Antioch in Pisidia that "the disciples continued to be filled with joy and with the Holy Spirit" (Acts 13:52), and here at Iconium the name of Jesus was beginning to spread in a marvellous way, for since his first appearance in the synagogue, there had been a steady flow of converts: "a great multitude of Jews and of Greeks believed." Naturally enough, the rabbis were alarmed at their losses, for Paul had succeeded in taking many God-fearing souls from them and starting a new "synagogue" in opposition to theirs. The result was that the city became divided into two camps, the supporters of the Jews and the defenders of Paul, and the air was filled with arguments, false accusations, insults and threats. Meanwhile, Paul and Barnabas went on teaching, baptizing, and adding to the number of Christians, until one day

[2] XI, 1.

hostile crowds began to gather around the house where they were exercising their ministry. Gradually the mob increased, surging like an angry sea about the building, shouting imprecations, brandishing cudgels, and clutching stones. The rabbis, perhaps taking advantage of the indignation aroused by the garbled reports about Thecla, had finally succeeded in stirring up the populace against the two strangers, and were already sure that they would be killed by the crowd. But the missionaries were able to frustrate the plans of their would-be assassins by leaving the house secretly and escaping from the city.

Moving toward the southeast, the two friends penetrated further into the plains of Lycaonia, a region where Roman influence was less felt and where, since there were no great commercial centers, there were few if any of those Jewish communities which most hindered the preaching of the Gospel. Here the people were simple, poor and uncultured, and among the hills there were wandering groups, half-bandits, half-warriors, who gloried in their turbulent but independent way of life. About thirty miles' distance from Iconium, there was a small city, Lystra, which was situated at the foot of a high, gloomy mountain, and about forty miles farther to the southeast lay Derbe, built on the shore of a lake. Paul and Barnabas concentrated on these two centers of population and, since no one interfered with their apostolate, they quickly formed a church in each city, from which the news of the Gospel spread to the villages of the shepherds and fishermen in the neighboring countryside. In fact, so great was the fame which the missionaries earned here that they had to hold in check the indiscreet enthusiasm of the crowds.

Among Paul's most attentive listeners was a cripple who feared God and was eager to learn the truth about Him.

One day the Apostle, having spoken to the people, approached this good man, looked fixedly at him and in a loud voice said: "Stand upright on thy feet." Immediately the man, who had never been able to walk, feeling that he was cured, sprang to his feet and began to walk and to leap for joy.

St. Luke, the author of the Acts of the Apostles, is loath to mention miracles, for he wishes to impress upon us that the Gospel is to be approached more through reason than through wonder at prodigies. When the supernatural intervenes, it does so primarily to encourage the preachers of the Faith, to make them see that heaven is confirming their words and that therefore they are not mistaken. On this occasion, the crowd misinterpreted the cure of the cripple, which struck them dumb with amazement and made them imagine that the gods of Olympus had come down to speak with them. When they recovered their voices they broke out in delirious cries: "They are gods! The gods have come down to us in the likeness of men!"

According to their traditions, Zeus and Hermes had travelled through the land, stopping in the huts of the shepherds and deigning to partake of their coarse food. The royal wayfarers, however, sought good will most of all, and therefore they had rewarded with long years of life the devout reception given them by Philemon and Baucis, but had turned Lycaon into a wolf because he had mocked them when he had seen them crossing the country in the pouring rain. Why, then, couldn't the Olympians continue to walk the earth as in bygone ages? And hadn't the crowd just seen the effects of their sovereign power? "They are gods!" the people kept repeating in their wild enthusiasm, while the most observant of them added: "Zeus and Hermes are once again among us!" and all prostrated themselves reverentially in adoration before the missionaries.

In Barnabas' noble bearing the Lycaonians thought they could perceive the majesty of Zeus, and concluded that the smaller of the two, the healer of ills, the master of persuasive words, *dux verbi*, energetic, pentrating, boldly daring, with piercing glance and commanding, vigorous appearance, could only be Hermes, the god of health, the swift messenger, the patron of eloquent orators. This was the Oriental concept of divinity, for in the East he who remains solemnly seated without speaking or acting is given pre-eminence and greatest dignity, whereas in the West, the more energetic, the originator of both ideas and actions, is considered the leader. That is why, in the Oriental religions, the father of the gods always appears secluded, far from the world, with which he comes in contact only through his messengers and subordinates. This reaction of the Lycaonians confirms the traditional description of the Apostle of the Gentiles: he was ugly and of medium height, bald, with pale copper-colored skin, aquiline nose, grey beard and blue eyes. But when he began to speak, his voice was so commanding, his glance and bearing so forceful, that he could easily be mistaken for a god.

The joyful shouts of the crowd continued to ring through the streets of Lystra; more people joined in the tumult and the general frenzy increased. Without understanding clearly the meaning of all the hubbub, since the mobs were crying out in their local dialect, Paul and Barnabas took advantage of the confusion to return to their lodgings. But suddenly their way was blocked by a strange procession headed by the priest of Zeus, the guardian deity of the city whose temple was near the principal gate, accompanied by his helpers carrying the instruments of sacrifice—knives, ropes, amphoras and vessels. One acolyte brought the salt, another bore the flour on a silver platter, while a third carried the incense. Everything needed for the sacrifice was there: the sacred choir of cantors, the band of flute-players, and, of course, the victims acceptable to the god, white bulls decked out in flowers and multi-colored ribbons.

When they were confronted with all this strange pomp, the missionaries understood what was happening, and they rushed into the crowd, tearing their garments as a sign of indignation and endeavoring to avert the sacrilege with all the means at their command. "Men, why are you doing this?" they cried out. "We also are mortals, human beings like you, subject to death and suffering, bringing to you the good news that you should turn from these vain things to the living God who made heaven and earth and the sea and all things that are in them. In the generations that are past he let all the nations follow their own ways; and yet he did not leave himself without testimony, bestowing blessings, giving rains from heaven and fruitful seasons, filling your hearts with food and gladness." (Cf. Acts 14:14–17.)

In these words St. Paul summed up the proofs of God's existence which he used when preaching to the pagans. Here, as later when he addressed the Thessalonians, he told the Lycaonians to relinquish their idols and turn to the living God who, though He permitted mankind to wander for a time, did not abandon them completely or forever. The preaching of the Gospel was the beginning of reconciliation between creature and Creator, although the world itself had always been a mute witness to the divine magnificence. St. Paul alludes only passingly to the cosmological argument for the existence of God, and stresses the physical argument which is easily understood by the crowds, since the concept of causality is more concrete and personal in this sphere. The order which reigns in the universe has its own eloquence, but the fatherly solicitude of Providence speaks more appealingly to the mind and heart, for God shows His goodness to us in a thousand ways, making the earth fertile and causing joy to bud in the heart of man by giving him an abundance of crops. That is the testimony to His existence which He gives us, a testimony that shows us His transcendence, His creative power and His benevolent providence.

But all this reasoning could not change the mind of the mob. They were so entrenched in their error that they persisted in giving divine homage to the strangers, and they could not bring themselves to acknowledge that they had been mistaken in their wild assumption that their gods had come again to walk among them. The missionaries almost had to resort to force to make the priest return to his temple with his incense and compel the butchers to lead away the sacrificial victims. Paul finally won the day, but not without revealing the profound contempt he felt for pagan mythology and the loathing with which he regarded its rites. His attitude doubtless aroused anger and resentment, for although many of the people may only have laughed at the ludicrous outcome of the affair, the fanatics must have felt humiliated in their deepest convictions. The priest of Zeus, in particular, would not forget the disrespect shown for the sacrifices which brought such prosperity to his temple. It was from this moment on that the popularity of the missionaries began to wane.

Matters became worse with the arrival of certain Jews who had come from Antioch in Pisidia and Iconium for the express purpose of hindering the spread of the Gospel.

With their insidious talk they turned the people against Paul and Barnabas, alleging that they were two shameless mockers, two common impostors who deceived simple women and led the populace astray with their magical practices. The troublemakers went on to tell how the missionaries had been at the point of being stoned in Iconium, and how the municipal authorities of Antioch in Pisidia had had to expel them as agitators and undesirables. The mob, always fickle and now in an ugly mood, believed these calumnies, and their idolatry turned into murderous hate directed particularly against the more aggressive of the two preachers. The trouble came to a head one day when the enraged crowd, armed with stones and cudgels, fell upon Paul, reviling him, striking him, dragging him through the streets and, finally, believing him dead, casting him out of the city. But the Apostle, though beaten into unconsciousness, was not dead. When he revived, he found himself surrounded by a group of disciples who tenderly lifted him up and helped him back into the city. He thought it prudent not to inflame his enemies' anger again and so the next day, although he was still badly bruised from the blows of the crowd, he and Barnabas left Lystra for Derbe, forty miles to the southeast.

The travellers were now nearing the border of Galatia, for Derbe was the last frontier stronghold, a city well fortified against the terrible ravages of the half-savage tribes who dwelt among the nearby Isaurian hills. Almost the only strangers who came here were the well-armed legionaries, for the territory was both poor and dangerous, with no appeal even for Jewish merchants. Thus freed of the interference of their compatriots, Paul and Barnabas were able to devote themselves undisturbed to their mission. No one hindered their teaching or sowed distrust among the people: the inhabitants of this upland region treated them kindly and many were converted to the new religion.

From the time they had set foot in the market place at Perge, the missionaries had undergone many trials and borne many sufferings; yet Paul was always to regard with special tenderness the churches which he founded on this missionary journey, for they were the fruits of his first apostolic labors. One of the things which made these churches in Asia Minor appealing to him was the fact that they were almost entirely free from Jewish influence. Among the Galatians, as he, the Roman citizen, called all the inhabitants of the Roman province of Galatia (although they were Pisidians, Phrygians or Lycaonians according to the ancient lines of demarcation), he was free from the Semitic atmosphere of Palestine and Syria, for this was a region where Greek was spoken by every moderately educated person, where Graeco-Roman ideas and customs were widespread, and where even the Jews allowed themselves to be influenced and almost absorbed by the cultural atmosphere surrounding them. It is true that the conflicts in which Paul had hitherto been involved here had been caused by his compatriots, but not once did the question of Mosaic rites arise while he was in Asia Minor. He tells us that he preached the Gospel in all its purity: ". . . the gospel which was preached by me is not of man. For I did not receive it from man, nor was I taught it; but I received it by a revelation of Jesus Christ" (Gal. 1:11-12). Here the seed fell on virgin soil, and so there was no need to speak of circumcision and the unprofitable practices of the Law. In conformity with their character, the people of Israel had received from God only a crude rudimentary outline of doctrine, which was to disappear in the face of the salvation brought by Christ. The Christian was to be a new being, animated and moved by the Spirit of God, and instead of the old, abolished practices, he was to cultivate the twelve fruits of the Holy Spirit: charity, joy, peace, patience, benignity, goodness, longanimity, mildness, faith, modesty, continency and chastity. (Cf. Gal. 5:22-23.)

In a short space of time, the semi-civilized inhabitants of the Taurus uplands became capable of understanding the sublime teachings of the Gospel. It is true that their instructor had worked so heroically to accomplish their spiritual formation that he could compare his labors to the pangs of childbirth, but these simple, upright people never failed to co-operate with him. They consoled him in the midst of persecutions; they remained faithful to him despite every kind of calumny; they lovingly cared for him and did not fear to risk their possessions and even their lives for his sake. Furthermore, in the crisis of his illness, during those violent and frightening bouts of chills which accompanied his fever, far from abandoning him as one accursed by God, they had surrounded him with every imaginable attention without considering expense, labor or sacrifice. Later he was to recall with emotion their kindness to him: "For I bear you witness that, if possible, you would have plucked out your very eyes and given them to me" (Gal. 4:15). His words are a vivid reflection of the spirit of love which he was able to instill into these early Christians, an indication of the joy which inflamed their hearts and of the generous enthusiasm with which these men, tired of pagan darkness, greeted the light of truth. He reminded them of their happiness at the time, recalling their first transports of joy in the Faith. (Cf. Gal. 4:15.) They were happy even in the midst of sufferings, which served only to bring them closer to each other and to form the tie that most strongly bound the Apostle to them. Many years later, when writing to Timothy from his prison in Rome, Paul called to mind the trials of his apostolate, dwelling especially on the persecutions that had befallen him at Antioch, Iconium and Lystra, and gratefully witnessing that "out of them all the Lord delivered me" (2 Tim. 3:11).

Although the thought of taking leave of his beloved new disciples pierced him to the heart, the Apostle had to start making plans to depart. It was two years since he and Barnabas had had any news of their companions in the apostolate, and they wanted to consult once more with them about the Lord's work, to tell them how the world of Greek culture was receiving the Gospel, and outline a more ambitious program for the spiritual conquest of the world. With one accord, therefore, Paul and Barnabas decided to return to Palestine. The easiest route to follow would have been that which led across country, through Cilicia, to the capital of Syria; in three or four days they would be able to cross the Taurus Mountains by the Cilician Gates to Tarsus, and from there on the stages of the journey were well known to them—Antioch, Apamea, Damascus and Jerusalem. Nevertheless, the two missionaries chose to retrace their steps to the coasts of Pamphylia, a decision which was both daring and of great importance to the Church, for upon it depended the consolidation of the work they had started. The organization of the new congregations had to be completed, a hierarchy established, and the new converts, whom the Apostle called his "dear children" (Gal. 4:19), confirmed in their faith until Christ was formed in them.

Since Paul and Barnabas did not have to present themselves in the synagogues or preach in the streets on this return journey, their work was done quietly and without attracting attention. In each city along the way there was a group of believers who met from time to time behind closed doors, and who spread the faith so unobtrusively that their neighbors were scarcely aware of their activities. Even if the pagans did pay any attention to the religion which was being slowly diffused among them, they never imagined for a moment that the worshippers of a God who had been executed would be able to transform the world! In any event, it was an accepted fact that all the other religious cults had their meetings and brotherhoods of various degrees of popularity and prosperity. Paul and his companion were able to revisit the churches in those places from which they had been expelled before, since the general populace and even the Jews had forgotten them and the riots in which they had almost lost their lives. No doubt the travellers took every precaution, entering the cities under cover of evening, avoiding their enemies and celebrating the Eucharistic banquet only among trusted friends.

Yet even though they had to proceed cautiously, they visited all the churches, "reassuring the disciples and exhorting them to continue in the faith, and reminding them that through many tribulations we must enter the kingdom of God" (Acts 14:21). Since the pagan mentality considered religion as a charm against adversity, they related their perilous adventures in the cities of Galatia for the benefit of the new converts, who would not be able to understand easily how men who had consecrated themselves entirely to the cause of their God could be so hated and persecuted. Of course in the well-known fable, Hercules had to complete his twelve labors before ascending the heights of Olympus, but in this he was only obeying the inexorable law of fate and did not suffer out of love. He may have slain monsters with his mace, but he did not conquer his own flesh, or sacrifice himself for the salvation of the world, or meditate on the beauty of virtue. Paul, on the contrary, could show "the marks of the Lord Jesus" engraved on his body and, consumed by love and suffering, "present [his body] as a sacrifice, living, holy, pleasing to God" (Gal. 4:17; Rom. 12:1).

He and Barnabas paid a quick visit to each church, spoke some words of exhortation and consolation to the congregation, offered the Eucharistic sacrifice, and after praying and fasting, proceeded to the election of the leaders of the local community. In these elections there was no mention of prophets and teachers as in the church at Antioch, the reason being that these latter offices depended on divine grace, and the Church accepted them when they were granted, but did not herself designate any person to hold them. As St. Luke tells us, the election of leaders was a fundamental part of the organization of the primitive churches, and the elected officials were impartially called presbyters, bishops and elders. The system of church government was modelled on the Jewish priesthood, each church being presided over by a group of grave and virtuous men who, as in the synagogue, watched over the temporal affairs of the community, reprimanded and excommunicated unworthy members, supervised the use of common funds, and defended the church's interests before the local magistrates and the Roman authorities. But their duties went still further, for they were charged with the very delicate and highly important task of guarding the deposit of Faith (cf. 1 Tim. 6:20), that is, the body of truths committed to them by the Apostles, the formulae of the Mysteries, and the ceremonies of common prayer and the sacraments. Judging by the expression used in the original text of St. Luke, the election of the church officials must have been similar to that of the Roman magistrates, in which the president proposed the candidates to a general scrutiny, while reserving to himself wide powers as regards the definitive selection. To Paul and Barnabas belonged the right of imposing hands on those elected, thus ordaining them and passing on to them the powers or orders. Each of those chosen to rule the church and be ordained had to be "blameless as being the steward of God, not proud or ill-tempered, or a drinker, or a brawler, or greedy for base gain; but hospitable, gentle, reserved, just, holy, continent; holding fast the faithful word which is in accordance with the teaching, that he may be able both to exhort in sound doctrine and to confute opponents" (Tit. 1:7-9).

At the end of the year 48, the two missionaries re-entered the low-lying lands of Pamphylia, after having "commended [their converts] to the Lord in whom they had believed" (Acts 14:22). Conditions were better here now than when they had first arrived, and they were able to traverse the region, sowing the seed of faith. Many in Perge believed in Christ and gave up the worship of Diana, patroness of the city, whose temple, filled with thankgiving offerings and gifts, stood on the highest point of the Acropolis. Then Paul and Barnabas finished their mission by making their way to Attalia, where they boarded a ship that brought them to Seleucia. Antioch lay only a few hours' walk from the port, and soon they were greeting the brethren by whom "they had first been entrusted to the grace of God for the work which they had now finished" (Acts 14:25).

Paul and Barnabas spoke with generous enthusiasm at their first meeting with the faithful at Antioch. Although the area they had covered had not been large—the island of Cyprus and about three hundred miles into the interior of Asia Minor—they had been long away and there were many things to tell. They looked with high hopes to the future, and told their listeners how God "had opened to the Gentiles a door of faith" (Acts 14:27). The pagans were thirsting for truth, wearied as they were with the vagueness of their philosophers and the futile efforts of their priests to reveal to them the secrets of the next life. They wanted certitude, and provided that they could conquer death and attain the happiness which some of their wise men said existed, they did not recoil from the austerities imposed by the new religion.

Such was the radiant, hopeful vision which Paul had at the completion of his first missionary journey. Before his mind he held the concept of a great Church which would be the union of all the local congregations. Hitherto the word "Church" had meant only the individual community, the group of brethren set up in each city and organized into a body similar to the city itself. Paul already had the clear concept of a society of brethren scattered over the whole world, and with true philosophical instinct he sought the appropriate term for the new idea. However, though he did not wish to make innovations and though the word "Church" was used in the very text of the Gospel itself, no one felt the unity, universality and grandeur of the Church as much as he. He speaks to us of the "church of God that is at Corinth," to make us understand better the essential unity of all the disciples of Christ—the part in the whole and the whole in the part. In this he was thinking of the organization of the Roman Empire in which each group of citizens who had united to form a Roman colony was considered as a part of the great concept of Rome. When a Roman citizen arrived at a provincial city possessing such a group, he was welcomed as a member of the whole. Paul's idea was not difficult to envisage, since the Empire was an existing example of what he desired—an organization which retained its vitality and character in its scattered colonies as strongly as within the circle of Rome's own walls. But Paul succeeded in giving his theory a consistency and a unity which the Empire never possessed. And it is a fact that the grandiose plans of the politicians and law-makers of Rome were fully realized only in that Church which Paul was organizing throughout the Roman provinces.

CHAPTER XI

False Brethren

Paul had arrived in Antioch at a moment that was critical for the internal life of the Church, for although he did not meet with any opposition from the synagogue on this occasion, there was no lack of conflict and contradiction within the Christian community itself. Christianity had arrived at that difficult stage of growth which is inevitable in every organism that is marked for a great future, and upon which the organism's destiny and even its very existence depends. When Islamism came to this point in its development, it split into two great branches; a similar division weakened Buddhism. Was this to be the fate of the Church? Her Founder had guaranteed that she would be safe from destruction, but He had not made her immune from attack by the powers of darkness. Since Christ, being God, had allowed Himself to be tempted, surely it was His disciples' duty as men to face trials bravely, and on many occasions He had seemed to indicate that the ship of the Church would be rudely buffeted by the wind and the waves.

The cleavage in the Church began in Antioch. The Jews there were powerful, but they were too immersed in their material interests to take time to observe attentively the importance of the new force that was breaking off from the synagogue. Furthermore, association with Greeks in an atmosphere saturated with paganism and laxity had made them tolerant and lenient toward others, and remiss in their following of the practices of the Law. Almost all of them had had to abandon their traditional observances, since anyone in such a community who wished to adhere to the Pharisaical ablutions would have had to renounce social life entirely or spend most of his time purifying himself. This careless attitude toward the Law disposed the Jews for entry into the Church, and at the same time prepared them to live in harmony with converted pagans.

In Antioch many of the Jews had embraced the Faith and, replacing their rigid Pharisaism with the liberty of the Gospel, they associated amicably with the baptized Gentiles without requiring them to follow the observances of the Mosaic Law, much less to submit to circumcision. Even before he had embarked on his first missionary journey, St. Paul had singled out as a future fellow-worker a young man called Titus, who was not circumcised, was of pagan parentage, and had not a single drop of Jewish blood in his veins; yet no one had been scandalized at his being chosen by the Apostle.

But there was a different reaction among the faithful in Jerusalem, for they were already reading St. Matthew's Gospel, which seemed to favor those who were bent on harmonizing the Church and the synagogue. The evangelist told how the Lord said that He had not come to destroy the Law but to perfect it, that not one jot or tittle of it would be forgotten or lost, and that, although the scribes and Pharisees did not act on their own teaching, their teaching should be obeyed: "All things, therefore, that they command you, observe and do" (Matt. 5:17–18; 23:2–3).

The literal interpretation of these texts gave rise to a rigid puritanism whose followers forgot the other teachings of our Lord and regarded Peter's vision at Joppa as unimportant. These Christians, all sons of Abraham and some of them Pharisees to boot, maintained close connections with the Temple, the Sanhedrin, and the orthodox schools with all their rites and doctrine. Perhaps that was why they were not involved in the persecution which had given the Church its first martyr, for the Jews of Jerusalem (and of the cities of Galatia) were more angered by the outrage offered to their national pride in the abolition of the Mosaic privileges and the raising of the Gentiles to equality with the Chosen People, than they were by the Christians' faith in a crucified God.

A conflict was therefore to be expected between Jerusalem and Antioch, the representative centers of the two opposing tendencies. Soon after the return of Paul and Barnabas, some Christians from Judea appeared in Antioch, alarmed by the rumors that were circulating about Paul's teaching and the consideration with which he had treated the Gentiles on his journey through Asia Minor. These newcomers had no official standing, but went around calling themselves disciples of St. James to bolster their claim as defenders of the Law. Paul described them as "false brethren who were brought in secretly, who slipped in to spy upon our liberty which we have in Christ Jesus, that they might bring us into slavery" (Gal. 2:4). The troublemakers, angered at the spirit which prevailed in the Antiochean community, did not hesitate to condemn it publicly and to launch anathemas against its principal promoters, Paul and Barnabas. They accused the two friends of betraying the truth so as to facilitate the conversion of the Gentiles, but at the same time they conveniently forgot the missionaries' prodigious labors, the sufferings and hardships they had undergone, their journeys by land and sea. And they always finished their haranguings of the faithful of Antioch with the dire threat: "Unless you be circumcised after the manner of Moses, you cannot be saved" (Acts 15:1).

From the start Paul saw the fatal consequences which this doctrine could have; it was undoing not only his work but the work of Christ, for to place salvation in the practice of the Law was to make void the merits of the Passion and destroy all the advantages of the Gospel. Furthermore, "the curse of the Law" (Gal. 3:13) would inevitably compromise the future of Christianity, since circumcision made the Jews the laughingstock of the Gentiles among whom they dwelt. Martial, for example, ridiculed the circumcised in bitingly witty verses, and about the same time Petronius wrote: "Although a Jew adores the divinity under the form of a pig and invokes the animal with the long ears, if he is not circumcised he will be expelled by his people and will have to flee to some Greek city where he will be dispensed from the Sabbath fast. Among the Jewish people the only nobility and the only proof of freedom is to have had the courage to be circumcised."

Hence, if even among the Jews themselves there were some who did all they could to avoid the painful rite, it is not surprising that few Gentiles were willing to submit to it.

Insistence on the observances of the Law was making it impossible to preach the Faith, the grace of the Gospel was being rendered sterile, and the immense riches of the Redemption were being shut up in the coffers of Judaism. Well aware of the storm that was brewing about him, Paul went on preaching "the Gospel of the uncircumcised" with his usual fearlessness. The emissaries from Judea were bent on combining the Church with the synagogue, a course of action which was equivalent to absorbing and nullifying Christianity. Against their propaganda, the Apostle proclaimed unequivocally that the works of the Law were useless, that the grace of baptism was the only remedy for sin, and that even circumcision, the symbol of Abraham's faith in the Redeemer, lost all its meaning from the very instant the Redeemer appeared on earth. The controversy soon became a bitter quarrel; the Gentile converts were not sure where to turn, and the converts from Judaism joined the fanatical advocates of Mosaic orthodoxy. The result was that the church at Antioch was divided into two factions which prayed and celebrated the Breaking of Bread apart from each other and under the direction of different pastors.

It was at this point that St. Peter, the Prince of the Apostles, arrived in Antioch, perhaps for the express purpose of restoring peace. However, warm-hearted, generous and impressionable as he was, he allowed himself to be influenced by the advocates of circumcision and his attitude was on the point of making matters worse when Paul intervened. St. Paul himself describes in vivid yet impartial words the trying occasion on which he and Peter faced each other: "But when Cephas came to Antioch, I withstood him to his face, because he was deserving of blame. For before certain persons came from James, he used to eat with the Gentiles; but when they came, he began to withdraw and to separate himself, fearing the circumcised. And the rest of the Jews dissembled along with him, so that Barnabas also was led away by them into that dissimulation" (Gal. 2:11–13).

Paul was now alone, and the cause seemed lost. All the

leaders of the Church avoided his company and even Barnabas, the faithful companion of his persecutions and apostolic triumphs, had deserted him. The excuse for the rift was the Mosaic legislation concerning clean and unclean foods, a law that was sacred not only because it was contained in the Book of Leviticus, but also because of the moral teachings and the symbolic reasons which the rabbis had read into the words of the Pentateuch. For example, the Law said that the hare was not to be eaten because it was a four-footed animal whose paw was not cloven like the hoofs of sheep, but the schools of Jerusalem added that this creature was particularly unclean because of its filthy habits. Yet, although it was a great sacrifice for a Jew to bring himself to eat the flesh of such unclean beasts, Peter had done so when admonished by the voice from heaven. But the vehemence of the Jews from Jerusalem had influenced his kindly heart and, fearing to scandalize the dissidents, he finally withdrew from the table of the Gentiles. His action sowed disquiet in the community, because all the Jews followed the example of him to whom Christ had said: "Feed my sheep," and also because the Gentiles seemed to be obliged to accept the legal observances if they were not to be reduced to an inferior position among the disciples of Christ.

Paul protested publicly against Peter's attitude, not because he wished to lower the dignity of the Prince of the Apostles, but solely because he wanted to take quick and decisive action to avert the consequences which could follow from Peter's momentary weakness. He knew that Peter's beliefs and his were, and had to be, identical, and he felt it was necessary that the chief Apostle manifest his true convictions in order to put an end to the ambiguous and painful situation. St. Paul himself describes the famous scene in unforgettable words:

But when I saw that they were not walking uprightly according to the truth of the gospel, I said to Cephas before them all: If thou, though a Jew, livest like the Gentiles, and not like the Jews, how is it that thou dost compel the Gentiles to live like the Jews? We are Jews by birth, and not sinners from among the Gentiles. But we know that man is not justified by the works of the Law, but by the faith of Jesus Christ. Hence we also believe in Christ Jesus, that we may be justified by the faith of Christ, and not by the works of the Law; because by the works of the Law no man will be justified. But if, while we are seeking to be justified in Christ, we ourselves also are found sinners, is Christ therefore the minister of sin? By no means. For if I reconstruct the things that I destroyed, I make myself a sinner. For I through the Law have died to the Law that I may live to God. With Christ I am nailed to the cross. It is now no longer I that live, but Christ lives in me. And the life that I now live in the flesh, I live in the faith of the Son of God, who loved me and gave himself up for me. I do not cast away the grace of God. For if justice is by the Law, then Christ died in vain (Gal. 2:14-21).

Paul's unpolished but vibrant and impassioned eloquence had the desired effect. St. Peter saw that his action had been unwise, and he used the whole weight of his authority to support his fellow-Apostle without ceasing to love him like a brother, despite Paul's public correction of him. His moment of vacillation caused two outstanding incidents in the history of the primitive Church: the humble simplicity with which he magnanimously recognized and bowed to the truth, and Paul's sublime oration, one of the peaks of

human eloquence, the expression of his towering personality, an example of irresistible reasoning, springing out of
a holy indignation which expressed itself in sentences that
will never die: "With Christ I am nailed to the cross. It is
now no longer I that live, but Christ lives in me." On hearing these words, Peter felt the old wound in his heart re-
opening and a fiery dart of sweet pain transfixed him,
causing tears of joy and love to spring to his eyes as he
remembered his beloved Master's forgiveness of his betrayal. We can well believe that as Paul finished speaking
Peter impulsively embraced him as a gesture of approval,
esteem and affection.

The incident had an immediate effect: indecision disappeared, peace of mind was restored, and the false
brethren's preaching lost its influence. Thus Antioch was
saved, but the fire had already begun to spread among
the recently-founded churches beyond the mountains of
Cilicia. Taking advantage of Peter's passing weakness and
its disconcerting effect, the Judaizers had rushed in to win
to their cause the new communities in Asia Minor. Their
emissaries were even then traversing the regions of lower
Galatia, Pisidia, Lycaonia and Isauria, preaching the necessity of circumcision as an essential condition for salvation,
or at least as the perfection and completion of Christianity.
They lauded the advantages of participation in the prerogatives of Israel; they insisted on the splendor of the Jewish
solemnities, and they stressed the necessity of uniting the
two parties in the Church. But since Paul was the preacher
of the Gospel of liberty, they endeavored more than anything else to destroy his prestige, depicting him as an in-
consequential partisan who wished to win popularity by
sacrificing the most sacred principles. They pointed out
that he had not spent long years under the direction of the

Master, but was only a pupil of the disciples, and they claimed that he was not teaching what he had learned. Finally, they accused him of being in opposition to the Twelve, to the "pre-eminent Apostles," as they called them to humiliate him.

When he heard of their insidious campaign and the havoc it was causing among his Galatian disciples, Paul, already aroused by the happenings in Antioch and now trembling with new indignation, wrote the first of his Epistles [1]—that rushing torrent, that irresistible marshalling of all his powers, that document in which are combined irrefutable arguments, biting irony, devastating logic, the vehemence of anger and the tenderness of fatherly love. As he wrote, he suddenly realized that letters such as the one he was now composing were the most effective means of maintaining his influence over the most distant churches, of speaking once more to his "dear children," of defeating his enemies and of bringing peace to wavering minds. This was truly a monumental discovery, an absolutely new thing of its kind, with a new vocabulary and a new style comprised of teaching, exhortation, argument and "diatribe," pointed up by the pouring out of innermost feelings and the exposition of sublime ideas.

It would be hard to find pages in which admonition and affection, exquisite delicacy and terrible warnings are blended together so vividly and so effectively as in the Epistle to the Galatians. For the first time we hear St. Paul

[1] Translator's note: There is a wide divergence of views concerning the date of this Epistle. Some critics place it first, as the author does; others place it last, while the majority place it immediately after the Thessalonian Epistles. The more probable opinion is that 1 Thessalonians was Paul's first Epistle, written about the year 51, while Galatians was written from 53 to 57. Cf. Fernand Prat, S.J. *The Theology of St. Paul*, I, p. 163.

speak his own ardent words as they come to his lips and not as they are summarized by the historian of the Acts. We hear him defending his apostolate in a life-and-death struggle. "Paul? And who is he?" shouted the contradictors: "Who made him an Apostle?" Conscious of his power, he takes up the challenge, raises his piercing eyes and begins proudly: "Paul, an Apostle, sent not from men nor by men, but by Jesus Christ and God the Father who raised him from the dead." Then, after a few words of salutation and prayer, and without further introduction, he plunges with assurance into the heart of the matter: "I marvel that you are so quickly deserting him who called you to the grace of Christ, changing to another gospel; which is not another gospel, except in this respect that there are some who trouble you, and wish to prevert the gospel of Christ. But even if we or an angel from heaven should preach a gospel to you other than that which we have preached to you, let him be anathema!"

After launching this imprecation against those who accused him of seeking the favor of the Gentiles, he continues to present his defense by addressing his detractors ironically: "Am I now seeking the favor of men, or of God? Or am I seeking to please men?" And remembering all he had abandoned when he heard the voice of Christ— his influence as a Pharisee, his bright future in the world, his very flesh and blood—he throws his enemies' accusation back in their faces: "If I were still trying to please men, I should not be a servant of Christ." Then, after defending himself and setting down his doctrine, he adds, with indignation that ends in sarcasm: "But I, brethren, if I still preach circumcision, why am I still persecuted? Then is the stumbling block of the cross removed? Would that those who are unsettling you would mutilate themselves!"

His Gospel is not of men but of Jesus Christ, for he was taught by revelation by the Lord Himself. John, James and Peter had acknowledged the validity of his vocation and had confirmed his doctrine, making an alliance with him by giving him the right hand of fellowship when he had visited them in Jerusalem fourteen years after his conversion, on the occasion of his bringing the alms from the faithful at Antioch. (Cf. Gal. 2:9–10.) As we have already seen, Luke refers to this errand of mercy, but Paul adds new details about how the question of the legal observances was discussed, and how he was given complete liberty. Furthermore, Titus, the Gentile convert who had accompanied Paul and Barnabas to Jerusalem, was not compelled to undergo circumcision, although the champions of the Law vehemently demanded it: "The men of authority laid no further burden on me. On the contrary . . . they said that to me was committed the gospel for the uncircumcised, as to Peter that for the circumcised. . . ." We have seen that Peter later wavered for a time; yet when Paul had admonished him, he took a firm stand, as the whole community at Antioch could attest.

After recalling these incidents in his life, Paul confronted his converts once more with the words:

O foolish Galatians, who has bewitched you, before whose eyes Jesus Christ has been depicted crucified? This only would I learn from you: Did you receive the Spirit in virtue of the works of the Law, or in virtue of hearing and believing? Are you so foolish that after beginning in the Spirit, you now make a finish in the flesh? . . . Know . . . that the men of faith are the real sons of Abraham. . . . But that by the Law no man is justified before God is evident, because "he who is just lives by faith" . . . Christ redeemed us from the curse of the Law . . . that the blessing of Abraham might come to the Gentiles. . . . Before the faith came we were kept imprisoned under the Law, shut up for the faith that was to be revealed. Therefore the Law has been our tutor in Christ that we might be justified by faith. But now that faith has come, we are no longer under a tutor. . . . We . . . when we were children, were enslaved under the elements of the world. But when the fullness of time came, God sent his Son . . . that he might redeem those under the Law, that we might receive the adoption of sons.

Then, abandoning for a moment his line of argument, the Apostle makes a touching appeal to the bonds of affection that unite him to his disciples:

Become like me, because I also have become like you, brethren, I beseech you! You have done me no wrong. And you know that on account of a physical infirmity I preached the gospel to you formerly; and though I was a trial to you in my flesh, you did not reject or despise me, but you received me as an angel of God, even as Jesus Christ. Where then is your self-congratulation? . . . Have I then become your enemy, because I tell you the truth? . . . My dear children, with whom I am in labor again, until Christ is formed in you! But I wish I could be with you now, and change my tone, because I do not know what to make of you.

Resuming the exposition of his doctrine, he uses an allegory based on the story of the two wives of Abraham, Agar and Sarah, the slave girl and the free, to explain more clearly man's condition before and after redemption, pointing out that Agar's son, the symbol of the Law, was a slave like his mother, while Sarah, representing the Church, begot a free race of men. Then he urges his disciples to follow the instructions of Scripture and cast out the slave and her son so that they themselves may live according to the promise as sons of liberty and light.

"Stand fast," concludes the Apostle, "and do not be caught again under the yoke of slavery. Behold, I, Paul, tell you that if you be circumcised, Christ will be of no advantage to you." In his later Epistles, Paul was content to add only a few words in his own hand by way of signature, but on this occasion, fearing that he had not said enough, he wrote a kind of summary of what he had just dictated:

See with what large letters I am writing to you with my own hand! As many as wish to please in the flesh compel you to be circumcised simply that they may not suffer persecution for the cross of Christ. For not even they who are circumcised keep the Law, but they desire you to be circumcised, that they may make a boast of your flesh. But as for me, God forbid that I should glory save in the cross of our Lord Jesus Christ, through whom the world is crucified to me, and I to the world. . . . Henceforth let no man give me trouble, for I bear the marks of our Lord Jesus in my body.

This letter, a prodigy of inspiration, logic and charity, is the spontaneous outburst of a soul wounded by the hypocrisy of some and the unfaithfulness of others. Yet in it Paul shows himself to be no less a diplomat than he is an author and orator. Perhaps his eloquence would have the desired effect; perhaps the Galatians would repent of the false asceticism which caused them to adopt the Jewish observances; but whatever the outcome, it was necessary to have an authorized document which would silence the critics, assure future obedience to the Apostle's preaching, and declare solemnly the conformity of his doctrine with the teaching of the Twelve. These considerations awoke in Paul's mind the idea of going to Jerusalem to resolve the problem that had originated there. In the Holy City he would find the pillars of the Church, James the Less, John, the beloved disciple, and Peter, the chief of the Apostles. Despite his independent character and his consciousness of the special mission entrusted to him, Paul reverenced these men and, good statesman and administrator that he was, always regarded them as the heads of the Church unified and organized about its leader. Therefore he now had recourse to their tribunal, confident that they agreed with him and would give him their approval.

With him went Barnabas, repentant of his recent humoring of the Judaizers and prepared to go on sharing the trials and the glories of his companion's ministry. They journeyed south through Phoenicia and Samaria, relating everywhere the story of "the conversion of the Gentiles"; but when they entered Judea, they decided to discontinue their preaching, for Paul, with his fine sense of diplomacy, did not want to awaken further suspicions in Jerusalem. He exercised this exquisite tact throughout his stay in the Holy City, proceeding slowly, maintaining a prudent reserve and giving his listeners plenty of time to reflect upon and absorb the truth of his contentions.

First he spoke with each of the leaders, but without referring to the privileges and divine favors which he had received, with humble self-distrust, asking them for advice, "lest perhaps [he] should be running, or had run in vain" (Gal. 2:2). This image of the runner competing for the crown in the arena was to remain one of his favorite illustrations, and neither Peter, James nor John took offense at its Hellenistic flavor, for they had seen their tireless fellow-Apostle's sincerity and valor and were completely in accord with him. Yet all around them they felt the pressure of the Judaizers, or as St. Luke calls them, "the Pharisees' sect" (Acts 15:5), who had watched jealously the enthusiastic and brotherly reception which the Apostles gave the two mighty preachers of the Gospel. There was a public demonstration in which most of the faithful took part under the leadership of their dignitaries, and Paul and Barnabas took advantage of the occasion to tell of the great works God had done through their ministry. The audience was overjoyed to hear about the new world that was accepting the doctrine of Christ; yet some dissenting voices were raised above the clamor of applause and congratulations. No one could deny the missionaries' success but, the objectors said, their work was actually incomplete, since they had not obliged the Gentiles to undergo circumcision and to keep the precepts of the Law of Moses. (Cf. Acts 15:5.) Thus it was Paul's enemies themselves who proposed the problem that he had come to discuss.

After a series of preliminary meetings, the solution to the difficulty was reached at a general assembly of the Apostles and elders in which Paul showed his usual strength of character and adaptability during the long and often heated debates. First the protagonists of the Law spoke, upholding their own point of view and condemning the liberalism of the teachers at Antioch. No doubt they recalled Israel's prerogatives, referring to the curses pronounced by famous doctors of the Law against those who violated the rabbinical precepts, and quoting those words of Christ which they used as one of their main arguments:

"I have not come to destroy but to fulfill" (Matt. 5:17). However, the discussion was turning into a personal attack on Paul when Peter, with the authority which all recognized in him, raised the debate to a higher plane. Although he defended the liberal party, he knew that his words had to be words of peace and charity and, with wise moderation, he neither upheld nor condemned the Law. The beginning of his discourse was an echo of what Paul and Barnabas had been saying since they arrived in Jerusalem; that one thing was plain—God wished to treat the Gentiles in the same way as the Jews, that He had purified their hearts by faith and had poured out upon them the grace of the Spirit. The conclusion was therefore obvious: for the Jews as well as for the Gentiles, there was only one means of salvation—the grace of the Lord Jesus. "Why then," Peter continued, "do you now try to test God by putting on the necks of the disciples a yoke which neither our father nor we have been able to bear?" Here he was using an argument similar to that which Paul had used against him in Antioch: "If thou, though a Jew, livest like the Gentiles, and not like the Jews, how is it that thou dost compel the Gentiles to live like Jews?" That was the simple question which, a short while before, had made a deep impression on his noble and faithful heart, and he now employed it in a more general form to channel the debate in this first Christian Council.

In his speech Peter showed that he was, as usual, the personification of sound common sense, and when he finished, a profound silence reigned in the assembly. Then Paul and Barnabas stood up and continued the chief Apostle's argument by relating in further detail the marvels that God had wrought in confirmation of their preaching in the churches of Galatia. This was the missionaries' most powerful defense of their ministry, for if their work had prospered, if miracles confirmed their efforts, and if the evangelical virtues ousted the vices of idolatry from men's hearts, then God was with them and their doctrine was the Gospel of Christ. No doubt Barnabas spoke with his usual persuasive mildness, while Paul was vehement and incisive, causing the sect of the Pharisees to renew their protests as he urged the assembly to adopt a favorable resolution of the problem.

James, the Lord's "brother," was present at the assembly also, and one wonders if it could be said of him that he had not been able to support the burden of the Law, for he was a perfect Israelite, of spotless life, fidelity to tradition, dignified and majestic bearing, impressive address, continual prayer and frightening austerity. No Nazarene had lived more strictly than he, for he never ate meat or drank wine, he never wore shoes, or cut his hair, or bathed, or anointed his body with oil. With truth he was called "the Just," and both Jews and Christians revered this man in whom adoration of "the Father of Lights" (James 1:17), who revealed Himself in His Son Jesus Christ, was joined to profoundest love of the Law of Moses, "the royal Law, the perfect Law which condemns prevaricators; the holy Law, that cannot be broken even in one point without the whole being violated." (Cf. James 1:25; 2:10.) No wonder then that the Judaizers had placed all their hopes in James, since his intervention on their behalf would have been a terrible blow to the liberals. But they were to be disappointed, for James' intransigence faded in the face of Peter's arguments and the story of Paul's and Barnabas' triumphs for the Faith.

He rose to address the assembly, beginning by referring respectfully to Peter's speech and then going on to show that the Gentiles' entrance into the Church was only the fulfillment of the ancient prophecies, proving his point by quoting a text of Amos in the Septuagint version, although the most important words in his proof are not found in the original Hebrew. It is very interesting to note that this champion of Hebrew traditions was familiar with the Bible in Greek and used its variant text to make his point. He supported Peter in the fundamentals: "Therefore my judgment is not to disquiet those who from among the Gentiles are turning to the Lord." But at the same time as he spoke against "the disquieters of souls," he pleaded for some concessions on Paul's part and, with his practical wisdom, proposed that the Gentiles be given "written instructions to abstain from anything that has been contaminated by idols and from immorality and from anything strangled and from blood." His reason for asking for these concessions was that the Jews were scattered throughout the world and might be scandalized at seeing the prescriptions of the Law violated. Actually, these regulations were to mollify the Judaizers and prevent a large section of the Jews from breaking with the Church. Paul accepted these conditions without demur, although he was later to state clearly that one of them was not obligatory except when the higher law of charity required its enforcement. (Cf. 1 Cor. 8.) He understood that such regulations were necessary to allow the Jews and Gentiles to live together amicably in the newly-founded churches, for each party had to yield in some respects to the other. The Law could not be imposed on the Gentiles, but if they were to live in fraternal harmony with the Jewish converts, they would have to bear in mind the horror inspired in the Israelites by unbled meat, the blood of animals and the flesh that was sold in markets after it had been offered to idols. The precept concerning immorality did not refer to sins of the flesh, which were already condemned by the natural law, but to marriage within the forbidden degrees of kindred, and this first step toward applying Hebrew legislation to Christian marriage was to have a profound effect on later ecclesiastical law.

All the members of the Council accepted James' proposal, and even the sect of the Pharisees, those false brethren who had entered the Church to spy and destroy, did not dare protest, although they were by no means satisfied with the verdict. The outcome of the Council's deliberations was set down in the famous document which, although addressed solely to the churches in Syria and Cilicia, had the force of law in all the cities where Jewish and Gentile converts lived together. The document opens with a denial that any authority had been given to the sowers of discord, who had said that they had been sent by the Apostles. Then it goes on to give high praise to Barnabas and Paul, "men who have pledged their lives for the name of our Lord Jesus Christ," and it continues with the Council's decree, prefacing it with the imperative and sovereign formula: "The Holy Spirit and we have decided. . . ." Those selected to promulgate this decree in Antioch were not the two missionaries to the Gentiles, but two Jews from Jerusalem, Silas and Judas Barsabbas, "leading men among the brethren," who were chosen with the object of precluding protests and murmuring among the Judaizers and of giving more authority to the decisions of the Council.

As he left Jerusalem after the assembly had disbanded, Paul could repeat the words which he had written some months before in reference to his previous visit to the mother-church: "The men of authority laid no further burden on me" (Gal. 2:6). The essentials of his thought remained intact, and his preaching to the pagans had once more been approved and recognized as completely orthodox; he had "not yield(ed) in submission, no, not for an hour, that the truth of the gospel" and the name of Christ be eclipsed (Gal. 2:5). And from now on, Peter's prestige and supreme authority, as well as the leading Apostles' support, would be behind him in his campaign to spread Christian theology. The advocates of circumcision would continue to hinder his work but he was no longer alone, for he could always use the definitive statement of the august assembly to foil the hatred and subtle trickery of these wily plotters and to silence the barking of these "dogs." When he had been alone and abandoned by all, his life, which he had described as being submerged in the life of Christ, had reached the highest peaks of greatness, and in the end he had reaped the fruit of his efforts. From now on he was to feel the full strength of the Church and her leaders supporting him.

Thus ended the famed question of the legal observances, an incident which marked a solemn moment in the development of the primitive Church. With his keen mind, St. Paul had been the first to see the importance of the apparently minor dispute about the legal rites, and he knew that in reality it was a question of deciding whether Christianity was simply a continuation of Judaism, a system of proselytizing for circumcision, or whether it meant the advent of a new people.

To have retained the Law would have been to renounce the conquest of the world, and, what was more important, it would have meant denying the transitory character of the old economy, the sufficiency of the Redemption, the value of the Blood of Christ, and the efficacy of grace. If it had been kept within the porches of the Temple, the wonderful plant of the Gospel would have been stifled, deprived of the light of the sun and the gentle breezes from far-off seas. The gigantic tree, in whose branches the birds of the air were to find shelter, as the Lord Himself had said in His parable, would have been but a lowly shrub, and the Christian community just one more sect destined to fade out after a few years of fruitless agitation. But in that critical moment the figure of St. Paul appeared, destroying and anathematizing the past to make way for a limitless future. He fought valiantly yet meekly, reasonably and with diplomacy, and when Peter's wavering threatened to wreck his cause, he succeeded, with his energy, humility, and passionate love of the Savior, in maintaining the vital unity of the Church by faith in the living Christ.

CHAPTER XII

"Timothy, My Dearly Beloved Son"

When Paul and Barnabas returned to Antioch, all the brethren gathered together, eager to hear the news and the decrees from Jerusalem. The two delegates of the assembly read the Apostles' letter, the Magna Carta of Christian liberty, and it was received with great joy, for it set the Antiocheans' hearts at ease and confirmed them in their faith.

After some time had passed, Paul was assured that peace was restored to the church at Antioch and he said to Barnabas: "Let us return and visit the brethren in all the cities where we have preached the word of the Lord, to see how they are doing." This was Paul's method: first, sow the seed; then water the plant, care for it, and clear away the weeds from around it—that is, increase the converts' love of God, awaken their fervor, and take measures to preserve their purity of life. But the journey he now proposed to take had still another object: to let the churches of Asia Minor know the decisions of the Council at Jerusalem.

Barnabas accepted the suggestions gladly, but imposed one condition: that his nephew, John Mark, go with them.

170

The young man had come to regret his former weakness and was now willing to suffer all the labor of the apostolate; but Paul still regarded him as an inefficient worker and considered his presence as an obstacle, for after putting his hand to the plough, he had looked back. It is possible, too, that Paul feared Mark's influence over Barnabas' kind heart; at any rate, a sharp contention sprang up between the two friends. The uncle was naturally more indulgent toward his nephew than was Paul, and was perhaps more aware of his fidelity, intelligence and virtue, with the result that he defended the young man as vehemently as the Apostle attacked him. The argument grew more heated, reached what the Greek text of the Acts calls a "paroxysm," and the two missionaries sorrowfully and regretfully concluded that they could not set out together on this second campaign. But, though they separated, it was without rancor or ill-feeling, for ten years later, John Mark was to appear once more at the Apostle's side, and Barnabas' name was to be mentioned with affection in the Pauline Epistles. As St. Jerome observed: "Paul was the more severe; Barnabas, the more clement. Each was convinced that he was right; yet the discussion contained an element of human frailty."

Barnabas and Mark left for Cyprus, and Paul had to choose a companion from among the teachers at Antioch. He could have selected Titus, who had followed him for some time with admiration and fervent loyalty; but Titus was the son of Gentiles and uncircumcised, and so he would not be able to help the Apostle on a mission which would bring them into frequent contact with Jews. On the other hand, there was an Israelite from Jerusalem in Antioch at the time, one of the most important personages of the Church, none other than Silas, who had been sent hither by the Apostles with the Council's decree, and who was already attracted by Paul's personality. This man fulfilled all the conditions required by the circumstances: he was loyal, generous, broad-minded, free of nationalistic prejudices, and he combined the prestige of a prophet with the advantage of being in the confidence of the elders of the mother-church and of having witnessed the deliberations in the assembly at Jerusalem. Moreover, he was a Roman citizen, no small recommendation in view of the persecutions which they would almost inevitably meet with on their journey.

It was the spring of the year 51 when Paul, taking Silas with him, left the city of Antioch to begin his second mission, and his first thought was to inspect and strengthen the churches already established. Crossing the Amanus Mountains through the Syrian Gates, he came upon the first Christian communities at Mopsuestia, Adena and Tarsus, cities in which he had undoubtedly preached during the years which he spent in his home-country after his first apostolic efforts in Damascus and Jerusalem. From place to place he and Silas went, quickening spiritual fervor and spreading the news of the decision reached by the Apostles and elders of the Holy City. "So the churches grew stronger and stronger in the faith and increased in numbers daily" (Acts 16:5).

Once again the imposing crags of the Taurus Mountains reared their rocky heights in Paul's path, but neither he nor his companion was daunted, for their hearts were stouter than the oak trees that flourished on the mountain slopes. Following the Roman road that wound along the course of the Cydnus, they crossed the Cilician Gates which opened the Lycaonian plateau to them. When the sun's rays became unbearable, they rested in the shade of the trees and rocks; when thirst came, they drank from a mountain spring; and when night descended on them, they sought lodgings in the hostelries along the road, finding a place to sleep among the confusion of cargo and equipment belonging to muleteers and camel-drivers, soldiers and merchants. As they traversed the sunlit uplands they could see in the distance the metallic glint of placid waters, for they were now approaching the land of the lakes, and their hearts beat high with hope and love at the thought of meeting the disciples, those brethren among whom Paul had lived the glorious springtime of his apostolate. Derbe, Lystra, Iconium, Antioch in Pisidia—what memories the names awakened! What emotions, joys, and sufferings they recalled!

In Lystra, for example, Paul had sowed the first seeds of his blood and had reaped a precious harvest. He had been insulted, dragged through the streets, stoned and left for dead; but when he recovered consciousness, he found himself in a modest dwelling where two women and a youth attended him solicitously. The women were Eunice and Lois, and the youth was Timothy, Eunice's son. All three were fervent Israelites, but the virtue and eloquence of their guest had so impressed them that soon they asked to be baptized.

Now, on re-entering Lystra, Paul found in Eunice's home the same faith, the same hospitality and the same enthusiasm for Christianity. Especially in the case of Timothy, the seed planted by Paul had grown prodigiously, and the young man had become noted for the sincerity and profundity of his religious convictions, having attained "perfect manhood . . . the mature measure of the fullness of Christ" (Eph. 4:13). The Apostle saw that this was a privileged soul, richly endowed by nature and by grace, and he wished to have him as a fellow-worker. Accordingly, he and the priests of the city laid their hands on the young man, and grace descended upon him with an abundance that he was never to forget. In the last months of his life, Paul spoke of this grace as of a fire that had consumed in his disciple every trace of fear, every relic of the Old Covenant, and had substituted the Spirit of Christ, the spirit of strength, of love and of wisdom.

But Timothy had been born of a Gentile father and therefore was not circumcised, a fact which would hinder his ministry among the Jews, since they would not allow an uncircumcised person to ascend the tribune in the synagogue to comment on the Scriptures. However, this was an obstacle which Paul overcame with his usual swift decisiveness: ". . . he took [him] and circumcised him on account of the Jews who were in those parts" (Acts 16:3). The Apostle's action was both a gesture of conformity and a stroke of diplomacy, for, in spite of the persecutions of his compatriots, he did not wish to change the recognized tactics of preaching the Gospel. He had to fulfill the command of Christ and at the same time follow the dictates of human prudence by approaching first the children of the Chosen Race, for a Jewish traveller was always sure of being well received by his own race in any of the large cities, and he would be entertained, admitted to the synagogue and, if necessary, given work. Therefore it was natural that the first missionaries should go from ghetto to ghetto throughout the civilized world, seeking out their compatriots. Paul wanted to preach first to the Jews because they were of the same blood as he, and because to them was due the first announcement of the realization of Israel's hopes. If his compatriots rejected his teaching, he could turn to their neighbors, the Gentiles, who were better prepared to receive the Gospel and who, disgusted with pagan practices, were attracted by Jewish monotheism and thirsted for a purer life.

These were the motives which caused Paul to circumcise Timothy after he had defended so violently the cause of liberty. The exterior rite mattered little to him, but he did not want to stultify his apostolate by being foolishly stubborn: "Circumcision does not matter, and uncircumcision does not matter; but the keeping of the commandments is what matters" (1 Cor. 7:19).

Now that Timothy was irreproachable in Jewish eyes, he could follow his teacher, and "as child serves father . . . [serve] with [him] in spreading the gospel" (Phil. 2:22). From this moment on, he drew increasingly near to Paul as his beloved disciple and the most faithful of his collaborators. The Apostle called him his true son, his son most loving and faithful in the Lord, the sharer of his spirit, his very soul, his other self, his companion, his brother, the slave of Christ, and the perfect imitator of the apostolic virtues. Although Paul and Timothy were of quite different temperaments, they seemed to have been made for mutual understanding. Undoubtedly the disciple was not inclined to impetuous action as was the master, for his was a gentle character, easily moved, impressionable, delicate and very sensitive, wholly averse to contention and instinctively inclined to maintain a timid reserve. But what he lacked in boldness and aggressiveness he made up in fidelity, deep, sincere loyalty, complete self-denial and thoughtfulness for others, so much so that the Apostle could say of him when writing to the Philippians: "I have no one so like-minded who is so genuinely solicitous for you" (Phil. 2:20). Their association was a precious boon to both, for Paul's manly spirit communicated to Timothy a great strength of thought and doctrine, while the Apostle received from his disciple that undivided and unquestioning devotion which the greatest geniuses need. In place of those "sisters" who ministered to the other Apostles, God had given Paul the young Lycaonian, a pure, lofty, luminous soul, capable of understanding his apostolic fervor and of participating in his prodigious activity; and although the Apostle came to regard Titus more highly as a valiant worker in dangerous missions, it was Timothy whom he loved with deepest affection. The young man was to serve him better with his undying, fervent devotion than he could ever have with cold intellectual brilliance. He was to be the Apostle's consolation in the painful crises of his illness and in the manifold trials of the apostolate. He was to be his assistant, confidant, nurse and secretary, taking down his letters, carrying the packs on their journeys, attending him in prison and being imprisoned with him, watching at his bedside, always content in the knowledge that Providence had placed him by the side of so great a man. He was to give his master unfaltering devotion and unwavering friendship, which were only to be increased and made more sublime by their common toils and sufferings.

Timothy began his missionary career in Iconium, and from thence he went with Paul and Silas to Antioch in Pisidia. The party travelled swiftly, stopping only to inquire into the state of the community, to correct abuses, to encourage further advances, to plan future developments, and to read and comment on the Council's decree. On leaving Antioch they began to penetrate into unknown territory, Paul's objective being proconsular Asia Minor, a thoroughly Hellenized region dotted with rich, populous cities, traversed by wide, well-kept lines of communication, and abounding in Jewish colonies. There lay the powerful land of the territory of Ionia, noted for its literary and artistic traditions. Ephesus was the capital of this region which boasted many other great cities—Smyrna, Perga-mum, Hierapolis, Laodicea, Miletus, Sardis and Philadel-phia. A strategic and commercial highway linked the highlands of Pisidia and Lycaonia with these famous cities on the Aegean coasts, and it was natural that the three missionaries should follow this road which led to a country that had every appearance of being a fruitful field for the Gospel.

But suddenly the Holy Spirit forbade them "to speak the word in the province of Asia," and therefore they changed the direction of their journey, turning toward the north, where they preached in the land of the Phrygians. Arriving at Ancyra, one of the most important cities of Asia Minor and famed for its temple of Augustus, they found themselves in the center of the province of Galatia, the land of the "Great Mother," Cybele of the bloody and lewd rites, whose priests, the real arbiters of the region, mutilated themselves, and howled and danced around their goddess to the sound of cymbals. The abominable rites and supreme sovereignty of this goddess of germination and fruitful nature extended from the peaks of the Taurus Range to the shores of the Black Sea. In the hostelries, Paul and his companions had more than once met pilgrims who were travelling, bearing gifts and carrying their sick to Pessinus, the sacred city where the divinity was adored under the form of a black stone that had fallen from heaven. These pilgrims were dark-skinned Phrygians clad in ample tunics; or shepherds from the steppes of Pontus mounted on small, shaggy horses; or blue-eyed, fair-haired Galatians, the descendants of the restless hordes that had come from the lands of the Rivers Garonne and Seine and had reached the coasts of Asia Minor two centuries before the Roman conquest.

Paul addressed himself to these people who were simple, inquisitive, innately upright, and eager for thrills and novelties. In this central region there were few Jewish colonies, since it was rough territory, difficult of access, and so the missionaries did not need to employ the subtle argumentation of the synagogues or search the prophets for proofs of their teaching, as they were accustomed to do when preaching to their compatriots. Instead, in their addresses to the pagans, they stressed the darkening of religious consciousness and described the lowering of moral ideals. They tried to give their listeners a clear idea of Christ, who was at once God and man, endeavoring to make them understand the redeeming power of His sufferings and death; and they pointed out the necessity of repentance and of faith as the basis for the supernatural life and the essential condition for a happy immortality. These fundamental ideas were the foundations of Paul's teaching, the theme of his conversations along the roads and at the inns, and of his discourses in the streets and beneath the colonnades. Often, while the mule and camel drivers shouted at their animals in front of the wide gates of the hostelries or military posts, he would hang his rain-soaked mantle above the fire and, finding a seat among the travellers who clustered around the blaze, he would tell them the story of Christ's life, relating to his wide-eyed listeners the marvels of his Lord's spiritual kingdom, comparing the pure teaching of the Gospel with the shameful practices of the local religion which fostered and instigated all the works of the flesh and the fruits of death, "immorality, uncleanness, licentiousness, idolatry, witchcrafts, enmities, contentions, jealousies, anger, quarrels, factions, parties, envies, murders, drunkenness, carousings, and such like" (Gal. 5:19-21).

Constantly preaching and organizing groups of disciples, the three missionaries crossed the center of Anatolia to the desolate borders of Pontus, where they turned back, keeping to the north of the way they had come. In due course they arrived in the neighborhood of Dorylaeum, having crossed and recrossed the River Sangarius, and in front of them rose the imposing crest of the Asiatic Mount Olympus, towering above the fertile fields of Bithynia dotted with flourishing cities such as Nicea, Chalcedon, and Nicomedia, for which a glorious future was in store. But here again "the Spirit of Jesus" stopped them: heretofore He had only forbidden them to speak the word in the provinces of Asia, but now He would not let them even set foot in Bithynia.

Thus all roads except that which led to the West were closed to them, and Paul began to see that his voice was calling him toward Europe. Accordingly, the party set out across Mysia, a sparsely-inhabited region which had little to detain them. Passing near the great lakes, they reached the famed heights of Mount Ida, from which they could see for the first time the dark waters of the Aegean Sea. They were now in the Troas, on the plains of Ilium and the renowned banks of the Scamander River, which had been immortalized by their association with Hector and Achilles. This was the land through which Caesar and Alexander had passed, building temples, offering sacrifices and recalling legends as they went. But the ancient witnesses to Greek glory drew only indifferent glances from Paul and his companions as they hurried toward the port to set sail over unknown seas, wafted on their way by the breath of the Spirit.

Their point of embarkation was Troas, a new city which had replaced Ilium of the epic, and which had been favored with all kinds of privileges by the Roman emperors, who were, according to mythology, the descendants of Aeneas. Later on, Paul was to make it a center of apostolic forays, but now he came seeking only a ship to carry him and his companions to the West. But where were they to go? It seems certain that, from the time of his first missionary journey, his ambitious gaze had been directed toward all the Roman provinces that extended along the coasts of the Mediterranean from Syria to Macedonia and from the deserts of Arabia to the pillars of Hercules. His eyes always ranged high and far, for he never had the least doubt about Christianity's power of expansion. Inspired by profound faith and passionate love for Christ, he conceived great plans and almost incredible projects, and the only bounds which he set to his conquests were the limits of the world itself.

Now, as he rested from his long journey of almost two thousand miles, he weighed the advantages of the different courses open to him. On the other side of the Aegean Sea lay legendary Greece with all the glory of her history and literature, but neither the wonders of art nor the splendors of poetry had any great attraction for a man of action such as he. He was much more taken with the spirit of Rome, which was so like his own—enterprising, daring, yet with high ideals and deep love of order and liberty. The Roman legionaries had always impressed him with their discipline and contempt for death, and he ardently longed to convert the capital of the world. "I have often intended to come to see you . . ." he wrote in his Epistle to the Romans, "having had for many years a great desire to come to you" (Rom. 1:13; 15:23).

But again the Spirit of Jesus turned his steps elsewhere, and in a vision he received instructions where to preach the Gospel. One night he had an apparition of a young man clad in an ample cape and wearing a wide-brimmed hat, evidently the dress of the people beyond the sea. And sure enough, the young man addressed him, saying: "Come over into Macedonia and help us." The missionaries interpreted the vision as a manifestation of the divine will, and resolved to take the first ship sailing for Europe.

CHAPTER XIII

The Prison Gates Swing Wide

"So sailing from Troas, *we* ran a straight course to Samo-thrace, and the next day to Neapolis" (Acts 16:11). We know by this sudden use of the word "we" in the Acts that the author had joined the missionary group, so that now Paul had three companions: Silas, Timothy, and a Greek, "Luke, our most dear physician," as the Apostle later called him, a man of refinement and great culture, an upright and generous soul. In him Paul found a faithful friend and an ardent collaborator who was to remain all his life under the spell of the Apostle's personality. Luke had realized that the Gospel teaching satisfied all his ideals, and to it he consecrated his life, his reflective and observant tempera-ment, and his cultivated, graceful and marvellously concise literary style. He joined the mission band at Troas, and from there on he began to take part in the drama of the Acts of the Apostles. His meeting with Paul and the others was unpremeditated, since the missionaries had been guided to Troas by the divine plan. It has been said that Luke also had come from Antioch, perhaps by a different route. The historian Eusebius tells us only that the physician was in some way related to the Antiocheans. But if we examine the Acts of the Apostles closely, we find reason to suspect

182

that he also had some connection with the city of Philippi, and perhaps he was the Macedonian whom Paul saw in the dream which made him decide to leave the coasts of Asia Minor. At any rate, the hero and the historian joined forces at Troas, and from that moment on the narrative of the Acts becomes more vivid, more detailed and more animated.

The wind from the south filled the ship's sails, driving it straight for its destination. From now on we are told exactly what occurred on the party's voyages from one port to another, for Luke had the Greek feeling for the sea, a feeling which develops spontaneously on the coasts of the Aegean where the waters are so tempting, the winds so regular and the sunsets so glorious; where the surface of the sea is like oil, heavy and with a metallic glint, and so thick and dark in appearance that it seems to invite the traveller to walk upon it. Luke recorded nothing of their journeys by land, but once he set foot on a ship's deck, images crowded into his mind and words flowed from his pen. It was not nautical experience or skill as a sailor that made him so love the sea; rather it was an inborn attraction, a personal characteristic which he had inherited from his seafaring ancestors.

In those days sea journeys were very irregular, swift when the winds were favorable, interminably slow when they were contrary. On one occasion it took Paul five days to go from Troas to Neapolis (cf. Acts 20:6), but on this first voyage he had to spend only two days en route (16: 11). Toward evening on the first day, the vessel reached a point opposite the island of Samothrace, and since night travel along these coasts was dangerous, the captain decided to seek shelter in the lee of the island's mountains. Moreover, some of the passengers probably wanted to go ashore on the island, which was famous as the dwelling-place of the Cabiri, gods who were said to protect men against the anger of the waves, the poison of snakes, and the plague. Devotees thronged to this home of the gods to leave offerings in thanksgiving for having been saved from shipwreck, or they came to be initiated in the terrible mysteries that would give them immunity from harm. On the deck of the ship, where the poorer passengers spent the day, St. Paul undoubtedly heard his fellow-travellers speak about the marvels of the prophetic mountain, and when on the following morning the vessel weighed anchor and skirted the northern shore of the island, he could sense the presence of the devil in the sanctuary on the heights.

Finally the ship reached port and the small group of missionaries stepped ashore at Neapolis, nowadays called Kavalla. The seacoast town held little to interest the travellers; so they passed through it and, following the Egnatian Road, one of the principal highways of the Empire, arrived in Philippi after a little more than three hours' walk. This was the great city which they were seeking, "the principal city of a part of Macedonia, a Roman colony" (Acts 16:12), first made famous by the gold mines in the nearby mountains and later by the battle in which Octavius decisively defeated the republican army of Brutus. Since then, Philippi had become a colony of veterans proud of their privileges and their Western background; when Paul arrived, there were many Romans in the city, although the main body of the population was made up of the natives— a sober race, simple and somewhat lacking in culture, yet orderly and accustomed to hard work—descendants of the great warriors who had conquered the world under the leadership of Alexander the Great.

There were also Israelites in Philippi, but since there

were not enough of them to warrant a synagogue, they met for prayers and ablutions in an oratory outside the walls of the city near the River Gangites, amid gardens perfumed by roses with a hundred petals which had been brought from the nearby Pangaeus where, according to the legend, Dionysus had roamed with the nymphs and muses. After a few days of uncertainty, the missionaries learned of the existence of this Jewish *proseuché*, and, on the next Sabbath, they went there to preach the Gospel. They found only a few women praying and singing psalms; "and we sat down," writes St. Luke, "and spoke to the women who had gathered there" (Acts 16:13). The small congregation listened to them with respect, but there was one who believed immediately and was baptized with all her household. She was a "worshipper of God," a very good woman who had left her native land of Lydia to set up a shop in Philippi and who, consequently, was called "Lydia," "the woman from Lydia," or "the seller of purple" since, besides other cloths, she sold expensive purple material which she bought in her native city, Thyatira, famed in antiquity for the beauty of its fabrics. In Thyatira there was a large and long-established Jewish colony, and it was undoubtedly there that Lydia had learned about the Mosaic revelation and had become one of those Gentiles who feared God. Since she was a rich and generous woman, she said to Paul and his companions: "If you have judged me to be a believer in the Lord, come into my house and stay there," and at her insistence the missionaries took up their abode in her household.

Thus the establishment of the seller of purple became the first Christian church in Macedonia, where the converts met to break bread and celebrate the Banquet of fraternal love. Soon the newly-baptized were joined by other neophytes, such as Epaphroditus, whom Paul came to call "my brother and fellow-worker and fellow-soldier" (Phil. 2:25), and Clement, "[who] toiled with [him] in the gospel" (Phil. 4:3), and many others "whose names are in the book of life"—all upright, industrious Macedonians, descendants of the legionaries of Octavian and Antony, members of the Roman-Italian colony, so proud of their liberties that the Apostle thought it necessary to remind them that "our citizenship is in heaven from which also we eagerly await a Savior, our Lord Jesus Christ" (Phil. 3:20). And since the Jews there had little influence, the new community grew quietly, peacefully, and without hindrance, so that the *proseuché* was virtually turned into a Christian oratory.

But one day as the missionaries were walking to the place of prayer, they met a girl who began to follow them, crying out: "These men are servants of the most high God and they proclaim to you a way of salvation." They quickened their pace but the girl kept following them, repeating the same cry. This happened day after day, so that they could scarcely venture out without being assailed by the noisy homage. They concluded that the girl was a "pythoness" or fortune-teller possessed by a "divining spirit" which spoke through her, foretelling the future and revealing hidden things. Some pagans of the city had banded together to exploit these powers of hers, and they were deriving a sizeable income from the clients she attracted.

Paul was moved by the girl's unhappy state as a plaything of men and devils, and remembering what Christ had done on a similar occasion, he said to the spirit possessing her: "I order thee in the name of Jesus Christ to go out of her." The devil left her, and from that moment on she lost her prophetical powers, her influence over the crowds disappeared, and she could no longer speak wonders as she did before. As a result, people stopped coming to her to have their fortunes told, to ask her help in recovering things they had lost or to consult her about their affairs of the heart. Her masters were furious at the missionaries for cutting off their income, and seizing Paul and Silas, they dragged them into the market place to the tribunal of the Duumvirs. Since the law was very severe on sorcerers, it would have been useless for the profiteers to accuse their prisoners of having lessened the slave girl's value by casting out her devil. Instead, they cleverly accused Paul and Silas of sowing disorder in the city by preaching doctrines that were a danger to the security of the Empire. "These men," they said, "are . . . advocating practices which it is against the law for us to adopt or observe, since we are Romans." And they added slyly, "They are Jews," knowing full well that the universally-hated Jews were just then passing through a crisis in their relationship with the Empire, and that the Emperor Claudius had recently expelled them from Rome.

While these accusations were being made, a crowd of idlers and scoffers had gathered around the tribunal, hurling insults at the missionaries. The rabble caused such an uproar that the magistrates could scarcely make themselves heard, and they tore their garments in that unjudicial gesture for which Horace satirized the provincial judges. Then, without going through even a pretense of trial, without giving the accused a chance to defend themselves or proclaim their Roman citizenship, the Duumvirs called the lictors to scourge the prisoners. After the scourging, when their backs had been torn and flayed by the rods and their whole bodies covered with wounds and blood, the missionaries were thrown into the public jail which stood nearby, not far from the Egnatian Road which divided the city in two. Even today, in the midst of a heap of ruins— the shapeless remains of one of Alexander's imposing edifices—there are some pillars still standing to mark the site of these events.

Although lacerated and bleeding, Paul and Silas were radiant with joy as they were cast into prison. So jubilant were they that despite the unbreathably foul atmosphere and the scurrying rats and other vermin, they were still praying and singing hymns when midnight came. The prisoners in the cells above them were listening to them, unable to understand the cause of their rejoicing, when "suddenly there was such a great earthquake that the foundations of the prison were shaken" (Acts 16:26). The shaking of the walls caused the bars to fall from the doors and broke the stocks which held the captives. All the prisoners crowded out on to the stairway, and the jailer, who had been rudely awakened from sleep, drew his sword to kill himself when he saw that his charges, whom he was obliged to guard with his life, were escaping. But before he could plunge the blade into his breast, one of the prisoners stayed his hand by calling out commandingly: "Do thyself no harm, for we are all here." The jailer recognized the speaker as Paul, the Jewish preacher, and calling for lights, he fearfully entered the cells where he found none of the prisoners missing, although the doors were open, the walls split, and the fetters lying on the floor. No one could tell him what had happened, for everyone was half-stupefied with shock. Only Paul and Silas remained calm, and their composure in the face of such an upheaval so impressed the jailer that, bringing them out of the dungeon, he fell on his knees before them saying: " 'Sirs, what must I do to be saved?' And they said, 'Believe in the Lord Jesus, and thou shalt be saved, and thy household.' "

The jailer forthwith asked for baptism, and he and all his family were baptized at a nearby fountain. Full of joy and gratitude, the new converts cleansed the missionaries' wounds, transferred them from the underground cell and did all they could to serve them. In their happiness at having found the truth, the jailer and his family had no fear of what the magistrates could do to them, and they were quite willing to accompany their teachers to the dungeon if that were necessary. But fortunately, as it turned out, their kindness to the missionaries did not earn them punishment. When day came, a loud knocking was heard at the outer door, and the jailer went apprehensively to open it. On looking out, he found himself face to face with the lictors who had scourged the two preachers the day before, but he had nothing to fear, for they had come only to give him the curt message: "Let these men go."

No doubt the terrifying earthquake had made the magistrates reflect on the injustice they had done to the unfortunate strangers whom they had condemned and scourged without even the semblance of a trial. Perhaps Lydia had been at work, too, pleading the prisoners' innocence and telling the judges that the victims were Roman citizens. This piece of information must have filled the local government officials with panic: all unknowingly they had used the punishment of the rods against two representatives of the Empire's lawmakers; they had insulted the majesty of Rome, and if the prisoners complained to the proconsul, the consequences would be drastic for all connected with the crime.

When the jailer heard the lictors' message, he ran back into the house and told Paul and Silas: "The magistrates have sent word that you are to be released; now therefore come forth and go in peace." But Paul took a stand that was to be expected of a man of his noble and lofty character. Summoning the lictors to him, he said in a tone of severe condemnation: "They have beaten us publicly and without trial, although we are Romans, and have cast us into prison; and now are they going to put us out secretly? By no means, but let them come themselves and take us out."

The lictors departed, and it was not long before the magistrates arrived, ready to make what amends they could. Humbly they presented their excuses to the strangers and, leading them with every mark of honor out of the prison, they besought them to leave the city as soon as possible, lest they should cause more disturbances. Paul saw that their request was reasonable and agreed to accede to it, for he knew that after what had happened, his ministry in Philippi was at an end. However, he was comforted by the thought that the community of Christians was already well-organized and would continue to grow into a flourishing church. But before leaving he went to Lydia's house, where he found his disciples gathered. He consoled and reassured them, broke with them the Eucharistic Bread, and after giving them his last recommendations, set out with Silas. Timothy and Luke stayed with the fervent converts, who were to remain so faithful to their master's teaching that he called them his joy and his crown (cf. Phil. 4:1); many years later, from his prison in Rome, Paul testified to the fact that they had always obeyed his word and never ceased to be solicitous for him in all his needs.

CHAPTER XIV

As a Father Comforts His Children

Leaving Philippi at the request of the magistrates, the tireless traveller once more set out along the imperial highways. More than eight months had passed since he had left the coasts of Syria, and it was now toward the end of the year 51. During the spring and summer he had visited the cities of Asia Minor, then crossed to Europe at the beginning of autumn, and now he was heading for the south amid the fogs of winter and the cold Thracian winds. Accompanied by Silas, he passed under the triumphal arch that commemorated the battle in which the Triumvirs had wiped out the last representatives of the republican ideal. For the next five days they followed the Egnatian Road which ran near the seacoast; at the end of the first day they came to a large city, Amphipolis, but they decided to continue on without tarrying.

As the road unfolded before them, valley gave way to mountain and mountain to lagoon. At times the paved highway took them through pasture land; at times it plunged into thick forests. As they journeyed, they passed a tomb, set deep amid oak and plane trees, bearing the name

191

of Euripides the tragedian. Even if this monument had no significance for them, they were surely reminded, when passing through Stagira, of the philosopher of the *Organon* whose theories about matter and form were not unknown to Paul. When they reached Apollonia, the most important city on the Chalcidic peninsula, they did not pause because they wished to push on "to Thessalonica, where there was a synagogue of the Jews" (Acts 17:1).

Thessalonica had attracted the Jews because of its commerce, trade, industries and wealth, for since its founding by Cassander, the son of Antipater, who had named it after his wife, Thessalonica, it had been a trading center between East and West, a meeting place for religions and races, a halfway-house for the merchants, legionaries and prefects who were sent by Rome to the lands of Asia Minor. The Egnatian Road and the ships of the archipelago not only transported merchandise from city to city, but also spread ideas and new theories, and an echo raised in the Macedonian metropolis carried far. Thus, some months after he had left them, St. Paul could write to the Thessalonians: "From you the word of the Lord has been spread abroad, not only in Macedonia and Achaia, but in every place your faith in God has gone forth . . ." (1 Thess. 1:8). Of particular interest to Paul the craftsman was the fact that there were then many weavers in the city who made brilliantly-colored woolen rugs, as well as rough goat-hair cloth like that woven in Tarsus.

Today, Salonika is still a city full of life, as it was in the times of the Roman Empire, and on one of its bare, dark hills, it preserves a relic of St. Paul's visit, a simple oratory sheltered by a few trees. One winter's day, the two missionaries descended the hill to the city, having travelled more than ninety miles from Philippi. A Jew named Jason, perhaps an acquaintance of Paul's or Silas', generously offered them the hospitality of his home. They set to work immediately, preaching and teaching, and when Paul as usual attended the synagogue on the Sabbath, he was invited to speak. He "reasoned with them from the Scriptures, explaining and showing that the Christ had to suffer and rise from the dead, and that this is the Christ, even Jesus, whom I preach to you" (Acts 13:3). On the next two Sabbaths he again addressed them, using a similar approach and endeavoring to clear their minds of the idea of a conquering Messias, resembling a Roman emperor, which the rabbis tried to read into the Messianic prophecies. But his words were in vain, and only a few of his hearers asked to be baptized, while the rest grew so indignant at the thought of a mocked and crucified Redeemer that they would not allow the missionaries to return to the synagogue. Fortunately the two preachers had already made a very large number of converts among the proselytes and the religious-minded Gentiles. St. Luke makes particular mention of a select group of high-born women, and he also makes a similar reference when speaking of the other churches in Macedonia, for here women had more liberty and influence than in the other Hellenized regions. The number of converts increased daily, and they came, for the most part, from among the common people, the unlearned but honest artisans and weavers. Paul instructed them, "coming and going among them," walking through the gardens, passing along the streets and, above all, working in their houses, especially in the house of Jason, his host. In order not to be a burden to anyone, he toiled at the loom day and night to earn his living, so much so that, when his disciples at Philippi found out that he was in such need, they sent him alms on several occasions for his missionary projects. And while his hands were busy manipulating the carder and the shuttle, he spoke about Jesus, exhorting his fellow-workers, "entreating and comforting each one of [them], acting toward them like a father toward his children, declaring to [them] that [they] should walk worthily of God, who called [them] unto his kingdom and glory" (1 Thess. 2:11–12). In this intimate and homely way Paul won men to Christ.

The tenderness of a great soul has an almost irresistible charm, and when, as in the case of Paul, it is accompanied by daily self-sacrifice, its power of attraction cannot be withstood. In a voice that vibrated with a sacred passion, the Apostle urged his converts on to a life of heroism, to the desire to suffer and be persecuted for the sake of Christ. He created around him an atmosphere of holy democracy based on the charity of the Gospel. Although he did not encourage the ingenuous communism of the Church's early days in Jerusalem, he knew how, by example, to incline the hearts of the rich to the needs of the poor and to unite, in the celebration of the Mysteries, the humble, unlettered working people with the noble, cultured ladies whom he had taught to cherish the virtues of self-sacrifice and mercy.

His preaching was full of love for his disciples, but without flattery or coddling. He did not speak to them of theological subtleties, but taught them the basic truths of the Faith simply and clearly, condemning avarice and lust, teaching the commandments of Christ, and exhorting them to lead lives of virtue and fraternal charity. "This is the will of God, your sanctification," he would say to them; ". . . for God has not called you unto uncleanness, but unto holiness" (1 Thess. 4:3, 7). On few occasions in his life did the Apostle make more complete conquests than here in Thessalonica. He himself said later that they received his preaching not ". . . as the word of men, but, as it truly is, the word of God" (1 Thess. 2:13), and the seed he sowed among them bore such fruit that the church at Thessalonica grew and flourished, becoming rich in virtues, abundant in prophets, and favored with all kinds of heavenly gifts and wonderful works.

Thus several months passed in peace until the Jews, implacable in their hatred, judged that the right moment had come to strike at the missionaries. One day, Jason's house was surrounded by a ragged mob recruited from the idlers and cutthroats who are always to be found hanging about the streets in great seaports. This gang had been picked from the lowest quarters of the city, given money and told what to do. Fortunately Paul and Silas were not in the house, but the crowd seized Jason and some disciples who were with him, and with ear-piercing shouts they dragged them before the municipal dignitaries or politarchs, as they were called in Thessalonica, which was a free city within the Empire. When they reached the palace of justice the rabble cried out their accusations against the prisoners: "These men who are setting the world in an uproar have come here too . . . and they are all acting contrary to the decrees of Caesar, saying that there is another king, Jesus" (Acts 16:7).

The charge was a very serious one, for in those days the least word of disrespect for the ruler, even a gesture or the merest suspicion of disloyalty, easily became a capital crime. In his palace on the Aventine, Claudius, surrounded by eunuchs and plotting women, was nearing the end of his career, and everywhere people were asking themselves who would take over the reins of office when they fell from his nerveless hands. This was the atmosphere of intrigue and uncertainty which brooded over the land where Paul raised his disciples' hearts above worldly pre-occupations by saying to them: "Your real king is Jesus." A few declarations of this sort were seized upon by the Jews to be used as evidence of the missionaries' disloyalty to, and disrespect for, the Emperor.

Although the politarchs were impressed by the gravity of the charge, they did not act with the same haste as the magistrates at Philippi. The Roman governor's presence in the city heightened their zeal for the imperial dignity, but at the same time they did not fail to notice the violent bias of the accusers. And since the captive disciples were not the ringleaders of the alleged sedition, the judges contented themselves with demanding that Jason pay bail as a guarantee that he would keep the peace in the future. This was the most humane solution to the difficulty, as well as the most prudent; yet it made it impossible for Paul and Silas to remain in the city. The riot might break out again at any moment, the enemies of the Church would not balk at assassination if it were necessary, and the Christian community itself would be exposed to the danger of persecution. Therefore, at the urging of the brethren, the two missionaries resigned themselves to leaving Thessalonica. They set out by night for fear of the spies who lurked about Jason's house, and some of the disciples accompanied them to a safe place. This disruption of his plans was one of the most painful trials of St. Paul's apostolic career, and throughout his life his thoughts and his heart often turned longingly to that city where he had experienced so much consolation. Some months after his departure he wrote yearningly to the faithful Thessalonians: "We . . . have made more than ordinary efforts to hasten to see you, so great has been our desire. For we wanted to come to you—

I, Paul, more than once—but Satan hindered us" (1 Thess. 2:17–18). The guarantee given by Jason and the other leaders of the local church was to remain as a barrier between Paul and his spiritual children, and until the politarchs relinquished their office or changed their attitude, the gates of Thessalonica were to be closed to the Apostle.

After leaving the city, Paul, Silas and their companions headed for Beroea, an inland town, peaceful and industrious. Two days' journey brought them within sight of its flowering gardens with their plane trees and rosebushes, their fountains and waterfalls. Beyond the city soared Mount Olympus on whose summit dwelt the gods whom the approaching fugitive was to dethrone and destroy. There was a synagogue in Beroea, and although he well knew what usually happened when he preached to the Jews, Paul went there, for nothing could swerve him from his purpose. On this occasion, however, his tenacity was rewarded, and his compatriots received his teaching with admiration and agreement. It is true that they were at first surprised by the idea of a Messias without glory which the newcomer presented for their consideration, but being men of good will, they searched the Scriptures and held daily discussions, with the result that a large number of them opened their hearts to the Faith. In this they showed a nobility of soul which St. Paul did not find again among the members of his race, and which has been repeated but rarely in a history of twenty centuries. To this day, the sons of Israel remain obstinate in their blindness, refusing to acknowledge their redemption by the Man of Sorrow, the humble, peaceful and suffering Envoy of God, whom their prophecies foretold, described and praised. For, according to their crude interpretation of Scripture, the shadows and sorrows contained in their prophecies are only symbols and personifications of the calamities with which God will punish His people.

But in Beroea a large part of the Jewish colony asked for baptism, and their example was followed by the noblest and most prominent women of the city and by many of the pagans who were stifling in the demoralizing atmosphere of their idolatrous cults, for the gods of Olympus could no longer satisfy even their nearest adorers. However, in the midst of his great success, Paul received disquieting news from Thessalonica where a storm had broken out against the newly-formed church, plunging it into "persecutions and tribulations" (2 Thess. 1:4) that were to continue for a long time thereafter. The Jews' hatred had not died down, and they were the principal instigators of the persecution, as can be inferred from St. Paul's indictment: "The Jews . . . both killed the Lord Jesus and the prophets, and have persecuted us. They are displeasing to God, and are hostile to all men, because they hinder us from speaking to the Gentiles, that they may be saved. Thus they are always filling up the measure of their sins, for the wrath of God has come upon them to the utmost" (1 Thess. 2:15–16). By these words, the Apostle kept fresh the memory of the prophecy about the destruction of Jerusalem and the downfall of the whole Jewish nation in order to stir up the faith of the first Christians. At the same time, he consoled those who were being persecuted by showing them that opposition was the inseparable companion of the Christian life. "For you, brethren," he used to say to them, "have become imitators of the churches of God which are in Judea in Christ Jesus, in that you also have suffered the same things from your own countrymen as they have from the Jews . . ." (1 Thess. 2:14).

There were also internal difficulties in the church at

Thessalonica which caused the Apostle perhaps even more pain than the onslaught of persecution. In his preaching he had told his neophytes about Christ's prophecies regarding the end of the world, and since the time of his vision of the Lord on the road to Damascus, he had had a constant presentiment of the *parousia,* the second coming of Christ. He longed with all his heart for that momentous event which would make the world happy. "Come, Lord, Maranatha," were expressions which were frequently on his lips, and which he derived from the first Oriental churches. His most fervent wish was that the Lord Jesus would come "with the angels of his power," and in the splendor of His glory, "to be glorified in his saints" and to inflict well-deserved punishment on those who did not listen to the Gospel. (Cf. 2 Thess. 1:8-9.)

All the primitive churches were preoccupied with the second coming of Christ. The Roman world was being shaken by tragic terrors; madmen or imbeciles ruled the Empire; there was talk of comets, showers of blood, and the birth of monsters, and the infamies of the imperial palace sowed panic in men's hearts. Jews and Christians alike considered all these things as omens of a world-wide catastrophe or a great social revolution. Had not the Redeemer spoken clearly of His second coming? And after the clouds had closed behind Him as He ascended to heaven, had not the last words of the angels been an explicit reference to the *parousia:* "Jesus . . . will come in the same way as you have seen him going up to heaven" (Acts 1:11)? Therefore, the Christians who were suffering persecution could not understand why He delayed His return, and in the midst of their sorrow they would cry out: "How long, O Lord (holy and true), dost thou refrain from judging and from avenging our blood on those who dwell on this earth?" (Apoc. 6:10). And the seer of Patmos consoled them, saying: "Wait still a little while, until the number of your brothers be complete." (Cf. Apoc. 6:11.)

The faithful at Thessalonica were the most impatient of all for the second coming, and some of them wrongly interpreted the Apostle's words, either out of malice or false mysticism, disturbing their fellow Christians by saying that the world was going to come to an end any day. People began to ask themselves: "How will it happen? What will the resurrection of the dead be like? And how will the living be gathered before the Supreme Judge?" Such questions as these were discussed in the community assemblies, and not a few of the faithful came to the conclusion that if everything were going to be destroyed, it was a waste of time to work. Under the pretext of praying as recommended in the Gospel, many of the workers in the cloth industry and on the docks gave themselves over to spurious mysticism, gossiping, idleness and begging.

About the same time that St. Paul heard the first rumors of these internal disturbances in the church, a group of Jews appeared in Beroea, sent from Thessalonica to hinder the preaching of the Gospel. The newcomers used the methods that had achieved such good results for them in the metropolis—that is, they represented the Apostle as an enemy of Caesar, and they paid the rabble to stir up trouble. The magistrates intervened, using perhaps the same procedure as had their counterparts in Thessalonica, and Paul had no other course but to leave the city. Since the Jews' hatred was focused on him alone, he was able to allow Silas to remain, and also Timothy, who had just come from Philippi. Then, accompanied by a few disciples, he set out in secret to cover the twenty miles between Beroea and the coast.

CHAPTER XV

The Unknown God

The tumult at Beroea forced Paul to leave Macedonia and made it clear that, at the instigation of the agitators from Thessalonica, all the synagogues in that region were plotting and intriguing against him. Hitherto Silas and Timothy had been at his side, but circumstances permitted them to remain in Beroea while he alone had the privilege of being the object of the violent hatred of the Macedonian Jews. After leaving Beroea, he turned south to the land of Hellas, so renowned for its thinkers and artists. He followed the plan of penetration which he had used from the beginning of his apostolate, and like a wise campaigner did not stop to conquer each little village he came to, but pressed on to gain the strongholds and thus win the whole country. He concentrated on the strategic points, the busiest seaports and the cities along the great commercial routes, so that by lighting the beacon of faith on the highest peaks he would be able to illuminate the surrounding territory.

In St. Paul's time, Athens, the city of Pericles, was still the intellectual center of the world, although it had lost its political importance centuries before and had ceased also to beget philosophers and to produce artists and poets. Yet it remained a city of beauty, a mecca for travellers, an

201

emblem of the glorious past and a university center through which all the distinguished young men of the Empire had to pass before finishing their careers. Vergil and Cicero, Atticus and Pompey, Caesar and Varro had walked the streets of Athens and had steeped themselves in her philosophy and poetry. These and many others, famous and obscure, came to admire and recall the grandeur of the past, to enrich their minds with the beautiful national myths and to feast their eyes on the masterpieces with which generations of artists had embellished the streets, the gardens, the market places and the sanctuaries. In the city too, there was a swarm of grammarians, rhetoricians and masters of subtle argument who called themselves philosophers.

After a week's sailing over the sea where the Athenian fleets had made famous the names of Marathon and Salamina, the Apostle landed at Piraeus and took leave of the disciples from Beroea who had accompanied him on the voyage. For the first time in his long years as a missionary, he was without a companion to share his thoughts and trials. He was alone in a city given over to the enjoyment of beauty, to the mad pursuit of pleasure and the mental gymnastics of subtle argument. But, intent on becoming all things to all men in order to gain all, he set himself to win the Athenians by meeting them on their own ground, and the part of the Acts which St. Luke devotes to this, the culminating point of St. Paul's second missionary journey, lets us see the Apostle in a light that is genuinely Attic in its delicacy and clarity. Paul summed up his surroundings and put himself in harmony with them with that facility for adapting himself to circumstances which was one of the characteristics of his genius. His doctrine was always the same, but he did not teach it in the same way to both Jews and pagans, nor was he going to approach the pagans of

Athens as he had those in Lystra. Although he was of a passionate temperament, he knew how to restrain his impulses and to hold in check his Jewish prejudices, and when he faced the Athenian philosophers he did not adopt the contentious attitude which his successors, the apologists of the second century, used to such good effect. Instead, he followed the line of conduct which he prescribed for his disciples in these noble words: "Walk in wisdom as regards outsiders, making the most of your time. Let your speech, while always attractive, be seasoned with salt, that you may know how you ought to answer each one" (Col. 4:5-6). One may say that this method of procedure made "Attic salt" a part of the Christian ethic, and that courtesy and good manners came to be classified thenceforth as an important part of the religious life. When writing to the Philippians, St. Paul expressed this thought in an even more exquisite form when he said: "For the rest, brethren, whatever things are true, whatever honorable, whatever just, whatever holy, whatever lovable, whatever of good repute, if there be any virtue, if anything worthy of praise, think upon these things"—observe them, imitate them wherever they are found (Phil. 4:8-9).

That was to be his strategy in the capital of the Hellenic world, although what he saw there filled him with repugnance and disgust. As St. Luke expressly says: "He was exasperated to see how the city was wholly given to idolatry" (Acts 17:16). Never before had he realized more clearly how great was the influence of paganism on souls. Here were the most intelligent people on earth, who had penetrated farthest into the truths of theodicy, and yet they, more than any other race, were dominated by the spell of their idols, those works of art which shone with the magic light of irresistible beauty. The imposing mass of the

Acropolis rose commandingly above the city, and on its summit the columns of the Parthenon seemed to come to life when the sun rose out of the sea. Some dazzling, vibrant emanation, like the air that quivers at the tip of a flame, seemed to radiate from the sacred hill, giving strangers the feeling that they were looking upon immortal things.

But what delighted and moved other visitors only filled the Apostle with pain and horror. No doubt he, too, was approached by idlers who offered to show him for a drachma the temple of Asklepios and the Sarmatian breastplate which was said to be made of horsehide; or the statue of Athena Polias, that masterpiece from the chisel of Phidias, and near it an ancient chair, the work of Daedalus; or the Persian cavalry leader's sword which was kept in the Temple of Victory. And although he indignantly rejected the guide's services, he could not escape seeing the temples, shrines, votive-offerings, monuments, and the statues of gods, goddesses, heroes, satyrs and cyclopes. The innumerable false deities, beautiful and serene, reigned in every porch, every sanctuary, and on every street corner, so that Petronius, writing a few years after Paul's visit to the city, could say that in Athens it was easier to meet the immortals than it was to meet men. Of what interest to the Apostle were harmony of line or grace of form or the splendors of chiselled marble, when they all signified only a sacrilegious usurpation of the glory due to the God who had sent him to Greece? Later he was able to say: ". . . the Greeks look for 'wisdom'; but we, for our part, preach a crucified Christ—to the Jews indeed a stumbling-block and to the Gentiles foolishness, but to those who are called, both Jews and Greeks, Christ, the power of God and the wisdom of God" (1 Cor. 1:22-24).

He suffered the same disenchantment when he turned

from the temples and statues to the people themselves, so celebrated for their genius and vivacity. The inhabitants of the city were certainly intelligent and high-spirited, but they were also giddy and fickle-minded, brilliant but superficial, more boastful than patriotic, more restless than vigorous. They had an inordinate love of pageants and spectacular displays; they were passionately fond of beautiful speeches. The majority of the citizens spent their time seated in the *agora* or walking beneath the colonnades, confronting strangers, discussing the news or laughing at the latest novelty. As in the time of Demosthenes, "What is the news?" was the formula which occurred in every conversation. Exterior devotion had replaced true religious feeling, and it was only because of their love of statuary that the Athenians could pride themselves on not having forgotten any of their gods, even the humblest and most obscure. One day, walking through the city and out along the road which led through plane trees and rosebushes to the ancient port of Munychia, Paul came upon an altar which interested him more than any other religious monument in Athens because of the dedication written upon it: "To the Unknown God." The discovery gave him plenty of food for thought and he was not long in taking advantage of his find. At last he saw a ray of hope; all the city's temples and statues had been erected to gods which the citizens had made to their own image and likeness; the effigies of the gods were only frail human symbols of the forces of nature, incarnations of man's passions and instincts, personifications of power and pleasure. But by erecting this altar, they had perhaps meant to honor the one perfect God envisaged by some of their sages, the Infinite and Merciful God whom Paul had come to reveal to them.

Despite the discouragement which had been weighing

on him since he set foot in this region, he had now found some reasons for confidence. As usual, he had already begun to speak at the meetings of the Jews and the "worshippers of God," but these first audiences remained deaf to his call, neither agreeing with him nor opposing him, but displaying complete indifference, an attitude that pained him far more than outright hostility. Even the synagogue seemed to have been tainted by the frivolous spirit that reigned in the city.

While he was trying to gain a footing in the synagogue, he also made it a point to enter into conversation with the people who swarmed in the *agora* at all hours of the day. There he found idlers strolling around, rhetoricians holding forth, and philosophers peddling their knowledge; he rubbed shoulders with magistrates and common citizens alike, for the *agora* was a center of exchange for ideas and news, as well as a market place for goods. Amid the stalls of flowers, perfumes and books, amid the shouts of the slave-traders, of vendors selling figs from Caria, oysters from Chios, or honey from Mount Hymettus, poets recited their verses and teachers expounded their doctrines. One teacher, calling himself a disciple of Plato, would be explaining his fantastic theories about the transmigration of souls, the expiations of Hades and rebirth into a higher world; while another pedagogue, a disciple of the Stoics, would be speaking of the mysterious force which exists in nature as an essential condition of matter and which gives every object its unity, activity and form; still another preceptor, a supporter of Epicurus, would be presenting his philosophy of pleasure, saying that it was to be sought prudently, following one's natural instincts, but moderately and without abuse since excess begot pain, destroyed the balance and disturbed that tranquillity of the soul which was to be deemed the most secure of pleasures. Here in

Athens, as at Rome and Tarsus, the Stoics and the Epicureans were predominant, and although the one party was entrenched in brutal egoism and the other sunk in gross materialism, they continued to argue with each other, using refined subtlety and poisoned words.

Paul made it his business to mingle with each of these parties in turn, joining in their discussions and expounding his doctrine at every opportunity. In the city of Socrates, who still lived on in his philosophy, the disciple of the rabbis became a follower of the philosopher. He understood the special psychology of his listeners and tried to present the Gospel in its most luminous and joyous form. He spoke of Christ, certainly, but he laid more stress on the glory of His Resurrection than on His humiliation. However, the word "resurrection"—*anastasis*—confused his listeners, for they thought that he was referring to some goddess who had to be adored along with Christ, and they imagined that he was the champion of a new pair of divinities like Zeus and Hera, or Isis and Osiris. At first they listened curiously, diverted by the sight of the strange Jew striving with quick gestures and ardent speech to reveal some new secret of the Orient. But when they wrongly concluded that the newcomer was trying to add another god to their Pantheon, they shook their heads mockingly and strolled away saying: "He is a herald of strange gods. He is announcing the coming of Jesus and Anastasis." Others laughed at him and called him a "spermalogue," that is, a gatherer of seeds, meaning thereby that he was a parasite, a hanger-on, and they compared him to the sparrow, that impertinent, tenacious and importunate bird which hops about, feeding on the crumbs of food dropped by passers-by. Paul continued to walk through the market place looking for the men of good will who had been

destined to believe. But his words fell on deaf ears, because
the Athenians' habit of constantly listening to all the
rhetoricians, charlatans and theorists who flocked to their
city had left in them a deposit of skepticism and fickleness
that prevented them from hearing the voice from heaven
now ringing out above the babbling of their sophists.

Nevertheless, the Apostle did not relax his efforts, and
one day he found a group of serious-minded people who
listened attentively to him. "And they took him," says St.
Luke, "and brought him to the Areopagus, saying, 'May
we know just what this new doctrine taught by thee is?
For thou bringest some strange things to our ears: we wish
therefore to know what these things mean'" (Acts 17:19–
20). These men were disciples of Zeno and Epicurus, professors of the university who wished to test the foreign
philosopher's ability to argue with them, thinking that he
was one of the many ambitious intellectuals who were continually flocking to the great cultural center in search of
fame and fortune. They were interested in him because
they were curious about, and also somewhat suspicious of,
his new teaching. Hence they brought him to the council
of the Areopagus, whose function was to watch over public
teaching, approve professors, and ensure the education of
youth. It was the Areopagus which, at Cicero's request,
issued a decree inviting Cratippus, the peripatetic philosopher, to give classes in Athens; and Quintillian speaks
of a young man condemned by the same assembly for
amusing himself by putting out the eyes of quail.

Although Paul was not seeking titles or degrees from
the council, the invitation gave him a wonderful opportunity for preaching Christ before the cream of Athenian
society in the very place where, according to the legend,
the gods had gathered to pass judgment on Ares. Therefore

he willingly accompanied his questioners up the marble stairway which leads from the *agora* to the hill of Ares in the western part of the Acropolis. A noisy crowd fell in behind them, eager for a feast of words and looking forward to being entertained by brilliant imagery, refined style, well-rounded phrases and subtle word-play. The Areopagites, the most noted men in the city, were already in their seats carved out of the rock, which they occupied in accordance with the age-old tradition of the great tribunal. Paul was placed in the middle of the semi-circle formed by the members' seats, and all eyes were turned expectantly on him. Before him rose the majestic columns of the Parthenon, and on either side stood other world-famed temples and monuments: the Erechtheion, the Propylaeum, the sanctuary of Themis the avenger; in the background lay the city with the most illustrious literary history of any in the world; and, farther off, was the glinting sea and the dark outline of the mountains: the sharp spur of the Pnyx, the pointed summit of Mount Lycabettus, and the elongated crest of the Hymettus, rich with the scent of thyme and marjoram.

The immortal name of Christ, the Conqueror of Olympus and the Parthenon, was about to ring out solemnly across the memorials of the dead gods, in the presence of those whom Euripides called the "happy sons of Erechtheus who walked in a pure atmosphere full of sweetness and light." "Men of Athens," began Paul in a powerful voice that carried to the multitudes gathered at the foot of the hill and in the porches of the temples, "I see that in every respect you are extremely religious. For as I was going about and observing objects of your worship, I found also an altar with this inscription: 'To the Unknown God.'

What therefore you worship in ignorance, that I proclaim to you."

Paul's introduction of his subject was very skillful. His opening words caused a murmur of curiosity among the crowd, and his allusion to the citizens' religious-mindedness was both praise and irony, for the word which he used meant "superstitious" as well as "devout." His reference to the altar of the Unknown God with which both Greeks and Romans tried to attract the benevolence and protection of the unrecognized deities, was also designed to catch the audience's attention. His whole speech was a marvel of rhetorical elegance in the exact sense of the word, elegant in the novelty, clarity, precision, and swift flow of expression and thought—all intended to produce a maximum effect with a minimum of words. Surely the pagan philosopher Longinus had this famous oration in mind when he placed Paul of Tarsus among the greatest orators of Greece.

The crowd was hanging on the Apostle's words, eagerly awaiting the solution to the mystery of the Unknown God. "God, who made the world and all that is in it, since he is Lord of heaven and earth, does not dwell in temples built by hands; neither is he served by human hands as though he were in need of anything, since it is he who gives to all men life and breath and all things."

The audience was not pleased to hear this line of argument, for they were proud of their temples and statues; but the ambassador of Christ was compelled to preach the truth to them, whether it was palatable or not. He set forth his doctrine in the clear, logical language that the cultured Greeks best understood, and although, later on, he was to include idolatry in the anathema which he launched when writing to the Romans, now in the Areopagus his phrases were more gentle, more veiled and less vehement. He did not dwell on the proof of the existence of a supreme God, since, thanks to the influence of the Neo-Platonists, it was already known, at least theoretically, in almost all the Greek schools. Instead, noticing that there was a large number of Stoics and Epicureans in his audience, he stressed the dogma of Providence which both of these philosophical schools distorted. And speaking of the nature of God and our relationship to Him, he added: "From one man he created the whole human race and made them live all over the face of the earth, determining their appointed times and the boundaries of their lands; that they should seek God, and perhaps grope after him and find him, though he is not far away from any one of us. For in him we live and move and have our being, as indeed some of your own poets have said, 'For we are also his offspring.' "

Here were more truths bound to wound the Athenians' pride. Unlike the pagan accounts of creation, the doctrine of unity of the human race would make the Greek and barbarian equal, erasing all difference between men. There is one God who watches over all peoples, dividing them into groups by means of rivers and mountains, and maintaining the rhythm of the seasons that produce prosperity and fruitfulness: this was the view of Providence which Paul placed before them. The God who was unknown to the Greeks, despite the fame of their wise men, is within reach of human reason. We must seek Him, and it is possible for us to know Him, since He is in us and we are in Him: even the Stoics used similar terms, although they tended to fall into pantheism. We are in Him, not only because we are lost in His immensity, but because He is the Efficient Cause that infuses life, movement and being into us at every moment of our existence. The Greek poets had said that we are His offspring, made in His image and likeness, and although neither Aratus in his *Phenomena* nor Cleanthes in his hymn to Jupiter used this expression in the same sense as Paul, their words did contain a profound truth. Having presented God's immensity reflected in His sovereign dominion over heaven and earth, the orator went on to deduce His spirituality from His being the exemplary cause of man: "If therefore we are the offspring of God, we ought not to imagine that the Divinity is like to gold or silver or stone, to an image graven by human art and thought."

In spite of their audacity and originality, all these considerations fell within the field of philosophy, and although they were opposed to the listeners' ideas as symbolized in the Pantheon, they were received with respectful silence. But it was difficult, not to say impossible, to expect such an audience to listen without protest to the exposition of the basic concepts of the Gospel, which was precisely the principal object of the discourse. In fact, Paul was able to set forth only the beginning of his argument when he was forced to leave it incomplete for all time. First he said a few words which must have grated on the ears of those gathered at the very feet of Pallas Athena in a citadel of intellectual tradition: "The times of this ignorance God has it is true overlooked"—the times of Solon, Thales of Miletus, Epicurus, Zeno, Socrates and Aristotle! What was this Jewish nonentity going to say that these great teachers had not already said? The listeners stirred restlessly and looked at each other in astonishment when the speaker thus cast a slur on the very philosophers of whom he himself had reminded them, if not by his elegant style, at least by his great originality and unusual command of language. They had been very favorably impressed by his reference to their poets, and by his use of the technical expressions which they themselves employed in their discussions and polytheistic rituals. Undoubtedly the pantheists of the Stoa were glad to hear a declaration such as: "In Him we live and move and have our being." The term "the Divinity" must have appealed to the Athenians too, because their philosophers and poets used it to express their vague, confused concept of the superior and transcendent nature of God. Paul had used these words, certainly, but he had given them a different meaning, filling them with precision and clarity and the riches of the spirit of Christ.

However, the audience's attitude had quickly changed. If they had understood aright, this stranger had called them ignorant people—they who were the teachers of the world's conquerors! Some of them laughed mockingly at what they considered the speaker's insolence, while others gave vent to their anger in biting, disdainful words. Yet they still seemed disposed to listen to the great revelation which had been unknown to the founders of their schools. And what was that revelation? That they would have to blot out the past and on bended knees humbly confess the depths of their ignorance! "The times of this ignorance God has it is true overlooked, but now he calls upon all men everywhere to repent; inasmuch as he has fixed a day on which he will judge the world with justice by a Man whom he has appointed, and whom he has guaranteed to all by raising him from the dead" (Acts 17:30-31).

Paul did not wish, just yet, to pronounce the name of Jesus or to call Him God, believing perhaps that in this way he would retain the good will of his listeners. But his last words, so familiar to us after twenty centuries of Christianity, raised a storm of protest, mockery and insults among the Athenians. They thought his allusions to resurrection and the last judgment unworthy of a philosopher, although some of them may have recalled that the great Plato himself had said that a dead fly would return to life if a handful of ashes were thrown over it. However, in general, they regretted having made so much of the Jewish dreamer, and now raised such an uproar that they drowned out Paul's words. Some of them stood up in their places, others made their way back to the *agora*, while a few, less boorish than the rest, overcame their disappointment sufficiently to remark to Paul, not without irony: "We will hear thee again on this matter."

The whole spirit of Athens was opposed to the religion of Christ. Art, beauty and the joy of living were what mattered most to the Athenians, and they had no wish to hear about the beatitudes of the Gospel or the happiness of the next life. It was useless to speak about the kingdom of heaven to these people who had made their own heaven on earth, and it would be absurd to preach about the divine beauty of a scourged and crucified God in a place where the greatest philosophers had said that one should adore any man who possessed the beauty that was reflected in Phidias' statues. Ever since his first entry into Greece, Paul had felt himself oppressed by a growing weight of despair, and after his reception at the Areopagus, he found he could no longer bear with the Athenians' frivolity, light-mindedness and incapability of attending to the serious and profound aspect of life. Accordingly, he set out alone from Athens, having spent scarcely a month in the city. Timothy had recently arrived with the disquieting news that the Jews in Thessalonica were still persecuting the faithful, and the Apostle had had to send him back to comfort and strengthen the sufferers. Paul's heart ached for the persecuted brethren, and later he wrote to them: "When I could bear it no longer I sent in order to know your faith, lest perhaps the tempter might have tempted you, and our labor might come to naught" (1 Thess. 3:5). As a result of his work in Athens, he could count only a small group of neophytes, among whom was a member of the Areopagus called Dionysius who later became the first bishop of the city, and a woman named Damaris who may well have been a distinguished and cultured courtesan, for in the city of Aspasia, it would have been difficult for a lady of good position to have found an opportunity to hear the Apostle.

CHAPTER XVI

Conflicts Without, Anxieties Within

"After this," writes St. Luke, "[Paul] departed from Athens and came to Corinth" (Acts 18:1). The Apostle passed along beside the purifying waters of the Ilissus, skirted the walls of Eleusis, famed for its mysteries, and went by Megara; or it may be that he took ship at the wharves of Piraeus and sailed across the Saronic Gulf, on his way to another of the great cosmopolitan centers of the Roman Empire. As he approached the city, he could make out the eminence crowned by the citadel which was no longer the breeding ground of warlike arrogance that it had been two centuries before, when its defenders had thrown filth on the envoys of Rome. Now it was the scene of ritual prostitution and mystical orgies in the temple on the hill where the citizens adored their patroness, Aphrodite Pandemos, the personification of all man's bestial instincts. This temple was served and the worshippers welcomed by thousands of priestesses who were so skilled in robbing the pilgrims that artists and poets depicted them as having the fangs of a lion and the claws of an eagle. Many devotees lost all their money there, and as a result the people along the coasts of the Mediterranean had a saying: "Not everyone can go to Corinth." Not everyone could come to Corinth, but many who could afford it did so—illustrious patricians, wealthy pilgrims, rich travellers from the Tiber and the Nile, and young thrill-seekers eager to enjoy the excitement of the city's sports which were held every two years under the title of "The Isthmian Games," and which were to make a deep and lasting impression on the mind of the stranger from Tarsus.

Corinth was not only a city of pleasure, but also a wealthy trading center, and although it had been completely destroyed during the Greeks' last fight for independence in 146 B.C., it had been rebuilt and had come to rival Alexandria. Caesar favored it with his protection, and Marcus Tullius called it "the luminary of all Greece." Motley hordes of colonists, freedmen, soldiers, artisans, sailors and gladiators had poured into the city to form its turbulent, hybrid population. It was a meeting ground for East and West—one head, as it were, with two restless and powerful arms, the two seaports, Cenchreae which overlooked the Asiatic sea, and Lecheum, where ships from Italy and Spain dropped anchor. Five hundred thousand slaves toiled in and around the city, transporting cargoes from the ports, rowing the innumerable barges, making the renowned Corinthian amphoras for which the Roman senators paid exorbitant prices, and fashioning the reddish ingots of Corinth's famed bronze, which were exported for the decoration of beautiful houses all over the Empire. Softly caressed by its surrounding sea and under the indulgent smile of its own goddess, Corinth worked, gathered in treasure, amused itself and played at dice.

As Paul entered the city, he was full of hope, for the power of Mammon and the demons of the flesh seemed less to be feared than the pedantic pride of false knowledge he had faced in Athens. As usual, he went seeking lodgings in the Jewish quarter, and there he met a married couple who offered him the most generous hospitality. The husband's name was Aquila and the wife's Priscilla; they were natives of Pontus and were engaged in tent-making, being members of that class of wandering craftsmen who went from city to city as trade dictated. We shall meet them again in Ephesus, from whence they ultimately returned to Corinth to set up business once more in that district. When Paul first met them they had come from Rome, where the Emperor Claudius had issued a decree forcing the Jews to leave. As Suetonius puts it: "Claudius drove from Rome the Jews who were continually agitating the city at the instigation of Christ." In the capital of the Empire there had been a repetition of the events at Antioch, Antioch in Pisidia, Thessalonica and all the cities where a church had sprung up despite the synagogue. The Jews of Rome had been angered by the new religion and their attempts to destroy the Church had broken the peace of the city, with the result that they had brought down the Emperor's wrath upon themselves and not upon the Christians. It is true that opposition to the name of Christ had been the cause of the conflict, but the historian Suetonius mistakenly thought that the Savior was an agitator who was sowing discord in the Roman ghetto.

When Aquila and Priscilla had arrived at Corinth from Rome, they had rented a house and set up their business. They could not have been working there more than three or four months when the Apostle came to their door seeking hospitality and finding not only a warm welcome but employment in a Christian household, for it seems that the couple had already been baptized in Rome. They were devout followers of Christ and were to figure among the most self-sacrificing members of the primitive Church. When writing to the Romans in later years, Paul penned this magnificent eulogy of them: "Greet Prisca and Aquila, my helpers in Christ Jesus, who for my life had risked their own necks. To them not only I give thanks but also all the churches of the Gentiles" (Rom. 16:3-4).

The Apostle became a worker in Aquila's establishment, for although his host wished to spare him toil and material preoccupations, he did not want to be given privileges or be exempted from labor. Untiringly and industriously he worked day and night, as he said himself, in order not to owe anything to anyone. Rather than live in the midst of plenty, he preferred to suffer hunger and thirst and wear old, patched garments, as was often to happen during his stay in Corinth. Every Saturday he went to the synagogue where he spoke with his compatriots, "bringing in the name of the Lord Jesus and try(ing) to convince Jews and Greeks," and although he was in a sophisticated Greek city, the seat of the proconsul of Achaia, his preaching was austere and simple.

As a result of his experience in Athens, he had resolved to approach his audiences not with beautiful speeches or the trappings of eloquence and human wisdom, but with a simple explanation of the Gospel teachings. He himself later wrote to the Corinthians: ". . . when I came to you . . . I determined not to know anything among you, except Jesus Christ and him crucified" (1 Cor. 2:1-2). This method of presentation produced very heartening results, but as conversions increased, opposition to the Church began to grow. After a few weeks Paul could no longer speak in the synagogues, because the moment he mentioned the name of Christ a storm of insults and blasphemies would break out, drowning out his words and obliging him to stop preaching. On one such occasion, before he left the speaker's rostrum, he shook his cloak over the blasphemers and pronounced these fearful parting words: "Your blood be upon your own heads; I am innocent of it. Henceforth I will go to the Gentiles" (Acts 18:6).

It happened that near the synagogue there lived a Latin proselyte named Titus Justus, and it was in this man's house that Paul established the first sanctuary in Corinth. Here he offered the Sacred Mysteries and preached whenever he was free from his manual labor in Aquila's workshop. After he had spent some time in Corinth, however, Silas and Timothy came from Macedonia to join him, bringing alms from the churches there, so that he was able to devote more of his time to the instruction of the catechumens. In St. Luke's vivid phrase: "He was possessed by the word."

God was showering His blessings on the Apostle's work, for when Paul turned his back on his compatriots in the synagogue many Jews followed him, among them Crispus, the leader of the synagogue, who was baptized with all his household. The converts increased in number daily and were drawn from all classes of society, rich and poor, Roman colonists and people from the poorest sections of the city. Later, their teacher was to tell them frankly that their ranks had contained fornicators, idolaters, adulterers, effeminates, sodomites, thieves, the covetous, drunkards, the evil-tongued and the greedy. "But," he added, "you have been washed, you have been sanctified, you have been justified in the name of our Lord Jesus Christ" (1 Cor. 6:9–12). Apart from some persons of distinction, the new-born community was composed mainly of slaves, the poor and humble of birth, lacking in power, riches, nobility and learning. (Cf. 1 Cor. 7:21; 11:30; 12:13.) Among the new

Christians were Tertius, who was St. Paul's secretary when he wrote the Epistle to the Romans; Chloe, a rich matron who owned important business establishments in Ephesus and Corinth; and Phoebe, the servant of the Church, the first of the deaconesses, who, as the Apostle wrote, "has assisted many, including myself" (Rom. 16:2). He taught this varied assembly of converts to live in fraternal harmony, and he brought together the leader of the synagogue, Crispus, the wealthy Jews, the ladies of rank, the shopkeepers and the dock-workers for the weekly Breaking of Bread, preceded by the *Agapé,* or love-feast. All felt themselves dominated by his energy, his faith, his abounding charity, and the marvellous gifts with which God had favored him—the ability to read hearts, the power of working miracles and of looking into the future.

But there was yet a new storm brewing around him. The Jews of Corinth were as vengeful as those of Thessalonica, and their anger was fanned to white heat by the success of his preaching, which was disorganizing the synagogue, winning over their proselytes and robbing them of the best of their fellow-Israelites. Consumed with envy, they did their utmost to destroy his work by undermining his prestige with intrigue and calumny, calling him a sower of discord, an enemy of peace and a deceiver of simple women. To his external battles were added bodily sufferings, the "thorn for the flesh," that chronic illness brought back and aggravated by the Corinthian summer which was so oppressive, enervating and injurious to those suffering from fever. In consequence, a wave of sadness engulfed the Apostle's great heart: "I was . . . in weakness and in fear and in much trembling" (1 Cor. 2:3). He was already contemplating leaving the field of battle and had almost made up his mind to seek a new country wherein to preach the Gospel when one night, as he was at prayer and weighed down with discouragement, he heard the Lord saying to him: "Do not fear, but speak and do not keep silence; because I am with thee, and no one shall attack thee or injure thee, for I have many people in this city" (Acts 18:9-10). Heartened by these words, he threw himself into his work with renewed energy, and remained in Corinth "a year and six months, teaching the word of God among them." Not only that, but he extended his activities to the seaports, to the city of Argos, famed in the Greek epic, and to other parts of the surrounding country. His disciples grew into the large and enthusiastic group of "the saints that are in the whole of Achaia," a closely-knit union of "the churches of God" animated by the same breath of life (2 Cor. 1:1; 2 Thess. 1:4).

While he was working in Corinth, Paul's thoughts often turned toward the north and the cities of Macedonia, where he had founded churches the year before. He was especially concerned about the church in Thessalonica, so long and sorely tried by the persecution of the Jews. Timothy and Silas had just brought him the consoling news that the Thessalonian converts were facing the tempest of hatred without shrinking and that their faith was admirable, their constancy unswerving, their fervor exemplary and their fraternal charity without blemish. Such a glowing account filled the Apostle with joy and caused his heart to pour out a canticle of thanksgiving and a flood of tenderness in the document we know as the First Epistle to the Thessalonians —the second of those wonderful letters which, better than any historian's narrative, preserve for us his vigor of mind and his depth of feeling. How sweet and full of grace are the words which his love inspired him to write in this moving letter to his disciples! Here we see him as a father exhorting and encouraging each of his sons, and showing the tenderness of a mother caressing her beloved children. He had already given his cherished neophytes truth and happiness, but he wished to give them all he had, placing his very life and soul at their disposal. "We live, if you stand fast in the Lord. For what thanks can we return to God for you for all the joys wherewith we rejoice for your sakes before our God?" (1 Thess. 3:9–10).

In addition to the persecution of the Jews, the Thessalonian Christians were beset by inner disquiet as regards the fate of their dead and the second coming of Christ. It is an undeniable fact that the Christians of the Apostolic age lived under the continual impression that the world was liable to end at any moment, and even St. Peter felt obliged to justify the Savior's delay in reappearing. (Cf. 2 Pet. 3:9.) Perhaps St. Paul shared the same illusion, but although he ardently longed for the *parousia*, he declared formally that it was not as near at hand as many believed. However, he was not dealing with that precise point when writing his Epistle, for he wished only to relieve the fears of the church at Thessalonica by making it clear to them that the dead would have no cause to envy the living on the last day, and that there was no reason why the Christians should trouble themselves about this matter "even as others who have no hope." In support of his doctrine he referred to the Lord's word which he must have heard in one of his mystical revelations: "For this we say to you in the word of the Lord, that we who live, who survive until the coming of the Lord, shall not precede those who have fallen asleep. For the Lord himself with cry of command, with voice of archangel, and with trumpet of God will descend from heaven; and the dead in Christ will rise up first. Then we who live, who survive, shall be caught up together with them in clouds to meet the Lord in the air, and so we shall ever be with the Lord. Wherefore, comfort one another with these words" (1 Thess. 4:12-18).

The Apostle then went on to remind the Thessalonians of the necessity to watch, because "the day of the Lord is to come as a thief in the night. . . . But you, brethren, are not in darkness, that that day shall overtake you as a thief; for you are all children of the light and children of the day. . . . For God has not destined us to wrath, but to gain salvation through our Lord Jesus Christ, who died for us in order that, whether we wake or sleep, we should live together with him" (1 Thess. 5:2, 5, 9-11). The Epistle ends with many beautiful counsels which reflect the loving intimacy and family spirit which reigned in the first Christian communities: "Be at peace [among yourselves]. . . . Comfort the fainthearted, support the weak. . . . See that no one renders evil for evil to any man. . . . Rejoice always. Pray without ceasing. In all things give thanks. . . . Do not extinguish the Spirit. . . . May your spirit and soul and body be preserved sound, blameless at the coming of our Lord Jesus Christ. . . . Brethren, pray for us. Greet all the brethren with a holy kiss . . ." (1 Thess. 5:14-26).

This Epistle quieted the fears of the church at Thessalonica about the fate of those who died, but in doing so, it aroused greater anxieties among them on other points. It was read, re-read and pondered by everyone, and, because some of the disciples interpreted it falsely, it revived the fatalists' conviction that the end of the world was near, and that the voice of the archangel was liable to ring out at any moment. Many spurious additions were made to Paul's words, and the whole erroneous interpretation was supposedly confirmed by private revelations. In their ecstatic prayers in the presence of the assembly, the prophets, that is, those who felt themselves moved by the Spirit or who had the gift of tongues, used to repeat the favorite formula of the first Christians:—"Maranatha!" "Yes, come quickly!" And this invocation, which was simply the expression of a wish, came to be interpreted as an announcement of the coming of the Lord, with the result that the Thessalonians were more disturbed and perplexed than ever. They discussed the matter endlessly, commenting pessimistically on the happenings in Rome, looking for premonitory signs in political upheavals, and finding dark omens in natural phenomena. The multitude of workmen and artisans that formed the bulk of the community threw down their tools, abandoned their trades, and went begging from door to door, for why should they work when everything was going to be consumed in the flames of the approaching conflagration?

Alarmed at this turn of events, St. Paul dictated another Epistle to them, stronger and more severe than the first. He re-affirmed the second coming of Christ, but made it clear that no one could know, even approximately, the moment of that coming. Meanwhile, they were to rest assured that it was not as close as they believed, because first the apostasy had to come and the man of iniquity had to manifest himself, the son of perdition, the adversary who would be exalted above all that is called God in order to seat himself in the place proper to the Divinity. In veiled terms whose enigmatic brevity has given commentators much food for thought, St. Paul speaks about "the mystery of iniquity that is already at work," the two great crises that would precede the coming of the Son of Man—the rebellion of the world against the divine order and the appearance of Antichrist.

But he made it clear that the sons of light would have nothing to fear in the final catastrophe. Their task was to preserve the light in peace and without apprehension, to follow the ordinary pattern of their daily lives, praying fervently, working tranquilly, and eating their bread in the sweat of their brow. With great asperity, the Apostle reprimanded the irresponsible babblers, the pessimists, the alarmists who spread fantastic rumors. He reminded the idlers that he toiled and sweated day and night while he was living among them in Thessalonica, and that although he had a right to be supported by those to whom he was dispensing the bread of truth, he had preferred to give an example of honest labor to his disciples. He exhorted and charged them to work, since idleness dulls the brain, blinds the heart and destroys one's sense of proportion. And he ended his advice to them with a saying that is very Jewish in character, and yet very Christian: "If any man will not work, neither let him eat"—a dictum which had a very real significance for him, the tireless laborer in the vineyard of the Gospel, whose work was his whole life. Finally, because the so-called visionaries were issuing false documents in his name to support their fantastic theories, he concluded his Epistle with the words: "I, Paul, greet you with my own hand. This is the mark in every letter. Thus I write" (2 Thess. 3:17).

We are beginning to know the heart of the Apostle from these first Epistles and from the way he addressed the churches he had founded. Later on we shall come across other letters of his, more vibrant, more profound and more theological, but these documents written to the Thessalonians already display the general characteristics of the literary genius with which he has won the admiration of men of all ages. We see that he is affectionate, courteous, sensitive, and yet at the same time commanding; that he is vigorous and full of verve, a master in the use of irony, skilled at touching hearts, at sharing other people's joys and divining and mitigating their sorrows, endowed above other men with what has been called the gift of sympathy. There is nothing in epistolary literature that can compare with St. Paul's letters, which, ironically enough, reveal a sovereign disdain for all literature. In his writings there is no striving for effects, no affectation, no literary preoccupations; yet seldom has language been used so nobly and so tellingly. He combines depth of thought with vigorous argument, tenderness with lively strength, and sublime eloquence with delightful spontaneity, so that in the same page, sometimes in the same sentence, one can find almost paradoxical contrasts, such as the profoundest theology alternating with references to the familiar things of daily life. His commentators, both ancient and modern, are often at a loss when confronted with his unorthodox yet irresistible style. St. Irenaeus reproaches him for his use of inversion, while Origen says he is obscure. St. Epiphanius taxes him with pouring out a confusion of words and ideas which get mixed and tangled together, and St. Gregory of Nyssa comments on his use of unusual words. St. John Chrysostom accuses him of carelessness in sentence structure, and St. Jerome says that he does not always employ the right word, that he commits solecisms and uses Cilician expressions and neologisms. Sometimes his critics exaggerate, as does Bossuet when he speaks about Paul's ignorance in the art of fine writing, his rough speech and his foreign turn of phrase. But it is a fact that they are all won over in the end by the power of this singular man, and that they come as docile pupils to the school of this "barbarian." St. Jerome praises the power and energy of "the thundering of Paul"; St. John Chrysostom is dazzled by the brilliance of his style; St. Augustine wonders at his conquering eloquence; and the pagan Longinus comes to regard him as one of the greatest exponents of vigorous reasoning and passionate oratory. Truly they can praise Paul, for he had a thorough knowledge of contemporary Greek, and he could use it skillfully and lend it the warmth of his own great heart. His method of composition explains many of his faults. He was not concerned with ceremonious phrasing, classical ornamentation or beautifully contrived perorations. For him, writing meant dictation, often done rapidly, perhaps after escaping from the hands of a mob in a street riot, and before taking up again his usual work of catechizing. The words sprang to his lips and poured out in incomplete sentences bristling with unfinished clauses, parentheses, and sudden changes of subject. The main thought is often obscured beneath a flood of accessory ideas, and then reappears only to be lost again. And when he read over a newly-dictated Epistle he further complicated the style by adding new details, new thoughts and new digressions. We can imagine him pacing back and forth as he spoke, gesticulating as if he were preaching directly to his disciples in Thessalonica, Ephesus, Corinth or Galatia. He knew them all so well and pictured them so vividly before him that he talked as familiarly and as animatedly as if they were present. Each of his Epistles is a conversation at a distance, a conversation which reveals the preacher with his questions, his hyperbole, and his devices for holding the attention of his audience. In some of the Epistles, there are pages so full of animation that they read like dialogues; objections are dealt with in the form of questions and answers; the same ideas are presented in several different ways in order to impress them more deeply, and sometimes important words are repeated like a chorus, with magical effect. Yet there is never any appearance of artifice. There is no sign of patient word-weaving, marshalling of ideas or retouching and polishing of style. The Apostle always spoke out of the rich fullness of his soul and sometimes under the stress of a sudden emotion, as when he had just heard some alarming news which moved him to the depths of his being, bringing a flood of ideas to his mind and a torrent of words to his lips—a torrent that burst forth so strongly, impetuously and tumultuously that no channel of grammar or style could contain it. At such times his eloquence has the impact of a volcanic eruption—forceful, fiery, spontaneous, irresistible, and awe-inspiring in its grandeur.

CHAPTER XVII

Before the Judgment Seat
of Gallio

When St. Paul concluded his Second Epistle to the Thessalonians with the words, "Pray for us . . . that we may be delivered from troublesome and evil men . . ." he was referring to the Jews of Corinth, the malicious race, as Seneca called them, who, in the words of Tacitus, were always unremitting in their hatred of the rest of mankind. They were consumed with the desire to avenge themselves on their compatriot, Paul, whom they regarded as a traitor and an enemy of their traditions and national honor. Accordingly, they hounded him from city to city, making life unbearable for him wherever he tried to settle for a time. They sought to discredit him by spreading all sorts of calumnies against him; they set traps for him and tried to make use of Roman justice to further their own despicable plans. From the moment the Apostle escaped their hands by having himself let down the walls of Damascus in a basket until he was decapitated in Rome, the Jewish nation never ceased to persecute him.

However, in spite of their influence in the capital of Achaia, the Jews did not dare to proceed directly against

Paul. In Thessalonica they had succeeded in winning over
the municipal authorities to their side, and here in Corinth
they were pursuing a similar policy by trying to interest
the representative of Rome in their scheme. Rome's delegate in Achaia, who bore the title of proconsul, was a
Spaniard, a brother of Seneca, a good man named Marcus
Annaeus Novatus, who had been adopted by the rhetorician Junius Gallio, whose name he added to his own. For
some years he, Seneca and their nephew, Lucan the poet,
had been in disfavor with the Emperor, but in the year 50,
Seneca was recalled from exile and named praetor of Rome;
in the spring of 52, his brother came to Achaia with the
title of proconsul, a post which he filled until the year 53.
The date of Annaeus Novatus Gallio's appointment is of
capital importance in the tangled chronology of St. Paul's
life, and St. Luke's historical accuracy on this point is borne
out by the text of a letter written by the Emperor Claudius
in the spring or summer of 52 and recently discovered in
Delphos.

The Jews, as usual, began their final onslaught against
Paul by creating a public disturbance. One day as the
Apostle was passing along a street in the city, an unruly
mob, well coached by the chiefs of the synagogue, fell
upon him and, guarding him closely, brought him before
the tribunal of the proconsul. Gallio was noted for his
affability, so much so that in the literary circle presided
over by his brother and among the patricians of Rome he
was known as "gentle Gallio." He was devoted to literature, well-versed in the natural sciences as had been Sergius
Paulus, the proconsul of Cyprus, and was one of those
cultured aristocrats who, when they were made magistrates, exercised their authority with all the broadminded-
ness of philosophical liberalism. The writers of the time

praise his whole character, for he was an enemy of adulation, ingenious in his decisions and intent on acquiring stoical calm. Like his brother, he despised the Jewish rabble for their avarice, their animosity, their fanaticism and their endless disputes.

Some members of this troublesome race were now gathered before him, shouting and jostling in the hall where he held audiences. The one who appeared to be the leader, Sosthenes, the president of the synagogue, whom the multitude hated more than the others because of the special brilliance of his Jewish qualities, approached the proconsul and, pointing to Paul, made his accusation: "This fellow is persuading men to worship God contrary to the Law."

The charge was an ambiguous one, since it did not specify which law the accused was breaking by his preaching. Perhaps Sosthenes meant that the majesty of Rome was involved in the subversive doctrines of the stranger, but Gallio did not take that meaning from the charge. No doubt the proconsul thought that it was a question of one of the many theological and casuistical arguments which were constantly arising in the ghettos between the disciples of Hillel and those of Shammai, between strict Jews and Hellenizers, or between the Pharisees and the Sadducees. At any rate, he was irritated and angered by this quarrelsome pack of Jews that had burst into his audience-chamber, and, just as Paul was about to speak in his own defense, the proconsul interrupted him by saying: "If there were some question of misdemeanor or serious crime, O Jews, I should with reason bear with you. But if these are questions of word and of names and of your Law, look to it yourselves; I have no wish to decide such matters."

Gallio's reply greatly pleased the crowd of onlookers who had pushed into the hall and who had no reason to love the Jews. Though Sosthenes doubtless wanted to press the charge, the proconsul made a sign to his lictors to clear the court, and in the midst of the confusion, Paul escaped his captors and started back in safety to Aquila's house. Meanwhile, an ironically humorous scene was taking place at the gates of the hall of justice, for when the crowd of spectators saw the accusers being expelled by the pro- consul's guard, they took advantage of the occasion to pay off long-standing religious and commercial grudges. Shout- ing out their hatred, they surrounded Sosthenes and beat him unmercifully in the presence of the magistrate, who pretended not to see what was going on and contented himself with having everyone driven from the hall.

When the Jews saw that their plans had miscarried, they thought it best to forget their arrogance and assume an appearance of submission, with the result that Paul sud- denly found himself free of persecution in Corinth. For the first time he had emerged the undoubted victor in a clash with his own race. Unfortunately, however, his triumph was not due to any sympathy on Gallio's part with the religion of the Gospel, but was the result of that tolerance, not to say indifference, in religious matters that was spread- ing among the upper classes in Rome. We do not know if Gallio had any other dealings with Paul, nor do we know if he spoke to his brother Seneca, causing the philosopher to examine with interest the new teaching from the East.

However, that was what many people in the Middle Ages believed had happened, and they went on to say that Seneca was converted by the Apostle's eloquence, although the testimony of history was against them, since we know that the philosopher died after offering sacrifice to Jupiter Liberator. There are letters which are alleged to have passed between the servant of Christ and the representative

of Caesar, but they are only forgeries, begotten of misguided zeal for spreading the Faith and regret at seeing outside the Church such noble and beautiful souls as Vergil,
the poet of Mantua, and Seneca, the thinker of Cordova.
Even in modern times, learned men have amused themselves
by comparing certain of St. Paul's expressions with some of
the philosopher's sayings, but although the words are sometimes similar, the meaning is completely different. There
is a wide gulf between Seneca's stoicism and Paul's moral
teaching, between the personal God of the Apostle and the
other's pantheistic system. It is possible, however, that the
philosophical school of Tarsus influenced Paul more than
is generally believed, and it is a fact that Athenodorus, the
most important member of the Tarsian group, did influence
Seneca. Both Paul and Seneca looked upon life as a battle
and described man's striving for the good as a conflict with
the flesh. So did Athenodorus, one of whose passages Seneca
had in mind when he wrote the following words which
could have come from a Pauline Epistle: "Live among men
as if God saw you; and speak with God as if men could
hear." [1] For the rest, we can be sure that Gallio's liberal
policy and the generous freedom which the Roman magistrates allowed Paul were due in great part to the broad
outlook of Seneca, the teacher of Nero, reigning arbiter of
the Empire's destinies.

Paul remained some time longer in Corinth, and a few
months after his appearance before the tribunal, Gallio
relinquished the government of Achaia and returned to
Rome to be raised to the dignity of the consulate. Paul
thought it was time for him, too, to leave the city and carry
the message of the Gospel to other lands. The people whom
God had promised him had been gathering together little

[1] *Epist.* x.

by little, so that now he had a large congregation, well-organized and protected by the tolerant attitude of Rome. The time had come for him to return to Jerusalem, as he had done after his first mission, and to renew his contacts with the churches of Syria and Palestine. Furthermore, he had a personal reason for presenting himself as soon as possible at the Temple. As a mark of thanksgiving to God for the favors he had received during his second missionary journey, for having been protected from many dangers and for the success of his preaching, he had taken the vow which Jewish tradition called the Nazarite's vow. A Nazarite had to abstain from wine for thirty days, have his head shaved at the end of that period, and, if he was then outside Jerusalem, keep the shorn hair until he could throw it on the fire of the Mosaic sacrifices during one or other of the great solemnities celebrated in the Temple. Thus we see that Paul was not opposed to the customs of his nation, so long as they were not contrary to the Gospel; he was not a fanatic but a man who, for all his passionate devotion to the Gospel, possessed great flexibility of soul. Moreover, this attitude, besides being an act of religion, was an effectual way to silence his enemies and prepare the ground in the Jewish colonies through which he meant to pass on his way to the Holy City.

Accordingly, at the beginning of the year 54, he embarked at Cenchrae, accompanied by a few disciples among whom were his hosts, Aquila and Priscilla, who had become so attached to him that they wanted to remain as long as possible with him. The couple planned to go with him to Ephesus, where they would be able to hear him preaching before his departure and, at the same time, resume their trade with perhaps more success than in Corinth, for Ephesus had a centuries-old reputation for its tents, which were so highly esteemed that Alcibiades had not been content until he had added one to his equipment.

The ship bearing the Apostle and his companions crossed the Aegean Sea in three or four days, and a short while before they came to the coasts of Asia Minor, the passengers could see to their right the island of Patmos, whose name was to be associated for all time with the beginnings of Christianity. At Ephesus, Aquila and Priscilla disembarked with Paul; as in Corinth, the couple rented a house and established their business, while the Apostle took advantage of the few days' break in the ship's journey to observe the spirit that reigned in the Jewish colony. He presented himself at the synagogue, spoke of Jesus and held discussions with the rabbis, making such an impression on all that they begged him to stay longer with them. He replied that he had to continue on to Jerusalem, but promised to return: "I will come back to you, God willing." He was unable to stay in Ephesus because at every port of call the ship was taking on passengers who were making the pilgrimage to Jerusalem for the solemnity of the Pasch, and he did not want to lose his place. After leaving Ephesus, he sailed for two weeks across the Mediterranean and, disembarking at Caesarea, went up to Jerusalem, where he greeted the brethren. Then he offered the prescribed Nazarite sacrifices in the Temple, and, returning to Antioch, remained there some time.

St. Luke's narrative seems to indicate that the faithful in Jerusalem, enmeshed in the cold and sterile practices of the Law, did not give Paul the cordial reception due him as a mighty propagator of the Gospel. In contrast, however, the church at Antioch, proud of its Apostle, greeted him with joy, gathered eagerly about him to hear the story of his missionary travels and conquests for the Faith, and

encouraged him to continue his spreading of Christ's kingdom. It was here in Antioch that he rested and made plans
for the Christian communities which he was going to create
across the Empire.

It was probably in Antioch, too, that the short manual
known as *Didache* or *The Teaching of the Apostles* was
written some years later, before the end of the first century.
This book gives us an accurate account of the inner life of
Paul's companions and of the first disciples, and it allows
us to penetrate into those primitive Christian communities,
with their organization set up along the same lines as the
synagogues of the Diaspora, with their directors and
teachers, their liturgical meetings, their common fund for
the poor, their arbiters to settle disputes, their judges, their
penances and excommunications.

But the spirit that animated the first Christian communities was very different from that of the synagogue. The
churches were not simply scattered groups of believers, as
were the proselytes who lived in the shadow of the synagogues, nor were they a series of independent schools like
those which wandering mountebanks formed in all the
principal cities of the Empire; nor were they a spiritual
movement analogous to that which was to be spread a
century later by the Montanist heretics. It is true that there
was an exceptional outpouring of extraordinary gifts or
charismata, to use the word employed by St. Paul; but
among all the *charismata*, among all the vital actions of the
Mystical Body of Christ, the first and most sublime was the
apostolate, which, like the other gifts, had its origin in
divine grace, and which was destined for the building up of
the Church. "And [Christ] himself gave some men as
apostles, and some as prophets, others again as evangelists,
and others as pastors and teachers, in order to perfect the

saints for a work of ministry, for building up the body of Christ . . ." (Eph. 4:11-12).

Since the first days of the Church these two elements, the hierarchical and the spiritual, have been essentially united, and when Protestant apologists try to prove that there is a radical opposition between the Church of the Spirit and the Church of authority, they disregard or repudiate all the authentic sources of the history of Christian beginnings. Thus, when St. Paul was asked for a letter of recommendation as proof of his apostolate, he replied with the following words, which show us what his views were on this indissoluble union of the hierarchical and the spiritual elements in the Church: "You are our letter, written on our hearts, which is known and read by all men; clearly you are a letter of Christ, composed by us, written not with ink but with the Spirit of the living God, not on tablets of stone, but on fleshly tablets of the heart" (2 Cor. 3:2-3).

The supernatural budded forth on all sides in that joyous springtime of Christ's spiritual kingdom, and the Spirit lived among the faithful as Jahweh had associated with our first parents in the earthly paradise. In union with the Apostles, the Spirit foretold the future; He manifested Himself in dreams, visions, ecstasies, prayers and hymns; He poured out His power in all kinds of unusual graces which at times alarmed the communities. The Church in those days was like a vigorous young tree whose sap broke through the bark and overflowed in unstaunchable streams. It was a time of marvellous spiritual richness, of promises, fervor, hopes, inspirations and illuminations.

This phenomenon of the *charismata* was so important that the author of the Epistle to the Hebrews presents the preaching of Christianity as being based on the *charismata* as much as on the testimony of Christ's disciples. Yet we see the churches reacting against that impetuous current and striving to channel and restrain it. St. Paul, who lived in constant communication with the Spirit, did not consider these manifestations of His grace as sovereign and beyond discussion, and when joyous outbursts of faith took the form of a delightful naïveté, as they sometimes did, they seemed childish to him. The incomprehensible discourses of those who spoke "with tongues," their sweet-sounding streams of words as musical as the murmur of gushing springs, at times became just an incoherent, confused noise. Hence the Apostle pointed out to the Corinthians that if a pagan were to enter one of their assemblies when everyone was speaking a different language, he would take them for a collection of lunatics. Therefore the *charismata* ought to be subordinated to two principles: the true Faith, and the edification of all. Of the other gifts of the Spirit, he preferred the gift of prophecy, since the prophet spoke to men in clear words, edifying, encouraging and comforting them. With his practical common sense, St. Paul had no great esteem for sterile marvels: "But now, brethren, if I come to you speaking in tongues what shall I profit you, unless I speak to you either in revelation, or in knowledge, or in prophecy, or in teaching? . . . If the trumpet give forth an uncertain sound, who will prepare for battle? . . . If I pray in a tongue, my spirit prays, but my understanding is unfruitful. . . . I thank God that I speak with all your tongues; yet in the church, I had rather speak five words with my understanding, that I may also instruct others, than ten thousand words in a tongue" (1 Cor. 14:6-19).

St. Paul did not by any means scorn supernatural gifts, but he wished the assemblies of the faithful to be conducted with becoming decorum and orderliness. After the common prayers or the reading of a portion of the Old Testament or of the "Recollections of the Apostles," as the Gospels were then called, someone might wish to rise, transported by a sudden inspiration, to interpret the hidden meaning of a sentence, to announce some revelation, to stir the fervor of the brethren with a canticle or to give a discourse in a strange tongue interspersed with cries and invocations. The Apostle laid it down that this was permissible provided that "all things be done unto edification" (1 Cor. 14:26). But only two or three were to speak, only two or three were to prophesy, and while one was speaking or prophesying, the rest were to remain silent, "for God is a God of peace, not of disorder" (14:33).

We catch further glimpses of these enchanting early days of the Church in the prayers, hymns, psalms and spiritual canticles about which St. Paul speaks elsewhere (Eph. 5:19; Col. 3:16), compositions which possess a youthful grace, freshness, inspiration and, above all, a jubilant confidence that introduced a completely new note into the traditional themes of the synagogue. The prayers which we find in the *Teaching of the Apostles* are of this type. For example, one of them begins with these words, full of a lyrical ardor: "We give Thee thanks, O Heavenly Father, for the holy vineyard of David, Thy servant, which Thou gavest us to know through Jesus, Thy Son! Glory to Thee through the ages! We give Thee thanks, O Father, for the life and knowledge which Thou gavest us to know through Jesus, Thy Servant! Glory to Thee through the ages!" [2] And in the evening hymn, which goes back to the first days of the Church, the disciples of the Apostles prayed: "O glorious light of the holy and immortal glory of the Father, holy

[2] *Didache*, x, 2–5.

and blessed Jesus Christ! Having come to the hour of sunset and seeing the star of the evening appear, we sing to the Father, to the Son and to the Holy Spirit of God. Thou art worthy to be hymned through all time by the voices of the saints, Son of God, who givest life; therefore the world glorifies Thee." [3]

One of the Apostle's main concerns was to make charity flourish in the churches which he founded. "Be . . . persevering in prayer," he wrote to the Romans; "share the needs of the saints, practicing hospitality" (Rom. 12:12-13). In actual fact, Christianity developed among its members a social solidarity which was hitherto unknown even in the Jewish communities, and which was one of the things the pagans most admired in the first disciples of Christ. Missionaries, merchants and poor travellers went from one church to another bringing alms, counsels, news, messages of affection, edifying letters, and help of all kinds. The Christians' unity of mind and their fraternal solicitude for each other was reflected in this constant flow of communication between the churches. Financial aid was freely given, and the communities encouraged and consoled each other with testimonies of the most fervent personal affection, sharing their sorrows and partaking in each other's joys. In a word, a new era of human solidarity and reciprocal love was dawning.

The fraternal charity that reigned among Christians had its origin in their love of Christ and their adherence to one Faith. With divine originality, Christianity began on earth not as a charismatic and prophetic movement, nor a society for the exchange of assistance and love based on any distinction between peoples and races, but as a religious revelation, a rule of morals divinely inspired, a compact

[3] Cf. Dom F. Cabrol, O.S.B., *La prière antique*, Appendix.

of hopes shared and lived out in common by the faithful, the brethren, the elect of each church and of all the churches. And Christ Himself was the center of these beliefs, these endeavors, these hopes.

During the first years of the Church's growth, more than at any other time, Christians were alive to the nearness of Christ, whose memory still remained fresh and vivid among His disciples. His name was the instrument of miracles, the motive of persecutions and the inspiration of patience. He was the central object of faith, and through Him came pardon for sins and eternal salvation. Christ is in a very special way the center of St. Paul's doctrine: the Church is the Body of Christ, baptism is His Resurrection, and the Christian must preserve himself from fornication because his body is the temple of Christ. Marriage is holy because it represents the union of Christ with His Church, and husbands must love their wives as Christ loves His Church. Servants must obey their masters as they would Christ, while the rich should be generous to the poor, thus imitating Christ who, being rich, made Himself poor for our sakes. And all who have been regenerated by the blood of Christ know that they no longer live for themselves, but for Him who lived and rose from the dead for them, Christ, the Lord of the living and the dead. "For in him were created all things in the heavens and on the earth. . . . He is before all creatures, and in him all things hold together. . . . He is the head of his body, the Church; he, who is the beginning, the firstborn from the dead, that in all things he may have the first place. For it has pleased God the Father that in him all his fullness should dwell, and that through him he should reconcile to himself all things, whether on the earth or in the heavens, making peace through the blood of his cross" (Col. 1:16–20).

CHAPTER XVIII

The Doctor of the Gentiles

St. Paul's character is a rich and complex one, presenting many different facets and containing the most diverse qualities. He is the very personification of sound common sense, yet his language is full of paradoxes and abrupt changes of subject. We know him to be a formidable logician, yet we often find him laying aside logic and using instead his wondrous power of intuition, and although he is at times so outspoken that he strikes us as being harsh, narrow and uncompromising, he is also able to soar to the highest peaks of idealism. Perhaps he would have been indignant if anyone had called him a poet; nevertheless we shall find many pages of sublime poetry in his Epistles. He possesses such a deep sense of rhythm that he frequently clothes his thought in measured, musical forms, not, however, after the manner of Greek and Roman poetry, but with the modulations of Hebrew prosody, parallelism, analogy, antithesis of thoughts and of words, cadences, and balanced sentences. For example, his eulogy of charity in the First Epistle to the Corinthians is so vibrant with emotion and so full of lyrical flights that it reads like an ode. In fact, the whole collection of the Pauline Epistles enshrines a poetic enchantment that is unique in literature. It is true that the Apostle's writings do not abound in original images; yet they are marvels of light, vigor and color. He imparts life to the most abstract of subjects, and makes inanimate things move, speak, breathe, argue and do battle. The Law, sin, nature, and death do not appear simply as concepts, but as living beings which take their part in an immense drama and share in the construction of that great spiritual temple, that masterpiece of harmony and art envisaged by the Apostle.

This skillful awakener of emotions who can, with one sentence, open up undreamed-of perspectives in the world of the heart and the world of the spirit, is also a supremely practical man, undeviating in the enunciation of principles, and discreet in their application. He never loses contact with reality; he is circumspect, balanced, and so much master of himself, so temperate, that despite his passionate nature he can, when occasion demands it, appear to be coldness itself.

It is during his third missionary journey, the culminating point of his amazing career, that we come to see in all their brilliance these seemingly contradictory traits in St. Paul's character. He was still the conqueror, but old age was approaching, and the sword began to gleam afar off on the horizon, so that he had to hasten to consolidate his work, weed out the cockle and make the future secure. Therefore he now became the organizer, the writer, the man of authority, the Doctor of the Gentiles. He increased his activity, preaching with his lips and with his pen, combating error, reproving, encouraging. With eyes always straying toward Asia Minor and Europe, he thought constantly of the communities which he had founded during ten years of toil and suffering. He had to remedy abuses, lay down laws, arrange for the collection of alms, and forestall dangers—all with tact, prudence, and consummate psychological skill. The characteristic note of this period of his life can be described in his own words: "My daily pressing anxiety [is] the care of all the churches" (2 Cor. 11:28).

St. Paul left Antioch accompanied by a disciple as on the other occasions when he had set out from that city. Silas was no longer with him, for it seems that this valued co-worker had yielded to a secret yearning to remain attached to the church in Jerusalem; and like John Mark, from this time on he appeared among Peter's followers, to remain with him as an assistant and messenger. Timothy was on the other side of the Aegean Sea, going from port to port, strengthening the faith of the churches recently founded in Achaia and Macedonia. However, in the community at Antioch, Paul had found a new travelling-companion, his disciple Titus, now a perfect man, mature in character, persevering in toil and expert in managing the affairs of the churches, about whom he could later say to the brethren: "Has [he] not walked in the same steps [as I]?" (2 Cor. 12:18). Titus was a Gentile, and therefore he had not taken part in the Apostle's second missionary journey, but on this third venture the possible murmuring of the Jews was no longer of such great importance.

After leaving Antioch, the Apostle paid a visit—his last as it turned out to be—to his native city of Tarsus, and then once again crossed the rugged heights of the Taurus Mountains. Arriving in Asia Minor, he set about retracing the route he had followed on his second journey, for he wished to visit "in turn," as the Acts say, the churches already founded, "strengthening all the disciples" and putting them on their guard against the intrigues of the

Judaizers, who were still sowing discord and unrest among the converts. Rapidly he paid visits of inspection in Cilicia, Lycaonia, Pisidia, Phrygia, and the cities of upper Galatia, where he was received with the same respectful reverence as he had enjoyed on his former appearance here among his spiritual children. Once again all showed themselves zealous in the good cause (cf. Gal. 4:18); they had learned how to discern beneath his stern words of correction a profound tenderness and a deep love, and they had finally come to realize the truth and justice of his vehement reproof: "Have I then become your enemy because I tell you the truth?" (Gal. 4:16).

After three or four months of travel, the two missionaries arrived at the western end of the peninsula of Asia Minor, and with scarcely a pause in the great cities that lay along their way—Synnada, Thyatira, Sardis, and Philadelphia—they descended toward the sea and, following the valley of the Cayster River, "the wide field of Asia," as Homer called it, they arrived at Ephesus, the capital of proconsular Asia and one of the most important cities of the Empire. Paul had promised to return to this region, and now he had arrived to fulfill that promise. Here he found an ideal center for his apostolate and an unequalled strategic point from which to begin the spiritual conquest of the East. An idea sown in that fertile soil, beneath that blue Ionian sky, was sure to spread along the imperial highways and reach every city on the Mediterranean. When he had stopped here a year before on his way to Jerusalem, he had seen representatives of many races swarming about the huge wharves and had noticed ships from every port in the Empire lying at anchor in the harbor. Now, in the spacious *agora* dominated and protected by the heights of Mount Coressos, the Apostle observed the same variety of peoples and tongues, of customs and dress—negroes from Africa; yellow faces from central Asia; Greek women gracefully clothed in the traditional *pepla;* Cynics with unkempt beards; sailors and merchants; clowns, musicians and dancers; priests of the great goddess with their novices, clad in silken, hyacinth-colored tunics; Jews in filthy gowns, and Ionians gorgeous in purple or saffron fabrics woven in diamond-shaped patterns.

Neither in Tarsus nor in Corinth had he found such a picturesque mixture of races. Ephesus rivalled Antioch in bustle and activity, and Corinth in luxury and license; and, some years after Paul's sojourn there, it was to leave an indelible impression on the mind of St. John: ". . . merchandise of gold and silver, and precious stones and pearls, and fine linen and purple, and silk and scarlet, and all thyine wood, and all vessels of ivory, and all vessels of precious stone, and of brass, and of iron, and of marble, and cinnamon and amomum and spices, and ointment and frankincense, and beasts of burden and sheep and horses, and chariots and slaves, and the souls of men" (Apoc. 18:12–13).

Today, Ephesus is not even a shadow of its famous past, for sifting sands have buried its palaces and the silt of centuries has blocked its harbor. Capricious fortune has turned its back on the city of Diana and now showers its favors on nearby Smyrna, its ancient rival. The traveller can still see relics of past greatness scattered over the historic site—the ruins of magnificent theaters, of immense stadiums, of famous "gymnasia." The streets, adorned with *stelai* and monuments, still display their dazzling white pavements, and among the porches, one may still discover the Library with open shelves along the walls, a memorial to the Ephesians' wealth and love of learning. But if it

were not for the ancient inscriptions, it would be impossible
to find the site of the great temple, one of the seven
wonders of the world. When Paul came to the city, a
splendid building stood in place of the ancient sanctuary
which Erostratus, in search of immortality, had burned to
the ground. The rebuilt temple was resplendent with
marble from Paros, bronze from Corinth, wood from
Cyprus and gold from Arabia. There the luxury of the
Asiatic world, the graceful genius of Greece, the inspiration of such great artists as Polycletus and Praxiteles, had
been placed at the service of an absurd and monstrous
goddess, the Artemis of Ephesus, who was an Asiatic
imposition on the spirit of Greek Ionia, for she bore no
resemblance to the goddess of the woods, the divine
huntress of the girt-up tunic and wind-blown hair, but was
a sister to the idol of Paphos. The lower part of the goddess' statue was a roughly-shaped column covered with
magical inscriptions, the bust was many-breasted to signify
fruitful nature, and the head was crowned with a battlemented tower to symbolize resistance and power. Fortunately, however, a purple veil hid this fetish from the
hundreds of thousands of pilgrims who came from all parts
of the East to make their offerings and vows to the divinity.

As he had done in Corinth, Paul went seeking work with
Aquila and Priscilla, who had established their business near
the hill where the goddess' temple stood and where the
first nucleus of Christians in Ephesus was to be formed.
The modern name of this hill, Aïa-Solouk, "the Holy
Theologian," still recalls the name of another Apostle of
Christ, St. John, who was to continue the work which St.
Paul was now about to begin. It was St. John who, from the
Ephesian Acropolis, raised aloft the light of faith over that
populous region, but Paul had first to prepare the way.

Some months before the Apostle's arrival, there had come to the city an Alexandrian Jew named Apollos, who had learned the art of commenting on the Sacred Scriptures in the school of Philo and who was justly renowned for his graceful speech. This man was a fervent proselytizer and very much preoccupied with the thought of the Messias, so much so that he devoted his life to travelling among the Jews of the Diaspora and re-awakening their religious fervor. On his journeys he had met some disciples of John the Baptist who told him about their master's connections with Jesus of Nazareth, and taught him about the baptism of penance, the fulfillment of the prophecies and the coming of the Messias whom John, the prophet of fire, had pointed out on the banks of the Jordan. Marvelling at this revelation, Apollos had accepted it fully and adopted it thenceforth as the principal theme of his teaching. Aquila and Priscilla went to hear this good man preach in the synagogue at Ephesus, and although they were overjoyed to hear him speak so fervently and eloquently about Jesus, they were also very surprised to find that his knowledge of the Messias was rudimentary and incomplete. "He . . . used to speak and teach carefully whatever had to do with Jesus," but he did not know about the baptism of the Holy Spirit, the baptism that was given in the name of the Three Divine Persons. And so when he was leaving the synagogue, Aquila and Priscilla approached him and brought him to their house, where they "expounded the Way of God to him more precisely" (Acts 18:26). They told him about Paul and his adventures in Corinth, and so enthusiastically did they describe the effects of the Apostle's preaching in the capital of Achaia, that they awoke in their guest the desire to visit the church there in order to speak with the elders and find out more about the Gospel. Accordingly,

Apollos went to Achaia, and "on his arrival there he was of great service to those who had believed" (Acts 18:27).

This was the episode which Aquila and Priscilla related to Paul in one of their first conversations with him after his arrival at Ephesus. It was the first he had heard of the Alexandrian teacher, but soon he found palpable proof that Apollos had been in the city, for he came across a group of Jews who had heard the travelling preacher and had been won by his eloquence. These men, like their master, had only a fragmentary knowledge of the Gospel, and although they lived lives of penance and seclusion, their faces did not shine with the joy of the true Faith. "Did you receive the Holy Spirit . . .?" Paul asked them.

"What is that?" they queried in surprise.

"With what baptism, then, were you baptized?"

"With John's baptism."

"Then Paul said: 'John baptized the people with a baptism of repentance, telling them to believe in him who was to come after him, that is, in Jesus.' On hearing this they were baptized in the name of the Lord Jesus; and when Paul laid his hands on them, the Holy Spirit came upon them, and they began to speak in tongues and to prophesy. There were about twelve men in all" (Acts 19:1-7).

Thus John's preaching was still preparing the way of the Lord, for the germ of Christianity which his words had contained necessarily led men to the Church. This is what had happened in Palestine with the Baptist's first disciples, and it continued to occur in the centers of reform set up in the synagogues of the Dispersion by men of good will who were witnesses of the voice that cried in the desert.

Paul, following his customary plan, began his campaign in Ephesus by speaking in the synagogue, but after three months many of those who, shortly before, had urged him to stay with them, now refused even to listen to him. Yet, despite their fickleness, the Jews of Ephesus were less intolerant than those of Thessalonica, for at least they did not plot to kill him. Some indeed still listened to him with interest, but others launched violent imprecations against his doctrine, so that in the end he could not speak before them without arousing an uproar in the synagogue. Seeing that further efforts were useless, the Apostle gathered together his disciples, both Jews and Greeks, and leaving the synagogue, made a clean break with the unbelievers. A teacher of philosophy and rhetoric named Tyrannus offered him his school at one of the "gymnasia" as a meeting place, and the first Christian church in Ephesus was established in this spacious hall. A specimen of such a "gymnasium" may still be seen among the ruins of the city, with its semi-circles of seats, its hollowed-out steps and its playing field.

For more than two years, both the Gospel and the categories of Aristotle were taught in the same building. Daily, from eleven in the morning until mid-afternoon, Paul instructed his disciples. Before dawn each day he was up and at his loom in Aquila's house, earning his daily bread; and when classes were over he resumed his apostolic work of going from house to house, strengthening the waverers, arguing with adversaries, and correcting the wrong-doers, "[keeping] back nothing that was for [their] good" (Acts 19:9-10; 20:20). Always fatherly and loving, he gave himself "night and day" to the service of the brethren, "with tears . . . admonish[ing] every one of [them]"; and the love which vibrated in every nerve and fibre of his travel-hardened body overcame all resistance.

The efforts he expended were great, but the fruit of his

toil filled his heart with joy, and he expressed the deep satisfaction he felt in the following words which he wrote to the Corinthians: "A door has been opened to me, great and evident. . . . (1 Cor. 16:9). This is the image evoked also by the Acts, for in the great city of Ephesus, gateway to Asia, not only did citizens frequent Tyrannus' "gymnasium," but so also did many outsiders from Rome, Egypt, Greece and Syria. Some listened to Paul for a while and then took themselves off, laughing derisively, or rose up against the herald of the new religion. But others found much food for thought in what they heard and, impressed by the Apostle's message, they carried the seeds of spiritual renewal to far-off lands. The greater part of Paul's audience, however, were inhabitants of proconsular Asia, and St. Luke tells us that "all who lived in the province of Asia, both Jews and Gentiles, heard the word of the Lord" (Acts 19:10). Numerous and wealthy were the cities that were growing up in that region, so proud of its fertile valleys, its busy industries, and its rich trade in rare marbles, bronze, beautiful rugs, engraved metals, glowing fabrics and thousands of other costly articles which were eagerly sought after by the Roman patricians. Here Grecian genius was combined with Asiatic extravagance, and the cities of Pergamos, Halicarnassus, Smyrna, Miletus, and Samos rivalled the most illustrious centers on the other side of the Aegean Sea in the glory of their artistic and literary traditions.

Undoubtedly it was about this time that those great churches were born which St. John the Evangelist found flourishing when he visited this region some years later. The divine word spread from the shores of the Mediterranean to the seacoast of Pontus and the province of Bithynia, where Paul had wished in vain to tarry during his second missionary journey and where, just half a century later, Pliny the Younger saw paganism fading rapidly and was forced to admit that "the temples are abandoned, the old religious feasts are no longer celebrated, the priests are left without livelihood since no one buys the flesh of the victims. The whole land, not only the cities, but even the villages and the countryside as well, has been subjected to the Christian superstition." [1]

The evolution of the Church in the valley of the Lycus is a good example of the way in which the Gospel spread so rapidly and so far afield. There were three famous cities in that part of Phrygia which lay in the shadow of Mount Cadmus: Hierapolis, "city of gold, holy city, divine nymph," renowned for the water of its fountains, which turned everything to stone; Laodicea, its rival, on the other bank of the river, world-famed for its dyed fabrics; and finally, Colossae, whose riches lay in its fertile pastures and the thick fleeces of its sheep. Some of Paul's audience in the "gymnasium" at Ephesus brought the first rumors of the "good tidings" to this region, arousing curiosity in some of their fellow-countrymen and enthusiasm in others. The most notable of these bearers of the light was a native of Colossae named Epaphras, who was aided in his missionary work by a rich landowner called Philemon, and by Archippus, who was a friend of Philemon, or may even have been his son. St. Paul was filled with joy when, as he wrote to the Colossians, he "heard of [their] faith in Christ Jesus and of the love that [they bore] toward all the saints. . . ." "The word of the gospel truth" had grown and borne fruit among them since the day they "heard and recognized the grace of God in truth" (Col. 1:4, 5, 6). And the Apostle went on to praise the diligent preacher who deserved the

[1] *Epistolae* x. 97.

eternal gratitude of the three cities for fostering in them this splendid upsurge of divine life. "Epaphras . . . a servant of Jesus Christ, who is ever solicitous for you in his prayers, that you may remain perfect and completely in accord with all the will of God" (Col. 4:12).

Never before, perhaps, did the Apostle's preaching have such force of conviction, and never before did he find such favorable soil in which to plant the seed of faith. Moreover, the marvels that accompanied his teaching gave his words almost limitless power, and his hands seemed to radiate a divine element which, without his realizing it, cured men's bodies and souls, for his disciples took his "handkerchiefs and aprons . . . to the sick, and the diseases left them and the evil spirits went out" (Acts 19:12).

This supernatural power, which always made a deep impression on those who witnessed its effects, had a special appeal for the people of Ephesus, who were passionately devoted to magic. Professional dealers in the occult arts were more numerous here than anywhere else; there were prophets who cast themselves into a pseudo-mystical trance by chewing an herb which they called *omomi;* there were "theoleptics" with fright-filled eyes and dishevelled hair, who moved their heads and limbs spasmodically as they mouthed incoherent sounds; there were tricksters who told fortunes; quacks who offered to sell the elixir of youth and a balm to cure all diseases; wizards, "pythonesses," astrologers, diviners, snake-charmers; evokers of the dead, the shades and the infernal genii; sellers of amulets and all sorts of magical figurines; practitioners of the terrible art of chaining the powers of heaven and hell; vendors of those mysterious recipes, the famed Ephesian formulae which contained invincible elements capable of wresting from the spirits of the upper air and the lower darkness some of their knowledge and power. Roaming about among all these impostors, these heirs of Phrygian pseudo-mysticism, there were other sellers of secrets: Jewish exorcists who boasted that they possessed superhuman power, thanks to the secret words which some families had passed down through the generations from the time of Solomon. Among the best known of these were the seven sons of Sceva, who was one of the chiefs of the Jewish priestly class. With blind confidence, the Gentiles came to the brothers and they, unsure of their ancient formulae, resolved to invoke over the possessed the name of Jesus, by which Paul was working so many miracles. "We adjure you by the Jesus whom Paul preaches," they said to the devils; but their new formula had unexpected results, for the evil spirit replied: "Jesus I acknowledge, and Paul I know, but who are you?" And falling upon the exorcists, the possessed men struck and bit them, tearing their garments and showing such ungovernable fury that the brothers, bleeding, half-naked and humiliated, were forced to flee from the house they had selected as the stage upon which to display their talents.

The news of this event spread through the city among Jews and Greeks alike; it was exhaustively commented upon in the market place, and it greatly enhanced St. Paul's reputation. Some merely laughed at the discomfiture of the sons of Sceva, but others were filled with fear and glorified the name of Jesus. Many who had already received baptism but who were still devoted to superstitious practices, were now convinced of the emptiness of the impostors' claim to superhuman powers, and they came before the assembly of the faithful and confessed their sin. As a sign of their sincerity and to remove a source of temptation, they carefully collected their books on the occult arts, their formulae for incantations, their papyri containing instructions for satanic rites, and burned them in the presence of the brethren. Their willingness to destroy their precious books was a cogent proof of their sincere repentance, since they had paid dearly for these manuscripts, which were very expensive both because of the extraordinary power they were thought to confer and because the authors had to be reimbursed for the risk they ran of being punished by the law. One witness of the burning, as he watched the flames leap up in the garden beside Tyrannus' "gymnasium," calculated that the manuscripts being thrown into the fire were worth all of fifty thousand pieces of silver. (Cf. Acts 19:13–20.) Despite their great cost, however, these books were an evil and pestilential literature which even the pagan governors tried to stamp out as a prolific source of fraud and error. This incident was not the first of its kind, for, some years before, Augustus had ordered the burning of two thousand similar books in one of the squares of Rome.

CHAPTER XIX

Solicitude for All the Churches

While he was in Ephesus spreading the Faith throughout the provinces of Asia Minor, Paul still kept in touch with the churches he had founded during his previous missionary journeys. He was able to do so because Ephesus was a veritable listening-post to which news came daily from the farthest corners of the civilized world, and from which messages could be easily sent to the most distant towns and cities. During this time Paul's solicitude centered on the community at Corinth, one of his most successful ventures, which was now being shaken by many storms. He first heard of the alarming events there from some messengers of Chloe, the wealthy convert from Cenchrae, who told him that discord, disorders, quarrels and immorality of every sort were spreading in the church of the Corinthians. Immediately he sent Timothy to restore peace, but without success. Other travellers came to inform him that the trouble still continued, although less violently than before, and their account was confirmed by Apollos, the Alexandrian sage, who had just come to Ephesus to meet the Apostle.

Actually, it was Apollos himself who, all unwittingly,

257

had precipitated the difficult situation at Corinth. The Alexandrian teacher possessed all the qualities needed to draw the crowds, especially the frivolous and elegant crowds of the Greek cities. He had natural eloquence, religious fervor, pure and graceful diction, the ability to combine biblical teaching with the speculations of Greek philosophy, and great skill in elaborating subtle allegorical interpretations of Scripture. Consequently, it was not long before he found himself surrounded by a fanatical following who thought it necessary to despise all other teachers in order to exalt their own. They even went so far as to criticize the Apostle, pointing out the contrast between Apollos' elaborate discourses and Paul's simple, familiar style, full of faults, bare of oratorical pomp, sometimes harsh and uneven. Paul's defenders answered these critics sharply, but they found that there were some among the brethren who went even further, comparing unfavorably his authority with that of Peter, the chief of the Apostles, who had lived in close friendship with Christ. And as if that were not opposition enough, another faction appeared, inspired no doubt by the Judaizers, who boasted that they followed only the doctrine of Jesus and did not need intermediaries. With the same blind devotion displayed by the Greeks to famous teachers, with the same vanity that had formerly caused them to cry: "I am of the Stoa," or "I am of the Academy," each group of converts passionately defended its leader. "I have been informed . . ." wrote St. Paul in his first Epistle to them, "[that] each of you says, I am of Paul, or I am of Apollos, or I am of Cephas, or I am of Christ. Has Christ been divided up?" (1 Cor. 1:11–13).

There was no question of real schisms, since fundamentally all the faithful respected Paul's authority and celebrated the Eucharist together; nevertheless, the arguments and rivalries endangered charity and could go so far as to imperil the Faith itself. One of the factions thought that Paul's personality had been overrated; they maintained that he was neither a philosopher, a logician nor an orator. Yet they recognized his authority as a witness to Christ, and he could still address them in words that combined severity and affection. "I write these things not to put you to shame," he said to them, "but to admonish you as my dearest children. For although you have ten thousand tutors in Christ, yet you have not many fathers. For in Christ Jesus, through the gospel, did I beget you" (1 Cor. 4:14-15). Again and again he pointed out the foolishness of human wisdom in the face of God's wisdom, for his experience at Athens had taught him that neither philosophy nor eloquence nor the artifices of language could convert the world. He was not angry with Apollos, who, without wishing it, had found himself at the head of a party; on the contrary, the Apostle, like St. Luke, recognized the excellence of his preaching: "I have planted, Apollos watered, but God has given the growth." With refined irony he derided the weaknesses and the philosophical vanity of the Greek spirit, and answering those who were confident that he would not dare appear again in Corinth, he wrote: "Now some are puffed up, as if I were not coming to you. But I shall come to you shortly, if the Lord is willing, and I shall learn the power of those who are puffed up, not the promises. For the kingdom of God is not in word, but in power. What is your wish? Shall I come to you with a rod, or in love and in the spirit of meekness?" (1 Cor. 4:18-21).

Besides being swollen with pride, the Corinthians were guilty of immorality, and St. Paul remonstrated with them:

"It is actually reported that there is immorality among you, and such immorality as is not found even among the Gentiles, that a man should have his father's wife. And you are puffed up, and have not rather mourned that he who has done this deed might be put away from your midst. I indeed, absent in body but present in spirit, have already, as though present, passed judgment in the name of our Lord Jesus Christ on the one who so acted—you and my spirit gathered together with the power of our Lord Jesus —to deliver such a one over to Satan for the destruction of the flesh, that his spirit may be saved in the day of our Lord Jesus Christ" (1 Cor. 5:1-5).

The Apostle had already forbidden the Corinthians to have any dealings with people of this type, but they had not wanted to understand his real meaning. "We would have to leave the world altogether," they had said, laughing at his command. St. Paul replied that this was not what he meant, since it was not a Christian's duty to judge sinners who were outside the Church. God would judge them, and the brethren had but to exclude them from the community: "Expel the wicked man from your midst." The incestuous man was therefore to be excommunicated. The Apostle then went on to refute those who, claiming to despise the body, asserted that everything was permitted to them: "The body is not for immorality, but for the Lord. . . . Shall I then take the members of Christ and make them members of a harlot? . . . Do you not know that your members are the temple of the Holy Spirit . . . and that you are not your own?" (1 Cor. 6:15-19).

In addition to all this, strange scruples had begun to affect some of the Christians who dwelt in that city of Corinth, where corruption was so widespread and virulent, and some of the extremists went so far as to condemn marriage, saying: "It is good for man to avoid all contact with women." Thus, as had happened before in other places, extreme laxity of morals began to provoke violent reactions. The Epicureans, despairing of reforming human nature, gave free rein to all their instincts, while the Stoics and rigorists strove to destroy every passion and emotion. St. Paul condemned both of these opposing moral systems which were later to do battle with each other for predominance among the Gnostics. He denounced fornication, went on to defend marriage, and concluded by proposing a higher ideal, the ideal of virginity: "I would have you free from care. He who is unmarried is concerned about the things of the Lord, how he may please God. Whereas he who is married is concerned about the things of the world, how he may please his wife; and he is divided. . . . Now this I say for your benefit, not to put a halter upon you, but to promote what is proper, and to make it possible for you to pray to the Lord without distraction" (1 Cor. 7:32-35).

All these doubts, dissensions, worries and rivalries that divided the church at Corinth had a disagreeable echo in the assemblies, in the liturgical ceremonies, and even in the Eucharistic Banquet. As Christians, the Corinthians could not participate in any other sacred meal or sit at the table of demons or eat the food sacrificed to idols. Christian worship, like Christian faith, is exclusive; the Christians' God and Lord is One, and one also is their sacrifice which is, like that of the pagans, a meal, but a heavenly meal: "The cup of blessing that we bless, is it not the sharing of the blood of Christ? And the bread that we break, is it not the partaking of the body of the Lord?" (1 Cor. 10:16). But there were some who received unworthily the Body and Blood of the Lord, without understanding the gravity of their fault; and, furthermore, the fraternal love feast which preceded Communion, the mystical symbol of a holy love and a triumph of the equality and fraternity of Christ's disciples, had, at times, been turned into one of those profane banquets which used to follow the sacrifices in the pagan temples. Besides the ecstatics who were caught up by the Spirit, and the poor, who remained fasting because they had nothing to eat, there were present also prophets eager to catch the eye of the assembly, vain women with unveiled heads who talked and gesticulated, and wealthy people who ate abundantly and drank until they were befuddled with wine. "What am I to say to you?" asked St. Paul. "Am I to recommend you? In this I do not recommend you" (1 Cor. 11:22).

Not only did he not recommend or praise them, but on the contrary censured and severely reproved them for their faults. And to those who were puffed up on account of the *charismata* they possessed, he proposed a higher ideal, the real treasure of the Christian: divine love which unites man to Christ. In a transport of sublime poetic creation, he dictated one of the most beautiful passages of his whole literary career, infinitely superior to the art of pagan wisdom which the Corinthians admired so much, and more exquisite than the eloquence of Apollos:

If I should speak with the tongues of men and of angels, but do not have charity, I have become as sounding brass or a tinkling cymbal. And if I have prophecy and know all mysteries and all knowledge, and if I have all faith so as to remove mountains, yet do not have charity, I am nothing. And if I distribute all my goods to feed the poor, and if I deliver my body to be burned, yet do not have charity, it profits me nothing.

Charity is patient, is kind; charity does not envy, is not pretentious, is not puffed up, is not ambitious, is not self-seeking, is not provoked; thinks no evil, does not rejoice over wickedness, but rejoices with the truth; bears with all things, believes all things, hopes all things, endures all things.

Charity never fails, whereas prophecies will disappear, and tongues will cease, and knowledge will be destroyed. For we know in part and we prophesy in part; but when that which is perfect has come, that which is imperfect will be done away with. When I was a child, I spoke as a child, I felt as a child, I thought as a child. Now that I have become a man, I have put away the things of a child. We see now through a mirror in an obscure manner, but then face to face. Now I know in part, but then I shall know even as I have been known. So there abide faith, hope and charity, these three; but the greatest of these is charity (1 Cor. 13:1–13).

This First Epistle to the Corinthians is of great value, not only for the truths it affirms, but also for the Christian life which it reveals. St. Paul's dogmatic exposition shows us, as St. Cyril of Alexandria pointed out, "the man in whom God speaks, the minister of the sacred mysteries," and at the same time gives us a highly instructive insight into the character of the Corinthians, those wayward disciples so beloved by him, so favored by God, and yet so carnal, so unruly. If we examine the lives of these Christians, we shall come to the conclusion that it is easier for God to make miracle-workers than to form saints. But the more we consider their waywardness, the more we shall admire the Apostle's method of teaching, for although he is patient and can pardon delinquents, yet he can also be uncompromisingly firm. When he is confronted with abuses he does not hesitate to speak out freely and condemn categorically, but always in the name of the Faith, his ultimate and sovereign reason for acting. Thus, when he is reproving the Corinthians, he does not censure their degrading vices as debasing and weakening their stock, undermining their health and destroying their human dignity, but as being opposed to the fundamental principles of the supernatural order: "Do you not know that your bodies are members of Christ . . . that your members are the temple of the Holy Spirit . . . ?"

When this Epistle was finished, Paul took the pen from his secretary's hand and wrote these words by way of signature: "I Paul greet you, with my own hand. If any man does not love the Lord Jesus Christ, let him be anathema. Maranatha. . . ." But it pained him to leave his disciples under the weight of this threat, and he added: "The grace of our Lord Jesus be with you. My love is with you all in Christ Jesus. Amen."

He entrusted his message to some of the faithful who were about to leave for Corinth. He had wished Apollos to go with these travellers, but the Alexandrian refused to accept the perilous mission, alleging that his presence would only reawaken the dissensions there. The Apostle then turned to Titus, the self-effacing disciple from Antioch, who was usually fearless in the face of danger and calm in his acceptance of the unexpected. But even Titus wavered for a time, momentarily deterred by the ill-fame of the Corinthians. Paul reassured him, however, pointing out the qualities of his character that would win the esteem of the Corinthians and finally convincing him by entrusting to him another mission no less delicate, namely, the collection for the Christians of Jerusalem, who continued to be hard-pressed by poverty. The Apostle pitied the brethren in the Holy City and wished to show them that all his disciples, both Jews and Gentiles, were united to them by the bonds of love. Furthermore, his appeal to the Corinthians for these alms was a sound psychological method of disarming suspicion and fostering good-will.

In starting his project on behalf of the church at Jerusalem, he showed the skill of the practical Jew and the sure touch of the master psychologist. He prepared the ground by announcing the collection in his first Epistle, then waited for some time, and when no one objected, he brought up the matter again. "Remember," he said in effect, "that we are members of the same body. Is it just that some should be in want while others live in abundance? Salvation comes from Jerusalem and it is in Jerusalem that Christ must manifest Himself in His glory. And seeing that the brethren of that city have given you spiritual goods, is it not natural that you should give them part of your material goods?" These arguments based on the Faith were the primary reasons for generosity, but honor and enlightened self-interest were also cogent motives: "Look at the Macedonians; they are poor yet they have given generously and even more than they can afford. Will you allow yourselves to be outdone in generosity? I have boasted to them about you, saying that all Achaia has been ready. But if some of them come with me on the visit which I intend to pay you and if they see that I have been mistaken, how shameful it will be for me and for you! Therefore be open-handed and give abundantly. He who sows bountifully will also reap bountifully. Your largesse will make you pleasing to the Lord, and by depriving yourselves in this way you will really make yourselves richer." (Cf. 2 Cor. 8–9.)

With characteristic delicacy he advanced these considerations and made arrangements for the actual gathering of

the money, showing thereby that he was a man of fore-
sight and a vigilant administrator: "On the first day of the
week, Sunday, let each one of you put aside whatever he
can so as not to put off this matter until I am actually in
your midst." (Cf. 1 Cor. 16:2.)

As we follow the course of St. Paul's life, we see him
emerge both as an eminently practical man and a sublime
teacher, the Doctor of the Gentiles, the architect of a theological system that is a marvel of harmony and immensity,
and a storehouse so rich that it has not been exhausted by
twenty centuries of investigation. In it we do not find a
moment of vacillation, superficiality or hypothetical discussion such as occur in the systems of Plato and Aristotle, for
absolute firmness is one of the Apostle's most characteristic
traits. The foundation of the towering structure is the
dogma of original sin. Sin, embedded, as it were, in the
flesh, makes slaves of men and gives them eternal death as
their wages. The mystery of the first disobedience, in
which the whole of humanity partook in the person of its
first father, demanded a redemption which could come only
from God. Man needed a propitiator to intercede for him,
since by himself he could not do or will anything toward
salvation.

For St. Paul, these brief concepts summarize long ages.
The history of the human race is the history of fallen man,
whose portrait he paints for us in the Epistle to the
Romans; it is the history of the Fall and the Redemption,
a story divided into two parts, the present and the future,
representing respectively the old man and the new, the one
corrupted, the other reborn in Jesus Christ. The moment
when the Cross was raised on the summit of Calvary
marked the climax of the Messianic era, the kingdom of
grace, the dispensation of the Holy Spirit, the new hu-

manity, and the establishment of love in the kingdom of darkness. By His death Christ reconciled man to God. He took the form of a slave in order to redeem slaves, and by making Himself in their image, He made it possible for them to become images of God. He rose again from the dead so that all might arise in Him, recovering supernatural life, the seed of eternal life, a pure gift of God's goodness which, since it is a gift, is called grace, the light of the mind and the strength of the will.

In St. Paul's theology these truths, already contained in the Gospel, are presented to us closely linked together, set forth in a sweeping sequence, formulated in precise terms, and illuminated by marvelous insight. To him we are indebted for such expressions as these: "The gifts and the call of God are without repentance . . ." and, "If by reason of the one man's offense death reigned through the one man, much more will they who receive the abundance of the grace and of the gift of justice reign in life through the one Jesus Christ . . ." (Rom. 11:29; 5:17).

In this Epistle to the Romans, the Apostle gazes with steady eyes into the unfathomable abyss of the dogma of predestination. God is just; He created man and desires his salvation; yet, while some obtain the privilege of life in Christ, others are disinherited. Why is this? But the clay cannot ask the potter why he makes it "a vessel of dishonor." Here Paul is thinking of the Jews, always rebellious enemies of the light, whose inheritance would be darkness, and who, faithless to the truth, would be rejected and condemned. Before the creation of the world, God, moved only by love, rested His gaze on the chosen. They were predestined, called and justified, and they will be glorified in order to praise the wonderful manifestation of grace, that is to say, they will be saved for the glory of God. But this glorification demands, as a necessary condition, union with the Mystical Body of the Universal Church, participation in the rites and sacraments and the invisible solidarity of the Communion of Saints. And as a pledge of predestination we already have the Spirit, who speaks within us and who guarantees us the enjoyment of our blessed inheritance.

CHAPTER XX

"Great Is Diana of the Ephesians!"

St. Paul had spent about three years in Ephesus, years of toil and suffering, of miracles and victories without precedent in his missionary life. He had preached daily, gathering disciples, uniting them to Christ and giving them new life through the Spirit, not so much by swaying crowds as by his conversations with individuals, his visits to the households of the faithful, his personal encouragement and the fervor of his unquenchable love. Some months later, when he had departed from Ephesus and was passing through Miletus, he was able to sum up this period of his life in his address to the Ephesians who had come to visit him at his request: "You know in what manner I have lived with you all the time since the first day that I came into the province of Asia, serving the Lord with all humility and with tears and in trials that befell me because of the plots of the Jews; how I have kept back nothing that was for your good, but have declared it to you and taught you in public and from house to house, urging Jews and Gentiles to turn to God in repentance and to believe in our Lord Jesus Christ" (Acts 20:18-21).

His struggle with the local synagogue must have been long and hard, for he later compared his predicament at that time to that of the unfortunate victims whom the Romans threw to the lions in the amphitheater for the amusement of the crowds: "I fought with beasts at Ephesus" (1 Cor. 15:32). And the fury of his enemies had even wrung from him this cry of pain: "I die daily" (1 Cor. 15:31). The anguish, the anxieties, the sufferings, the fears and stresses of those years pulse through these words of his First Epistle to the Corinthians: "To this very hour we hunger and thirst, and we are naked and buffeted, and have no fixed abode. And we toil, working with our own hands. We are reviled and we bless, we are persecuted and we bear with it, we are maligned and we entreat, we have become as the refuse of this world, the off-scouring of all, even until now!" (1 Cor. 4:11-13).

After three years, then, Paul saw that his stay in Ephesus was coming to an end. It was not that his indomitable soul quailed before persecution, for, inured to suffering and serene amid agonies of body and soul, he had, as often before, cheerfully risked torture and death for the sake of Him whose name he preached. But the church at Ephesus was now solidly established, and the voice, which for many years had been sounding in the depths of his soul when he had to make an important decision, now made itself heard insistently and clearly. "To Rome, to Rome!" it said to him, and pointed out the principal stages of the long journey—Macedonia, Achaia, Jerusalem, and then to one of the ports of Syria or Palestine to take ship for the West. Thus at the end of the year 56, the Apostle said to his disciples: "I must . . . see Rome," but he waited until the feast of Pentecost of the next year before undertaking the journey, because in the spring the great festivals of Diana would be celebrated. The devotees of the goddess would come down from the mountains with their baskets of flowers; the valleys of the Cayster and the Meander would be left deserted by their inhabitants, who would flock to the shrine with sacred offerings; pilgrims and sightseers would arrive in thousands, and from all the eastern provinces would come the unemployed and the very rich, those lovers of music and feasting, eager for the orgies and displays that Ephesus had to offer during a whole month of concerts and theatrical shows, exotic dances, horse racing and athletic and gladiatorial contests. Even now, at the beginning of the year, the asiarchs, who acted as stewards in the confraternity of the goddess and organized the feast, were bustling about, engaging acrobats, singers, animal trainers, and companies of all kinds to ensure that the month of festivities would be celebrated with the greatest possible splendor.

This great concourse of people would be a magnificent opportunity for making catechumens and for sowing the Gospel seed afar. Paul, knowing by experience the value of the occasion, did not want to squander it, and so he postponed his departure until after Pentecost. It is true that he would have to witness the orgiastic pomp of the annual commemoration, the wild enthusiasm of the crowd for their favorite contestants, and the triumphal procession of worshippers through the city: the choir of virgins, servants of Diana; the eunuchs of the temple; the bands of heralds, trumpeters, harpists and flute players; the battalion of horsemen leading the march; the charming groups of children swinging censers and scattering flower petals; and, finally, the statue of the goddess, symbolic of creative fidelity with its bizarre headdress, its clustered breasts, its rudely shaped base adorned with winged bulls, griffins, lions and

bees. However, Paul was accustomed to all the horrors of
the pagan cults, and it was sights such as this procession at
Ephesus that inspired him to raise his voice in paeans of
praise to God in which we can see a fervent protest against
the widespread adoration of devils: "To the king of the
ages, who is immortal, invisible, the one only God, be
honor and glory forever and ever. Amen" (1 Tim. 1:17).

An unexpected and deeply disturbing incident hastened
St. Paul's departure on his long-planned journey to Rome.
The cult of the goddess provided a living not only for the
priests, the priestesses and the other members of the temple
staff, but also for a large guild of artists who shaped silver,
stone, wood and clay into all sorts of objects which the pilgrims bought as souvenirs of their visit to the city or as
thank-offerings to hang on the walls of the sanctuary—
medallions, amulets, figurines, and statuettes of Diana in
her niche, as well as miniature replicas of the famous temple.

For some time now the ceramic workers, silversmiths,
sculptors and engravers had noticed that the sale of their
images had fallen off considerably, and they were not long
in pinning the blame on the Jewish missionary who had
said that the divinity has nothing to do with gold, silver,
stone or any sculpture produced by the art and imagination
of man. (Cf. Acts 19:26.) Eager to put an end to such
unorthodox teaching and to recoup his losses, Demetrius,
one of the most noted silversmiths in the city, who no
doubt owned his own establishment, gathered his fellow workers together and said to them: "Men, you know
that our wealth comes from this trade; and you see and
hear that not only at Ephesus but almost over the whole
province of Asia, this man Paul has persuaded and turned
away numbers of people, saying, 'Gods made by human

hands are not gods at all.' And there is danger, not only that this business of ours will be discredited, but also that the temple of the great Diana will be regarded as nothing, and even the magnificence of her whom all Asia and the world worship will be on the decline" (Acts 19:25-27).

This harangue of the silversmith's marks the beginning of one of the most picturesque episodes in the book of the Acts, a sequence of events which is recorded with the keenest psychological observation, that sure indication of the eyewitness, and which enables us to gauge the fruitfulness of Paul's apostolic activity, which in such a short time had spread the Gospel so widely that it threatened to ruin the business of the idol makers. The speaker's words took immediate and startling effect, and the craftsmen rushed furiously into the street shouting at the top of their voices: "Great is Diana of the Ephesians!" With every passing minute the angry crowd increased, the clamor grew louder, and in streets and squares the swirling mob gathered new members who were swept along, crying out, without knowing why, "Great is Diana of the Ephesians!"

The crowd made for the house where Paul was staying, but when they broke in they did not find him there and had to content themselves with seizing his companions, Gaius and Aristarchus, instead. Carried away by what was to them a holy anger, the demonstrators rushed to the amphitheater, which was the accustomed place for public meetings and was one of the most spacious in the world at the time, capable of holding about fifty thousand spectators. Even today the traveller can admire its ruins at the foot of Mount Coressos, the stage still intact with fragments of walls, bases of columns and of statues, while the countless lines of seats remain, cut out of the rock.

Like the roaring waves of an angry sea, the crowd

surged into the theater. The confusion was indescribable, for although many of the mob did not know why they were there, they did not cease on that account to cry up the glory of Diana. The Apostle, appalled at the danger which threatened his companions, felt the urge to plunge into the riotous throng to rescue them. It would not have been the first time he had succeeded in quelling a riot, nor would it have been the last. Moreover, this great gathering of Ephesians offered him a wonderful opportunity for proclaiming the name of Christ before an immense audience. His disciples did all in their power to restrain him, but he desisted only when implored by some asiarchs who were friends of his and who pointed out to him the terrible consequences of the conflict with the Roman authorities which was bound to occur if he appeared on the scene.

Among the rioters there were many Jews, happy that at last they had a chance of annihilating the hated apostate, and it is possible that they had used the guild of the silversmiths as a tool in their devious machinations. Nevertheless, it looked for a moment as if this riot were going to end as unpleasantly for them as the incident at Gallio's court. Here in Ephesus, as before in Corinth, they had been plotting against Paul and had succeeded in precipitating that sharp crisis which forced him to exclaim: "If the dead do not rise at all . . . why do we stand in jeopardy every hour? I die daily, I affirm it, by the very pride that I take in you, brethren, in Jesus Christ our Lord. . . . If the dead do not rise, 'let us eat and drink for tomorrow we shall die'" (1 Cor. 15:29-32).

Now the hatred of the Jews, united with the interests and the anger of the crowd, seemed near to triumph. However, there were many in the mob who were not able to distinguish the Christians from the Jews, who were as hostile to the idols of paganism as the disciples of Paul. Hence, above the mad, confused clamor of the riot, a few voices were heard to shout, "Death to the Jews!" One of the Israelites, Alexander, a copper worker and a mortal enemy of the Apostle, was pushed forward by his compatriots to act as spokesman, and he succeeded in ascending the tribune with the intention of defending his people. But his efforts at making himself heard were fruitless, and although he shouted and waved his arms he only added fuel to the rage of the crowd. Someone cried out: "He's a Jew!", and the mob, as if taking the cry for a signal, shouted louder than before, over and over again, "Great is Diana of the Ephesians!" making the nearby mountain slopes ring with the echo of their thundering voices.

For about two hours the citizens' vociferous affirmation of their faith rolled in deafening waves about the city, growing weaker at times only to surge up again with increased violence. Then the *grammateus* or chancellor of the city, who usually presided at popular assemblies, appeared on the proscenium and was greeted with a storm of applause and a murmur of expectancy. Calm was restored quickly; the strident voices were silenced, so that the official was able to make himself heard all through the theatre. "Men of Ephesus," he said, "what man indeed is there who does not know that the city of the Ephesians is a worshipper of the great Diana and of Jupiter's offspring? Since therefore this is undeniable, you ought to be calm and do nothing rash. For you have brought these men here who are neither guilty of sacrilege nor blasphemers of your goddess. Therefore, if Demetrius and the craftsmen with him have a complaint against anyone, court days are kept and there are proconsuls; let them take action against one another. And if you require anything further, it shall be settled in the lawful assembly. For we are even in danger of being accused of riot over today's uproar, since there is no culprit whom we can hold liable for this disorderly gathering" (Acts 19:35-40).

These words reminded the inflamed mob that they lived in the shadow of Rome's authority, and they trembled at the thought, their anger turning to fear. The official, seeing that his warning had taken effect, took the final bold step of dismissing the assembly. Once again Paul's cause had triumphed over its enemies, but his position in Ephesus had become untenable. His friends among the asiarchs and the official whose intervention had saved his life, all advised him to withdraw from the city, for the accumulated hatred of the Jews, artisans and temple eunuchs continued to be an imminent danger to his life, and it was during this period that both Aquila and Priscilla had been close to death on his account.

In the calm that succeeded the storm, St. Paul gathered his disciples together, exhorted them to persevere, and having embraced them, embarked for Europe. He had not relinquished his plan of going to Jerusalem, but only wished to visit his disciples in Greece and Macedonia before setting out for the Holy City. His ship put into port at Troas, where he hoped to find Titus with news of the churches beyond the Aegean Sea. The situation at Corinth weighed heavily upon him, and he was anxious to find out how the church there had received his envoy, and what had been the effect of the letter which Titus had brought them, that letter written "in such affliction and anguish of heart, with many tears" (2 Cor. 2:4). But since Titus had not yet reached the seacoast, the Apostle, still beset by uncertainty, continued on across the Aegean to Philippi. (Cf. 2 Cor. 2:12-13.) Not even the sympathetic attitude of the inhabitants of Troas toward the Gospel was able to restrain him from resuming his journey, and when his ship put out to sea, a large group of his new disciples gathered on the beach to wave farewell until the vessel was out of sight.

The crossing was a sad and painful one for Paul. There are occasions on which even the bravest souls feel crushed beneath the weight of their destiny, and this is what now happened to the tireless warrior of Christ. The whole world seemed armed against him, while his inner life was a perpetual holocaust of ineffable love. Behind him he left the hatred of Jews and pagans who thirsted for his blood; in the churches that lay ahead, he knew he would find envy and ingratitude; everywhere there were false brethren, enemies of the Cross of Christ, men filled with ambition and self-interest, heretics and Judaizers who dogged his footsteps in order to destroy his work, and about whom he could speak only with tears: ". . . whose god [was] their belly . . . [and who] mind[ed] the things of earth" (Phil. 3:18-19). He was exhausted even physically, and was to write a few weeks later: "Our outer man is decaying" (2 Cor. 4:16). He described the principal cause of his sorrows in the following words: "We would not, brethren, have you ignorant of the affliction which came upon us in Asia. We were crushed beyond measure—beyond our strength, so that we were weary even of life." But he goes on to reveal the secret of his constantly renewed strength, of his unalterable serenity, and of that gentle, trusting and self-sacrificing charity which urged him on to undertake superhuman tasks: "We have been carrying, within our very selves, our death sentence; in order that we may not trust in ourselves but in God who raises the dead" (2 Cor. 1:8-10).

His trials continued as he made the rounds of the European churches, and he was persecuted so constantly that he seemed like a fugitive driven from place to place. Indeed, his life at this period reminds us forcibly of the continual harrying suffered by the Wandering Jew of the legend. Yet he was neither a fugitive nor an aimless drifter, but the tireless missionary, the providential sower of truth whom the Spirit guided through the world to spread the Gospel despite all opposition. "When we came to Macedonia," he wrote after arriving at Philippi, "our flesh had no rest; we had troubles on every side, conflicts without and anxieties within" (2 Cor. 7:5).

However, he did not lack great consolations, for in the port of Neapolis two of his most self-sacrificing disciples, Timothy and Luke, had been on hand to greet him. Furthermore, Titus had arrived soon after with the comforting news that his mission to Corinth had been a complete success. Thanks partly to the disciple's tact, St. Paul's Epistle, far from being contemned, had touched the hearts of the Corinthians, and when it had been read in the assembly it had had unhoped-for results. The hostile factions were reconciled, the rebels were moved to repentance, Paul's calumniators were obliged to beg his pardon in order to avoid punishment, the incestuous man whom he had condemned in the Epistle did penance and made his peace with the brethren. Titus, who was naturally inclined to be gentle, had been able to accomplish his mission in a spirit of reconciliation and forgiveness, and although the Corinthians at first regarded him with fear and distrust, he had soon won them over so completely that they outdid themselves in generosity when contributing to the Apostle's collection for the poor in Jerusalem.

When he heard Titus' account of his success at Corinth, St. Paul was overjoyed, and in his second letter to the church there he wrote: "God, who comforts the humble, comforted us by the arrival of Titus. And not by his arrival only, but also by the comfort which he himself experienced in you. He told us of your longing, of your sorrow, of your zeal for me, so that I rejoiced yet more. Wherefore, although I made you sorry by my letter, I do not regret it. And even if I did regret it, seeing that the same letter did for a while make you sorry, now I am glad; not because you were made sorry, but because your sorrow led you to repentance" (2 Cor. 7:5-9).

But the glowing picture of the Corinthian church was not without its shadows. Titus had to tell the Apostle of the destruction being wrought by some agitators, about whose origin and preaching we can only guess. These men were strangers, "great apostles," as St. Paul ironically dubs them, false prophets, missionaries full of cupidity and hypocrisy. If they did not change the Gospel, they exploited it for money and tried to undermine the Apostle's prestige by meaningful silences and open calumny. "His letters," they said, "are weighty and telling, but his bodily appearance is weak and his speech of no account." "He is usually stubborn and intractable," they continued. "The haughtiness with which he refuses to take gifts from you is a sign of his arrogant ambition. And the way he announces plans for his journeys and never carries them out is a sign of his lightmindedness and inconstancy." "Don't be afraid that he'll present himself here," these envious men assured the Corinthians. "He wouldn't dare!" And they added: "If you want to see true apostles, be faithful to the disciples of Jesus, to the twelve privileged souls who lived close to Him for three years. They are not tyrannical in their rule, nor cunning in their preaching nor arrogant in their speech, as is the missionary from Tarsus." They even went so far as to cast doubts on his motives in taking up the collection for the church at Jerusalem. "Who knows," they asked, "in whose pocket this money will end up?"

Rising above these paltry personal attacks, Paul continued to rejoice at the Corinthians' repentance; yet he well knew that he would have to strengthen them against the wiles of his enemies and refute the accusations made against him. With both these ends in view, he immediately dictated to Timothy, in Philippi or Thessalonica, the most eloquent, moving and passionate Epistle of his career. Christians down through the centuries have blessed the malice of those pseudo-apostles which spurred the Apostle on to write such vibrant pages.

This Epistle begins with a hymn of joy, a canticle of thanksgiving for the restoration of peace. With fatherly pride and tenderness Paul opens his heart to his children, praising, thanking, encouraging, exhorting and counselling them, rebuking them affectionately, and gently insisting that they carry out his wishes in regard to the alms for the poor in Jerusalem. And when he has made himself master of the situation and has ensured the sympathy, receptivity and obedience of the Corinthians, he turns on his adversaries, joining battle with them, annihilating them, crushing them with sarcasm and searing them with the flames of his wrath. Critics have observed that Demosthenes followed a similar pattern in his discourse *De corona*, but what in the Greek orator was a refinement of art, is in St. Paul the spontaneous inspiration of his profound knowledge of men.

Pitilessly he unmasks the agitators, letting the Corinthians see that these enemies of his are deceitful workers masquerading as apostles of Christ, envoys of Satan who make themselves out to be ministers of justice in the same way as their master transforms himself into an angel of light. They are ruled by love of money, and for them the Gospel is only a tool to be used for gain. They harass, weaken, prey upon and devour Christ's flock, and if any of the brethren dares to oppose them, they do not hesitate to strike him across the face. They take all the credit for other men's success and push themselves forward, unlike Paul who is the first to acknowledge his weakness and insignificance.

Referring to his method of addressing the Corinthians, the Apostle says: "I am speaking foolishly." His eloquence ebbs and flows in obedience to paradoxical impulses which his enemies call contradictions. At times, perhaps, his illness and exhaustion influence his attitude toward and dealings with the Gentiles; yet all his thoughts are in "captivity to the obedience of Christ" from whom all his strength comes. "For when I am weak, then I am strong."

His enemies have accused him of vanity and arrogance, but he takes pride in the accusation, because it is not he whom people praise, but his Lord. He could boast of his advantages according to the flesh, for there is not one drop of pagan blood in his veins; he is a Jew of illustrious lineage; he has labored harder than anyone else for Christ, and he has received the blessing of divine favors. Yet he wishes to glory in one thing alone—his weakness. Calumny has forced him to make his apologia, and he now uses all the rhetorical devices to justify his boasting, or as he calls it, his foolishness. His detractors have contrasted his ministry with that of the Twelve, and he readily accepts the comparison, for as a representative of Christ he is inferior to none. To prove his point he relates, with great feeling, his apostolic labors, his superhuman efforts, and his awesome struggles. The condensed and restrained narrative of the Acts tells only a few of St. Paul's adventures and trials and leaves us to suspect that there were many others. It tells us about the stoning at Lystra, the imprisonment at Philippi, the picturesque and hazardous escape from Damascus, the dramatic disturbance at Ephesus, the hasty flights from Jerusalem, Antioch in Pisidia, Iconium, Thessalonica, Beroea, and Corinth. But it does not give us an account of the three shipwrecks which preceded the one described by St. Luke with such unforgettable detail and color, nor of the thirty-nine lashes which the Jews gave St. Paul on five different occasions, nor of the three scourgings which, in spite of his Roman citizenship, he had to suffer at the order of the imperial governors. And we know nothing, or almost nothing, of another of his claims to honor, namely, his visions, revelations and mystical raptures, and his marvellous flight through the regions of Paradise. The reticence which holds him back from recounting these mysteries is an indication that he regards them as precious treasures which the soul should guard jealously as a secret between itself and God.

However, in spite of all he could have boasted about, St. Paul wishes to glory only in his infirmities. "I have become foolish!" he says. "You have forced me. For I ought to have been commended by you, since in no way have I fallen short of the most eminent apostles, even though I am nothing" (2 Cor. 12:11). He speaks out solely because it is necessary for the edification of his disciples and the defense of the best of his conquests, that is, for the benefit of the church of Corinth, for which he is "jealous . . . with a divine jealousy. For [he] betrothed [it] to one spouse, that [he] might present [it] a chaste virgin to Christ" (2 Cor. 11:2).

Nowhere else do we see Paul's personality and eloquence

so clearly as in this Second Epistle to the Corinthians. He reveals himself as a man who is as direct, as warm and as vibrant as a beam of light. When roused in defense of the right, he cannot contain himself, and in the violence of his indignation he reveals the depths of his soul. He says what he has to say, like a man thinking aloud, without plan, without worrying about elegance or even grammatical correctness. We see a succession of the most diverse emotions mirrored on his countenance as he dictates—sorrow, anger, irony, tenderness. He goes from one extreme to the other, and in the space of a few moments he runs the whole gamut of human feeling. In his terse, vigorous, turbulent language he lays bare his sorrow-riven yet always loving and generous heart. He says he is "speaking foolishly," and at the same time he attains such sublime heights of eloquence that Demosthenes' reply to Aeschines seems cold and colorless when compared with his fiery vehemence.

CHAPTER XXI

The Mystery of Life and Death

Paul's second visit in Macedonia was not simply a tour of inspection. Always ambitious in his plans, he took advantage of the journey to extend the frontiers of Christianity, going beyond Beroea and along the Via Egnatia to the confines of Illyria and founding churches in the cities on the coast of the Adriatic—Apollonia, Dyrrachium and Lissus. He may even have penetrated into Dalmatia, that land of pirates and brigands whom Rome had difficulty in subduing, and among whom Titus was to labor some years later. But this mission must have been brief, because at the close of the year 57 St. Paul finally paid his long-promised visit to the Corinthians. On this journey to Corinth he was accompanied by a larger following of disciples than he had ever before travelled with, for he was bringing envoys from the churches in Macedonia to present the brethren's offerings in Jerusalem and to stop the mouths of his enemies. In all, his company numbered twenty and included his most assiduous co-workers in the mission field—Timothy, Titus, Luke, Erastus, the treasurer of the city of Corinth, Tertius, one of his secretaries, and Gaius the Corinthian, at whose house the Apostle stayed during this, his third sojourn in the capital of Achaia.

These days in Corinth were days of peace and joy, a breathing space in Paul's turbulent and energetic career as well as a preparation for a new series of works and enterprises. It seemed to him that his task in the Eastern world was finished, for the Gospel was firmly planted in Antioch in Pisidia, Ephesus, Corinth, in the principal cities of Asia Minor, Illyria and Macedonia. (Cf. Rom. 15:19.) The seed had been sown, and time and the breath of the Spirit would scatter it to the furthermost corners of those regions. There was no longer anything for him to do in the East; the West was calling to him, and the name of Rome was resounding more imperiously than ever in the depths of his heart. Beyond Rome, he could visualize Spain on the borders of the world, to which he in his zeal wished to extend Christ's kingdom. But first he had to go to Jerusalem to present the alms collected by his converts, and now he was only biding his time until spring when the dangerous winter storms would have ceased and the ships would be able to resume their traffic across the Mediterranean.

In Rome itself the Gospel already had a large following. At first the church there had been made up of Jews from the districts of Trastevere and Suburra, humble shopkeepers and rich merchants, date sellers and fishmongers, physicians and actors, courtesans and women fortunetellers like the one Juvenal saw on the Via Aurelia reading the future for the passersby in exchange for a few copper coins. Now it included soldiers, perhaps from the Italian cohort, as well as Roman travellers who had heard St. Peter's sermon on Pentecost Day, and imperial employees from the Eastern provinces.

In Rome, as elsewhere, the proselytes, or those who feared God, had gathered in the shadow of the synagogue, which thus, all unconsciously, served as a rallying point for future Christians. These proselytes, when invited to the wedding feast, eagerly accepted and assented to the Gospel teaching with such alacrity that the fanatical Jews were alarmed. Then, when the inevitable break between the church and the synagogue came, it gave rise to such violence that the Emperor Claudius expelled all Jews from the capital. However, although the imperial decree included also those who adored Christ, the Christian community continued to add to its membership, particularly from among the Gentiles, so that eight years later it was so flourishing that "[its] faith [was] proclaimed all over the world" (Rom. 1:8).

Paul had not founded the church at Rome and, consequently, in accordance with his rule never to interfere in another's domain, he had resolved not to preach when he arrived. Moreover, he had not yet heard the voice within him say, as it did later, "Just as thou hast borne witness to me in Jerusalem, bear witness in Rome also" (Acts 23:11). Nevertheless, he had already made up his mind to pass through Rome on the way to Spain, not because he was drawn by the fascination which the capital of the world had for provincials, but because he was impelled by a mysterious inner force and perhaps also by the presentiment that that city, the mistress of the earth, was destined to be the center of the Church. Furthermore, he had many friends and disciples there, such as Andronicus and Junias, his compatriots and companions in captivity; Urban, his associate in the work of Christ; his beloved Persis, "who . . . labored much in the Lord"; Narcissus and all his household; Mary, who had done much work in the Roman community; his beloved Stachys; Apelles, faithful to Christ, the family of Aristobulus, and many others who had come from Macedonia, Achaia or Asia Minor to live in Rome. Aquila and Priscilla also awaited him there, for they were now making and selling their tents on the banks of the Tiber. (Cf. Rom. 16:3–15.)

Before setting out for the Empire's capital, St. Paul wished to give his friends there notice of his intended visit, in order to forestall the rumors which his enemies might circulate about his journey, and to nullify any attempts they might make to stir up trouble in that prosperous and peaceful church whose members were "filled with all knowledge, so that [they were] able to admonish one another" (Rom. 15:14). Moreover, he wished to set down his teaching on the mystery of salvation in a letter to the inhabitants of that center of world civilization, "that great city . . . that strong city" (Apoc. 18:10) whose influence was such that it would send his words echoing through all the regions of the Empire. Such were the motives which inspired the Epistle to the Romans. The circumstances of its writing were solemn, for Paul was in Corinth, a territory which he himself had conquered; behind him lay the whole Greek world already sown with the Gospel seed, while before him were Rome and the far West. But between Greece and Rome stood Jerusalem, whither he intended to direct his steps, although with deep misgivings. He wrote in the belief that perhaps this letter would be his testament; at least, like a clasp of gold, it would close one period of his life with the definitive exposition of the Gospel of liberty for which he had toiled and suffered.

The central idea of the Epistle is summed up in these sentences from the first chapter: "I am not ashamed of the gospel, for it is the power of God unto salvation to everyone who believes, to Jew first and then to Greek. For in it the justice of God is revealed, from faith unto faith, as it is written, 'He who is just lives by faith' " (Rom. 1:16–17). For Paul, the Gospel illuminated the whole history of mankind; sin entered the world at the beginning of history through the action of one man, and with sin came death. No degree of natural justice could save man. The pagans were able to know God through His works, but they freely followed all the aberrations of the human mind; they did not acknowledge God, they did not glorify or thank Him, and He, to punish them, gave them over to their shameful passions, to unnatural vices, to filth and infamy. With burning words St. Paul describes the state of these idolaters sunk in corruption: "filled with all iniquity, malice, immorality, avarice, wickedness; being full of envy, murder, contention, deceit, malignity; being whisperers, detractors, hateful to God, irreverent, proud, haughty, plotters of evil; disobedient to parents, foolish, dissolute, without affection, without fidelity, without mercy" (Rom. 1:29–31).

No doubt here Paul was recalling what he had seen in his travels about the East, and the thought of the scenes in the groves of Daphne in Antioch and in the temples at Paphos and Corinth made his voice ring with anger as he dictated to Tertius this terrible catalogue of sins. Rome, too, if he had seen it, would have left the same nauseating impression upon him. It is true that there were still Romans with the fidelity of Lucretia and the integrity of Cato; but the most eloquent commentaries on the Apostle's description of pagan degradation are to be found in the epigrams of Martial and Juvenal; in the descriptions given by Tacitus, the tragic historian and psychologist, who wrote with the insight and virtuosity of the artist; in the unpolished, starkly realistic accounts given by Suetonius of the court of Nero and Caligula; in the paintings and sketches at Pompeii; and in Petronius' *Satyricon,* which describes the most terrible perversions with the calmness of complete amorality.

The pagans were sunk in impiety and shameful impurity. But had the Jews, in contrast, found the path of justice? They believed they had, but implacable reality accused and condemned them: "But if thou art called 'Jew,'" writes St. Paul, "and dost rely upon the Law, and dost glory in God, and dost know his will, and dost approve the better things, being informed by the Law, thou art confident that thou art a guide to the blind, a light to those who are in darkness, an instructor of the unwise, a teacher of children, having in the Law a pattern of knowledge and of truth. Thou therefore who teachest another, dost thou not teach thyself? Thou who preachest that men should not steal, dost thou steal? Thou who sayest that man should not commit adultery, dost thou commit adultery? Thou who dost abominate idols, dost thou commit sacrilege? Thou who dost glory in the Law, dost thou dishonor God by transgressing the Law? 'For the name of God,' as it is written, 'is blasphemed through you among the Gentiles'" (Rom. 2:17-24). Actually, the Jews were more culpable than the Gentiles, because they had more motives for acknowledging God; they had the Law, the prophecies, and enjoyed the privileges of the Chosen Race. They were the men of promise, and to them belonged "the adoption as sons, and the glory and the covenants and the legislation, and the worship and the promises; who have the fathers, and from whom is the Christ according to the flesh" (Rom. 9:4-5). But they were unfaithful to the divine call, and extinguished the light which was given into their hands.

"For there is no distinction, as all have sinned and have need of the glory of God. They are justified freely by his grace through the redemption which is in Christ Jesus" (Rom. 3:22-25).

St. Paul then proceeds to describe the unfolding of the divine plan and to show that if God permitted the whole of humanity to fall into the abyss, it was because He had the means of saving it. "God has shut up all in unbelief, that he may have mercy on all. Oh, the depths of the riches of the wisdom and of the knowledge of God! How incomprehensible are his judgments and how unsearchable his ways!" (Rom. 11:32-33). These immense perspectives, before which man stands in awe and fear, prepare him to understand the mystery of his redemption. This is the kernel of St. Paul's mystical theology, and it is in this Epistle to the Romans that he expands it with greatest force, clarity and insight. "Where the offense has abounded, grace has abounded yet more; so that as sin has reigned unto death, so also grace may reign by justice unto life everlasting through Jesus Christ our Lord" (Rom. 5:20-21).

St. Paul's central idea is that Christ has died and risen again, and that by baptism the Christian, incorporated into Him, dies and rises with Him, thus becoming a son of God and taking on a new life. The washing in baptism is a purification and a new birth, no mere symbol but a profound reality which reaches into the very depths of our being. However, while we are on earth, neither this death nor this new life is perfect, because although the interior man, that is to say, the new man, enjoys union with God, he still remains under the influence of a power which chains him to the law of sin: "Unhappy man that I am! Who will deliver me from the body of this death?" (Rom. 7:24). But man is saved by hope; "And hope does not disappoint, because the charity of God is poured forth in our hearts by the Holy Spirit who has been given to us" (Rom. 5:5). For the rest, grace is given us to overcome all our weaknesses, and the trials of this world are insignificant when compared with the glory that awaits us.

The Spirit is with us, making us live and giving us the victory. "If anyone does not have the Spirit of Christ, he does not belong to Christ. But if Christ is in you, the body, it is true, is dead by reason of sin, but the Spirit is life by reason of justification. But if the Spirit of him who raised Jesus from the dead dwells in you, then he who raised Jesus Christ from the dead will also bring to life your mortal bodies because of his Spirit who dwells in you" (Rom. 8:9–11).

This sublime doctrine has an echo in the moral life of the Christian. St. Paul is a great moralist, and his ethical teaching is closely bound up with his theology and eschatology. Thus the exhortations which he never fails to put at the end of his Epistles are not vague platitudes, but express a very concrete ideal which he proposes to his disciples, or, rather, to all the disciples of Christ. All perfection is an imitation of Christ, of Christ dead and buried as well as of Christ living and glorious; and this divine ideal is presented to us in a strikingly gracious and compelling manner. In this Epistle we find, perhaps for the first time, that secret sympathy which constantly inclines the Church toward what can be called humanism in the noblest sense of the word. We already know the respect which Paul, the Jew and Pharisee, had for the best features of Graeco-Latin civilization, and it is not strange to find that the Hellenic ideal influenced his conception of moral perfection. It could be said that having broken the bonds of Pharisaical

formalism, he wished also to destroy the Jewish pattern itself, and to form a humanity more free and more complete
than that legislated for in Leviticus; that he wished to make
a new mold to produce the masterpiece he dreamed of, at
once divine and human, a model of perfection for Greek
and Jew alike.

Elsewhere he says: ". . . whatever things are true, whatever honorable, whatever just, whatever holy, whatever
lovable, whatever of good repute . . . think on these
things" (Phil. 4:8). Here, in the Epistle to the Romans, he
warns them that while seeking after these good things they
should be careful not to become ensnared by the false
attractions of the world: "Therefore, brethren, we are
debtors, not to the flesh, that we should live according to
the flesh, for if you live according to the flesh you will die;
but if by the spirit you put to death the deeds of the flesh,
you will live" (Rom. 8:12-13). And a little further on, his
sublime theology resolves itself into superbly clear-cut
maxims: "Bless those who persecute you; rejoice with
those who rejoice; weep with those who weep. . . . 'If
thy enemy is hungry give him food, if he is thirsty, give
him drink; for by so doing thou wilt heap coals of fire
upon his head.' " (Cf. Rom. 12:20-21.)

Unlike the nationalistic Jews who, with their stubborn
fanaticism, were continually trying to throw off the yoke
of Rome, St. Paul counselled respect for authority. He
advised his disciples to be exemplary citizens, "not only
because of the wrath, but also for conscience' sake" (Rom.
13:5). His line of argument seems to presuppose that
Roman authority acted justly; "for it is God's minister, an
avenger to execute wrath on him who does evil." Although
the grandeur of Rome did not dazzle him as it did Josephus,
a man of his character was bound to admire the Empire, for

it possessed order, strength, continuity, a sense of organization, a spirit of equity, and the logic of action—all of them ideas which had molded his own personality. Yet although he was a Roman citizen, he rarely used his title, perhaps disdaining to live under the protection of the lords of the world. However, he understood that the imperial unity of government opened up prodigious horizons to his work, and that Rome's genius for organization had made it possible for him to journey over the imperial highways in safety. An indefatigable traveller, he was so well aware of the chaos that reigned in the countries of the East that he never even considered carrying the Gospel to lands where the Roman legionaries had not penetrated.

At any rate, his command to obey the authorities is general, and is part of a mystical certitude that the ruler is the representative of the divine attributes of power, justice and mercy. And to this precept which he had to set down because there were so many secret rebels, he added another no less necessary, that is, distrust of those who fomented divisions and scandals, of the Judaizers, the false prophets and those who spread evil: "Now I exhort you, brethren, that you watch those who cause dissensions and scandals . . . and avoid them. For such do not serve Christ our Lord but their own belly, and by smooth words and flattery deceive the hearts of the simple" (Rom. 16:17-18). In Corinth such men had already wrought havoc, and although they had not yet come to Rome, it was necessary for the Christians there to be prepared to repulse them and their poisonous whisperings: "For your submission . . . has been published everywhere," continued the Apostle. "I rejoice therefore over you. Yet I would have you wise as to what is good, and guileless as to what is evil" (Rom. 16:19).

In our constant striving toward Christian perfection, the Spirit strengthens our weakness. We do not even know what we should ask for, but "the Spirit pleads for us with unutterable groanings. And he who searches the hearts knows what the Spirit desires. . . ." Furthermore, we are not alone, "for all creation groans and travails in pain," trembling in expectation of that new life. (Cf. Rom. 8:26–27; 8:22.) Thus St. Paul reveals to us the unity of the world and its inhabitants, for everything created was wounded and corrupted by sin, and all is renewed by the action of Christ, through whom it returns to God. God and man, heaven and earth, are combined in the Apostle's theology, which is at once human and cosmic.

God is the beginning and end of all things. It is true that in St. Paul's doctrine Christ is pre-eminent, but He Himself comes from the Father and leads us to Him, so that, contrary to what has been alleged, the Apostle's teaching on Christ and on God are inseparable in this magnificent theological panorama. Christ is God, and transformation into Christ means transformation into God, for "Christ . . . who is over all things, [is] God blessed forever" (Rom. 9:5). And this infinite gift of transformation into Christ is applied to each Christian by a particular pre-destination which St. Paul expounds in burning words.

By a mysterious election the soul is admitted to participation in the privileges of the new Israel, an election by which God chooses one and leaves the other, loves one and hates the other: "Jacob I have loved, but Esau I have hated" (Rom. 9:13). This stern and mystery-filled doctrine is in wonderful harmony with St. Paul's own determined character. He affirms it joyfully, repeats it, proclaims it in all its severity, and recalls it with great rejoicing, for it changed him from a persecutor and blasphemer into a vessel of election, and he is enraptured by the inscrutable wisdom of the divine decrees. He does not tremble or grow fearful in the face of the arbitrariness of a selection that could only be good and just; on the contrary, the thought of grace's victory over sin fills him with confidence and love, and causes him to exclaim daringly: "For God hath shut up all in unbelief, that he may have mercy on all" (Rom. 11:32). He exalts the justice which was given us by a sovereign love, and his heart brims over with exultation at the sublimity of the mystery which he describes in these unforgettable words:

For those whom he has foreknown he has also predestined to become conformed to the image of his Son, that he should be the firstborn among many brethren. And those whom he predestined, them he has also called; and those whom he has called, them he has also justified, and those whom he has justified, them he has also glorified. What then shall we say to these things? If God is for us, who is against us? . . . Who shall make accusation against the elect of God? It is God who justifies! Who shall condemn? . . . Who shall separate us from the love of Christ? . . . I am sure that neither death, nor life, nor angels, nor principalities, nor things present, nor things to come, nor powers, nor height, nor depth, nor any other creature will be able to separate us from the love of God, which is in Christ Jesus our Lord (Rom. 8:29–39).

This Epistle is actually a profound treatise on theology in which flashes of genius illuminate the fundamental dogmas of Christianity—the necessity of faith, the gratuitous acquisition of justice, the action of grace in sanctification, the distinction between the Three Divine Persons, the mystery of original sin, the universality of the Redemption, the unity of the Church, and the incorporation of the Christian with Christ. The general tone of the Epistle seems to indicate that St. Paul did not write it in just a few hours as he did some of his other letters, but that he meditated long upon it. The difficulty of the theme, the abundance and careful linking of the ideas, the terseness of the style, the profusion and aptness of the quotations, the subtlety of the arguments, and the absence of repetition, are signs of prolonged labor performed on a plane above all local controversy and sweeping indignation such as had inspired the Epistle to the Galatians, in which the Apostle expresses similar ideas.

The Epistle to the Romans is the ripe fruit of that winter of the year 58 which the Apostle had to spend in Corinth, since traffic on the high seas did not recommence until the beginning of spring, or, at the earliest, the first weeks of March. His plan was to embark as soon as possible in order to reach Jerusalem before the Passover, but at the last moment he found out that the Jews were plotting to assassinate him on the ship or, failing that, to throw him overboard during the voyage. They still hated him enough to want to kill him, but now they had perhaps an added motive for waylaying him, namely, the money which he was carrying to his brethren. The Apostle had already hinted at these dangers in the conclusion of his Epistle to the Romans, and had also intimated there that he was not sure of his reception in the Holy City: "Now I exhort you, brethren . . . that you help me by your prayers to God for me, that I may be delivered from the unbelievers in Judea, and that the offering of my service may be acceptable to the saints in Jerusalem . . ." (Rom. 15:30-31).

Despite these forebodings, Paul decided to put his head in the lion's mouth. But instead of going by sea, where he could easily fall prey to the plotting of the powerful Jewish merchants and shipowners, he resolved to make the journey on foot, at least as far as Macedonia, thereby renouncing the opportunity of celebrating the Pasch in Jerusalem. Accordingly, he set out accompanied by more than a dozen disciples, and, skirting Thebes, then reduced to an insignificant village, went through the pass of Thermopylae to the plains of Thessaly. They stopped in Thessalonica long enough to salute the brethren, and here the party split up, some of them taking ship for Troas. Paul, with the rest, pushed on to Philippi, where he wished to spend the week of the unleavened bread out of regard for the Jewish Pasch and in order to solemnize the anniversary of the death of Christ, our true Paschal Lamb whose immolation should be celebrated "with the unleavened bread of sincerity and truth" (1 Cor. 5:8).

From Philippi, Paul and the remainder of his companions journeyed to the seaport of Neapolis, and there, taking every precaution to throw his would-be assassins off the trail, he and his friends embarked as inconspicuously as possible. With the party went Luke who, ever fascinated by the sea, has left us an interesting note on the journey. The beginning of the voyage was not favorable, since the ship was buffeted by contrary winds and could not leave the Bay of Thasos, so that it took five days to reach Troas, three days at least being lost in fighting the head winds. At Troas, where the rest of the party had already arrived, they had to change ships, and another week went by before they found a vessel to carry them from port to port down the coast of Asia Minor.

The week they spent in Troas was passed in conversation with the brethren of the church there, and on the evening of the last day, which was a Sunday, Paul gathered the faithful "for the breaking of bread" in a large upper room or cenacle. Since he was to leave on the next day, the Apostle addressed the congregation at considerable length, giving them many counsels and instructions. The heat in the room was stifling, for the assembly was close-packed and many lamps were burning. All the windows were wide open to catch the sea breeze, and on one of the window sills was seated a young man named Eutychus, "the man of good fortune," listening and fighting the drowsiness induced by the heat and the fatigue of his day's toil. Suddenly there was a commotion in the assembly and Paul's discourse was interrupted by women's screams, for Eutychus had fallen asleep and toppled into the street. The brethren rushed out to his assistance, but finding only a shattered, lifeless body, they began to weep and lament. Paul came down to see what had happened and when he saw the young man lying dead, he recalled the example of the ancient Hebrew prophets. Asking to be left alone with the corpse, he stretched himself face down upon it for a moment; then, returning to the assembly, he announced: "Do not be alarmed, life is still in him." Without further reference to the event he continued his discourse, ate the *Agapé* with his disciples, consecrated and distributed the Body of Christ, and as the first light of dawn paled the sky, he descended from the cenacle to continue his journey to Jerusalem.

His companions took ship immediately, but he preferred to travel the next stage on foot, and at nightfall rejoined his friends at Assos, a small town whose ruins can still be seen on a rocky point jutting out into the sea. The next day they all boarded the ship and set out toward Lesbos, the island of Sappho. From Mitylene, its capital, to Chios took one day's sailing; from Chios to Samos another, and on the third day they passed Ephesus without stopping and reached the next port, Miletus, where the ship had to put in for several days because of trade commitments. On each island that they passed, in every bend of the coast, there were sonorous names which awakened memories of great feats and echoes of poetry. Every night, the ship lay to along this historic coast, and continued its journey only with the advent of dawn, when the north wind again filled the sails.

No sooner had the Apostle set foot on land at Miletus than he sent a message to the leaders of the church at Ephesus, asking them to come to see him. They arrived the next day, eager to hear him once again, and he gathered them together in a building near the wharves, probably in one of the warehouses built there for storage purposes. He spoke to them at length, exhorting them to watch over the Church of God and preserve unchanged the doctrine he had preached to them. St. Luke has recorded for us the essential parts of that celebrated discourse, which throbs with the emotion of a final leave-taking, and in which the Apostle pours out his love for his disciples. If his speech on the Areopagus in Athens was a revelation of his genius, his address at Miletus shows us his heart. This scene has been compared to the one in Euripides' *Alcestis* in which Hercules, about to depart, bids farewell to King Admetus, to the woman he has saved, and to the people he has made happy. But St. Paul's words enshrine a greater light, a more profound emotion, a tenderness that is more intimate, more natural and more human.

"You know," he said, "in what manner I have lived with you all the time since the first day that I came into the province of Asia, serving the Lord with all humility and with tears and in trials that befell me because of the plots of the Jews . . ." (Acts 20:19). Like a father speaking to his children, he recalled his anxieties, his labors, and the care he had taken of each one of them, and, confiding to them his forebodings, he added: "And now, behold, I am going to Jerusalem, compelled by the Spirit, not knowing what will happen to me there, except that in every city the Holy Spirit warns me, saying that imprisonment and persecution are awaiting me. But I fear none of these, nor do I count my life more precious than myself, if only I may accomplish my course and the ministry that I have received from the Lord Jesus, to bear witness to the gospel of the grace of God" (Acts 20:22-24).

Each sentence of this farewell went straight to the hearts of his listeners, impressing them with his deep simplicity, making them partners in his greatness, increasing their admiration for his courage and generosity, revealing to them his profound humility and patience, and drawing them closer than ever to him by giving them new evidence of his sound judgment and self-forgetfulness. "And now, behold," the Apostle continued, "I know that you all among whom I went about preaching the kingdom of God, will see my face no longer. Therefore I call you to witness this day that I am innocent of the blood of all; for I have not shrunk from declaring to you the whole counsel of God. Take heed to yourselves and to the whole flock in which the Holy Spirit has placed you as bishops, to rule the Church of God which he has purchased with his own blood. I know that after my departure fierce wolves will get in among you, and will not spare the flock. . . . Watch, therefore, and remember that for three years night and day I did not cease with tears to admonish every one of you" (Acts 20:25-31).

As he spoke, Paul gesticulated, now with vehemence,

now with pathos; if he had not done so, he would not have been an Oriental, he would not have been himself. Sensitive, energetic and highly demonstrative, he was able to externalize vividly the innermost feelings of his heart. Thus, when the pagans at Lystra had taken him for one of the gods from Olympus, he had torn his garments as a sign of his angry disapproval, and later, in Caesarea, when he spoke before Festus and Agrippa, he held up the chains that bound him and said: "I would to God that . . . not only thou but also all who hear me today might become such as I am, except for these chains" (Acts 26:29). And when he described in vibrant tones the sufferings of Christ, he appeared more like a prophet than a preacher.

Now, as he finished his farewell to the disciples from Ephesus, his voice became increasingly tender and appealing, until his listeners' hearts were breaking within them: "And now I commend you to God and to the world of his grace, who is able to build up and to give the inheritance among all the sanctified." Then, stretching out to them his work-hardened hands, he added: "I have coveted no one's silver or gold or apparel. You yourselves know that these hands of mine have provided for my needs and those of my companions. In all things I have shown you that by so toiling you ought to help the weak and remember the word of the Lord Jesus, that he himself said, 'It is more blessed to give than to receive'" (Acts 20:32-35).

No one who reads these words will be surprised at the emotions they awoke in his audience, at the tears the disciples shed and the moving scene which followed. "Having said this," relates St. Luke, "he knelt down and prayed with them all. And there was much weeping among them all and they fell on Paul's neck and kissed him . . ." (Acts 20:36-38). But the time for parting had come and he had to tear himself away from them. Stricken with grief, the Ephesians stood like statues, tears pouring down their cheeks as they watched the ship draw away from land, keeping their eyes fixed upon it until it disappeared below the horizon.

After leaving Miletus, the ship bearing Paul and his companions made a straight course for Cos, where it arrived before nightfall of the same day and cast anchor to await dawn and the morning winds. On the following day, the vessel reached Rhodes after rounding the peninsula of Cnidus, a finger of land reaching out into the Sea of Greece. Ahead rose the snow-capped mountains of Lycia, and one more day's journey brought the travellers to land at Patara, the city on the Xanthus River, shaded by groves of palm trees and famous for its temple of Apollo. They arrived just in time to catch a larger ship which was about to sail across the eastern Mediterranean to the coasts of Phoenicia. ". . . We went on board and set sail," writes St. Luke. "After sighting Cyprus and leaving it to the left, we sailed for Syria and landed at Tyre, for there the ship was to unload her cargo" (Acts 21:3-4).

CHAPTER XXII

The Prisoner

The travellers' forebodings increased as they drew nearer Jerusalem. In Tyre, the Phoenician metropolis which the prophets of Israel had anathematized and which was now fallen from its ancient greatness, the Holy Spirit reiterated His predictions. "Having looked up the disciples," says St. Luke, "we stayed there seven days. And they told Paul through the Spirit not to go to Jerusalem. But when our time was up we left there and went on, and all of them with their wives and children escorted us till we were out of the city; and we knelt on the shore and prayed. And having said farewell to one another, we went on board the ship and they returned home" (Acts 21:4–6). Sailing south along the coast, Paul and his companions came to Ptolemais, where they left the ship and spent a day with that small community of brethren. From there they made their way among the coastal foothills, passing Mount Carmel and coming out onto the fertile plain of Sharon, near the northern end of which lay the city of Caesarea. Paul, sure now of reaching Jerusalem for the feast of Pentecost, wished to pass the days that remained to him in the church at Caesarea. Philip, "the evangelist," as St. Luke calls him, one of the first seven deacons, lived in the city with his

303

four unmarried daughters, all of whom possessed the gift of prophecy, and he threw open his house to the Apostle. Thus in this city on the plain, Paul found a man who had been an intimate friend of the martyred Stephen, and a generous, broadminded Hellenistic atmosphere.

The calm of those happy days was broken suddenly by the advent of a man who came down from Judea. Paul recognized the newcomer as the prophet Agabus who, fifteen years before in Antioch, had foretold famine and sorrow. Once again the seer presaged misfortune, for one day when the faithful were gathered together he appeared in their midst and, without a word, approached and took the cincture from about the Apostle's waist and bound his own hands and feet with it. Everyone watched him uneasily, at a loss to know what he was about, until he explained his actions by announcing: "Thus says the Holy Spirit: 'The man whose girdle this is the Jews will bind like this at Jerusalem, and they will deliver him into the hands of the Gentiles'" (Acts 21:11).

These words fell like a thunderbolt upon the assembly, changing their presentiments into certainty. With tears in their eyes, Paul's companions and the brethren of Caesarea crowded around him, begging him not to go to Jerusalem. But the Apostle, feeling the irresistible call of God, remonstrated gently yet firmly with them. "What do you mean by weeping and breaking my heart?" he asked. "For I am ready not only to be bound but even to die at Jerusalem for the name of the Lord Jesus." In the face of this reply, which revealed both his deep love for them and his unflinching resolution, the disciples "acquiesced and said, 'The Lord's will be done.'" (Cf. Acts 21:13, 14.)

For a moment the disciples' natural instinct to save their master had seemed to stifle their faith in a Messias glorified by suffering, but far from fearing pain, several of them now showed their willingness to come to grips with it by accompanying the missionaries on their journey to Jerusalem. Yet concern for their teacher filled the disciples with sorrow, and only Paul appeared able to conquer fear completely and to look on the dark future with radiant joy. No doubt he was remembering his Master's last journey to celebrate the Passover in the city that had killed the prophets. He knew he was going to meet suffering too, but, without being able to foretell exactly what the future held for him, he seemed to hear an inner voice which hinted that his missionary work was not to end so soon.

When Paul and his companions arrived in Jerusalem, the inhabitants and the pilgrims had already begun to celebrate the commemoration of Moses' receiving the Law on Mount Sinai. There were signs of jubilant festivity everywhere—crowds of pilgrims, blaring trumpets, and streets strewn with branches and flowers. The Apostle and his friends went to live in the house of Mnason, a Cypriot who was free of legalistic scruples and who had joined them at Caesarea. Paul had a sister living in Jerusalem, but did not think it advisable to lodge with her, nor with the brethren of the local church, with whom his companions, almost all of whom were uncircumcised, would soon have clashed. Now that he was actually in the Holy City, a lively apprehension took hold of him, for soon he would be in the midst of that church from which his bitterest enemies had sprung—those false brethren who had attacked his work in Antioch, who had stirred up the churches of Galatia against him, and who had blackened his name in Corinth. He knew that his conduct had been irreproachable and his bearing without offense, for the more they had criticized him, the more he had striven to preserve the unity of the church and the good opinion of the community in Jerusalem. His present visit to them, and the collected alms which he brought them were new proofs of his desire for harmony in the household of God, and of his friendly intentions. But how would they receive him? He could not tell, although he no longer had to ask himself, as he had before, if he had "run in vain," for his accomplishments lay behind him, living and flourishing, eloquent witnesses in his favor. Yet it could happen that even here his opponents would go so far as to disown him and refuse the offering he wished to present to them, and in that case schism would be inevitable. He was sure of St. James' support and of his fidelity to the prescriptions laid down in the assembly years ago. But Paul was now surrounded by many enemies full of poisonous hatred, swollen with pride, and opposed in principle to his missionary methods, and Peter was no longer there to lend him the weight of his authority. This was the problem that disquieted him, a problem that weighed on him more than all the machinations of the non-Christian Jews.

The situation was relieved only after an official meeting of the elders had been called, and the Apostle had exercised all his tact and goodwill. On the day after his arrival, St. James called together in his house all the leaders, the presbyters and bishops of the community, and Paul and his companions presented themselves before the gathering. This was the critical moment. First, the customary greetings were exchanged, the kiss of peace was given, and the usual prayers were said in common. Then Paul, invited to speak, gave an account of his labors, his successes, the wonders with which God had blessed his apostolate, and the fidelity with which he had carried out the conditions agreed upon by the pillars of the Church. He concluded by presenting to the first among the churches, as a proof of his respect and affection, his collection of alms as a testimony to the unity of his disciples with the saints at Jerusalem.

The whole assembly listened kindly to his narrative, and when he had finished speaking, "they praised God." However, they still thought it necessary to exact from him some palpable and irrefutable proof of his adherence to the Law, in order to pacify those who had been alarmed and disquieted by his methods. The rigorists had accused him of having advised the Jews of the Diaspora to apostatize, and of telling them that they should not circumcise their children or observe the national traditions. It was important that he should dispel that rumor which could cause trouble, and therefore the elders of the assembly were of the opinion that he ought to silence his enemies by a public act of devotion. They themselves suggested what he should do: "We have four men who are under a vow; take them and sanctify thyself along with them, and pay for them that they may shave their heads; and all will know that what they have heard of thee is false, but that thou thyself also observest the Law" (Acts 21:23-24).

Paul could have refused, for he knew well that the murmuring raised against him came only from the evil-willed and hostile. He had always observed the Law as far as was compatible with the practices of Christianity, and he had prescribed the same course of action for the Jews who entered the Church. But his whole Christian life had been ruled by the principle of charity, which at times had led him to make concessions which his enemies could have interpreted as being scandalous: "Take care lest perhaps this liberty of yours become a stumbling-block to the weak." (Cf. 1 Cor. 8:9.) Yet had not he fulfilled the

Nazarite vow on his last visit to the Holy City? And now the assembly were asking him to do less than he had done before without prompting; they merely wanted him to present himself at the Temple as the sponsor and guarantor of four of the brethren, and in their name to pay for the victims demanded by the Law in such cases: a male lamb, an ewe lamb, a ram and a basket of unleavened bread.

However, Paul willingly acceded to the elders' wishes; on the following day he took the four Nazarites, "and . . . after being purified along with them he entered the temple and announced the completion of the days of purification, when the sacrifice would be offered for each of them" (Acts 21:26). Only those who have not sincerely examined the Apostle's teaching can see in this act of his a contradiction of his whole trend of thought. He certainly believed that true justice did not come from the Law but from faith; yet the Law, now superseded and destined to disappear, could still have circumstantial worth. Did he not often say: "Every man who has himself circumcised . . . is bound to observe the whole Law"? (Cf. Gal. 5:3.) For the rest, the Nazarite practices were an ascetical form of separation from the world and consecration to God which Christianity would not destroy, but rather would perfect. We can be sure that when St. Paul presented himself in the Temple to answer for the four brethren, he spoke with all the solemnity of a devout Jew and with deep devotion, for he knew the real significance of the rite, viewing it as he did in the light of the charity and liberty of the sons of God. Truly he made himself all things to all men: for the Jews he became a Jew, having in mind the punctilious believers to whom the elders of Jerusalem had just referred when they said: "Thou seest, brother, how many thousands of believers there are among the Jews, all of them zealous upholders of the Law" (Acts 21:20).

In the Temple there was a special place set aside in the inner court for the Nazarites, and it seems that the Apostle spent his first days in Jerusalem there, engaged in performing the sacred rites with his companions. He had already passed a week in the city without his presence causing the least disturbance, when one afternoon, as he was walking through the porches of the Temple, a group of fanatics gathered around him, shouting: "Men of Israel, help. This is the man who teaches all men everywhere against the people and the Law and this place." And they added this terrible calumny: "Moreover he has brought Gentiles also into the temple and has desecrated this holy place" (Acts 21:28). The agitators were Asiatic pilgrims from those synagogues of Ephesus which had caused the Apostle so much trouble the previous year. They had recently seen him in the city with one of his travelling companions, a man of Greek origin and a fellow citizen of theirs from the metropolis of Asia Minor. That was the slim evidence upon which they based the charge which they now shouted from the upper terrace of the Temple, thereby causing a commotion among the crowd of devotees and curious onlookers who gathered in the court below.

Their accusation was a very grave one, for every uncircumcised stranger who penetrated beyond the Gentiles' Porch was guilty of a capital crime, as was clearly indicated by the notices displayed in Greek and Latin on the doors of the inner court. The riot spread rapidly, and in a short time a mob had gathered in the Temple, shaking their fists and shouting denunciations. Paul tried to speak in his own defense, but the roar of the crowd drowned his voice and a handful of fanatics pushed and dragged him out of the

Temple, whose doors the Levites hurriedly closed lest the sacred edifice be desecrated by the taking of human life within its walls.

The aggressors were belaboring their victim when the swords of the Roman legionaries began to flash over the heads of the crowd. In a center of fanaticism such as Jerusalem, and especially at the times of the great solemnities, the Roman authorities were keenly vigilant. Therefore, when the sentinels on the walls of the Fortress Antonia had heard the enraged clamor of the mob and had seen the surging mass of humanity, they immediately sounded the alarm, and an official had run to the tribune of the cohort with the breathless announcement: "The city is in a tumult!"

The tribune quickly gathered a group of centurions and soldiers and led them at a run down the stone stairway which connected the fortress with the Gentiles' Porch. Then, brandishing his sword, he forced his way through the crowd to where Paul, covered with blood but still undaunted, faced his attackers. "Stand back!" the tribune commanded imperiously: "If he has done evil, he shall be punished." While the soldiers took the Apostle into custody and bound his hands, the mob kept on denouncing him and accusing him of so many different things that the tribune was unable to find out the real cause of the tumult. He heard his prisoner called "a disturber of the peace," "a revolutionary," "a deceiver of the people," and he concluded that he had on his hands the Egyptian Jew who, a few months before, had appeared on the Mount of Olives with several thousand ragged zealots whom he had persuaded that he was an incarnation of the Messias, and that the walls of the Holy City would tumble to the ground at the sound of his voice as had those of Jericho at the blare of the trumpets. The Romans had dealt quickly with this insurrection, but the pseudo-prophet had escaped their grasp, and now, seeing the mob's violent reaction to this stranger in the Temple, the tribune was sure that at last he had found the trouble maker.

Fearing that the crowd would lynch the prisoner, the tribune ordered the soldiers to take him to the fortress. When the angry Jews saw that their victim was being snatched from them they swarmed up the stairway after him, trying to break through the cordon of soldiers and recapture him. But they were beaten back, and the Apostle was finally deposited at the top of the stairway outside the door leading to the fortress. He was panting with exertion, covered with blood, sweat and dust, his beard and hair dishevelled, and his garments in shreds. For the first time, the tribune was able to take a good look at his prisoner, and he was examining the Apostle with a glint of amusement in his eyes when Paul addressed him in good Greek and with a tranquil, respectful air: "May I say something to thee?" A sublime idea had just suggested itself to the undaunted herald of Christ, the idea of witnessing to his Lord for the last time at the very gates of the Temple which was marked for ruin, and in the presence of an immense multitude in which, along with the upholders of Roman law, the whole of Israel was represented—priests, chiefs of the Synagogue, Jews from Jerusalem, pilgrims from all over Palestine, from Asia Minor, Alexandria and the far West. We have already seen examples of Paul's intrepidity in the face of danger, but never have we found him so much master of himself as at this moment.

The tribune's name was Lysias and he was a typical Greek: astute, keen, boastful, diplomatic, resourceful, haughty, and yet docile before the grandeur of Rome. He was not a bad man at heart, and he was always careful not to make a false step in wielding the authority entrusted to him by the lords of the world. His first reaction to the prisoner's request was surprise: he thought he had captured an ignorant peasant, but the few words Paul had spoken were enough to convince him that his prisoner was a man of culture, quite different from the unlettered eccentric he had taken him for. "Dost thou know Greek?" he exclaimed. "Art not thou the Egyptian who recently stirred up to sedition and led out into the desert the four thousand assassins?" Paul, serenely and with justifiable pride, answered: "I am a Jew from Tarsus in Cilicia, a citizen of no insignificant city. But I beg thee, give me leave to speak to the people." (Cf. Acts 21:37–39.)

The tribune, Greek that he was, and therefore curious and a lover of eloquence, gave his consent, motioning to the two legionaries who held Paul's chains to let him go. The Apostle turned to face the multitude which was still howling for his blood, shaking their fists and brandishing clubs. Raising his manacled right hand, he motioned for silence and the crowd quieted down, awed by the fiery glance and imperious gesture of this man whose short figure, standing high above them on the staircase and outlined against the grim massive bulk of the fortress, seemed like a reincarnation of the ancient prophets of Israel.

Speaking now in Aramaic, the language of the time, he began with a salutation and a plea for their attention and consideration: "Brethren and fathers, listen to what I have to say to you in my defense." His ringing, commanding voice cut across and quelled the murmuring of his audience, and in the deep silence that followed, he related once more the Pharisaical enthusiasm of his youth, the vision at Damascus that had rescued him from error, and his instruction and baptism by Ananias, "an observer of the Law, respected by all the Jews who lived there." With consummate skill he stressed everything Jewish, and thus succeeded in holding in leash the anger of his bloodthirsty listeners. He pointed out that his conversion was simply submission to "the God of our fathers," the God of Abraham, Jacob, Moses and David, and that although he had wished to remain in Jerusalem in the service of his fellow countrymen, he had not done so because while praying in the Temple he had heard the Lord's voice commanding him to preach to the Gentiles.

In making this point, the most delicate part of his defense, he had recalled to them Stephen's martyrdom, as if to emphasize his own former upholding of the Law. But his appeal was in vain, for upon hearing the hated name "Gentiles," the crowd, hitherto subdued and spellbound, broke out into a wild clamor of hatred, as if all their rabid fury had been once more unleashed by what they considered an insult to their patriotism. Like madmen they gnashed their teeth, shouted, waved menacing arms, tore their garments and cast handfuls of dust into the air, and above their incoherent clamor could be heard cries of "Away from the earth with such a one! It is not right that he should live."

The tribune saw that he had better put an end to the turbulent scene, and accordingly he ordered his soldiers to bring the prisoner into the fortress. Safe behind the barred door which shut out the noise of the mob, he decided that he would have to find out the reason for the riot and then pacify the fury of the Jews, which the representatives of Rome always feared. He had understood none of Paul's speech and was growing more perplexed every moment. He could have asked his prisoner to explain, but he was so angry with that disturber of the peace that he perversely made up his mind to use more violent methods of getting the truth. Therefore, thinking that he had to deal with a common agitator, a slave who had earned crucifixion, he ordered him to be scourged. Paul was stripped of his garments and his hands were stretched above his head and tied to a post, and when all was in readiness two executioners appeared with their fearsome scourges composed of long, flexible lashes bristling with spikes and leaden balls.

The victim seemed tranquil, even joyful, for his Master had suffered the same torment not far from the very spot where he now stood. He well knew what a Roman scourging meant, since on three previous occasions he had felt the lashes on his body. He did not quail before the pain but, weakened from the beating he had just received from the Jews, he feared that he would not be able to survive the torture which was now about to begin, and he still had much work to do in the world. Accordingly he fixed his eyes on the centurion who was in charge of the scourging, and said to him: "Is it legal for you to scourge a Roman, and that without a trial?"

The simple question was enough to stay the lashes, to send the centurion running to consult Lysias, and to bring the tribune back to interview the miserable looking prisoner whom he had taken for a footpad. "Tell me, art thou a Roman?" he asked.

"Yes," replied Paul dryly.

"I obtained this citizenship at a great price," said the tribune.

"But I am a citizen by birth," retorted Paul, and he showed his proofs of citizenship.

Thoroughly alarmed, Lysias sent away the guard and executioners and made his excuses to the Apostle. He had committed a crime by binding a Roman citizen to the scourging post without trial, and he fully realized his responsibility. But what would the people of Jerusalem say when they heard that he had sided with their hated enemy? Whatever way he turned he was compromising himself. Moreover he did not even know exactly what crime the prisoner had committed to turn the whole city against him. Suddenly Lysias saw the way to clear up the whole matter and put himself in the good graces of the Hebrew aristocracy. He would have the accused appear before the Sanhedrin, which would have to be content with inflicting a light punishment if a mere question of religion were involved. The tribune was pleased with his solution, the more so because he had detected a nobility and uprightness in his prisoner which, combined with the man's Roman citizenship, would commend him to the benevolence of the imperial authorities.

Early the next day, therefore, Lysias ordered the supreme tribunal of Israel to assemble. The presiding prelate was Ananias, of the family of Annas who had sentenced Christ to death, that family which the Hebrew books called "The Hissings of Vipers" in allusion to their covetousness, cruelty and scandalous sensuality. Lysias also took his place among the judges with some of his centurions, and it was for this reason that the assembly was being held at the gates of the Temple instead of in the inner hall, where Christ had been tried and where Paul had seen Stephen in ecstasy surrounded by the enraged Sanhedrists.

No doubt the Apostle saw again in his mind's eye the deacon, hemmed in by enemies and hurling his terrible indictment at them, and although the speech which he himself meant to make would not be less strongly phrased than Stephen's, he would do his best to present his defense without arousing the wrath of the Sanhedrin. "Brethren," he began, "I have conducted myself before God with a perfectly good conscience up to this day." Scarcely had he said these words when, from the presidential benches where the priests sat wrapped in their snow-white robes, an order was barked out to the bailiffs of the Sanhedrin: "Strike him on the mouth!" The command came from Ananias himself, who perhaps had been angered by the Apostle's opening word "Brethren," or who may have judged that the prisoner had committed a grave fault in beginning to speak before being questioned. Paul was conscious only of the insult and, surprised and stung by the arbitrary command, he replied hotly in words that were soon to prove prophetic: "God will strike thee, thou whitewashed wall. Dost thou sit there to try me by the Law, and in violation of the Law order me to be struck?" This was a severe pronouncement, reminiscent of Christ's own words, and it implicitly accused the high priest of hypocrisy. Time proved the Apostle right, for Josephus relates that the unworthy pontiff, hounded for his crimes, had to hide in an aqueduct where his enemies found and killed him.

But now, at Paul's trial, some of those present hastened to defend the high priest. "Dost thou insult God's high priest?" they said to the Apostle. And Paul answered: "I did not know, Brethren, that he was the high priest; for it is written, 'Thou shalt not speak evil of a ruler of thy people.'"

He spoke calmly, having mastered his spontaneous outburst of anger, and he quoted from the Book of Exodus to show the judges that he respected the word of God and so could not be accused of destroying the Law. However, the disagreeable incident caused confusion in the assembly, and a casuistical theological dispute began between the disciples of Hillel and the followers of Shammai, between Pharisees and Sadducees. Realizing that even the most eloquent defense would be useless to move these men who regarded him as an apostate and blasphemer, Paul gave up the idea of making a formal speech, and instead widened the breach between the warring factions by introducing the subject of the resurrection of the dead. "Brethren," he cried out, "I am a Pharisee, the son of Pharisees; it is about the hope and the resurrection of the dead that I am on trial." His plan succeeded, and a veritable storm of argument swept through the assembly, for the dogma of the resurrection was fundamental in the Pharisees' theology, while the Sadducees, on the contrary, denied it altogether. The discussion grew more bitter every moment, with everybody talking at once. Finally some of the Pharisees began to defend Paul because he thought as they did on the resurrection. "We find no evil in this man," they declared. "What if a spirit has really spoken to him, or an angel?" The Sadducees, on the other hand, insulted and threatened him, but while his enemies gesticulated and argued angrily, he smiled quietly at the effect of his stratagem. Some of the more fanatical members of the assembly tried to take advantage of the uproar to attack the Apostle, but Lysias saw the danger and, gathering his soldiers, escorted his prisoner from that den of assassins and shut him up in a dungeon of the fortress. Here Paul spent a sleepless, harrowing night, for he was sad and disheartened at the incurable stubbornness of his people; he had not seen one glance of compassion, and even the Christians of Jerusalem seemed indifferent to his sufferings. But suddenly "the Lord stood by him and said, 'Be steadfast; for just as thou hast borne witness to me in Jerusalem, bear witness in Rome also'" (Acts 23:11).

Meanwhile, more than forty Jews had come together and taken an oath not to eat or drink until they had killed Paul, and their scheme had been approved by the chief priests. The assassins planned to stab him while he was being brought by the legionaries from the fortress to the Temple for the continuation of his violently interrupted trial.

However, the Apostle's nephew, the son of his sister, heard of the plot and came with haste to tell him. At once Paul called the officer of the guard and said: "Take this young man to the tribune, for he has something to report to him." Lysias received the Apostle's nephew kindly, and when he had heard what he had to say, he sent him away with the warning, "Do not tell anyone that you have made known this scheme to me." Then, intent on saving his prisoner and more particularly on extricating himself from the whole vexatious affair, he called two centurions and gave them precise orders: "Get ready by the third hour of the night two hundred soldiers to go as far as Caesarea, and seventy cavalry and two hundred spearmen; and provide beasts to mount Paul and take him in safety to Felix the governor." (Cf. Acts 23:23–24.)

To the commander of the escort, Lysias gave a letter which read: "Claudius Lysias to His Excellency Felix the governor, greeting. Whereas this man had been seized by the Jews and was on the point of being killed by them, I came on them with the troops and rescued him, having learnt that he was a Roman. And wishing to know what charge they had preferred against him, I took him down into their Sanhedrin. I found him accused about questions of their Law, but not of any crime deserving death or imprisonment. And when I was told of an ambush which they had prepared for him, I sent him to thee, directing his accusers also to state the case before thee. Farewell" (Acts 23:26–30).

When night had closed over Jerusalem, Paul, with an escort worthy of a king, left the city of David, which he was never to see again. To supply the guard, Lysias had withdrawn a large part of the garrison stationed in the city for the purpose of maintaining order, for he was afraid, and the warning he had given Paul's nephew not to tell anyone else of the plot was an unwitting confession of his anxiety. St. Luke tells us the reason for his fear: "He was afraid that the Jews might seize [Paul] by force and kill him, and he himself should afterwards be slandered, as though he intended to receive money." (Cf. Acts 23:25.) Lysias was a far-sighted man and on the whole an honest one, and his judiciary report or *elogium*, as it was called, was couched in terms of open sympathy with the prisoner. Only in one small detail did he depart from the truth: he wished to have the governor believe that in rescuing Paul from the Jews he was defending the dignity of Rome, whereas in reality he had not known the Apostle was a Roman citizen when he plunged through the crowd to his assistance. His reason for giving this version of the incident was to ingratiate himself with the emperor's representative and to show him how much he appreciated his own title to citizenship, for which he had paid so high a price.

Day was breaking when the escort and their prisoner entered Antipatris, a fortified town which dominated the plain of Sharon. Behind them they had left the dangerous passes over the hills where ambush was always a possibility, but now that they had reached open country, the foot-soldiers were no longer needed and could be sent back to Jerusalem. Then, escorted only by cavalry, Paul continued on to Caesarea, and, a little before nightfall, reined in his horse in front of Herod's palace, which was then the residence of the procurator.

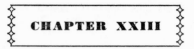
"I Appeal to Caesar"

There is still extant a painting of the tower of the Roman castle-palace where St. Paul was imprisoned on his arrival at Caesarea. The whole city, rebuilt by Herod the Great in honor of the Emperor Augustus, had a Western air about it, for its streets were laid out in a regular pattern, its houses had peristyles as well as inner patios shaded by trees, like those of Pompeii, and in its forum stood the temple of Rome and the statues of the Caesars.

On the very evening of his arrival Paul was brought before Felix the governor, and although Lysias' report contained no accusation against him, he was received with a certain coldness. Despite his fatigue after the long journey, he would have preferred to have his case decided as soon as possible, so great was his desire to embark for Rome. But the procurator merely asked him what province he came from, and then carelessly dismissed him, saying: "I will hear thee . . . when thy accusers have come" (Acts 23:35).

This man Felix was a Greek, a native of Arcadia, and, although born a slave, he had not had to buy his way to the heights of power he now occupied, but owed his success to the unbelievable favor enjoyed by his brother Pallas at

320

the court of Claudius. Josephus has left us an account of his extortions, adulteries and other crimes, while Tacitus describes him in one devastating sentence: "Antonius Felix, by all kinds of cruelty and licentiousness, exercised his kingly power with the spirit of a slave." Supported by his brother's influence but without the latter's skill in state-craft, he thought he could commit every atrocity with impunity. Thus, when he became enamored of the Jewess Drusilla, wife of King Aziz of Emesa and daughter of Herod Agrippa I, he did not rest until he had won her from her husband with the help of Simon Magus' sorcery and persuasion. And St. Luke's narrative, despite the sympathy which the Acts usually display toward Rome's representatives, adds more details about the unsavory character of this petty tyrant who for ten years was the ruler of Palestine.

Five days after Paul's arrival in Caesarea, his accusers, a party of Sanhedrists led by the high priest, came from Jerusalem. They brought with them a rhetorician and lawyer called Tertullus, who was to press their charge against Paul in conformity with the principles of Roman jurisprudence. Without delay the court was convened, and Tertullus launched into a well-prepared speech, setting forth in Greek his clients' accusations against the prisoner. Being a skillful advocate, the lawyer opened his address with all sorts of compliments to "most excellent Felix," praising his justice, his vigilance and the measures he had taken to ensure the peace of the country. No doubt the venerable Sanhedrists smiled to themselves at the lawyer's words, for they knew well that His Excellency the Proc-urator used to negotiate with the brigands in the hills of Judea for part of their spoils, at the same time promising the rich men of Jerusalem that he would stamp out these robber bands.

Then, coming to the reason for the trial, the Sanhedrin's lawyer described the prisoner as a fomenter of disturbances and seditions, as more of a threat to the nation than the plague, as an agitator well-known for his anti-Jewish prejudices, and finally, as a profaner of the Temple. The whole point of this speech was to prove that a crime had been committed against religion, and that consequently the prisoner should be turned over to the Sanhedrin, the only tribunal competent to judge such matters. "That is what would have been done at Jerusalem," concluded Tertullus, "and everything would have been conducted within the limits of strict justice, had not the tribune Lysias intervened and removed Paul from the jurisdiction of the Sanhedrin." It was a mistake for the lawyer to use this argument, which was bound to displease Felix because it implied that Lysias, his representative in Jerusalem, had complicated the whole affair by his hasty intervention. But nothing blinds people like fanaticism, and when Tertullus ceased his pleading, the Jewish delegation eagerly agreed with what their spokesman had said.

At a signal from the procurator, Paul began his defense, opening with a brief and dignified expression of restrained praise for the man who was to judge him: "As I know that for many years thou hast been a judge for this nation, I shall answer for myself with good courage." Then, calmly but forcefully, he replied to the three accusations formulated by Tertullus. That he was not a disturber of the peace could be proved by examining, hour by hour, his sojourn in Jerusalem. He had arrived there some twelve days before, and not once in that time had he disputed with anyone or caused the least disturbance in the streets or the synagogues. None of his adversaries could bring proof to support their accusations, and thus they had to let the first part of his defense pass unchallenged.

Taking up the next charge, Paul denied that he was a heretic, since he believed everything that was written in the Law and the Prophets, for Christianity was but the complete development of all the essential doctrines of Judaism. Finally, he denied that he was a profaner of the Temple, and declared that at the very time of his arrest he had been worshipping there and performing a sacred rite. Some Jews from Asia had seen him there, and it was they rather than the Sanhedrists who should stand before the procurator, since they had started the riot. "It is true," he added, "that I follow a way that they call heresy," but it was a way authorized by the Scriptures. "For the rest," he concluded, "I hope, just as they do, for the resurrection of the dead, of the just and the unjust, and I strive always to keep my conscience without reproach before God and man." (Cf. Acts 24:10–21.)

Paul's line of thought is ever the same in the presence of Jews and Gentiles alike. His teaching about the resurrection is not new, and "the Way" which he announces is the completion of the Law. He does not cease being a Jew because he is a Christian, nor does he renounce the sacred writings of Israel, for the risen Christ is the Just One, the Messias, the Son of God and man whom the prophets foretold.

Now that both sides had had their say in the trial, it only remained for the governor to give his verdict. However, that verdict was not forthcoming. Felix, who had ruled the land for almost ten years, had undoubtedly heard of the new religion and must have known of the upheaval it was causing in the Jewish world. Consequently, he was in a very good position to judge fairly the case before him. But actually, he was not interested in religious matters, and for him the crucial point of the affair was the popular uprising which had led to the detention of the preacher of the new sect. He therefore decided that he would have to have more information, and that only the tribune Lysias could remove his last doubts. This was his official reason for postponing the verdict, but he had a more compelling motive which he could not make public, that is, the money that would come to him from a long trial involving the chief men of Israel.

The delegates of the Sanhedrin could now return to Jerusalem, temporarily appeased, for their enemy would remain a prisoner in the tower of the palace until the trial had ended. The Apostle, however, being a Roman citizen, was not closely confined, so that the disciples were able to minister to his needs; sometimes his chains were taken off and his friends had free access to his cell. Nevertheless, his detention chafed him and disrupted his plans, although, fortunately, he was able to receive the faithful of Caesarea, speak with Philip the deacon, and send orders to the churches through the disciples who had accompanied him from Jerusalem. His most faithful followers were still at his side: Timothy, the best-beloved of all, Aristarchus of Thessalonica, and Luke the physician, who was already planning the writing of his life of Christ, studying the topography of Palestine and consulting with the witnesses of the word. From time to time delegates from the churches in the East arrived to console St. Paul, to ask his advice and to manifest their love for him. Thus from his prison the Apostle was able to go on preaching, directing, consolidating his work and making new efforts for the glory of Christ. Not for one day did his powerful voice fail to make itself heard. His majestic bearing impressed even his jailers, and his status as a Roman citizen added further weight to his words. It is not unlikely that the very soldiers who took their turn at guard duty were won over by their prisoner, as the keeper of the jail at Philippi had been. We can easily imagine how they would begin to call him "Master," to kneel before him as they loosed or replaced his fetters, and eventually to receive from his hands the Bread of Love.

The Apostle's personality seems to have had a profound effect even on the procurator and his household, for when Felix returned from a journey a short time after the first audience, he summoned Paul to his presence. When the Apostle came to the audience chamber he saw there the procurator and his wife Drusilla, of the family of Herod the Great, a young woman of great beauty, sporadically religious yet thoroughly wicked, who, although scarcely sixteen years old, had left her first husband for Felix, influenced by Simon Magus and lured on by the spell of ambition. Drusilla was curious about her compatriot who was disturbing the Sanhedrists, and she wished to hear him speak.

When she and her husband questioned him about his doctrine, Paul explained the principal points of Christianity. Filled with holy wrath at the ex-slave who ruled Israel, and his wife, the worldly Jewess who had betrayed her national traditions, the Apostle, like another John the Baptist, spoke with such fiery eloquence about "justice and chastity and the judgment to come," that the procurator's interest changed to fear and he hurriedly arose, cutting short the burning torrent of words with the curt phrase: "For the present go thy way; but when I get an opportunity, I will send for thee." Evidently Felix was not so immersed in evil that he could not feel some pangs of remorse; yet he feared that the Christian apologist's words might come between him and the woman he had stolen. Undoubtedly Drusilla, too, trembled and was unwilling to listen more to the sound of that voice which had the power to stir hearts to their depths. Years later, while still young and beautiful, she was suddenly to hear another voice more terrible than Paul's, a voice that came to call her away from what she most loved. It happened in Pompeii, on that fearsome night when Vesuvius erupted in flame and burning ashes; like so many others she tried to flee, but the glowing waves of lava swept over her, engulfing her and the son she had borne to Felix, the slave for whom she had left her rightful husband and the royal palace of Emesa.

However, Felix did speak with Paul on many other occasions, although he was interested less in the Apostle's doctrine than in his personality, the power and surge of his eloquence, his character, his originality of thought, his sincerity and fidelity of heart, and the brilliance of his conversation which sparkled with the jewelled memories of countless divine and human experiences such as had been granted to no other man. But the procurator was looking for something more than mere entertainment from his prisoner. He had been quick to estimate the influence wielded by Paul over an immense following of disciples spread throughout the East, disciples who, at a sign from their leader, would hasten from Philippi, Ephesus, Thessalonica, Corinth, even from Rome itself, bringing with them millions of sesterces. It was well known that money could settle any case that came before Felix's tribunal, and thus Josephus could say of him and his successor, Albinus, that "the only people [they] kept in prison were those who had given [them] nothing." But in spite of Paul's yearning to be free to spread the Gospel, he would have remained a captive all his life rather than bribe a magistrate. The result was that month after month went by without Felix delivering a verdict, to the great satisfaction of the Jews in Jerusalem, who were happy to see their greatest enemy thus condemned to inaction.

In Rome, however, the star of Pallas, the Empress Agrippina's protégé, had begun to wane, and on the political horizon a new light was dawning, namely Poppaea, a Judaizer who had succeeded in winning the heart of Nero. The Jews at Jerusalem accordingly took advantage of the change to accomplish the ruin of Felix, the unscrupulous foreigner who was ruling their country. They could not forgive him his extortions and, especially, the unfairness with which he had treated them in their quarrels with the Greeks. Only a short time before he had led his legionaries against them in the market place at Caesarea, wounding some and scattering the rest. At length, the plotting of Felix's enemies bore fruit and he was recalled to Rome, but before he went, he tightened the restrictions on Paul with a view to avoiding further reprisals by the Jews. But his precaution was in vain, for he was forced to relinquish his office and was lucky to escape with his life, thanks to whatever little influence his brother Pallas still retained.

Paul had now suffered unjust imprisonment for two years. The thought of Rome continued to fill him with great yearning, but, knowing that God's will had to be obeyed, he waited patiently for his hour to strike.

He was completely conformed to God's will. With a generous effort aided by grace, he had succeeded in establishing this supreme harmony within himself, and the peace which the angels promised to men of good will was his reward. Thus he could say to the disciples at Philippi:

"What you have learned and received and heard and seen in me, these things practice. And the God of peace will be with you" (Phil. 4:9). The rays of divine light which were shed upon his soul filled him with a joyful assurance, so that he sang as he had done in the prison at Philippi, and his poetic enthusiasm and mystical exaltation he voiced in words of moving sincerity such as these: "Rejoice in the Lord always; again I say, rejoice. . . . In every prayer and supplication with thanksgiving let your petition be made known to God" (Phil. 4:4–6). His joy was the fruit of his love of Christ, that love which intoxicated him, filled him with unbounded confidence, held out to him the greatest hopes and inspired him to undertake superhuman enterprises. What could his heavenly Father deny him after having given him His Son who had loved him so deeply as to suffer death on the Cross for him?

Felix's successor as governor of Judea was Porcius Festus, who was, according to Josephus, a just and energetic man, skilled in the art of ruling. The new governor's first care was to present himself in Jerusalem to win the support of the powerful Sadducees and scheming priests whose influence, always to be feared, had grown with their latest triumph, the removal of Felix. These leaders of the Jews all hastened to greet Festus with typical Hebrew courtesy, bowing deeply before him and flattering him with honeyed words. Foremost among the welcoming delegation was the high priest, Ismael, son of Phabi, who had just succeeded Ananias and whose main preoccupation was to renew the legal process against Paul. Two years of silence had not been enough to lessen the hatred of the Sanhedrists, and now they wished to renew their petition to have the prisoner handed over to them so that they could judge him according to their laws, that is to say, so that they could rid themselves of him once and for all. This was the price they were demanding from the procurator in exchange for their support.

But Festus had already guessed their intentions and knew, moreover, that they had a band of brigands waiting in the mountains of Judea to ambush his prisoner if he were to be returned to Jerusalem. Accordingly, he foiled their plan by replying courteously but firmly to their request: "I shall be returning to Caesarea shortly; let, therefore, your influential men go down with me . . . and if there is anything wrong with the man, let them present charges against him." (Cf. Acts 25:1–5.) Thus it was that several days later Paul once more appeared in the praetorium where his enemies, headed by the high priest, Ismael, began shouting insults at him and accusing him of many serious crimes. But the procurator silenced them by demanding: "Prove your charges." All they had done so far was to repeat to Festus: "He has profaned the Temple," and "He has broken the Law," as they had to Felix two years before, naming crimes which did not appear anywhere in the Roman code.

However, the Sanhedrists were not to be robbed of their prey: they now resorted to the same charge which Caiphas and his friends had launched against Christ, and which the Jews at Thessalonica had already used against Paul: "He has conspired against Caesar." They alleged that the Apostle was an agitator who was proclaiming, in Christ's name, an empire more powerful and beneficent than that of Rome, and saying that Rome itself was destined to destruction. They quoted him as saying that even the successors of Augustus would have to render an account to his king, who was the judge of all men, and that one could burn incense and offer the tribute of adoration to his God alone.

By these insidious allegations, the Jews wished to prove that Roman rule and the spiritual kingdom of the Gospel were incompatible. But Paul replied to his adversaries with a resounding denial that effectively silenced them. "Neither against the Law of the Jews," he cried, "nor against the temple nor against Caesar have I committed any offense." He spoke with such sincerity that, in spite of the wrathful insistence of the Sanhedrists, Porcius Festus was convinced that the whole affair was one of personal animosity on the part of the Jews, or at most a religious quarrel whose implications he was unable to fathom. It seemed to him, therefore, that the accusers were not wholly wrong in asking to have the prisoner judged by the highest tribunal of their nation. No doubt the venomous attitude of the Jews toward Paul made him fear that they would not be capable of following the peaceful processes of justice; but he could accompany the captive to Jerusalem to protect him in the presence of the judges and ensure his rights as a Roman citizen.

Thus Festus thought he had found a way to pacify the Jews without doing violence to his own conscience. "Art thou willing to go up to Jerusalem," he asked Paul, "and be tried there before me on these charges?" In a flash the Apostle foresaw the dangers of this proposition which had been made with the most honorable intentions: he thought of the possibility of ambush on the journey, riots in the city, prejudice in the court, intrigue, violence and coercion. He knew that if he ventured into the enemy's own camp he would not come out alive. But he knew too that no Roman magistrate could oblige a citizen of the empire to submit to trial by a foreign power. Aware of his rights, and seeing that the procurator apparently wished to be rid of the whole affair, he made a sudden resolve: "I am standing at the tribunal of Caesar; there I ought to be tried. To Jews I have done no wrong, as thou thyself very well knowest. For if I have done any wrong or committed a crime deserving of death, I do not refuse to die. But if there is no ground to their charges against me, no one can give me up to them; I appeal to Caesar."

The prisoner's words fell like a thunderbolt on the praetorium, and the Jews bowed their heads in furious defeat. The procurator briefly consulted with his council, and, relieved at the unexpected solution that freed him from compromises and worries, he turned to the accused and pronounced the legal formula: "Thou hast appealed to Caesar; to Caesar thou shalt go" (cf. Acts 25:9–12).

Paul had rejected his own people's tribunal in appealing to the justice of the enemies of Israel. Many years had passed since he had broken with the hair-splitting, rigorist Pharisees, the malevolent, epicurean Sadducees, and the haughty champions of theocracy who, ten years after his trial, were to cause the destruction of Jerusalem itself. That break, begun by the vision at Damascus, was now made definitive by his appeal to Caesar. Despite his long years of persecution by the Jews, he must have felt something within him snap when he took the step. He grieved for his fatherland as his Master had done and, unlike Tertullian, could never have penned the impressive words: "We Christians acknowledge no republic other than the world." He was proud of the dignity of his blood; he had striven to give his compatriots the light of faith, and he did not hesitate to make that whole-souled declaration which reveals the sublime selflessness of his patriotism: "I could wish to be anathema myself from Christ for the sake of my brethren, who are my kinsmen according to the flesh" (Rom. 9:3). But his love for his nation did not prevent him from seeing clearly that the glory of the Gospel exceeds all the privileges of blood, and without heeding the protests of egoistic Judaizers, he had upheld the doctrine of the spiritual Israel, the kingdom of God, where all peoples enjoy a holy equality and perfect union with each other. Romans and Scythians, Jews and Greeks, all were one in Christ. Membership in this kingdom of the spirit conferred a nobility that eclipsed all the privileges of the Chosen People and all the splendors of the Empire. Paul was first a disciple of Christ, then a Hebrew, the son of Hebrews, and finally, acknowledging the providential mission of Rome's political structure but without giving too much importance to human greatness, he was a citizen of that city which was giving the world the example of a well-governed empire, one which imposed order and laid down laws, one which had succeeded in welding into a single state a multitude of peoples differing vastly from each other in character, customs, interests and tendencies.

The Apostle's appeal to Caesar made possible the fulfillment of the desire he had long entertained; at last he was going to see the faithful at Rome, to preach Christ in the capital of the world, to appear before the Emperor and bring him the word of God. Although he knew that his accusers would pursue him, he was content. Now he had only to await the moment of departure, the arrival of a ship that would take him across the Mediterranean. A few days after his appeal, he was told that the procurator wished to see him. Joyfully he thought, "He wishes to say farewell"; but he soon found that he was mistaken and that he was only going to be submitted to another interrogation. Agrippa II, the king of a small territory east of the Jordan, a remnant of the kingdom once ruled by his grandfather Herod the Great, had arrived at Caesarea with his sister Berenice to greet the new governor. In the course of conversation with his guests, Festus had mentioned the extraordinary prisoner whom he had in his palace. The royal visitors knew Paul's name but had heard only some vague rumors about his stormy life, perhaps from their sister Drusilla, the frivolous wife of the ex-procurator Felix. These three, Agrippa II, Berenice and Drusilla, were the children of Herod Agrippa, the persecutor of the Christians, and were regarded with much disfavor in the religious centers of Israel because of their fawning upon the Roman authorities. Agrippa was one of those petty kings whom Rome had skillfully made its slaves, while Berenice, even more than Drusilla, was noted for her flitting from court to court, infatuating rulers with her beauty. After the death of her royal husband, she had married Polemon, King of Cilicia, and later she was to seduce "the austere Vespasian with the magnificence of her gifts" [1] and the magic of her charms, while later still, on the threshold of old age, she was to win the heart of Titus. But at the time of her visit to Caesarea she was living with her brother in a relationship that was a scandal to all good Israelites.

Berenice, like her sister, though a past mistress of allurement and wickedness, also had spells of religious fervor, and Josephus records that she once took the Nazarite vow and fulfilled it to the letter. The conflicting traits in her character seemed to arouse in her the desire to meet the preacher of the new sect of the Nazarenes. Agrippa was also curious about the prisoner, since he was interested in doctrinal discussions and the affairs of Jerusalem, if only because he had the power of designating the high priest.

---

[1] Tacitus *Hist.* ii. 81.

The procurator, in his turn, wanted to investigate further the whole affair, for he had to send the prisoner to Rome and he was not sure how he should make out the judicial report to the Emperor. "As far as I can ascertain," Festus said to his guests, "there is question of a controversy about their own religion and about a certain Jesus, who had died, but who Paul affirmed was alive." (Cf. Acts 25:19-20.)

The scene which met Paul's eyes as he was led into the audience chamber was more brilliant and formal than any ordinary reception, for it was adorned with the beauty of the young princess, the regal presence of her brother, the splendor of Festus' officials, friends and counsellors, and the prestige of the principal men of the city. The Apostle's humble appearance, his clothing threadbare and torn from imprisonment and penances, his fettered hands and worn face bearing the marks of years of persecution and toil, made a strange contrast to the smiling faces, the rustling silks, and the perfumed elegance of the company which awaited him. Yet his glance was serene and firm, and his eyes shone with an inner happiness. He did not enjoy being made a spectacle to satisfy the curiosity of these people, but the prospect of bearing witness to the Faith before such a select audience banished all personal preoccupations from his mind.

Festus opened the proceedings by making it clear to the assembly that they were not gathered for a judicial process, since the prisoner had already appealed to Rome. He explained that the purpose of the gathering was an unofficial interrogation which would enable those present, and particularly King Agrippa, to assist him in drawing up the report which he would have to submit to the Emperor. When the procurator had finished his brief introduction, Agrippa, moved by the Apostle's pitiful yet noble appearance, invited him to speak in his own defense. Paul extended his right hand which bore the manacle, symbol of his consecration to Christ, and closing his fingers in the accepted gesture of Greek orators, he claimed the attention of the assembly. "I think myself fortunate, King Agrippa," he began, "that I am to defend myself today before thee against all the accusations of the Jews, especially as thou art well acquainted with all the Jewish customs and controversies; I beg thee therefore to listen to me with patience" (Acts 26:2–3).

Then, as on other occasions, he related the story of his youth and conversion, emphasizing the harmony of the Gospel with Jewish tradition as regards the dogma of the resurrection, and showing that his teaching was in accord with the ancient prophecies: "And now for the hope in the promise made by God to our fathers I am standing trial; to which promise our twelve tribes hope to attain as they serve night and day; and it is about this hope, O king, that I am accused by the Jews. Why is it deemed incredible with you if God does raise the dead?" (Acts 26:6–8).

It had been a long time since Paul had had an opportunity of speaking before such a large and influential audience. As he recalled the memories of his youth his voice became more vibrant; carried away by his natural vehemence, he forgot that he was defending himself, and his speech changed from an apologia to an impassioned missionary sermon. As he described the scene on the road to Damascus, he seemed like a visionary, a man clothed with a compelling power that struck his listeners with fear. "King Agrippa," he continued, "I was not disobedient to the heavenly vision; but first to the people of Damascus and Jerusalem, and then all over Judea and to the Gentiles, I set about declaring that they should repent and turn to

God, doing works befitting their repentance. This is why the Jews seized me in the temple and tried to kill me. But aided to this day by the help of God, I stand here to testify to both high and low, saying nothing beyond what the Prophets and Moses said would come to pass: that the Christ was to suffer, that he first by his resurrection from the dead was to proclaim light to the people and to the Gentiles" (Acts 26:20-23).

Such language as this must have seemed senseless to the Roman patrician, Porcius Festus, who was a skeptic and a stranger to arguments about visions and revelations and to all the mysterious convolutions of Jewish speculation. If at first he thought he was going to hear a speech about the creation of the world, he was soon disabused, for he found that his prisoner was dealing with ideas that were incomprehensible to him, ideas such as judgment, resurrection and penance. He concluded that Paul was more a dreamer than a philosopher. But what seemed completely absurd to him was the speaker's attempt to remove the problem from the limits of Judea and to make it universal and of equal importance to Gentiles and Hebrews. What did Rome care about the prophets of Israel? It is possible that the procurator was angered by Paul's teaching and regarded it as a slur on the dignity of Rome, but not wanting to cause a scene before his distinguished guests, he contented himself with a disdainful smile and the remark: "Paul, thou art mad; thy great learning is driving thee to madness."

Unruffled by the brusque interruption, Paul turned to Agrippa for confirmation, knowing that the king was better informed than the procurator about the recent history of Israel and the teachings of the Jewish schools. "I am not mad, excellent Festus," said he, "but I speak words of sober truth. For the king knows about these things and to him also I speak without hesitation. For I am sure that none of these things escaped him; for none of them happened in a corner. Dost thou believe the prophets, King Agrippa? I know that thou dost." Agrippa was alarmed by the turn the audience was taking, for the Apostle's sudden question seemed like the opening of a religious discussion which might well lead him onto dangerous ground. Moreover, he did not want to appear in front of the pagan Festus as a man concerned with superstitions. Therefore he refused the prisoner's daring invitation by answering: "In a short while thou wouldst persuade me to become a Christian." This was simply a gracious compliment, the reply of a man of the world, uttered in a tone of charming courtesy, but not without ironical exaggeration. The prisoner's single-mindedness, the ardor of his speech and the sincerity of his convictions had impressed the king. Actually, Agrippa had as little interest in Christianity as he had in Judaism, but, knowing the high priests for what they were, he recognized that this man, their enemy, was much more worthy of esteem than they. To the king's compliment Paul made a bold and ingenious reply: "I would to God that, whether [the time] be long or short, not only thou but also all who hear me today might become such as I am," adding with a smile as he held up his fettered hands, "except for these chains." This famed episode came to an end with these words of brotherly charity and delightful humor which brought a murmur of applause from the audience, who had been captivated by Paul's personality but who, nevertheless, did not fully grasp all the sacrifice, love and generosity contained in the speaker's parting wish. "He has done nothing to deserve death or prison," the listeners said to each other, and Agrippa, who had been in haste to end the session, perhaps for fear of being asked another compromising question, gave his verdict to Festus when they were discussing the situation afterward: "This man might have been set at liberty, if he had not appealed to Caesar." But, as they both knew, whoever appealed to Caesar, guilty or innocent, had to go to Caesar.

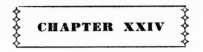

CHAPTER XXIV

In Perils in the Sea

Paul began his sea voyage from Caesarea to Rome as the autumn of the year 60 was drawing near. The days were bright and calm, cooled by gentle winds from the south, and the evenings were still and peaceful. When the Apostle's ship drew away from the land, he left behind him for the last time the coasts of Palestine, full of memories both bitter and sweet. The vessel had still two months of good sailing weather ahead before the winter storms set in, ample time for the voyage from the shores of Asia to the mouth of the Tiber. Paul was on his way at last, and he went joyfully, eager to appear before the imperial court which would decide his fate. He had spent two years in forced inaction, and he was restless with anxiety at the thought of his churches and of the thousands of pagans who did not yet know of the Gospel. Philip and the faithful at Caesarea had indeed showered upon him signs of their admiring love; his most beloved disciples had remained close to him day after day, and messengers from Asia, Greece and Macedonia had constantly come to his prison. But a soul such as his required a field of action as large as the world itself.

For the journey to the imperial capital, Paul had been

attached to a group of prisoners whom Festus was sending to Rome with a guard consisting of a detachment of soldiers under the command of a centurion. The prisoners belonged for the most part to that type of condemned felon whom the emperors were always requesting from the provinces for the purpose of amusing the people of Rome in the amphitheater. But the Apostle was a very different kind of prisoner, since he was a Roman citizen travelling under the protection of the imperial power, and the officer commanding the detachment, a centurion of the Augustan cohort named Julius, had received orders to treat him with every consideration. In addition, by special permission of the procurator, several of his disciples, Timothy, Luke, and Aristarchus of Thessalonica, had been allowed to join him as the "slaves" or servants who, according to Roman law, might accompany a citizen-prisoner. We can visualize the Apostle on the deck of the ship, buffeted by the wind or lashed by the rain, or in the damp, fetid hold of the vessel consoling the wretched prisoners crowded together there. All the incidents of this historical journey, however, seem to indicate that he was regarded by everyone on board as a person of importance. St. Luke, with his instinct for observation and his love of the sea, has recorded for us the events of the crossing, and his vivid, detailed narrative remains one of the most instructive documents on ancient seafaring.

Since there were no ships making a direct run to Rome from Caesarea, the prisoners and their guard boarded a coaster which plied between the ports on the Asiatic coast and which was headed for Adramyttium, near Troas, from which it had sailed a few weeks before. There would be no lack of direct communication with Italy in any of the great harbors of Asia Minor, and even if the party failed to find a suitable ship for the remainder of the journey, they could always cross over to Macedonia and travel by land along the Egnatian Road to Dyrrhachium.

The voyage began very auspiciously, and the vessel, running before a favorable wind, put in to Sidon at the end of the first day, after having travelled nearly ninety sea miles. While the crew discharged their cargo and reloaded the ship, Paul, with the consent of the centurion, who always treated him with unbounded kindness, went ashore to visit the brethren of the city, and was received by them with great affection.

Two years before, Luke had sailed from the coasts of Lycia to Tyre, leaving Cyprus on his left, and he thought that they would now follow the same route back. But he did not know that during the summer months in that region the winds blew constantly from the west and were dangerous to ships which ventured out on the high seas. Therefore, instead of turning west toward Lycia, the ship continued north, keeping the protecting mountains of Cyprus to windward, taking advantage of every opportunity to make headway while staying comparatively near the coast, and running in to land for shelter when the contrary winds grew too strong. Thus it was quite two weeks after leaving the country of his ancestors before Paul was able to make out in the distance the coast of Attalia and Perge, where he had landed on his first missionary voyage. How far he had travelled since then! How many peoples he had evangelized, how many trials and victories had been his! But he was not to set foot again on his first mission field, for the ship continued west until it reached Myra, where it anchored in that spacious and sheltered harbor.

In ancient times, Myra seems to have been one of the

principal stages on the commercial route between Asia and
Europe, and it boasted a temple to the god of the sea, a
building whose walls were covered with the thank-offerings of sailors and seafarers, the emblems of a cult whose
theme was retained in the Christian devotion to St. Nicho-
las of Myra, the protector of the shipwrecked and of all
who sail the sea. Ships going from Syria to the Black and
Aegean Seas used to put in to port at Myra, and frequently,
when the direction of the winds demanded it, vessels
carrying cargo from the banks of the Nile to those of the
Tiber also docked there. Thus it was that Paul's party was
quickly able to find a large ship, belonging to the imperial
fleet, which had recently come from Alexandria with a
cargo of grain for Italy. Julius the centurion straightway
transferred his soldiers and prisoners to this vessel, and the
voyage was resumed. However, the wind continued to
hamper their westward progress, so that after several days
of struggling with the gales, they succeeded only in reaching a point between Rhodes and the headland of Cnidus.
Then, being unable to sail straight for the Peloponnesus,
the ship swung sharply and ran south before the wind
toward the coasts of Crete. Reaching the island safely, they
rounded the promontory of Salmone into comparatively
calm water and, sailing along under the lee of the land,
they came to a small bay which then, as now, bore the
name of Fair Havens.

By this time, the voyagers had been battling contrary
winds for almost two months; the great fast of Yom Kippur
had already gone by, recounts St. Luke, who no doubt had
kept it with his master, and the autumn was drawing to a
close. It was now the middle of October, the time when
navigation in these waters began to be increasingly perilous, and the whole party knew that they would have to

winter in Crete; but despite its name, the port in which they had anchored offered only scant refuge from the south and west winds. The ship's captain was in a dilemma, since it was dangerous to remain in Fair Havens, yet impossible to venture out to sea again. To discuss the situation a meeting was called, to which St. Paul was invited as a distinguished passenger and seasoned traveller. The centurion presided, since the ship belonged to the imperial merchant fleet, and with him sat the captain and the supercargo. The captain proposed following the coastline of the island to the larger port of Phoenix, which was well-known to Alexandrian seafarers; the supercargo voiced the same opinion, adding that with suitable weather they could arrive at Phoenix in little more than a day. St. Paul alone opposed the idea, saying: "Men, I see that this voyage is threatening to bring disaster and heavy loss, not only to the cargo and the ship, but to our lives also." But no one heeded him, and Julius, guided by the experience of his two professional advisers, ordered the anchor to be raised and a course set for Phoenix.

Taking advantage of a south wind which had sprung up, the ship beat its way along, keeping close inshore but at a safe distance from the steep coastline against which the waves were dashing themselves to foam. In spite of Paul's predictions, the venture seemed to have every chance of success, when suddenly a furious tempest swept down upon the vessel. The first sign of trouble was a wind of hurricane force, a "violent wind" St. Luke calls it, which burst from over the island as if a door had suddenly been opened through the mountains. "The Euroaquilo!" the sailors cried in terror, for they well knew the ferocity of this northwest wind which now began to howl through the rigging, tearing at the sails, shaking the yards and shrouds, causing the timbers of the vessel to creak and groan, and threatening to snap the masts. Furiously the gale-driven waves crashed against the ship, throwing up plumes of spray which the shrieking wind flung into the terror-stricken faces of the sailors. Caught unawares as they were and carrying full sail, the crew had no course but to swing the vessel around and run blindly before the gale.

They had been careering along for twenty or thirty sea miles when they sighted a point of land rising out of the sea before them. The landfall gave them new hope, for the ship's pilot recognized it as the small island of Cauda, today known as Gozo, whose steep shores, though containing no harbor, yet offered the storm-tossed vessel some shelter from the blast. In the lee of this island they found calmer waters, and there they hove to in order to make such repairs as were necessary if they were not to founder.

St. Luke mentions first an operation in which he took part, the hoisting inboard of the longboat which until then had been towed astern, but which had shipped so much water that it was sinking and adding to the instability of the ship. Next, some of the sailors proceeded to run cables under the vessel's hull to strengthen it and tighten the timbers, which had begun to spring under the hammering of the storm. Meanwhile, other members of the crew were hard at work furling the sails, trimming them to suit the force and direction of the gale, and unshipping any parts of the rigging that offered resistance to the wind. All these hurried preparations were necessary to avoid running aground on the sand bars of the Libyan Syrtis, the terror of ancient seafarers, toward which they were heading, driven by the fury of the Euroaquilo. As an added precaution the sailors then put out a sea anchor to slow the speed of the ship and help to prevent it from being cast up on the shoals.

Thus the vessel was stripped almost to the hull, and carried only enough sail to stop it from broaching to. Despite these precautions, they were inexorably driven on before the gale, sinking into the trough of the waves and rising obliquely with a sickening lurch that threatened to send them to the bottom. Around them the hurricane continued to shriek and howl like a wild beast goaded on by a horde of demons, and scarcely were they out of sight of the island of Cauda than they were compelled to jettison part of the cargo. By dawn the next day the situation had become even more serious, and such was the panic of those aboard that they all lent a hand in throwing overboard the benches, the useless rigging, the sails and the wind-shattered yards, ending up by pitching the heaviest items of their baggage into the insatiable maw of the sea. Madly the ship ran before the wind, tossing and plunging about on that wide expanse of water which extends from Crete to Sicily, and which formed the Adria of the ancients. They were completely at the mercy of the elements, at times approaching the African coast, and at other times being driven north again by the storm. The pilot, straining at the steering oar and trying to keep the vessel from being swamped by the waves, saw that they were making headway, but only very slowly on a straight course, about a mile an hour, due to the ceaseless veering about. However, he could not tell where they were, since he could not see the sun by day or the stars by night, thus being deprived of the ancient seafarers' only guides. The whole sky was covered with clouds so low that they seemed to mingle with the leaping waves in an infernal dance. So passed three endless days, and since, as St. Luke puts it, "no small storm was raging, all hope of our being saved was in consequence given up."

All on board, save one, lived in a state of continual fear,

waiting apprehensively for that final wave to crash over them and send them to the bottom. Of the two hundred and seventy-six souls aboard some were ill with disease, others were overcome by seasickness, and all were exhausted from the buffeting and the strain. During those terrible hours only one passenger, St. Paul, remained calm and strove to reassure the others, for he was sure he would reach Rome, even if all the forces of evil conspired against him.

Yet at times the terror of the sailors, the cries of the soldiers, the white faces of the prisoners and the captain's uncertainty so affected the Apostle that he wondered if he were not the victim of an illusion. Therefore, saddened by his fellow-travellers' wretchedness, he fasted and prayed unceasingly, and after thirteen days of that unequal struggle with the raging sea, he was given the sign he was seeking. Looking around at his companions' weary faces he said: "Men, you should indeed have listened to me and not have sailed from Crete, thus sparing yourselves this disaster and loss. And now I beg you to be of good cheer, for there will be no loss of life among you, but only of the ship. For last night an angel of the God I belong to and serve, stood by me, saying, 'Do not be afraid, Paul; thou must stand before Caesar; and behold, God has granted thee all who are sailing with thee.' So, men, be of good cheer; for I have faith in God that it will be as it has been told me. But we are to reach a certain island." (Cf. Acts 27:21–26.)

Paul's words gave his companions new hope, even though the storm continued and the danger of shipwreck was heightened by the increased swaying of the mainmast, which had to be retained, however, to keep them off the perilous African sand banks. Circumstances such as these often cause one man to stand out from his fellows as a leader and restorer of hope and courage. This was the case with Paul, and, just as he had been a prudent counsellor before, so now, in the midst of panic and despair, he appeared as a messenger from heaven with a prophetic vision to reawaken confidence in his companions' hearts.

That same night the sailors heard a new sound close to the ship; it was the pounding of the surf on the rocks, indicating that they were close to land. Quickly they heaved the lead and found that they were in twenty fathoms of water; again they took soundings and got a reading of only fifteen fathoms. Fearing that they would be driven onto a shoal, they let down four anchors from the stern which immediately found purchase on the bottom. The time was midnight and the intense darkness increased the peril of the situation; they seemed to have escaped one danger only to fall into another, for the water was already coming through the timbers, and the vessel, held firm by its anchors against the blows of the waves, would be pounded to pieces in a few hours. Anxiously they awaited the dawn, but so terrible was the strain that the crew decided to desert their ship. Under the pretext of casting more anchors from the bow, they lowered the ship's boat into the sea with the intention of rowing ashore in it. But Paul, watching them from the deck, saw their maneuvering, and knowing that all would be lost without the assistance of experienced sailors, he warned the centurion and his soldiers: "Unless these men remain in the ship, you cannot be saved." Immediately the soldiers drew their swords and hacked through the ropes of the boat, letting her drift off.

Neither the captain nor the centurion was master of the situation now, but rather the small Christian preacher with the calm face, the commanding presence and the burning eyes, who reasoned with the crew, encouraged the soldiers and went from group to group speaking words of faith and consolation. His voice rose above the tumult of the sea as it had so often done before over the clamor of infuriated mobs, and his steady eyes reflected a compassion that lent a transfiguring beauty to his countenance. In the flickering rays of the swinging lanterns and the uncertain light of dawn he could discern the exhausted faces, the piteous glances and the swollen and trembling limbs of his companions. He had put their minds at ease, and now with his eminent sense of the practical, he set about comforting their bodies. "This is the fourteenth day," he said, "that you have been constantly on the watch and fasting, without taking anything to eat. So I beg you to take some food for your safety; for not a hair from the head of any one of you shall perish." Giving the example himself, "he took bread and gave thanks to God before them all and broke it and began to eat. Then all became more cheerful and took food themselves." (Cf. Acts 27:33–36.)

Now there remained only one thing to do, namely, to lighten the vessel still further so that it would not run aground on the coastal reefs. Everyone set to with enthusiasm, casting overboard the sacks of wheat that were left in the hold, the rest of the baggage and the food supplies. As daylight increased, they caught glimpses of land between the curtains of wind-driven rain and spray, but no one aboard could identify the place, even when they were able to see a small barren island in a deserted bay whose high rocky shores ran inland to a wide inviting beach.

Deciding to run into this bay for shelter, they slipped the anchors, unlashed the rudder which they had secured during the storm, raised the foresail and abandoned them-

selves to the sea current. The operation seemed to be suc-
ceeding, when suddenly the keel cut into a sand bank
formed by two currents at the mouth of the bay. The long-
feared shipwreck had come at last; the prow of the vessel
remained immovably rammed into the sand, while the stern,
battered by the waves, quivered and threatened to break
up at any moment. The only course left open to those on
board was to abandon ship and make their way ashore as
best they could by swimming or by floating in on parts of
the wreckage. The soldiers, whose duty it was to guard
with their lives the prisoners committed to their custody,
decided to put their charges to the sword, but the centurion, intent on saving Paul, forbade the slaughter, and
"ordered those who could swim to jump overboard first
and get to land," while the rest could make shift to struggle
ashore on planks torn from the breaking hull of the ship.
Paul had already been shipwrecked three times and had
once spent more than twenty hours alone, clinging to a
timber adrift in the sea; now he experienced once more the
violence of a struggle with the waves. Assisted by the wind
from the sea he got safely ashore with the others, not one
of the two hundred and seventy-six people aboard being
lost.

Probably some of the sailors had landed more than once
on these shores, but none of them could say with certainty
where they were. This was due, no doubt, to the fact that
they were confused and exhausted by their terrible experience. In addition, the bay into which they had swum
was some distance from the great port where at that time,
as in our own day, seagoing vessels usually anchored.
While the shipwrecked passengers and crew were discussing what they should do, the natives of the region, fishermen, shepherds or inhabitants of the nearby villages, arrived

at the scene of the wreck. St. Luke calls these people "barbarians," that is to say, those who did not follow the customs of the Greeks or Romans. They were of Punic origin for the most part and spoke in the guttural tones of their race. However, as was the case in all the seaports of the time, their Semitic language contained many Greek and Latin words which enabled the castaways to ascertain that they had landed on the eastern shore of an island known as Malta, or Melita, as it was called in ancient times.

The sky was still covered with dark clouds, the rain fell ceaselessly, while an icy wind froze and paralyzed the exhausted castaways. The kindly, hospitable Maltese therefore hastened to kindle a large fire to warm the travellers and, thanks to their generous initiative, soon a blazing pyre of underbrush, sticks and branches was built. Paul, always the man of action, joined in the search for wood, instead of remaining close to the fire as his companions were doing. He had gathered a bundle of sticks and was laying them on the blaze when a viper, aroused from its winter sluggishness by the heat, wriggled out of the faggots and sank its fangs into his hand. Without any sign of fear, he shook the dangling snake to the ground, crushed its head underfoot, threw it into the flames and went on with his work, but the bite had been so severe that the blood flowed freely from the wound. The natives of the island saw the incident, and being somewhat superstitious, they looked at each other and said: "What kind of man is this?" They had heard that the wrecked vessel was carrying a group of criminals condemned to the beasts, and they concluded: "Surely this man is a murderer, for though he has escaped the sea, Justice does not let him live." Certain that he would soon be overcome by the poison and fall to the ground in his death agony, they watched him with expectant curiosity.

But when nothing happened, their harsh opinion of him turned to admiration: they were astonished to see that his face did not grow pale nor his hand begin to swell, and that he even continued to smile calmly; not knowing how else to explain his miraculous escape from certain death, they exclaimed: "He is a god!" (Cf. Acts 28:3–6.)

Not far from the scene of the shipwreck lay the palace of "the head man of the island," the title given by ancient inscriptions and the Acts to the official who governed Malta in the name of the praetor of Sicily. This man, whose name was Publius, was as kind and generous as the people he ruled, and he received the strangers with patrician open-handedness, entertaining them for three days with gracious hospitality. "And it happened," says St. Luke, "that the father of Publius was laid up with fever and dysentery; but Paul went in, and after praying and laying his hands on him, he healed him" (Acts 28:8). This miracle added so much to the Apostle's fame that the people brought their sick from all parts of the island to be cured by the touch of his hands.

Paul spent three months on the island, during which time the people overwhelmed him with marks of gratitude, the principal families honored him with their friendship and all showed him the greatest respect. Of his missionary activities on Malta we know nothing, but it is probable that he did not fail to take advantage of his fame to combat the gross superstitions of the islanders and to sow the seed of the Gospel. After his sufferings in prison and the strain of the sea voyage ending in shipwreck, these months must have been very welcome to his exhausted and aging body. The gentle sea breezes and the warm Mediterranean sun combined with the friendliness of the island-dwellers to render that winter one of the most pleasant of his life. His heart had been made for danger and it yearned for struggle and hardship; yet when it came time for him to depart from the hospitable island, he and his disciples must have raised their hands over Malta and its people in blessing and gratitude. In its turn, the island was to keep fresh, century after century, the memory of the Apostle, and to receive with open arms the most valiant knights of the Cross as before it had welcomed its beloved missionary. Until the end of time, the Apostle's memory will be enshrined in the name "the Bay of St. Paul," the title given by the islanders to the inlet across which he had struggled to fall exhausted on the sand.

CHAPTER XXV

Ambassador in Chains

The party's sojourn on Malta came to an end at the beginning of the year 61, when the first signs of an auspicious spring and the soft winds from Africa invited them to put out to sea again. Thus, after three months of forced inactivity on the island, the centurion Julius set out once more for Rome with his band of soldiers and his prisoners. They boarded an Alexandrian ship like the one on which they had made their near-fatal crossing, a vessel under the protection of the Dioscuri, the twin sons of Jupiter and Leda, whose names it bore and whose images appeared on its figurehead. This vessel, having wintered at Malta, was in haste to leave "the island of honey" even before the season for navigation had really begun, in order to get her cargo of grain to Rome. But despite their haste, they had to wait three days in Syracuse on the island of Sicily because the wind had died down, and from there they followed the coast toward the straits of Messina to Rhegium (Reggio di Calabria). Two days later they anchored at Puteoli, the modern Pozzuoli, on one of the extremities of the Bay of Naples, and Paul set foot in Italy for the first time.

For many years he had dreamed of this moment when he could tread Italian soil. At last he was within reach of

353

Rome, the far-famed city whose providential destiny he seemed to have divined. Nevertheless, he did not feel the elation which comes from the definite prospect of realizing a long-cherished dream. It seems that once again, as in Troas and Philippi, he was enveloped in one of those dark clouds of discouragement which sometimes descended on him. Perhaps this wave of depression was due to fatigue after a long journey, or fear of the unknown, or apprehension at coming face to face with the terrible reality of that imperial Rome to which he was looking for support against the satanic hatred of the Jews in Jerusalem. Then, too, he was nearing the end of his career. For more than fifteen years he had ranged through the Empire, founding churches and struggling against subjection to the Jews. Yet his years of imprisonment in Caesarea had given him an opportunity of delving more deeply into those truths which, amid the noise of disputation, he had been able to see only in outline, as by intuition. Thus the mystery of the Incarnation now rose before his eyes in all its sublime grandeur, and the flickering lamps of the Temple at Jerusalem grew ever dimmer in the brilliance shed by the figure of Christ, the Eternal Priest, the eternally flowing Fountain of Life and the Fullness of the Godhead.

His thought was moving onto a higher and more serene plane, and with his thought, his whole being ascended and was transfigured. Little by little, the impetuous and highly sensitive scribe whom we met on the road to Damascus was approaching the regions of unalterable peace. His energy was greater than ever, but it was most noticeable in his absolute dominion over self. The thunderings of Paul, as St. Jerome would say, were now becoming more powerful but less reverberating. A heavenly clarity bathed his soul and imparted a more-than-earthly equilibrium to his senses.

Formerly, he had exulted in battle, brushed obstacles aside, shaken with indignation, reprimanded, rejected spiritless workers without a second thought, and later, in moments of trial, in the crises of illness, in the sorrow of isolation, he had trembled, wept, and felt that he was weak, useless, and an outcast. But now, incorporated with Christ, identified as it were with Him in the depths of his will, he was able to defy all the powers of evil, all the onslaughts of sorrow, all the terrors of life and death, of earth and hell. The love of Christ, the one passion of his life, had taken possession of all his faculties, had transformed and sanctified all within him, had endowed him with contrasting qualities, and had blended them into harmony, making him at once vehement and tender, affable and austere, brusque and courteous, prudent and daring, humble and haughty. No mere man has ever possessed to a higher degree than he this inner symphony composed of apparently discordant and incompatible notes, this spiritual unison which is indicative of moral perfection, for, as Pascal says, greatness does not consist in attaining one of two extremes, but in touching both at the same time and filling the space between.

". . . At Puteoli," says St. Luke, ". . . we found brethren and were entreated to stay with them seven days" (Acts 28:14). With extraordinary rapidity all the intellectual currents of the Empire reached and affected Rome, the head of that vast and complicated organism of which Puteoli was one of the principal centers of cosmopolitan influence, for it was as much a capital as Ephesus, Corinth or Antioch. A church had been founded there some years previously, and the Gospel was not long in reaching the nearby city of Pompeii, among whose ruins the first known sign of Christ's Cross was discovered centuries later, and where, a short while before the eruption of Vesuvius in the year 79, the Christians were already the target of street-corner wit.

The first welcome given Paul by the brethren of Italy was a source of consolation to him, but the faithful of Rome received him with even greater cordiality. He was travelling along the Appian Way with his guard and companions, and he was still more than forty miles from the capital when he was met by a group of disciples who had come out to welcome him at the Forum Appii, a town of seagoing folk, fishermen and small shopkeepers. A little farther on, at "the Three Taverns," there was another delegation. Such was the Apostle's first personal contact with the Roman community, and, as St. Luke relates, "when Paul saw them, he gave thanks to God and took courage," his face lighted up with joy and his lips poured forth his gratitude. The time was the end of February, in the year 61.

On arriving at Rome, the centurion handed over his prisoners to the commander of the prison camp (*Castra Peregrinorum*) where he and his soldiers were billeted. Then Paul was brought to the *Castra Praetoria* to await his turn with others who were being held there to appear before Caesar's tribunal. The praetorian prefect or captain of the imperial guard was Afranius Burrus, a man distinguished for his virtues as a Roman, stoical, austere, cultured and of irreproachable character. No doubt it was he who read the report on Paul written by the procurator of Judea, and heard from the centurion Julius' own lips the story of the eventful crossing and of the providential part played therein by his extraordinary prisoner.

We do not know if Burrus was interested enough to want to see Paul, but since both the procurator and the centurion spoke highly of him, the prefect ordered that he was to be treated with all the clemency possible under the law. Thus, instead of committing the Apostle to a public jail, he placed him under what was then known as military guard, that is, he was allowed to move about freely, but under the constant surveillance of a soldier to whom he was bound by a light chain. In these circumstances, therefore, he was able not only to receive his friends as at Caesarea, but also to walk through the city, live where he chose, and speak with all who came to visit him.

Taking advantage of this unexpected freedom, and after having spent some days with the brethren, Paul rented one floor of a house near the *Castra Praetoria* in the north-western district of the city, not far from the Via Nomen-tana. He took up residence here with the disciples who had accompanied him from Asia, being careful to leave available a large room in which to receive his numerous visitors, perform the liturgical functions and teach the Gospel. He began his apostolate three days after moving into his new home, starting as usual with the Jews. Since it would have been at the very least undiplomatic, if not impossible, for him to enter the synagogue chained to his Gentile guard, he sent word to the leading Jews that he wished to speak with them, and many of them came to his house, drawn by the same curiosity which the Ephesians had shown when they first saw him. No doubt the Jews of Rome had heard his name and knew of the protests which his preaching had aroused in the ghettos of the East, and therefore, without mentioning the past, he could begin immediately to explain to them how he had come to be a prisoner in their city. He related the circumstances of his imprisonment in Jerusalem, told of the humane treatment he had received from the Romans, saying that they had been ready to release him

because he had done nothing against the Jewish nation or
the customs of his ancestors; and he alluded discreetly to
the opposition of the Sanhedrin which had forced him to
appeal to Caesar. Then, repeating once more his customary
protestation of innocence, he declared: "For it is because
of the hope of Israel that I am wearing this chain" (Acts
28:20).

The purpose of his opening words was to dissipate his
compatriots' prejudices, forestall any calumnious accusations that might have come from Jerusalem, and prepare
the way for the preaching of the Gospel. The interview
took place in an atmosphere of cordiality, and the leaders
of the Roman synagogues, with every appearance of
courtesy and prudence, replied that they had not the least
complaint against their host, that they had received no
adverse comments about him from Jerusalem, and that it
grieved them to see a brother-Jew condemned to bear the
burden of captivity. And they added: "We want to hear
from thee what thy views are; for as regards this sect, we
know that everywhere it is spoken against" (Acts 28:22).

Paul did not wish to lose such a wonderful chance of
preaching his doctrine, so he and the Jews fixed a day for
the next interview. On the appointed date his audience was
more numerous than on the first occasion, and the meeting
lasted from morning to evening, during which time he
announced the spiritual kingdom foretold in the sacred
books of Israel, taking pains, as was his custom when
speaking to his compatriots, to show that Christ had fulfilled in His Person the Messianic prophecies, and that the
Gospel teaching was but the realization of their hopes.

As always, his hearers split into two factions, some
believing in the "good tidings of great joy," others, after
many objections, declaring that the Apostle's doctrine was

incompatible with the religious traditions of Israel. The discussion degenerated into a quarrel, and Paul, seeing that some rejected the truth while others went away laughing at his Messias or stayed to insult him and his Lord, indignantly addressed to the mockers the words which Isaias had hurled at their fathers: "With the ear you will hear and will not understand; and seeing you will not perceive. For the heart of this people has been hardened, and with their ears they have been hard of hearing, and their eyes they have closed. . . ." With sorrow and anger at their ingratitude for the divine call he added: "Be it known to you therefore that this salvation of God has been sent to the Gentiles, and they will listen to it." (Cf. Acts 28:26–28.) It was this willingness of the Gentiles to listen to the Gospel that consoled him for the rebellion of the Jews.

His detention continued, but he did not feel it a great hardship, for he was in Rome, the city which had been so much in his thoughts as he journeyed about the world; he was suffering for Christ, thus realizing anew one of his most ardent desires, and yet there was nothing to hinder his ministry. In the last sentence of the Acts, St. Luke sums up these two years of toil and victory: "And for two full years . . . he welcomed all who came to him, preaching the kingdom of God and teaching about the Lord Jesus Christ with all boldness and unhindered" (Acts 28:31).

The members of the Roman community came to him for light and consolation. His house had become a church, and conversions increased among the pagans, among the slaves of the great senatorial households, the "clients" and freedmen, and the humble laborers on the banks of the Tiber. Very soon he began to make disciples among the soldiers who took turns at guarding him, and his career, his doctrine and his present state were being discussed at the Praetorium: ". . . I suffer even to bonds. . . . But the word of God is not bound," he said (2 Tim. 2:9); and his words, dictated while he was chained in fetters, produced marvellous effects. A wave of fervor ran through the church at Rome, and if formerly there had been cowards who had to be reminded that one must do good not only before God but also before men, now the disciples rivalled each other in courage and enthusiasm in confessing the faith: "The greater number of the brethren in the Lord, gaining courage from my chains, have dared to speak the word of God more freely and without fear" (Phil. 1:14).

Unfortunately, not all were motivated by good intentions, for here, too, the sowers of cockle were active, those hardened Judaizers, those same false brethren who had fought so bitterly against him in the East. These enemies were joined by some of the established missionaries at Rome who considered that they were being eclipsed by the zeal and authority of the newcomer, and who, though they were working harder than ever, did so with an unreasoning bitterness that poisoned their ministry, their whole aim being to hinder the work of their adversary and minimize his successes. As Paul himself put it: "Some proclaim Christ . . . out of contentiousness, not sincerely, thinking to stir up affliction for me in my chains" (Phil. 1:16–17). But these unworthy men were thwarted in their hopes, for the whole church at Rome, in a spontaneous outburst of love, proclaimed the divine character of the Apostle's teaching, and recognized that his great heart was too generous to become embroiled in petty personal feuds. "But what does it matter?" he said, "provided only that in every way, whether in pretense or in truth, Christ is being proclaimed; in this I rejoice, yes and I shall rejoice." (Cf. Phil. 1:18.)

In spite of opposition and envy, Paul was experiencing

one of the happiest periods of his life. The rapid spread of the Gospel filled him with joy, the faithful of Rome listened to him with veneration, even the authorities of the Praetorium recognized the power of his personality, and he had with him, helping him in his labors and drinking in his doctrine, the most devoted of his friends: Luke, the "most dear physician," who was still preparing himself to be his master's biographer; Timothy, the best beloved of all the disciples; Aristarchus of Thessalonica, who had passed through the same dangers as Paul during the riot of the silversmiths at Ephesus. Even his former co-worker John Mark reappeared at his side, completely won over by the force of his personality. There, too, was Aquila, the dealer in tents, and "beloved Stachys," as well as many others whom the Apostle had known before he came to Rome. In addition, delegations came from the churches of the East to obtain his advice on their problems, to assure him of their affection and fidelity, and to show their respect for him as a prisoner of Christ.

From far-off Phrygia came one of his Ephesian disciples, Epaphras, who had founded the churches in the valley of the River Lycus, at Colossae, Laodicea and Hierapolis, and who continued to exercise a benevolent influence over them. This good man brought Paul consoling wishes, tender regards and ardent promises from the faithful of the churches he had established. But he also had alarming news to tell, for although the Judaizers' attacks were losing their virulence, a new danger loomed on the horizon there. Judaism, as it decayed, was not content merely to impose the obligation of dead observances, but was also becoming diluted with dangerous teachings which were becoming an added menace to the infant Church. The ravages of this new system of religion were already being felt in Colossae,

Epaphras' native city, where false teachers were trying to amalgamate with the Gospel the principles of a gnostic religion, a confused mixture of rabbinical traditions, Oriental theosophy and Hellenic speculations.

These theorists were the first heretics; they were still impregnated with Judaism, but a conciliatory, hypocritical Judaism that eschewed violence in order to insinuate itself more effectively. They spoke of the *pleroma*, the plenitude of the Divine Essence diffused throughout the universe in a multitude of *aeons* and forming a chain of links between matter and the absolute. They took delight in all sorts of disquisitions about angels, their hierarchies and genealogies; like the Judaizers they continued to venerate the legal observances, the fasts, feasts, new moons and Sabbaths, which were only, as St. Paul says, "a shadow of things to come, but the substance is of Christ" (Col. 2:16–17). They preached contempt for matter and introduced into Christian practices an asceticism of Essene origin which went so far as to condemn marriage.

This gnosticism adulterated and belittled Christ's teaching, regarding it as just one more emanation of the *pleroma*, and holding that its influence was limited by that of the stars, whose movements controlled men's destinies. Furthermore, the virtues of Christianity were eclipsed by a proud, austere puritanism.

An authoritative voice was needed to sound a warning against the evil and to exorcise it, and since St. John had not yet appeared in Asia Minor, that voice had to be none other than St. Paul's. That is what Epaphras pointed out to his master, and Paul, cut to the heart by the insult which the false teachers were offering to Christ, dictated to Timothy two new Epistles, one written expressly for the Colossians, and the second a kind of circular letter destined for the other churches in the valleys of the Lycus, the Meander and the Cayster Rivers, a document which has come down to us under the title of the Epistle to the Ephesians.

The plague of heresy could easily spread over the whole region about these rivers, and so it was essential to proclaim the true Faith once more throughout that district. Ionia, mother of thinkers and philosophers, was always seeking novelties and pursuing chimeras. Thales, one of its philosophers, had said that the world is an animal full of demons. Phrygia, ever noted for its tendency to the most extravagant illuminism, was a fertile soil for all kinds of fanatical excess and pseudo-mystical exaltation. This was a harsh, forbidding country, convulsed by earthquakes, pitted with volcanoes, and regarded from the dawn of history as the scene of gigantic battles between the forces of hell. St. Paul's voice would not succeed in stemming completely the ever-rolling tide of fanaticism and excesses, but his word would shed the light of sanity on the dark labyrinth of the teeming sects.

Stimulated by the absurd speculations of the heretics, his mind rose to luminous heights of thought and ranged over a wider metaphysical field than ever before. The Epistles to the Colossians and the Ephesians do not paint vivid pictures of daily life, but rather depict immense philosophical perspectives bathed in a warm serene light. In these letters the Apostle does not abandon entirely his usual polemical air; yet we are now very far from the Epistles to the Corinthians or the Galatians. His sallies against the false teachers remind us of the knights of old going forth to kill the dragon at the mouth of its cave in order to regain the immense treasure within. St. Paul slays the enemy, and his conquering lance, flashing as it plunges down, throws rays of light on treasures of truth that hitherto appeared inaccessible. Thus, in the Epistle to the Colossians, he has left us glowing pages on the mystery of Christ, and in the Epistle to the Ephesians, has delved deep into the mystery of the Church.

Writing to the Corinthians, he had said: "There is . . . one Lord, Jesus Christ, through whom are all things, and we through him" (1 Cor. 8:6). Now he simply developed this idea, throwing light on the divine designs and paying particular attention to the plan of redemption which saves the whole human race, calls all men to the inheritance of the kingdom, and makes them members of the Body of Christ. In order to cut short the overly-ambitious discussions of the Colossians, he wrote to them: "[God] has rescued us from the power of darkness and transferred us into the kingdom of his beloved Son, in whom we have our redemption, the remission of our sins. He is the image of the invisible God, the firstborn of every creature. For in him were created all things in the heavens and on the earth, things visible and things invisible, whether Thrones, or Dominations, or Principalities, or Powers. All things have been created through and unto him, and he is before all creatures, and in him all things hold together" (Col. 1:13–17).

In opposition to the "intermediate beings," the angels, and the *aeons* of the heretical speculators, Paul held up the image of the One Mediator, Christ Jesus, the Redeemer of all men, the Fount of all grace and the Principle of all life, both natural and supernatural. But unlike the other Apostles, who were content to recall and relate their memories of that Christ with whom they had conversed and broken bread, he concerned himself primarily with the heavenly Christ. This was an original and wholly new attitude which, however, did not prevent him from being in full accord with his companions in the apostolate. He stressed the fact that everything was created through and for Christ; just as everything proceeds from the Father, so also everything is through the Lord Jesus, who is King of the angels, who holds primacy of place in all things, and who, although He hid His majesty under a garment of flesh, is true God. Paul was not afraid to use the very expressions which his adversaries always had on their lips, as for example, the word *pleroma*, which, along with the word *logos*, then seemed to hold the attention of the teachers of the Hellenistic schools. These words were thought to sum up all light, power, perfection, grandeur, virtue and wisdom; about them was gathered everything reasonable, beautiful, ordered, charming, musical and harmonious. They were essential to any attempt to know the Divinity and, full of hidden meaning, they epitomized the philosophical and religious ideal of the epoch; but their vagueness and lack of precision served only to start discussions, formulate theories and raise insoluble problems.

The solution to the mysteries contained in *logos* and *pleroma* was supplied by the disciples of the Gospel. Soon St. John was to say that the *Logos* was Christ, living and personal, the Perfect Revealer and Eternal Wisdom; the *Pleroma*, St. Paul now declared, is the same Christ, the Summation and Principle of that fullness which the heretics thought was diffused through the visible and invisible universe. Christ is Infinite Perfection which manifests itself in an ineffable abundance of graces and benefits, majesty and perfections, "for it hath pleased God the Father that in him all his fullness should dwell. . . . In him dwells all the fullness of the Godhead bodily" (Col. 1:19; 2:9). To those who considered themselves pure and perfect because of their austerities and abstinence, he said: "By grace you have been saved through faith; and that not from yourselves, for it is the gift of God" (Eph. 2:8). The rest of the heretics' teaching, he declared, consisted of vain philosophies, human traditions, lying words, crude relics of Judaism, and at most the shadow of a reality which had taken on a bodily form in Jesus Christ. (Cf. Col. 2:8, 17.)

In order to describe the "glorious riches" of the Word-made-flesh, of "Christ's love which surpasses knowledge," and fills "unto all the fullness of God," Paul resorted to new terms, unusual images, digressions and circumlocutions. Here we find Pauline language at its most typical—concise, rapid, animated, yet so rich that it sometimes seems diffuse; here, too, we find Christianity's technical theological language being hammered out, as well as the Apostle's most difficult passages, and his most obscure and complicated sentences. His genius was striving to find words in which to express the sublime things he had seen and understood.

The shadows of mystery are accentuated in the magnificent portrait of the Church which is painted for us in the Epistle to the Ephesians. The Church is the fullness of Christ, just as Christ is the fullness of the Father; it is the very life of Christ being prolonged in the world and being perpetuated in souls. In these pages we find the full development of the doctrine of the Mystical Body, the vine with its branches, the olive tree with its offshoots, Christ the Bridegroom with the Church His Bride, the Body with its members. There is a natural Christ and a mystical Christ, the One redeeming us, the Other sanctifying us; the One dying for us, the Other living in us; the One reconciling us to the Father, the Other uniting us to all men in Him. And in order to make his ideas more palpable, the

Apostle clothes them in images and allegories. He visualizes the living stones of the edifice supported by the cornerstone which unites the two walls, Jews and Gentiles, forming from them a "temple holy in the Lord" (Eph. 2:21). He has recourse to the analogy of the human body, an analogy which was less clear to the Jews than to the Gentiles, who were familiar with the combats of the arena and the exercises of the gymnasium. He points out that if an organism is to be perfect it must possess a variety of organs, each aptly located and having its own special structure and function, all being united under a central principle of movement and life. He develops this analogy by observing that "the whole body (being closely joined and knit together through every joint of the system according to the functioning in due measure of each single part) derives its increase to the building up of itself in love" (Eph. 4:16).

In the course of his captivity in Caesarea, before he had come as a prisoner to Rome, during those long hours of forced inaction, of isolation and of inner activity, his thought had reached its full maturity, and his soul had taken bold flight toward the world of the divine, to return to earth familiarized with the ineffable mysteries of the Faith which he now presented in profound and original language, secure in the knowledge that the expounding of the truth would dissipate the darkness of error. His mystical gaze had penetrated into the essence of things visible and invisible, but he did not for that reason forget to clothe his ideas in the garments of simile and metaphor, and his heart remained, as always, solicitous, loving, full of compassion and tenderness. Thus to the Colossians he said, using an inelegant but expressive image: "Put ye on therefore, as the elect of God, holy and beloved, the bowels of mercy, benignity, humility, modesty, patience. . . . But above all these things have charity, which is the bond of perfection. And let the peace of Christ rejoice in your hearts, wherein also you are called in one body" (Col. 3:12, 14–15. Rheims version). At the end of this Epistle, he took the pen in his fettered hand, drawing the chain across the rough parchment as he wrote: "I, Paul, greet you by my own hand. Remember my chains. Grace be with you. Amen" (Col. 4:18).

He entrusted the delivery of these two epistles to Tychicus, one of his companions from Asia Minor, who had come with him from Palestine—"our dearest brother and faithful minister and fellow servant in the Lord" (Col. 4:7; cf. Eph. 6:21). With Tychicus went Onesimus, a slave from Colossae who had robbed his master and then fled to Rome where he hoped to hide among the motley, nameless denizens of the city's slums. But he had been observed and recognized by Epaphras, who had often seen him in the house of his owner, Philemon. This man, Philemon, was one of the most fervent Christians in Colossae, and also one of the richest. He had generously offered his house as a meeting place for his fellow-disciples, and he and his son Archippus had had great success in spreading the Gospel. Paul had met him during his sojourn in Ephesus, and their acquaintance had gradually grown into a warm friendship founded on mutual service.

Onesimus, exhausted by privation or perhaps stung with remorse, allowed himself to be led by Epaphras to the Apostle's house, where he was given shelter. He listened attentively to his host as he spoke of Christ and, finally convinced of the truth of the Gospel, begged for and received baptism. His case, however, was a grave one, and as a fugitive he would have to wear around his neck an iron

collar and have branded on his forehead the letter "F" to
deter him from running away again. In addition, as a thief
he was completely at the mercy of his master, who could
wreak the cruellest vengeance on him. Paul knew all this,
but was at a loss exactly how to proceed with the case of
his new convert. The immediate abolition of slavery was
not a part of his apostolic program, for he was mainly
concerned with achieving a doctrinal revolution, and did
not wish to cause sudden upheavals or changes in the existing social economy. To have proclaimed the immediate
emancipation of slaves would have started a bloody cata-
clysm in a society where free men were outnumbered by
those in bondage.

The Apostle was gravely concerned about this problem
of human slavery, and in his teaching he offered a solution
which, however, the jurists did not accept nor the philosophers advance. According to the law, the slave was a
beast of burden, a living machine, a household chattel. He
was bought like an animal and sold off when his usefulness
was ended; his master could have him thrown into the
tanks to feed the fish, could abuse his sense of decency or
even traffic in it, or let him be used for experiments in
vivisection. During Paul's first months in Rome an event had
occurred which clearly demonstrated the misery and hope-
less lot of the slaves. Pedanius Secundus, a senator and
prefect of the city, one of the most illustrious men of the
time, had been killed by one of his slaves, and, according to
the ancient custom, all the other slaves in the senator's
household were sentenced to death along with the
murderer. In this case the condemned numbered four
hundred, and although some of the senators protested
against such a slaughter, the traditionalists prevailed. The
citizens, angered by the cruel decree, tried to stop the

massacre, but the imperial forces attacked and scattered them. All the slaves, men and women, children and old people, were crucified or strangled.

Thoughtful people were already beginning to catch a glimmering of the truth that men cannot own other men as they would own cattle. A contemporary of Paul's from the valley of the Lycus, named Epictetus of Hierapolis, who had been the slave of a slave, declared sententiously: "If a man wishes to be free, let him not desire or shun any of the things for which he depends upon others; otherwise, he will necessarily be a slave." And Seneca exhorted Lucilius in words that are worthy of a disciple of the Gospel: "Are they slaves? No, they are men; they are friends in a humble state of life; they are colleagues in servitude, as you can see if you remember that their lot could have been yours. . . . He whom you call your slave had the same origin as you, enjoys the same sky, breathes, lives and dies just as you do. . . . You are free now, but you could become a slave, and your present slave could be your future master. . . . Such and such an individual is a slave, and yet he may have the soul of a free man. Is there anyone who is not subject to bondage? One serves lust, another binds himself to follow ambition, a third is held in thrall by fear." [1]

From all these considerations Seneca deduces that, although it be only from self-interest, the master should be good to his slaves, treating them kindly, seating them at his table and regarding them as part of the family. He also recalls the barbed question which Socrates asked one of his friends: "Why do you beat your slave so much?"

"Because he is a lazy glutton," replied the friend.

"Haven't you realized," retorted the philosopher, "that perchance you ought to beat your own self more?"

[1] Cf. *Epist.* xlvii.

St. Paul's doctrine on this subject was more radical in its principles and, above all, more firmly based than that of such pagan thinkers. He built his teaching on the words of Christ: "All you are brothers" (Matt. 23:8), brothers by nature, and brothers especially in the higher life of grace. Incorporation into Christ not only makes us sons of the same Father but binds us into a unity: "There is neither Jew nor Greek; there is neither slave nor freeman. . . . For you are all one in Christ Jesus" (Gal. 3:28). The Apostle knew that his present task was to spread this leaven of liberty and fraternity throughout the world; time would do the rest gradually and without riots or revolutions. Meanwhile, he urged masters to be mindful of humility, and slaves to cultivate obedience. "You, masters," he said, "look with love on all those who serve you, and give up threatening, knowing that their Lord who is also your Lord is in heaven, and that with him there is no respect of persons." (Cf. Eph. 6:9.) The slaves he admonished by saying: "Slaves, obey your masters . . . with fear and trembling in the sincerity of your heart, as you would Christ, not serving to the eye as pleasers of men, but as slaves of Christ, doing the will of God from your heart . . . " (Eph. 6:5-7).

As regards Onesimus, the escaped slave, Paul's first thought was to keep him at his side to help in the ministry, but later he concluded that it would be more considerate not to employ him without the consent of his master. And so, taking advantage of Tychicus' mission to the churches of Asia Minor with the Epistles, he sent Onesimus back with him to Philemon accompanied by a letter, the shortest of all his writings, and, in a certain sense, the most moving. In this Epistle to Philemon, Paul recognizes the rights which his friend has over the runaway slave, and makes a plea to stay his hand and avert the punishment he could mete out to the fugitive. He does not ask expressly for the slave's liberty, but he is counting on having it granted. By virtue of his paternal authority and the gratitude owed him, he could have commanded Philemon to free Onesimus, but he preferred to elicit a spontaneous act of generosity on his disciple's part. He does, however, request that the repentant fugitive be left unpunished, since he is now one of the brethren and a future sharer with them in the glory of heaven. Then he goes on to say that he will personally answer for Onesimus and take it upon himself to make good any debt the slave may have incurred. In contracting this formal obligation, he speaks half in earnest and half in jest, but not without hinting that, taking everything into consideration, Philemon himself is greatly indebted to him.

The Epistle opens with the words: "Paul, a prisoner of Jesus Christ, and our brother Timothy, to Philemon, our beloved and fellow-worker, and to Appia, the sister, and to Archippus, our fellow-soldier, and to the church that is in thy house: grace be to you and peace from God our Father and from the Lord Jesus Christ." Then, after praising his friend's charity, faith and generosity, the Apostle continues:

Though I am very confident that I might charge thee in Christ Jesus to do what is fitting, yet for the sake of charity I prefer to plead, since thou art such as thou art; as Paul, an old man—and now also a prisoner of Jesus Christ—I plead with thee for my own son, whom I have begotten in prison for Onesimus. He once was useless to thee [here St. Paul plays upon the name Onesimus, which means "useful"], but now is useful both to me and to thee. I am sending him back to thee, and do thou welcome him as though he were my very heart. I had wanted to keep him here with me that in thy stead he might wait on me in my imprisonment for the gospel; but I did not want to do anything without thy counsel, in order that thy kindness might not be as it were of necessity, but voluntary.

Perhaps, indeed, he departed from thee for a short while so that thou mightest receive him forever, no longer a slave, but instead of a slave as a brother most dear, especially to me, and how much more to thee, both in the flesh and in the Lord! If, therefore, thou dost count me as a partner, welcome him as thou wouldst me. And if he did thee any injury or owes thee anything, charge it to me. I, Paul, write it with my own hand: I will repay it—not to say to thee that thou owest me thy very self.

The Apostle wished these last words to be in his own handwriting in order to give his request more authority. Then, returning the pen to Timothy, he adds: "Yes, indeed, brother! May I, too, make use of thee in the Lord! Console my heart in the Lord! Trusting in thy compliance I am writing to thee, knowing that thou wilt do even beyond what I say."

This short letter, in which there is no surge of passion, no doctrinal discussion or argument, shows us how the Apostle bore himself in the intimate circle of his friends. Charity and tenderness combine with the humor, delicacy and psychological insight of a genius to make the Epistle to Philemon a masterpiece of homely eloquence, an exquisite pearl in the rich treasury of the New Testament, so much so that Erasmus, that exacting connoisseur of literature, declared that Cicero could not have been more eloquent here than Paul.

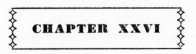

CHAPTER XXVI

To the Ends of the Earth

When Tychicus and Onesimus set out from Rome on their journey to Asia Minor, their departure cast a pall of sadness over the house of the prisoner of Christ. Still other disciples followed in their footsteps to carry his counsels to the churches scattered throughout the world. Thus Aristarchus, John Mark, Luke, all the most beloved of Paul's companions, had to leave their master's side to carry his messages, console the far-flung brethren, and combat the danger of heresy. With their help his triumphant words went ringing across the world, while he, seated in a corner of his house in Rome, kept in his mind's eye a multitude of peoples whom he wished to bind, not with fetters of iron such as he himself wore, but with the sweet yoke of Christ's love.

The departure of his friends and disciples saddened him: on the one hand, he wished to keep them with him, but on the other, he knew that he had to sacrifice his own feelings in the general interests of the Church. Epaphras, the missionary from the Lycus valley, whom he had formerly been able to call "my fellow-prisoner," had also returned to his own land, and soon Paul could say sadly: "For I have

374

no one so like-minded [as Timothy] who is so genuinely solicitous for you" (Phil. 2:20).

One of his great consolations during this trying time came to him from the church at Philippi, his first conquest in Europe and the most loved of all. The Philippians, happy at the thought of his predilection for them, sent him a sum of money to supply his needs while he was a prisoner, an alms which he received as "a sweet odor, an acceptable sacrifice, well pleasing to God" (Phil. 4:18). But more acceptable than the funds was the message of solicitous love which their ambassador Epaphroditus, one of the elders of their church, delivered in their name. From day to day, Paul had been expecting to hear from Philippi, but as time passed without any word from that city, he had begun to suspect that his dearest disciples had forgotten him. Later on, he intimated as much to them, adding with charming generosity: "Indeed you were always concerned, but lacked opportunity" (Phil. 4:10).

Even after the Apostle's envoys to the various churches had begun to return, Epaphroditus remained with him as his assistant and companion in arms. But soon the elder from Philippi became gravely ill and was at the point of death. "He was sick, almost unto death," St. Paul later wrote to the Philippians. "But God had mercy on him, and not on him only but on me also, that I might not have sorrow upon sorrow" (Phil. 2:27). Epaphroditus was indeed restored to health, but fell victim to that restlessness, that disquiet tinged with nostalgia, which is one of the aftereffects of the fevers of Rome. His homeland beckoned to him, and he seemed to hear his fellow-countrymen calling him to return with news of the capital. Paul therefore sent him back to Philippi with a letter to the church there, a letter that demonstrates clearly the personal character of the Apostle's spiritual illuminations, his kindliness, his delicate courtesy, and his more than fatherly tenderness. This Epistle to the Philippians is a father's heart-to-heart talk to his children, an intimate conversation in which ideas are expressed, not in logical sequence, but as they occur to the speaker. Here Paul exhorts, encourages, and comforts his disciples and, above all, opens his heart to them, so that as we read we get new insight into the depths of his affection for his spiritual children.

At other times we have seen him afire with just wrath as he fought his enemies; we have seen him downcast and weary of life. The austere outlook on the corruption of nature which he set down in the Epistle to the Romans might have made us regard him as a somber philosopher, had we not been allowed to see that his view of human life also included the splendors of a general rebirth. And it was this conviction of a regeneration of glory, founded on the grace of Christ, that enfolded him in a peace "which surpasses all understanding" (Phil. 4:7). If the external world was for him but "dung," if he showed himself indifferent to the pure delights of nature and art, it was because his soul was filled with another joy, a joy that was austere, certainly, but one that was more profound and on a much higher plane, undimmed by sacrifices and sufferings. It is this joy that shines out from every page of the Epistle to the Philippians. What do all the contradictions of the world matter when we carry within us the life of God? In words of poignant beauty, the Apostle describes how Christ had humbled Himself and had suffered before being exalted by the Father: "Christ Jesus, who though he was by nature God, did not consider being equal to God a thing to be clung to, but emptied himself, taking the nature of a slave and being made like unto men. And appearing in the form of man, he humbled himself, becoming obedient unto death, even to death on a cross. Therefore God also has exalted him and has bestowed upon him the name that is above every name; so that at the name of Jesus every knee should bend of those in heaven, on earth and under the earth, and every tongue should confess that the Lord Jesus Christ is in the glory of God the Father" (Phil. 2:5–11).

This being so, how could an Apostle of Christ play the coward when threatened with torture and persecution? "Have this mind in you which was also in Christ Jesus," St. Paul used to say to his disciples (Phil. 2:5). That was the reason why he loved his chains, those chains which were an inspiration, a source of strength and of glory for the faithful, and, for the Apostle himself, a new testimony to his likeness to Christ. He rejoiced in the sufferings he bore: "What is lacking of the sufferings of Christ I fill up in my flesh for his body, which is the Church" (Col. 1:24), for he was in haste to realize the definitive perfection of the Mystical Body, which will reach its fullness only when all the elect enter into the glory of heaven. He wished to obtain for the brethren an increase of fervor, peace, and joy, and hence he gladly accepted his pains, uniting them to those which Christ bore for the salvation of the world, and thus making them a continuation of the Savior's Passion.

His most ardent desire was to be freed from "the body of this death," because only thus could he enter into the full possession of the mystery which he had revealed to the world. Hence in these loving confidences to his disciples at Philippi, he uttered a cry which has since become the battle hymn of fervent Christians: "To me to live is Christ and to die is gain" (Phil. 1:21). Only love of souls restrained his longing to be dissolved and to be with Christ, and when he thought of the possible outcome of the long legal process which was slowly dragging itself out in Caesar's tribunal, a sublime battle began in his soul. He was neither elated at the prospect of freedom, nor downcast by the possibility of death; his only desire was that Christ should triumph, whether in his life or in his death. Thus he possessed the perfect balance of mystical peace, a noble indifference which conquered his natural desire to prolong his life, and rendered him perfectly willing to shed his blood as "the libation for the sacrifice and service of [his disciples'] faith" (Phil. 2:17). In a revelation of his innermost feelings, he confessed to the Philippians that he desired "to depart and to be with Christ, a lot by far the better; yet to stay on in the flesh is necessary for your sake" (Phil. 1:23-24).

It was God's will that for the present he should live. He had good cause to believe that the judges were favorable to him, so that when writing to Philemon, he had hinted that he would soon revisit the churches in Asia Minor and had asked his friend to prepare a room for him in his house. Now, writing to the Philippians, he expressed as a conviction what before he had only surmised: "I know that I shall stay on and continue with you for all your progress and joy in the faith, that your rejoicing in my regard may abound in Christ Jesus through my coming to you again" (Phil. 1:25-26). When he wrote these words he had already appeared several times before the judges, as seems to be indicated by his rather vague declaration: "The chains I bear . . . have become manifest . . . throughout the praetorium" (Phil. 1:13), that is to say, his case was known to all those at the court who, under the presidency of the prefect or prefects of the Praetorian Guard, had to decide his fate. He undoubtedly took advantage of these public appearances to present an outline of his doctrine, as he had done when defending himself before the procurator of

Judea. Therefore, it is possible that the Gospel made a deep impression not only on the soldiers charged with guarding him, but also on their illustrious commanders. In a sentence expressive of deep contentment, the Apostle intimated to the Philippians that the Faith was making headway among the members of the imperial court as well as in the Praetorium: "All the saints greet you, especially those of Caesar's household" (Phil. 4:22).

It may well have been these disciples in the royal palace who brought Paul the news that he would soon be free. He had already been in Rome for two years, but imperial justice was as slow-moving as that of the procurators of Judea. Of course, time had to be allowed for the accusers to arrive, but the religious authorities in Jerusalem, fearing that the existing atmosphere in Rome was contrary to their interests, had done all they could to retard the case. But the Apostle's presentiments proved correct, and in spite of all the influence his enemies could wield in the royal palace, and despite the suspicion with which the name of "Christian" was already being viewed, the Emperor's tribunal recognized his innocence and set him free. St. Luke does not say this expressly, but only hints at it before bringing the Acts of the Apostles to an abrupt end. Did the narrator stop here because he did not wish to record the subsequent condemnation of his hero by the Romans as being contrary to the thesis he had upheld throughout his whole work? Probably not, for it is reasonable to assume that he intended to add another book to the two into which the Acts appear to be divided, an assumption that provides a solution to the difficult problem set by the sudden cutting short of the narrative before the end was reached. From this point on, the figure of the Apostle is hidden from us in the mists of time, except for brief periods when we catch glimpses of him in his travels, or come across some marks of his passage, or hear the echo of his voice, now serene and experienced, but still vibrant.

On leaving Rome after his release, he apparently turned his eyes still farther toward the West, for it was now that he must have made the journey to Spain which he had mentioned in his letter to the Roman disciples. (Cf. Rom. 15:24–28.) The Spanish mission had been in his mind for many years, and it seems as if God Himself had committed it to his care when calling him to the dignity of the apostolate with the words: "I have set thee for a light to the Gentiles, to be a means of salvation to the very ends of the earth" (Acts 13:47). For, at that period of history, the end of the earth was Spain, one of the most Romanized regions of the empire, as is evident from the fact that, a few years later, the Emperor Vespasian granted the rights of an Italian colony to all the inhabitants. Furthermore, there were busy ports on the country's Mediterranean coast, and its great cities had swarmed with Jewish merchants since the days when Solomon's ships had come to Tharsis for precious metals.

Since he had received that commission from God, the years had been rushing on, and his life had been consumed by journeys and imprisonments, so that now he felt compelled to use his remaining days to such purpose that he could say when the final call came: "My mission is fulfilled; the whole earth has heard Thy name; come, Lord, come now!" An indication that he did travel far to the West is found in a passage from a letter written thirty years later, before the close of the century, by Pope St. Clement to the faithful at Corinth: "Paul, after having instructed the whole world in justice and having reached the ends of the

West, was withdrawn from the world." [1] These words, written in Rome, can mean only one thing—that the Apostle's long-cherished dream of journeying to the land of Spain had finally come true, and that the tireless herald of God, the valiant enemy of idols and infernal monstrosities, had fought the good fight in the land of the Pillars of Hercules. That he did so is further confirmed by an author of the second century who wrote that "Luke related only those things of which he was an eyewitness, as he clearly demonstrated by omitting the passion of Peter and the departure of Paul for Spain." [2]

Neither history nor tradition has preserved the least detail of this apostolic pilgrimage, but it is undoubtedly a fact that St. Paul trod the shores of Spain, that his prayer blessed that land, and that the crowds in the cities on the coasts, probably of Andalusia, heard from his lips the promises of the Gospel, while ships laden with silver and mercury, Andalusian oil and amphoras from Cadiz, lay at the docks waiting for a favorable wind to waft them to Rome or the ports of the East.

Everything seems to indicate that he travelled to Spain in the middle of the year 63, when he was finally freed from his confining chains. The sentence which we have just quoted from the Muratorian Canon appears to confirm this opinion by mentioning together the mission of the Apostle of the Gentiles and the passion of the Prince of the Apostles, which was the outstanding event of the first persecution launched by the imperial authorities against the Christians.

The storm that then burst about the Church had been

[1] *Ep. ad Cor.*, 5.
[2] Muratorian Canon, *ca.* 160; cf. L. Duchesne, *Les origines chrétiennes* (2e Ed.), p. 445.

gathering slowly, and it is probable that when St. Paul returned to Rome after his voyage to Spain, his accustomed sympathy with the imperial order waned. Afranius Burrus had died, and Seneca, one of the best governors in the empire, had been removed from office and was soon to receive the order to kill himself by opening his veins. Already Nero had broken all the bonds of sanity. His own mother, the Empress Agrippina, had been one of the first victims of his insane rage, and Tigellinus and Poppaea, his prefect and his favorite, were inciting him to further madness. Life on the Palatine was an unceasing orgy of blood and pleasure, an infernal merry-go-round of denunciations, confiscations, torture, murders, games, festivities, banquets and shameless depravity.

But the worst feature of all was that the life of the palace was being reproduced more or less faithfully in hundreds of patrician households. The rottenness of Roman society at that time is well illustrated by the figure of the fish which Juvenal imagined as battening on the filth of the sewer through which it swam up to the gutters of the Suburra.[3] In Petronius' *Satyricon*, we find another revolting picture of contemporary Rome which shows the city as a den of thieves and libertines, a swarming ant hill of robbers and buffoons, sodomites and prostitutes, where the poor starved in the streets while the rich feasted at banquets like that of Trimalchio at which the guests drank themselves into a stupor, only to wake and start the cup circulating again. All the refinements of pleasure were accompanied by the most exquisite cruelty, and the populace at large delighted in seeing prisoners thrown to the beasts in the arena. The most elegant society matrons thought nothing of trying on new gowns while the shrieks of their slaves

[3] *Satire* v.

under the lash rang in their ears, and, if we are to believe Suetonius, it was Nero's pleasure to give live victims to a certain Egyptian gourmet whose favorite dish was human flesh.

To St. Peter, Rome was a new Babylon, a name which was to be given it again a few years later by the author of the Apocalypse, while St. Paul alludes to the Romans in a general way as a depraved and perverse generation among whom the Gospel appeared "like stars in the world" (Phil. 2:15). There could not have been more of a contrast between the empire of Nero and Caligula, those sadistic and demented rulers, and the empire of Christ preached by the Apostle of the Gentiles. As the Jews of Rome had already observed, opposition to Paul's doctrine was springing up on all sides, and although an open persecution had not yet broken out against the Church, it was being regarded with suspicion. A short while before the Apostle had come to the city on the Tiber, an illustrious matron named Pomponia Graecina had attracted attention by her life of retirement and her aversion to pagan banquets and public functions. Rumor had it that she was addicted to "foreign superstitions," or, in other words, that she was "a disciple of Christ." A council of her family, however, decided that she was innocent of evil; her husband recognized her virtue, and her constancy in her austere way of life won her the respect of all. Nevertheless, the general public looked askance at the new sect, acknowledged it as being distinct from Judaism, and regarded it as a gloomy and inhuman cult.[4] They distrusted it because of the way its members sedulously avoided pagan amusements such as the games, circuses and the theatre, and perhaps also because the authorities already considered the Christians

---

[4] Cf. Tacitus *Annales* xiii. 32; Suetonius *Nero* 16.

dangerous to the Empire on account of their insistence on the worship of the One God and their refusal to adore the deities of the state.

Rome's resentment of the Christians was turned to open hostility by what seems to have been a chance happening. During the last days of July, in the year 64, three-fourths of the city was burned to the ground. The fire began near Trastevere and the Porta Capena, close to the labyrinth of narrow streets in the Jewish quarter. But the ghetto itself escaped unharmed, and some people began to wonder if the fire had not been started by the Jews to avenge the harsh treatment meted out by the Roman governors to their compatriots in Palestine. Others accused Nero of starting the conflagration in order to clear ground for the extension of his palace, and he, inspired no doubt by the coterie of Jewish women and actors whom he kept at his side, decided that the best way to clear himself of suspicion was to cast the blame on the Christians. Thus began a campaign of defamation in which the Jews played no small part. Dark rumors about the Christians began to spread. They were depicted as "hating the whole human race," [5] as being enemies of all joy, atheists, sorcerers, cannibals, rebels and conspirators. The Jews, as they had done before in the reigns of Caligula and Claudius, now intrigued against the disciples of Christ, representing them as cherishing thoughts of heavenly vengeance, widespread destruction by fire, and the end of the world. It seems that jealousy was one of their main motives for wishing to annihilate the Church, as it had been the motive of the Thessalonian synagogue for persecuting Paul and Silas, for in St. Clement's Letter to the Corinthians we read: "It was because of jealousy and envy that the greatest and most

[5] Tacitus *Annales* xv. 44.

righteous pillars of the Church were persecuted and fought to the death."

Nero, whether or not he was guilty of having caused or extended the burning of Rome, lost no time in presenting the populace with the victims of his insane prejudices, and he did it in a characteristically theatrical and bloody manner. Everything confirms Tertullian's statement that the Emperor issued a decree prohibiting the profession of Christianity: *Christiani non sint.* From that moment on it became a crime to be a Christian. There were mass arrests among all classes of society, from the imperial household down to the lowest quarters of Rome. There were no trials; a simple denunciation or a cry torn from a victim by torture was proof enough, and anyone who confessed himself a Christian was automatically convicted of having wielded a torch at the burning of Rome. According to the law, the supposed criminals should have been burned alive or have met death in the amphitheater; but Nero had a fertile imagination in devising tortures. He liked to play with his victims as a cat with a mouse, adding to his enjoyment, for instance, by clothing the condemned prisoners in the skins of wild animals to increase the ferocity of the savage hunting dogs he set on them. Now, wishing to turn the mass execution of the Christians into a spectacle, he held nightly festivals in his gardens at the foot of the Vatican hill, which the people of Rome applauded madly, paying tribute to the genius of their Emperor. There were living reproductions of Hercules in the flames, Ixion on the wheel, Orpheus being devoured by bears, and of Daedalus falling from the sky. Some of the young Christian women were made to play the part of the Danaides condemned to fruitless labors in Tartarus, while others were given the role of Dirce by being tied to the horns of a bull, dragged along the ground, trampled and pounded to a pulp. Every night, among the rosebushes and myrtle trees of the gardens, Christian martyrs were bound or impaled on high posts, covered with pitch, and set on fire to provide illumination for the games. And by the light of these gruesome torches, the imperial satyr drove through the gardens in his four-horse chariot, playing his harp or singing snatches of some ancient song. "A great multitude," so Tacitus estimated it, of men, women and children suffered the agonies of martyrdom, giving the people of Rome, who were so eager for spectacles, a glimpse of something they had never seen before—gentle smiles and unshakeable serenity in the midst of the most atrocious torments.

We do not know what effects this wave of persecution had on the provinces. Some have seen an allusion to this question in the following words from a document written some time later: "But call to mind the days gone by, in which, after you had been enlightened, you endured a great conflict of sufferings; partly by being made a public spectacle through reproaches and tribulations, and partly by making common cause with those who fared thus. For you both have had compassion on those in prison and have joyfully accepted the plundering of your own goods, knowing that you have a better possession and a lasting one" (Heb. 10:32-34). "Although you have not resisted unto blood," continues the author of this fervent exhortation, "it is necessary, in order to temper souls, to recall the torments suffered in the Old Testament by the prophets of the Messias and the precursors of the 'good tidings.' They were tortured, refusing to accept release, that they might find a better resurrection. Others had experience of mockery and stripes, yes, even of chains and prisons. They were stoned, they were sawed asunder, they were tempted, they were put to death by the sword. They went about in sheepskins and goatskins, destitute, distressed, afflicted—of whom the world was not worthy—wandering in deserts, caves and holes in the earth." (Cf. Heb. 11:35–38.)

These thoughts can be found in the beautiful work which has come down to us under the title of the Epistle of St. Paul to the Hebrews. And no one has better right than St. Paul, the eternal traveller who passed through the world like a nomad through a desert, to pen those haunting, nostalgic words, which we find in this document: "Here we have no permanent city, but we seek for the city that is to come" (Heb. 13:14). But this Epistle presents the critics with an insoluble problem, for the ideas expressed therein are Paul's, but the style is not. There is nothing further from the vivacity and spontaneity, the moving, vibrant passion, the formidable reasoning of the Epistles to the Corinthians or the Galatians, than this work which is at once didactic and oratorical, a model of majestic gravity, unvarying elegance and sustained dignity. Instead of Paul's usual bold and impetuous writing, full of life and, at the same time, of imperfections and abrupt transitions, we find a prose that is artistic, musical, carefully wrought, conforming to all the canons of rhetoric, which has reminded one writer, at least, of a work by Demosthenes amplified by Isocrates. In it there are no introductory salutations, no personal allusions except a terse reference to Timothy: "Know that our brother Timothy has been set free; with whom [if he comes soon] I will see you" (Heb. 13:23–24). After centuries of discussion and ingenious research, the commentators have found no more reasonable solution to the problem than the one proposed by Origen at the beginning of the third century, namely, that Paul conceived and inspired the Epistle, while one of his disciples or followers who had a greater command of literary Greek than he, such as Luke, Barnabas, Apollos or some other one of the brethren, set it down in writing.

It could be said that in this Epistle St. Paul wished to hide himself, so that his exhortation would have greater effect on the community at Jerusalem where, although he had been tolerated and even approved, he was never looked upon with real sympathy. Be that as it may, though the language is not his, the thought and doctrine are. It was as if he disguised his voice in order to preach once more to the Christians of his own race the all-encompassing value of the sacrifice of Christ and the fleeting character of the Old Testament, and as if he also wished to halt the Jewish Christians on the brink of the abyss that yawned before them. For, on the eve of the great national crisis, when Judaism was being shaken by death throes which might appear to some as the resurgence of new life, the Christians at Jerusalem would have to decide between making common cause with the fanatical patriots, or breaking completely with them and preserving intact the religion of Christ.

At this time more than ever before, the Pharisaical leaven threatened to corrupt the purity of the Gospel in the narrow-minded communities of Palestine. But suddenly this warning voice rang through the churches, the voice of the Epistle to the Hebrews, pointing out to them the danger which they ran, telling them of the consequences that would follow their desertion, and throwing into relief the contrast between the definitive, immutable, eternal and ideal religion of the new economy, and the dim twilight of the Mosaic dispensation. In measured tones of solemn admonition, the voice went on to show that the Jewish priesthood, being only a rudimentary image of a divine reality, was destined to disappear, and that Christ is the essential Mediator, the eternal Priest. "[Christ is] appointed heir of all things. . . . For the Law . . . is never able to perfect those who draw near. . . . He who is just lives by faith" (Heb. 1:2; 10:1; Rom. 1:17)—faith in Christ without whose blood there is no forgiveness, faith in the word of God, "living and efficient and keener than any two-edged sword, and extending even to the division of soul and spirit, of joints also and of marrow . . ." (Heb. 4:12).

The disciples of St. James hearkened to this austere but loving voice, even when it reminded them that "it is a fearful thing to fall into the hands of the living God" (Heb. 10:31). And thus it came about that the majority of them had taken refuge in Pella on the other side of the Jordan when, in the year 67, the legions of Titus descended on Jerusalem to fulfill the prophecies of Christ.

CHAPTER XXVII

"I Have Finished My Course"

The Empire had declared open war on the infant Church; the Christian community at Rome, so prosperous a year before, had been almost wiped out by the persecution, and the Prince of the Apostles had given his life for his Faith. One day the Master had said to him: "When thou wast young thou didst gird thyself and walk where thou wouldst. But when thou art old thou wilt stretch forth thy hands, and another will gird thee, and lead thee where thou wouldst not" (John 21:18). A venerable tradition whose first link is found in the writings of Tertullian, says that Peter extended his arms on the cross and that he was crucified head down, possibly in that macabre festival in the Vatican gardens or a little later. The earliest historians tell us that he died on the same day as St. Paul, though not in the same year.

In spite of the furious tempest that was threatening to destroy the Church, Paul continued to labor as zealously and actively as ever. With the minions of the Emperor no doubt dogging his footsteps, he went from city to city, from church to church, preaching and encouraging and completing the organization of the communities, for he

wished to pay a last visit to his disciples, who were undoubtedly deeply perturbed by Nero's decree of persecution, confused by the claims of innovators, and harried by
the partisans of the Mosaic observances. "Beware of the
dogs," he had said a short while before to his disciples at
Philippi; "beware of the evil workers, beware of the muti-
lation. For we are the circumcision, we who serve God in
spirit, who glory in Christ Jesus and have no confidence in
the flesh—though I too might have confidence even in the
flesh" (Phil. 3:2-3).

It may well have been during his travels at this time that
he sent his Epistle to the Christians of Jerusalem from an
Italian port where his ship had anchored. From Italy, he
sailed across the Mediterranean to the island of Crete,
where he had spent a week some years before his voyage to
Rome. No doubt he felt that he would be safest there from
the snares of his enemies; so he decided to stay until he had
received news from the mainland. Titus hastened to join
him there, and both set to work preaching the Gospel to
the people of Crete. There were Christian communities
already established on the island, but, lacking leaders, they
were in constant danger of departing from the purity of
the Gospel and were at the mercy of the agitators of
Pharisaism. Actually, these churches were little more than
groups of Christians who had drifted together and who
were content to go their way without making any sincere
attempt to spread the Faith. However, after a short time,
Paul was called away from Crete by the churches in Asia
Minor, but he left Titus to continue the work and establish
a hierarchy—a task which required delicate tact, for the
Cretans had earned a bad reputation for their character and
customs. The ancient writers described them as avaricious,
grasping, cunning and given to lying, and the impression

they made on St. Paul during the short time he spent among them was not a flattering one.

The defects mentioned by the old authors were evident also among the first Christians of the island, so that shortly after he left them the Apostle was able to say: ". . . Both their mind and their conscience are defiled. They profess to know God, but by their works they disown him, being abominable and unbelieving and worthless for any good work" (Tit. 1:15-16). The island did not lack charlatans who used the name of Christ to lend weight to the absurd ravings which they presented as subtle truths. The Faith mattered little to these impostors; all they wanted to do was to make money out of the Gospel, twisting it to suit their own ends, and, unfortunately, they deceived many people by their cunning. Spreading their nets for the unwary, "they upset whole households, teaching things they ought not, for the sake of base gain." (Cf. Titus 1:11.)

It was the spring of the year 66 when Paul visited Asia Minor, probably going to Colossae to stay with his friend Philemon, as he had promised. He also went to Ephesus, where he had to contend once more with false teachers. Eight years before, he had said to the Ephesians: "I know that after my departure ravening wolves will appear among you," and now his fears were coming to pass. Christianity had made such rapid progress in the intervening years that the city had begun to rival Antioch in the number and fervor of its disciples. But this extraordinary vitality had its own dangers. The converts, in their eagerness to know more about their religion, accepted everything that seemed to develop, explain or illuminate the basic doctrine they had learned, and there was no lack of preachers, badly instructed or Christians in name only, who adulterated the teaching of the Apostle under the pretext of expounding it. The ambition of these men was to give a literary and philosophical tinge to the Gospel by mixing it with myths, Hebrew fables, and interminable genealogies which the gnostics were soon to transform into chains of *aeons* and imaginary beings. They were also very fond of arguing about the resurrection of the dead, and they soon arrived at the conclusion that there was really no resurrection other than the spiritual rebirth effected by baptism.

During this, his second stay in Ephesus, Paul devoted himself particularly to rooting out error, arguing with the leading heretics and strengthening the faith of the unlettered and ill-instructed Christians who had allowed themselves to be led astray by brilliant, empty rhetoric. He also took care to warn all the faithful against the seduction of that pseudo-mysticism of the Judaizers which was so closely related to the vain speculations already condemned in his Epistle to the Colossians. In this campaign against error he met with heartbreak and great sorrow, for there were defections from the Faith and stubborn resistance to the truth. These were indeed heretics he had to deal with, and three of them, Hymeneus, Philetus, and a coppersmith named Alexander, who was the most obstinate of all, had to be excommunicated.

When writing to the Philippians, Paul had declared that he wished and hoped to visit them again, and now, in the autumn of the year 66, he was able to realize his desire. Once more he travelled along the Egnatian Road, pausing briefly at the churches to counsel and admonish them for the last time on a tour of visitation that was a father's farewell to his children, the last effort of an organizer deeply concerned about the future of his work. This concern is evident in two of his pastoral Epistles composed at this time which reflect the tempering effect of old age as well as the writer's unchanged fidelity to his principles. There is less vigor, less vivacity in these letters than in the dogmatic and polemical Epistles. They are clearer and more serene than the ones that preceded them, but they contain the same maxims, the same language, the same unorthodoxy of style, and, above all, the same doctrine. No longer does Paul argue; for the sectarians he has no syllogisms, only anathemas. To Titus, who was still working on the island of Crete and whom he had fashioned into a skillful organizer, he especially recommends an authoritative bearing when dealing with the unruly, and great vigilance in everything that concerns "foolish controversies and genealogies and quarrels and disputes about the Law." (Cf. Tit. 3:9.) He looks for energetic action more than for eloquent words: "Speak . . . with all authority. Let no one despise thee, since thou knowest what those islanders are. Epimenides, their prophet and compatriot, well described them when he said: 'Cretans, always liars, evil beasts, lazy gluttons.' " (Cf. Tit. 2:15; 1:12.)

At Ephesus, Timothy, now the leader of that community, was carrying on the struggle against the heretics, but although the memory of his master sustained him, he was dismayed by the insolence of the false teachers. Paul, knowing his beloved disciple's gentle nature, wrote to him from Macedonia encouraging and advising him in a letter that may be considered a manual of pastoral theology. The Apostle addressed his friend in an easy, familiar style such as he had used when they had talked together, sitting around the fire in the hostelries during their travels. He recalled to his mind the various aspects of his duties as head of a church—the duty of maintaining decorum and order in the liturgical assemblies, of showing respectful deference to the civil authorities, of exercising great care in the election of the community leaders, of promoting harmony, fidelity and purity in the homes of his people, and of being circumspect yet firm in maintaining the authority of "the Church of the living God, the pillar and mainstay of the truth." (Cf. 1 Tim. 3:15.) Above all else, St. Paul advised Timothy to be very diligent in combating the heretics' errors, lies and never-ending discussions, their "foolish fables and old wives tales," their "doctrines of devils" taught by hypocrites whose consciences were stained with vice despite the apparent austerity which led them to condemn marriage and the use of meat. Then, with affectionate solicitude, the Apostle suddenly inserts a recommendation to his disciple to take "a little wine for [his] stomach's sake," and possibly also for the purpose of avoiding even the appearance of that empty ostentation which the impostors assumed. The underlying thought is that external practices alone are worth little; true inner piety is what counts, piety useful for all things.

During these days a storm of rebellion was brewing in the ghettos of the large cities. The Jews in Palestine were restless under the yoke of Rome, and it is quite possible that the false teachers in Ephesus took advantage of the general unrest to spread sedition and disquiet, for St. Paul, in his advice to Timothy, recommends peace and submission to authority. And although the blood of his martyred Roman brethren was still fresh on their murderers' hands, and the insane fury of those who dwelt on the Palatine had left an indelible mark on his memory, he ordered the Christian assemblies to offer public prayers for the Emperor and the magistrates, "that we may lead a quiet and peaceful life in all piety and worthy behavior" (1 Tim. 2:2).

But the Apostle's greatest concern was the conduct of the elders who governed the community, for everything depended on them, on their unity of purpose, their vigilance, their zeal and their spirit of sacrifice. Now more than ever before, he gave thought to the firm establishment of the hierarchy, that indispensable condition for avoiding the evils inherent in every human society, and for cultivating the Gospel virtues without which the seed of the Christian life would remain sterile—that seed which, in the words of a Pauline hymn that may well have been sung in the primitive churches:

> . . . was manifested in the flesh,
> Was justified in the spirit,
> Appeared to angels,
> Was preached to Gentiles,
> Believed in the world,
> Taken up in glory (1 Tim. 3:16).

The hierarchy which we find in these pastoral Epistles was still imperfect and embryonic, and even the very terms used are obscure and indefinite in meaning. For instance, the title "deacon" was given to anyone who worked for the good of the church, and although the term "bishop" always signified a sacred minister, the name "presbyter" was given to any member of the church who was prudent and advanced in years. But one thing is certain—that Paul was considered as the head and ruling bishop of all the churches founded by him, and that no one could question his authority, received as it was from the Apostles and from Christ Himself. He possessed all the powers of Orders and jurisdiction, and could delegate his disciples to represent him in matters of government. Thus, whenever it was necessary to appoint presbyters or deacons in a church, he either did so personally or through his delegates who were travelling missionaries like himself—Timothy, on whom he had imposed hands; Titus, his most active co-worker; and Luke, who no doubt organized the church at Philippi. The college of presbyters and bishops, men of proven virtue and orthodoxy, had the task of presiding over and administering the local church, of preaching and consecrating, but lacked the power of ordaining. In the administration of the church's temporal goods and in the demands of preaching, the presbyters and bishops were assisted by the deacons and, on a lower plane, by the deaconesses who, although they were not allowed to preach in the assemblies, instructed the women privately, presided over the groups of virgins, and rendered valuable service in tasks befitting their sex. However, with regard to the role of women in the churches, St. Paul had severe words to say: "I do not allow a woman to teach, or to exercise authority over men; but she is to keep quiet. For Adam was formed first, then Eve. And Adam was not deceived, but the woman was deceived and was in sin. Yet women will be saved by childbearing, if they continue in faith and love and holiness with modesty" (1 Tim. 2:12-15).

In his Epistle to Titus, the Apostle had written: "Make every effort to come to me at Nicopolis; for there I have decided to spend the winter" (Tit. 3:12). There on the western coast of Macedonia, across from the shores of Italy, he wished to organize a new church and lay plans for the following year. During these closing years of his life, we find him particularly intent on preparing workers to carry on his mission after his death. We see that new disciples have joined the old—Linus, Artemas, Carpus, Pudens, and Zenas the lawyer, while Apollos still remained a member of the Apostle's cohort, which obeyed him with strict discipline. For the moment, Timothy was to continue his apostolate in Ephesus, Titus was to come to Nicopolis and then continue on to Dalmatia, being replaced at Crete by Artemas or Tychicus. Zenas and Apollos also received orders to come to Nicopolis to speak with their master. "Help Zenas the lawyer and Apollos on their way," Paul wrote to Titus, "taking care that nothing be wanting to them. And let our people also learn to excel in good works, in order to meet cases of necessity, that they may not be unfruitful" (Tit. 3:13-14).

In the spring of 67, Paul once more crossed the Aegean Sea from Europe to Asia Minor on his way to fulfill the promise he had made some months before of visiting his beloved Timothy. We know almost nothing about this journey. No doubt he passed through Corinth, where Erastus, one of his old fellow-workers, left him; he put in at Miletus, where he had to leave his companion Trophimus, who had fallen ill; and finally he arrived at his destination, Ephesus, whither he was drawn to give courage, aid, and experienced advice to Timothy, who was daunted by the responsibility of his task. After this voyage, the remainder of his life is more hidden than before by the veils of time. A short while later, however, we see him in Rome, destined to travel no more, for he had been made prisoner, possibly in Troas, the sentinel post at the time for the ports of Europe and Asia Minor. When he was arrested, the soldiers had apparently been so strict that they had not given him time to collect his cloak, books and parchments. Possibly they considered that he would not need these personal belongings, since he was as good as condemned to death as a leader of the incendiarists who, two years before, had paid for their alleged crime with their lives.

We do know that in the spring of 67 he was in Rome, laden with chains and lodged in a jail. This time his captivity was not as it had been before, surrounded by glory, crowned with success and alleviated by the company of his disciples. One of his friends, Onesiphorus, who no doubt had followed him from Ephesus, had succeeded in finding him only after many inquiries. (Cf. 2 Tim. 1:17.) The prisoner of Christ was completely abandoned, "suffer-[ing] even unto bonds, as a criminal." His former friends either did not dare to appear in public, or else did not know, or pretended not to know, where he was held captive. When writing to Timothy from prison, he mentioned particularly the defection of those from Asia Minor. "All in the province of Asia," he said, "have turned away from me, among them, Phigelus and Hermogenes" (2 Tim. 1:15). Those of his most intimate companions, such as Luke and Titus, who had been able to accompany him to Rome, were now engaged on various missions. Luke was to return soon, but meanwhile Onesiphorus was the only one who visited him and kept him company: "He often comforted me and was not ashamed of my chains" (2 Tim. 1:16).

It was now that his sensitive soul most needed the support of a friend. He could no longer hope for the former sympathy shown him by his judges, for the burning of Rome, the massacre of the Christians, and Nero's decree had intervened. Just then, the Emperor was in Greece making his ostentatious tour of the country, fighting the wild beasts in the circus, singing to the accompaniment of the harp in the theater and seeking applause and laurels for his fondly-imagined talent as an actor. But in the capital the government was still headed by the prefect Tigellinus and Aelius the freedman, the companions of the Emperor's orgies and worthy representatives of his policy of rapine and cruelty. It was these men who, directly or indirectly, influenced the tribunal that was to judge Paul, and St. Clement was able to say some thirty years later that the Apostle gave testimony under the government of the prefects.

From the first moment of his appearance before his judges, the prisoner was aware of the hostility that surrounded him. Everything in the court seemed to be working against him—the severity of the magistrates, the menacing attitude of the crowds, and the absence of his friends and disciples. No one came forward to defend him: "At my first defense no one came to my support, but all forsook me. May it not be laid to their charge" (2 Tim. 4:16). But he did not falter in courage, and seeing the attention with which the large, motley audience was following the unfolding of his trial, he took advantage of the occasion to preach the name of Christ. Thus those pagans, corrupt and proud, had to listen to the herald of an unchangeable empire before which the splendor of earthly kings grows dim. *The Acts of Paul*, despite its many obvious ineptitudes and inaccuracies, contains some sentences which may be an echo of this court scene: "Why did you enter the Roman Empire?" the Apostle was asked. "Why do you recruit soldiers, withdrawing them from imperial authority?" To which he replied: "I recruit soldiers in every inhabited land. I have been commanded not to exclude any man from the service of my King, a service which can save all of you who wish to submit yourselves to Him. For one day He will make war on the world."

However, St. Paul undoubtedly spoke more diplomatically than this, for he preached Christ so persuasively and made such a deep impression on all present that he was not then condemned. As he tells us himself: "The Lord stood by me and strengthened me, that through me the preaching of the gospel might be completed, and that all the Gentiles might hear; and I was delivered from the lion's mouth" (2 Tim. 4:17). This triumph of his may have encouraged some of the Roman disciples to resume relations with him: at any rate a few of them, such as Linus, the future bishop of the city, and Pudens, an illustrious patrician, spent several days visiting him in his prison, congratulating him on his stay of execution and offering him their services. But Paul was thinking of Timothy, the most beloved of all his friends, who was now far away.

The Apostle was under no illusions because of his temporary reprieve from death, and although he still retained some hope of living, the executioner's sword never ceased to gleam before his eyes. Wishing, therefore, to have Timothy at his side in this supreme hour, he wrote him a moving letter which has been considered his testament and in which he lays bare his heart on the eve of death. In this Epistle we see that his former impetuosity has died down, and we hear a note of sadness running through these unforgettable pages. He is still concerned with moral and dogmatic questions, but now he is an old man, prone to recall the past—his miraculous conversion, his first missions, his meeting with his best-beloved son and the faithful Lois and Eunice, the fervor of his own first days and the divine victories of his early years as a missionary. He reminds Timothy: "But thou hast followed my doctrine, my conduct, my purpose, my faith, my long-suffering, my love, my patience, my persecutions, my afflictions . . . such persecutions as I suffered, and out of them all the Lord delivered me" (2 Tim. 3:10–11).

Despite his years, he still retains his same stout heart and indomitable courage: "God has not given us the spirit of fear," he proclaims proudly, "but of power and of love and of prudence" (2 Tim. 1:7). A disciple of Christ must always be ready to fight and to suffer: "Do not, therefore, be ashamed of testimony for our Lord, nor of me, his prisoner. . . . I am suffering these things; yet I am not ashamed. For I know whom I have believed, and I am certain that he is able to guard the trust committed to me against that day [of eternity]" (2 Tim. 1:8, 12). He is not sure of seeing his disciple again, and therefore he gives him many counsels in which we can catch the echo of a father's last words to his son. He is concerned about having placed on Timothy's young shoulders a burden that was perhaps over-heavy. Tenderly he recalls Timothy's boyish face and, remembering his gentle nature, not yet steeled for the fray, he prays night and day for him, evoking his image with many tears. The Apostle has now but one wish in this life—that he may have his disciple with him before he dies.

It was this desire that moved him to write to Timothy to come as soon as possible, bringing with him the books and parchments left behind at Carpus' house in Troas, as well as the cloak, presumably the Apostle's only cloak, old, gray with the dust of many roads, worn threadbare from being used as couch and blanket in the rude hostelries along the imperial highways. No doubt he asked for his cloak because he judged that his imprisonment would be a long one, and he knew what the winter would be like in that dark, humid, pestilential prison, with his hands chafed raw by the irons, his feet clamped in the stocks and his whole body tormented by vermin. Yet he was even then offering his blood before the altar of God, believing that the moment had come for him to weigh anchor for his final journey, and feeling on his face the soft caress of that breeze from afar that would waft him to the shores of eternity. "I am already being poured out in sacrifice," he wrote, "and the time of my deliverance is at hand. I have fought the good fight, I have finished the course, I have kept the faith. For the rest, there is laid up for me a crown in justice which the Lord, the just Judge, will give to me in that day; yet not to me only, but also to those who love his coming" (2 Tim. 4:6-8).

How admirable the serenity of the old campaigner, the veteran athlete of Christ! He shows no signs of weariness, vacillation or fear; in his soul there is not the least shadow, in his voice not the smallest tremor. He has reached the end of the course; his convictions are stronger than ever, and his words express a peace that is a reflection of the better world to come. As they prepared for the final battle, future martyrs were to meditate upon these words that Paul wrote from his Roman prison, arming their souls with them, steeling their bodies for the lash, the flames and the fangs of the wild beasts. They were to drink in the spirit of the Apostle from the burning cup of his Epistles, and then defy the threats of the tyrants. Thus in the year 180, when the proconsul of Africa, Saturninus, asked the Scillitan martyrs: "What do you keep in your archives?" they answered: "Our sacred books and the Epistles of Paul, a most holy man."

We do not know if Timothy arrived in time to find his master still alive. Probably he did not. And the prisoner never came to need the old mantle he had requested, because one day even before the summer heat had begun, he was taken from his cell for the last time, escorted by a platoon of legionaries with drawn swords glittering in the sun. As he made his way through the streets under the curious eyes of some and the hate-filled glances of others, and with the gibes of his escort ringing in his ears, no doubt he caught now and then the sound of the suppressed sobs of some faithful disciple. His hair was dishevelled, his beard tangled and his clothing in rags; yet he was surrounded by a heavenly radiance and he advanced to his death like a valiant warrior, for, as he himself had said: "O death, where is thy victory? O death, where is thy sting. . . . Thanks be to God who has given us the victory through our Lord Jesus Christ" (1 Cor. 15:55, 57).

Tradition tells us that when the Apostle and his escort arrived at the Ostian Gate, to the southwest of the city, a woman of aristocratic bearing accosted him, sobbing out: "Paul, man of God, remember me in the presence of the Lord Jesus." Recognizing her as Plautilla, a noble lady who had sat near the slaves as she listened to him preach, the Apostle addressed her joyfully: "Hail, Plautilla, daughter of eternal salvation. Lend me the veil from your head to cover my eyes, and in the name of Christ I shall leave to your care this pledge of my affection." After the encounter, the escort continued along the Ostian Way near the banks of the Tiber and halted in a silent, deserted vale whose springs had earned it the name of *Aquae Salviae*, "healthful waters." There Paul turned toward the east and prayed; then, blindfolding himself, he knelt and bent his neck to the sword. The blade flashed down; the incomparable voice was silenced forever, and rest from journeying had finally come to the tireless traveller who, more than anyone before or since, merits to be called a citizen of the whole world.

CHAPTER XXVIII

The Man and the Saint

After Paul's execution, the faithful of Rome reverently took his body and buried it in the place where his basilica stands today. Down through the years they kept his memory green, and at the beginning of the third century a Roman priest was able to say to those who visited his church: "I can show you the trophies [*i.e.*, monuments] of the Apostles: if you go to the Vatican hill and then turn in the direction of the Ostian Way, you will find these trophies of the men who founded our Church."

The faithful throughout the empire, his neophytes, disciples, friends and companions-in-arms lovingly gathered together his Epistles, for in them they could hear once again his fearless voice and listen to the beating of his great heart. And it is in these Epistles, more even than in St. Luke's fragmentary narrative, that we, the Apostle's disciples of the twentieth century, can discover the greatness of that man, "whose like," as St. John Chrysostom says, "the world shall never see again." There we see him fully depicted with his all-embracing love, his quick sensibility, his brilliant mind, his upright, impetuous will, his impassioned love for truth. At first glance, his style is disconcert-

405

ing and his thought puzzling; his logic seems bewildering when compared with ours, which is so measured, prudent, cold, and accustomed to passing from one known concept to another. He thinks explosively, as if unable to confine himself to a narrow, rigid line of reasoning, and each of his thoughts—each of his words, even—bursts upon us like a ball of fire that expands as we watch it and lights up vast panoramas. But nothing in his scheme of thought is isolated from the rest, nothing is disconnected, nothing dissonant: the details are interlinked and in harmony with each other, like the drops of water in a current, like the instruments of an orchestra. Each of his phrases opens up infinite perspectives and discloses unfathomable depths, while at times, in one short sentence, he sums up a whole world of thought: "The Scripture shut up all things under sin" (Gal. 3:22); "Now we know that for those who love God all things work together unto good" (Rom. 8:28); "[God] purposed . . . to re-establish all things in Christ" (Eph. 1:10); "There is no intermediary where there is only one; but God is one" (Gal. 3:20).

His keen eyes look boldly into the depths of mystery; his visions are full of splendor. And when he endeavors to condense these infinite vistas into the small compass of human speech, he writes sentences that are so enigmatic, so laconic, that they have tried the patience of even his most devoted readers down through the centuries. Perhaps no one has read him with more loving attention than St. John Chrysostom, but even he had to admit: "The more I study Paul, the less I understand him." And it was to these obscure passages that St. Peter referred in his second Epistle when he said: "In these epistles . . . [of] our most dear brother Paul . . . there are certain things difficult to understand" (2 Peter 3:15, 16). But Paul's obscurity is only the darkness of a mine that encloses great treasures and inexhaustible riches; it is the darkness cloaking the intensity of life, the power, variety and exuberance of a world in formation.

As we have seen, the Apostle's personality presents us with as many facets and as many contrasts as his Epistles. As one writer has put it: "If we try to fill the centre of . . . [a] . . . church window with a portrait revealing the essence of his profound life, we must admit in advance that we are baffled by the grandeur and complex unity of a figure without parallel. . . . His features must epitomize such multiplicity and distinction of character that no plastic representation has ever been able to encompass the whole. The second-century medallion on which he is facing St. Peter, gives but a traditional mask: the curving nose, the bare forehead, and the prominent eyes express the tension of activity, but not the mystical meditation." [1] Down through the years, each artist who made the Apostle his subject, concentrated on the characteristic of his model that struck him most. Thus, one depicted St. Paul's prophetic majesty and superhuman serenity; another his enraptured gaze into the mysteries of God; a third his conquering strength and grave austerity; a fourth the luminous beauty of the contemplative. Some of these artists may have succeeded in reproducing on canvas that unique combination of steely resolution and fatherly tenderness that was his, but no brush has ever been able to capture his whole character—that marvellous blending of haughtiness and humility, dignity and meekness, common sense and mystical exaltation, fidelity to tradition and hatred of empty

[1] E. Baumann, *Saint Paul*, translated by Kenneth Burke (New York: Harcourt, Brace and Company, 1929), pp. 301–2.

formalism, irony and gentleness, flexible prudence and unyielding determination.

All of these traits come together to form the magnificently balanced character of the Apostle. If one of them predominates it is his impassioned vehemence, which is, however, not begotten of sheer impulse, but ruled by the principles of his Faith.

He believes; and he insists that others should believe like him and live like him, humbling themselves before the truth. His temperamentalism is not the result of his faith—but his faith turned his innate potentialities to purposes of its own. Even his faults have served divine ends; the quickness of his impressions exposed him to incontinence; his intense moodiness would tempt him to meet opposition with summary abruptness; his virile energy could have served carnal appetites; the strength of his convictions prepared him for fanaticism; the subtlety of his dialectic was the making of a sophist. But being directed towards righteous ends, his need of movement and his promptness in action hastened the march of the Gospel. Wherever necessary, his resolution and abruptness sundered the bonds of the old Law. His indomitable faith gave direction to the hesitant, and maintained unity among those whose frailty exposed them to discord. His adaptability enabled him to adjust his means of persuasion to the particular people whom he was converting, or to the errors he wished to combat. His infirmities helped him to remain humble. . . .[2]

In Paul we find the noblest of man's qualities raised to their perfection by sanctity. In him human genius combines with the divine influence to produce a perfect type of man, compared to which the greatest figures in the annals of

[2] Baumann, *op. cit.*, pp. 303–4.

philosophy and Christian history seem but incomplete copies. This fruitful union of thought and action closely co-ordinated in a vigorous personality explains the characteristics of his genius. God chose him to be the great propagator of the Gospel, the Doctor of the Gentiles, and the kindler of divine love in the infant Church. He armed and prepared His Apostle to accomplish the providential mission entrusted to him, and never ceased to assist him in a miraculous manner throughout his career. From the time of his vision on the road to Damascus, Paul received a continous stream of illuminations which unfolded to him the most profound mysteries of religion, and it was this supernatural light shining upon his mind that was the generating principle of his interior life as well as the inspiration of his methods in the apostolate.

This divine help also explains his unbelievable powers of endurance, for although weak and sickly in body, he was able to bear up under crushing fatigue, unrelenting persecution and fearful torture. Few men have possessed such sustained and rugged energy as his. His will, like his body, seemed made of steel, and no danger or threat could turn him from his purpose. His battle cry was: "Forgetting what is behind, I strain forward to what is before" (Phil. 3:13). In his dealings with others he was skillful and prudent, but never deceitful or cunning, for he performed his duty as Christ's ambassador with nobility, dignity, and fidelity. Whether he was speaking before the Jewish rabbis or the magistrates of Rome, his words were always suited to the sacred message he bore and the high cause he defended. In his bearing he was neither truculent nor fawning; in his speech there was no glossing over unpleasant facts, no subterfuge, no pandering to error. He declared the full truth, expounding it with the skill of the born orator and with the clarity of the seer. To adulterate truth in order to please men would have seemed to him both a blasphemy and a betrayal: he himself might groan under the weight of his chains but, as he proclaimed fiercely, the word of God is not bound.

Born to command, he naturally tended to express his thoughts with force and authority. His demeanor was that of a leader who sees things clearly and knows how to bend others to his will. His certainty that he possessed the truth lent his words and actions an imperative decisiveness, so that if we view some of his deeds and attitudes in isolation from the rest of his character, we see the Paul whom the Renaissance artists depicted—somber, grim, bitter, irascible and violent. It is true that his personality was overpowering in its strength and originality, that he defended his convictions with vehemence, that his tenacity never faltered before obstacles or resistance, that he demanded complete, unquestioning obedience in those who had to work with him, that he smote his enemies hard when he saw that they were malicious and perverse. But, as we have seen, this is only one aspect of his complex character, and we should not lose sight of the difficult, and at times, tragic circumstances under which his life unfolded. God had called him, and had made him an Apostle of His Church. The responsibility of that office was his; the glory of it belonged to Christ, his Lord. Therefore he demanded unity of effort and obedience to the plan of action which he had elaborated. For this reason, too, he never worked in another's territory if he could avoid it, and anyone who refused to carry out his orders found it impossible to remain with him. That is what happened to Barnabas, Silas and John Mark. Perhaps Titus and Timothy were less talented than those who left him, yet they worked in harmony with him, and so great was his vigilance and inspiration that, under his direction, an ordinary ability was capable of doing work of the highest order. Great indeed was the influence of that voice speaking words of celestial wisdom, of those toil-hardened hands, of that life composed of love and sacrifice, majesty and humility. Well could he command, he who was first into battle and who could with perfect justice say, as he did with charming directness: "Be imitators of me: do what I do." (Cf. 1 Cor. 4:16.) Truly he had all the qualities of a leader—clear-cut plans, swiftness in attack, alacrity in retaliation, boldness and decisiveness in action, a steely resolution to attain his object, but also the flexibility to change his goal or method if circumstances demanded it. The most important trait of all was his ability to set the example for his followers.

Even so, his most shining victories would have been use-less if, as he gained territory for Christ, he had not taken pains to consolidate his conquests. In his role as organizer he was as admirable, if not as brilliant, as in his work as an apostle, and the two skills combined in him to form the perfect missionary. He himself governed all the churches he had founded; he visited them, attended to their needs, protected them from danger, encouraged, counselled and directed them. But for the historian of Christian origins, his principal merit consists in his having understood from the start, and with greater clarity than any of the other preachers of the Gospel, the universal character of Chris-tianity. From the beginning of his apostolate, we see him possessed by the vision of a society embracing all mankind and bound together by the common tie of Christian fraternal charity; impelled by this vision he made a clean break with Jewish narrowness, thus making possible the conquest of the world. It would be wrong, of course, to regard him as the originator of Christian universality, for that is of the very essence of the Gospel teaching; he was, however, its most ardent champion and it was he who, by God's grace, finally made it triumph. Nor must we forget that his preaching was not his own personal doctrine, distinct from that of the other Apostles; yet he proclaimed the truths of the Faith with such vigor, clarity and originality that we can well speak of "Paul's Gospel."

The inflexible will that made him so great a general and organizer was guided by an intellect of surpassing brilliance, one which could analyze a problem minutely, and yet could also synthesize a host of apparently divergent elements into a living unity. His piercing gaze could penetrate into the very depths of men's souls, and then could soar to the heights of the Godhead; by comparing men's misery with the divine perfections, and by exploring their consciences in the light of faith, he was able to discover the root of their weaknesses and the fountainhead of their virtues. Again, we have frequently admired the irresistible march of his reasoning; yet logic served him only as a means to ensure the triumph of ideas which he had discovered by intuition. As one writer puts it:

He was essentially a man of intuition, and the characteristic mark and originality of his genius are found in this dominant quality of his cast of mind. For him religious truth was something to be contemplated; his intellect grasped it by direct vision and not by reasoning, for the great mysteries which he succeeded in understanding fully presented themselves to his mind without the intervention of symbols or images. His thought had its starting point and its terminus in God and in the world of supernatural realities, in which he moved as in his natural element. This direct and lasting contact with divine things strengthened and enriched him, giving him that twofold characteristic of certitude and clarity which a simple discursive knowledge could not have imparted to him in so high a degree.[3]

In this intuitive knowledge, Paul resembled the great mystics, whose ideal he realized in a sublime manner, living as he did continually under the action of the Holy Spirit, his gaze fixed in contemplation of the next world. When in his Epistles the need to develop an argument or explain some doctrine or settle some matter of discipline obliged him to leave this vision for a moment, he always returned to look upon it. Thus, on the one hand, he was one of the most practical men who ever walked the earth, while on the other, he lived in thought in the world of the spirit, which for him was more real and more true than the world of sense. His idealism reminds us of Plato, whose writings he probably did not know, but whose philosophy impregnated the atmosphere he breathed. He tells us that "this world as we see it is passing away." (Cf. 1 Cor. 7:31); he counsels us not to "look at the things that are seen, but at the things that are not seen. For the things that are seen are temporal, but the things that are not seen are eternal" (2 Cor. 4:18); thus we are put in mind of the demiurge of Plato's dialogue *Timaeus*, forming the eternal unchangeable archetypes of which sensible things are only imperfect copies, fleeting shadows, and passing reflections. The world of the spirit, which we are inclined to view as being inhabited by unsubstantial phantasms, was the world which most interested Paul. He looked upon Christ as a real, living Person; he meditated long upon the Spirit who guided him; he saw himself surrounded and penetrated by

[3] A. Tricot, *St. Paul, Apôtre des gentils*, 1927, p. 183.

the very essence of God; he viewed the meetings of the faithful as being honored and made joyful by the presence of the angels; and he could visualize the legions of devils, "the spiritual forces of wickedness on high" (Eph. 6:12), placing obstacles in the way of the Gospel and lying in ambush for souls on the road to God. It was this concept of reality that inspired him to use such expressions as: "The kingdom of God does not consist in food and drink, but in justice and peace and joy in the Holy Spirit" (Rom. 14:17); "God forbid that I should glory save in the cross of our Lord Jesus Christ, through whom the world is crucified to me, and I to the world" (Gal. 6:14).

After ranging through this higher world, St. Paul was able to describe its marvels to us in unforgettable words, for although his mind was essentially intuitive, his reason was not idle. He drew the majority of the ideas which form his "Gospel" from Hebrew tradition, the preaching of Christ, and personal revelation; but he welded them together into a coherent, harmonious system illuminated by the clarity of his vigorous logic. He did not build up theories just to satisfy his intellectual curiosity, but always with a practical end in view. We shall never be able to admire enough that method of argument in which his thought, stimulated by an antithesis of ideas, concentrates on the higher principle in order to unfold itself with irresistible force and invincible logic. But he never argued for argument's sake; he always had a very real aim in view— the annihilation of error, the salvation of a soul, the defense of Christ's glory. His teaching was always spirit and life, never a dead letter, "for the letter kills, but the spirit gives life." (Cf. 2 Cor. 3:6.) Yet even in these marvellous sweeps of reasoning, the central point is always a truth discovered or lighted up by immediate contact with the supernatural world.

The Apostle once said that he knew "no one according to the flesh." (Cf. 2 Cor. 5:16.) Does this imply that his surrender to Christ had torn from his breast every human affection? By no means, for his conversion, far from destroying his love for men, transformed it. "Paul's heart," says St. John Chrysostom, "is the heart of Christ." Truly, it was a great heart, one which, as Neumann observes, possessed the gift of sympathy, a gift which enabled him to live more in others than in himself, sincerely sharing their joys and especially their sorrows, working beside them, helping them in their needs, making himself little and laying aside his genius and his Apostle's mantle in order to be better understood and accepted by the humble ones of the earth. Each separation, each farewell, tore at his heart. In thought he followed his friends, converts and fellow-workers, and when he wrote to them he could not find, even in his rich vocabulary, words strong enough to express his love. He called Luke "the beloved physician," Titus "his beloved son," Timothy "his dearest son," and their absence was always a source of sorrow and pain. "My dear children, with whom I am in labor again . . ." he wrote to the Galatians; "I wish I could be with you now . . .!" (Gal. 4:19-20). As we have seen, he once arrived at Troas full of enthusiasm and dreams because God had opened wide the door of the Gospel to the Gentiles, and failing to find Titus whom he had hoped to meet there, he was so downcast and troubled that he interrupted his work to go to Macedonia in search of his disciple. (Cf. 2 Cor. 2:12-13.)

Not only did he love intensely, but he needed to be loved in return. He wanted his converts to share his feelings: isolation weighed heavily upon him. He wished others to feel the same waves of indignation, enthusiasm and joy that swept through his heart. "I trust in you all that my joy is the joy of you all." (Cf. 2 Cor. 2:3.) "I joy and rejoice with you. And in the same way do you also joy and rejoice with me." (Cf. Phil. 2:17–18.) It is a moving sight to behold this austere ascetic, this iron warrior, this mystic to whom God lent strength, requesting and, in a certain sense, begging for the affection of those around him. "Our heart is wide open to you," he wrote to the Corinthians. "In us there is no lack of room for you, but in your heart there is no room for us. Now as having a recompense in like kind— I speak as to my children—be you also open wide to us" (2 Cor. 6:12-13). These confidences, this opening of his heart, almost always had the desired effect, and his power of attracting people to him and the depth of affection that he inspired were extraordinary. Few teachers have been loved by their disciples as Paul was loved by his converts and fellow-workers. And few have appreciated their followers' devotion as he did, for, as he himself often said, the knowledge that he was loved and understood was one of his greatest consolations. (Cf. 2 Cor. 12:12-27; Gal. 3:26-28; Eph. 4:15–16.)

It is conceivable that, discounting the transfiguration wrought in the Apostle's heart by his constant intercourse with Christ, some twisted minds may read evil into these expressions and these sentiments of his. Undoubtedly he loved without measure, but "in the heart of Christ Jesus," to use his own phrase, the foundation of his love being the noble, fruitful idea of fraternal charity. Unceasingly he taught that all the faithful form one Mystical Body in union with the Divine Redeemer; all have been saved by the same Blood, all live with the same life, all take part in the same Sacrifice, and all are equal in the sight of God as sons of the same Father. Every difference of birth and fortune disappears before the fact of divine sonship: there is but one heavenly society, bonded together by the redeeming Blood, united by the Spirit of Jesus, who is the Spirit of Love. Thus Paul's individual life was intimately blended with the collective life of the Church. Extremely sociable by nature and by reason of this concept of sublime solidarity of the Spirit, he exclaimed: "Who is weak, and I am not weak? Who is made to stumble, and I am not inflamed?" (2 Cor. 11:29). His, too, is this maxim in which delicacy of feeling is rivalled only by beauty of thought: "Owe no man anything except to love one another . . ." (Rom. 13:8).

The ultimate reason for Paul's love, for his strivings, his sufferings, his constancy, his whole life of heroism and triumph, was Christ. From the moment he met his Lord on the road to Damascus, his whole desire was to imitate Him. Snatched up by Christ in the middle of his career, as he puts it himself, he was not content to follow his Captor as a prisoner, but gave himself completely to Him and lived with the constant aspiration of becoming a living image of Him. In order to realize this goal, he had to sustain harsh inner struggles, which have left ringing echoes in his Epistles; but little by little the old man was conquered, calm was restored by a resounding victory, and his love flung its confident challenge in the face of the powers of earth. In winning him, the love of God made a great conquest, more glorious than the conquest of Augustus' empire. Paul no longer saw or knew anything save love. He was an apostle preaching one doctrine, a theologian wielding one argument, a lover repeating one name, the adorable Name that was continually on his tongue, sometimes without apparent reason, the Name that sprang from his heart, that burned on his lips, the blessed Name of Jesus at which every knee bends in heaven, on earth and under the earth. For this Name he suffered, for it he conquered, for it he preached, for it he was consumed with zeal, for it he toiled with inexhaustible patience, the patience of those who never tire of hoping, a patience which never failed in him although, impelled by his desire to bring all men to recognize the Name he loved, he was the most energetic, the most impetuous, the most impatient of men. Christ was his obsession, his ever-present thought, his very existence; every aspect of his life, religious, intellectual, social and sensible, was reduced to a sovereign unity by the life of Christ. He lived by and for Christ, so that his own activity was replaced by the action of God. When he thought, when he loved, when he worked, he felt himself moved by a mysterious power, the power of God Himself, and thus with entire truth he could utter the words which he wrote in Rome and which the pilgrim can read today engraved upon his tomb:

Mihi vivere Christus.

INDEX

419

A NOTE ON THE TYPE

IN WHICH THIS BOOK IS SET

This book is set in Janson, a Linotype face, created from the early punches of Anton Janson, who settled in Leipzig around 1670. This type is not an historic revival, but rather a letter of fine ancestry, remodelled and brought up to date to satisfy present day taste. It carries a feeling of being quite compact and sturdy. It has good color and displays a pleasing proportion of ascenders and descenders as compared to the height of the lower case letters. The book was composed and printed by The York Composition Company, Inc., of York, Pa., and bound by Moore and Company of Baltimore. The typography and design are by Howard N. King.

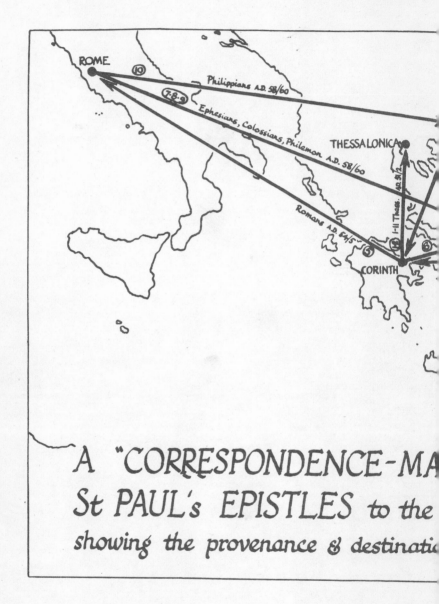

A "CORRESPONDENCE-MA
St PAUL's EPISTLES to the
showing the provenance & destinatio